Foxfire 10

Foxfire 10

**Railroad lore, boardinghouses,
Depression-era Appalachia,
chair making, whirligigs,
snake canes, and gourd art**

**Edited by George P. Reynolds, Susan Walker,
and Rabun County High School Students
With the assistance of Eliot Wigginton**

DOUBLEDAY

New York   London   Toronto   Sydney   Auckland

PUBLISHED BY DOUBLEDAY
a division of Bantam Doubleday Dell Publishing Group, Inc.
666 Fifth Avenue, New York, New York 10103

DOUBLEDAY and the portrayal of an anchor with a dolphin
are trademarks of Doubleday, a division of Bantam Doubleday
Dell Publishing Group, Inc.

Mission Statement of The Foxfire Fund, Inc.

The Foxfire Fund is a not-for-profit educational corporation based in
Rabun County, Georgia. Its mission is to model, refine, and
encourage methods of active learning, where students help design
work that engages the curriculum in meaningful, interdisciplinary,
elegant ways. This process, of necessity, involves the community,
teachers, and students in extended learning partnerships that are
cooperative, collaborative, and democratic.

Those interested in learning more about the Foxfire Fund should
write to:

The Foxfire Fund, Inc.
P.O. Box 541
Mountain City, Georgia 30562

The Foxfire Fund still publishes *Foxfire* magazine, as well
as other publications.

Library of Congress Cataloging-in-Publication Data
Foxfire 10 : railroad lore, boardinghouses, Depression-era Appalachia,
chair making, whirligigs, snake canes, and gourd art / edited by George
P. Reynolds, Susan Walker, and Rabun County high school students
with the assistance of Eliot Wigginton.
p.   cm.
Includes index.
1. Rabun County (Ga.)—Social life and customs. 2. Appalachian
Region, Southern—Social life and customs. 3. Folklore—Georgia—
Rabun County. 4. Folklore—Appalachian Region, Southern. 5. Han-
dicraft—Georgia—Rabun   County. 6.   Handicraft—Appalachian
Region,   Southern. I.   Reynolds,   George   P. II.   Wigginton,
Eliot. III. Walker, Susan W.   IV. Title: Foxfire ten.
    F292.R3F69   1993
975.8'123—   dc20   92-24634
                                                            CIP
ISBN 0-385-46910-1
Copyright © 1993 by The Foxfire Fund, Inc.

April 1993
First Edition
1   3   5   7   9   10   8   6   4   2

Dedication

When the students decided they wanted to dedicate this book to Bob Edwards, I thought, "Of course." For it was Bob, owner of the Kodak Shop in Clayton, who taught us how to print black and white photographs in 1966, let us use his darkroom thereafter until we had one of our own, carried our photographic charges on his books without complaint until we could pay them, loaned us equipment, and has greeted us, supported us, trusted us, encouraged us, and been a constant friend since our very first meeting. It has been—and continues to be—an extraordinary friendship.

We would also like to dedicate this volume to Ed Cross, who printed the very first issue of *Foxfire* magazine. He died in March of 1992.

—*B. Eliot Wigginton*

Table of Contents

Acknowledgments

This is the most pleasurable part of any book to write: the thank-yous. Over the years, hundreds of people have helped us with our work in gathering material for Foxfire magazines and books. Thanks go first, as always, to our contacts, whose names are gathered on a separate list at the back of this book. We are always glad when we have new friends to add to this list. And we miss the old friends who are no longer with us. We owe them all a tremendous debt of gratitude for sharing so much of themselves.

The students whose work appears in this volume are listed separately as well, after the contacts. Like the contacts, they are a resource from and with whom we have learned as they have shared themselves and their work for a quarter of a century.

The student editors who oversaw the production of this volume in the summer of 1991 are Robbie Bailey (Crafts), Julie Dickens (Tourism), Jenny Lincoln (Personality Portraits), Tim Martin (Transportation), Chris Nix (Crafts), Celena Rogers (Economic Revolution), and April Shirley (Economic Revolution, specifically the CCC). Eric Hollifield assisted with the U.S. Forest Service research. Lori Lee and Monica English researched and produced maps. All labored hard, in trying circumstances, with a tight deadline, and all were a pleasure to work with. Book-production veterans Jenny Lincoln and Chris Nix were extremely helpful at the eleventh hour. Rabun County High School, under the leadership of Principal Allen Fort, provided significant help as well as a hospitable base of operations for the book crew that summer—as indeed it has for many years.

Like everything else at Foxfire, this book represents a group effort, calling upon the talents of community, students, and staff. Among the latter, thanks go to Kaye Carver Collins for her help with the TF Railway; Ann Moore for her thoughtful remarks on boardinghouses; Robert Murray for his advice on spring pole lathes; Sheri Thurmond for transcribing most of the new interviews—a laborious task; Teresia Gravley for her help in transcription and manuscript preparation; Billy Parrish for his overall encouragement and help with final manuscript assembly; Teacher Outreach staff Lyn Ellen Eubanks, Hilton Smith, and Kim Cannon for information, assistance, and willingness to release Susan Walker's time for editorial help; Mike Cook for help gathering material; Susan Walker for editorial assistance; and, of course, Eliot Wigginton, for his keen eye and editorial support at critical junctures.

Former Foxfire student Dewey Smith helped with photographs and other needs. Former Foxfire student and photographer Al Edwards also contributed his photography and darkroom skills. Special thanks go to Jewell Murray, whose unfailing good humor, energy, and many and varied abilities contributed substantially to the production of this book (especially to the Tallulah Falls Railway section). Thanks, too, to her six-year-old son John Murray, who, during the last leg of production, wrote us a gently encouraging note: "Work Foxfire work!"

The following folks have been particularly helpful in providing information and assistance in compiling this volume: Suzy Angier, Barrie Aycock, Jo Anne Beck, Margie Bennett, James Bruce, Thomas Camden (Georgia Room, University of Georgia Library), T. J. Campbell, William Cannon, Louise Dillard Coldren, Gilbert Corbin, Robert C. Covel, Kyle Dampier, Jim Dillard, Mary Dillard, Frank Dyer, Herman Dyer, Thomas Ebright, Bob Edwards, Abby Ellard, Glenn Ellard, Rutherford L. Ellis, Jr., Beatrice Erwin, Mallory Ferrell, Thomas Fetters, Ann Foskey, Franklin M. Garrett, Ollie Glore, Terry Harkin, Marion Hemperly, Bill Henry, Gordon

Hunnicutt, William Hunnicutt, Jean Ivester, George James, Jr., Bill Jarrett, Joyce Kastner, Steve Keplinger, Jim Kidd, Peter Knepton, Robin Lakey, Anthony Lampros, Marion McConnell, Gail Miller (Georgia Department of Archives and History), Robert Mize, Delpha Moneypenny, M. M. Nate, H. G. Nelson, Kirk Newnan, Tim Nix, John Norcross, Betty Peardon, Joy Phillips, William Pippin, Jr., Fred Pitts, Jim Pitts, Cynthia Powelson, Marilyn Rogers, Pat Rogers, R. A. Romanes, Marty Roy, Tomy Short, Esther Smith, James A. Smith, Buck Snyder, Ernest Snyder, William Taylor, Chuck Wells, Cratis D. Williams, C. K. Williamson, Virginia Wilson, Jack Wynn.

Thanks, too, to Doubleday for being open to the students' desire to do a *Foxfire 10,* and to editor Charles Conrad and his assistant, Jon Furay, for their help in making it happen.

Introduction

Chris Nix: I am now a senior at Rabun County High School. I am seventeen, which means I wasn't even born when *The Foxfire Book* was first published in 1972. This past summer I was employed by Foxfire, along with seven other students, to put together *Foxfire 10.* I was one of two students in charge of the Crafts section, and, along with Jenny Lincoln, I helped put on the final polish and take care of some last minute details—up to the minute we left to deliver the manuscript to New York. I have been involved with Foxfire for three years now, and although I have not yet graduated from high school, I have already been a co-editor for two recent Doubleday releases: *A Foxfire Christmas* and *Foxfire: 25 Years.* Foxfire, and Wig (Eliot Wigginton) especially, made it possible for me to do important things and to travel to places I never dreamed I would get to visit. Together we went on many speaking engagements, one in Australia, for example, in the summer of 1989. I wanted to do something significant which would begin to repay Foxfire in some way for the opportunities it has provided me. Doubleday and Foxfire had planned at one time to end the *Foxfire* series with volume nine. This new volume of *Foxfire* came about, in part, because of the urging of a group of students who were hungry for *more.* That Doubleday and the Foxfire staff would respond to our urging is an important step, one of the first steps in forging Foxfire's *next* twenty-five years.

There are several reasons that *Foxfire 10*, to me, represents a humongous leap toward our future. To begin with, Wig was on a sabbatical leave from our program in Rabun County to teach education courses at the University of Georgia, so we had to put this book together largely on our own. We have had some apprehension: you know, that little voice in the back of the head that says: "It can't be done. . . ." It's a little scary. Second, whereas all of the previous nine volumes of Foxfire were put together using typewriters, scissors, and rubber cement, the copy for *Foxfire 10* was all typed and edited on Apple Macintosh word processing equipment, which we also use to produce our magazine. As far as I'm concerned, I have never worked on copy in any other way. The crafts persons I worked with for this book are different, too, from most of the contacts Foxfire worked with twenty-five years ago. Foxfire has been known throughout the country as a project in which students interview "old-timers" on their means of survival. Now, often as not, we interview people about what they do as a hobby—something they chose to do instead of practicing it as a way of life. What's more, it is not unusual to discover that people we interview do things based on what they have read in the Foxfire books.

George Reynolds: Since 1976 I've worked at Foxfire as music adviser, folklorist, and when the job demands, writing coach. Chris and I collaborated on this introduction as students and teachers do in most every aspect of our work at Foxfire. Those who have followed the process of Foxfire through the years will know that the books represent more than they appear to be on the surface. At first glance, this volume features the folklore, arts and crafts, and personal experiences of Southern mountain people. But, like the first nine volumes, this book is also the product of an educational process that takes place in classrooms in a public high school. For twenty-five years, Wig and his colleagues in the Foxfire program have been developing and refining an approach to classroom instruction that is spreading among teachers and their students from Washington to Maine to Florida. The approach, briefly, is based on the following notions: that people learn best when they are involved in real work with a real audience, that they should help plan strategies to meet a rigorous academic agenda, that their work should be honestly assessed, and that the work have aesthetic value and connect directly to the community where the learning is taking place (See Wigginton, "Foxfire Grows Up," *Harvard Educational Review,* Vol. 59, No. 1.).

Here's a brief update of what we've been up to since the last Foxfire book. Our main effort has been, I guess, our Teacher Outreach program, begun six years ago. Teacher Outreach director Hilton Smith offers a brief description of the program:

It started with the modest goals of offering courses in the Foxfire approach to classroom instruction at four or five colleges and universities, then supporting the efforts of participating teachers as they learned how to implement the approach in their classrooms.

Evidently the program struck a chord resonant with some very fundamental but untended notions about students, teachers, and schooling—notions which can elicit achievements by teachers and students well beyond what most educators have come to expect. It's that responsive chord that attracts teachers to this program, around two thousand to date, in levels K–12, all content areas, and all sorts of student constituencies.

We now offer graduate-level courses and staff development workshops at about twenty regional sites in twelve states, with a number of spinoff courses around each of those. In each region, the participating teachers have formed a network to provide continuing support of each other as they refine their own applications of the approach in their classrooms. Each network has a coordinator; several of the networks have developed area units or subdivisions to cope with the increasing numbers and geographic spread. The networks have become quasi-professional organizations, providing the kind of training and follow-up that those of us as teachers have always wanted and almost never received from our school districts.

Foxfire teacher networks are involved in collaborations with the Coalition of Essential Schools; Project Zero; the National Center for Restructuring Education, Schools, and Teaching; the

Program for School Improvement; and a number of state-level initiatives.

One reason our Teacher Outreach Program succeeds is that it is one of the few initiatives that is carried out entirely by teachers. Another is that we can draw on the accumulated, reflected-upon experiences of classroom teachers from an increasing variety of contexts. Beyond that, there is a conscious linkage of practice to pedagogy—a feature that empowers participants with the knowledge of why it works and what to do about it when it doesn't. [For more information, write to Foxfire Teacher Outreach, P.O. Box 541, Mountain City, Georgia 30562.]

Five years ago we planned to end the numbered series of Foxfire books, launching instead a new series, in collaboration with E. P. Dutton, that would go into some depth on special topics. We had already begun the effort with three titles: *Aunt Arie: A Foxfire Portrait* (1983; rpt. 1992), *The Foxfire Book of Appalachian Cookery* (1984; rpt. 1992), and *The Foxfire Book of Toys and Games* (1985). We continued with *The Foxfire Book of Wine Making*. We came to realize that books of such a specialized nature were more suited to a regional market, and we are now working with the University of North Carolina Press to reissue those titles and market them closer to home. Our continuing relationship with Doubleday has remained strong, however, with the publication of Wig's book for teachers, *Sometimes a Shining Moment* (1985), and two more recent titles Chris mentioned earlier—*A Foxfire Christmas* (1989), and *Foxfire: 25 Years* (1991), an oral history of the Foxfire Program focusing on the experiences of students through the years. With the publication of *Foxfire 10*, we return to a format much like that of the previous numbered volumes of Foxfire, but with a more unified theme.

Like Chris, all of my kinfolks for the last several generations made their start in the Appalachian Mountains. Though I grew up in the mountains of southwestern Virginia, I feel like "branch kin" to my northeastern Georgia students and their folks. As we worked on the book together, we realized that we have much in common: our ancestors faced a difficult world, while relying on their families, their neighbors, and their Maker for help and guidance. The stories in *Foxfire 10* reveal that our contacts used their wits, their creativity, and their traditional resources to respond to a changing world. In this respect we are all "branch kin."

As we collected the material for this book, the story emerged of a people coping with the irreversible changes that came to Appalachia by way of improved transportation, government decree, and corporate America. In this volume the issue of change clusters around five main topics. They include the history of the Tallulah Falls Railway, which entered Rabun County in northeast Georgia at the turn of the century; the era of the boardinghouses that sprang up to serve the tourists who came to the county by rail; a people's history of the coming of the hydroelectric dams, the Depression and its concomitant federal programs; personality portraits; and folk art and crafts. Much of the information in *Foxfire 10* was gathered from past issues of our student-produced quarterly, *Foxfire* magazine—which we still publish—and includes the work of students who were involved with Foxfire back in the early 1970s and throughout the 1980s. Of course, we also conducted additional interviews, some just weeks before the manuscript deadline.

Popular literature around the turn of the century created a romantic image of Appalachian people as naive illiterates, isolated from the rest of society, living in idyllic surroundings, and holding doggedly to archaic, Old World traditions. The media since that time have created another image of the same people, that of helpless victims, impoverished, ignorant, malnourished, genetically deficient, and sometimes sinister and dangerous. Neither is accurate, but nonetheless we have to deal with it. When I accompanied some students to Australia last summer to visit rural schools, the movie *Deliverance* played on network television; I found myself explaining to locals, "No, folks in North Georgia really aren't depraved, dangerous, and strange-looking." In examining the history of Appalachia, or of other regions where exploitation of natural resources has taken place, one will find that mainstream culture tends to deride yet romanticize those who live on the land being exploited. And people will believe what they see and hear in order to live with their social conscience.

There may have been a time when travel in Appalachia was difficult, but the region was never as isolated from the outside world as popular culture would have us believe. Since the indigenous Cherokees began to trade with the white man in the eighteenth century, people who live in the Appalachian Mountains have contended with successive waves of influence from the outside world. When we think of the American Industrial Revolution of the nineteenth century, we think of the factories in New England and the northern Midwest, but the Industrial Revolution came to Appalachia as well, in the form of railroads, and timber, power, and mining companies. From the turn of the century on, missionaries, settlement schools, and the popularizers of folk culture made their mark on Appalachian mountain communities. (For an examination of the politics of culture in Appalachia, see David Whisnant's *All That Is Native and Fine* [Chapel Hill and London: University of North Carolina Press, 1983]). In the 1930s the Depression hit, and Roosevelt's New Deal came to the mountains, bringing federal economic improvement programs. In the sixties the government's War on Poverty came to Appalachia with more programs designed to aid the economy. Today, the tourist and retirement home industries are alive and well in southern Appalachia, driving the economy in parts of the region.

Throughout *Foxfire 10* runs the common thread of mountain people interacting with the outside world. Many of the contacts illustrate how people coped with and participated in the workings of a changing world decades ago. Others, particularly the crafts people, address their situation as tradition bearers in today's world.

The first section of *Foxfire 10* is devoted to the Tallulah Falls Railway, referred to locally as the TF, which for fifty-four years was a major link to the outside world for communities between Cornelia, Georgia, and Franklin, North Carolina. Much of the cash economy in Appalachia has historically been linked to railways in some form or other until the four-lane highway began to change the picture. As early as 1882, the railroad had reached as far as Tallulah Falls, Georgia, inviting a brisk trade with tourists seeking a look at the "Grand Canyon of the East." Its completion in 1907 made a thriving timber business feasible in Rabun County. Foxfire students and staff put together the first story of the Tallulah Falls Railway in 1976, entitled *Memories of a Mountain Shortline*. Since then, students at Rabun County High School have made additions to the original work, and their combined effort is represented in these pages.

October, better known as "leaf season" in Rabun County, is one busy time. On balmy Sunday afternoons the glut of cars on U.S. 441 moves like rush hour in Atlanta. All along the roadside, vegetable stands advertise fresh cider, boiled peanuts, jams, jellies, and handicrafts. The harvest sale means a sure income to everyone from basket makers, to Boy Scouts, to banjo pickers. The Dillard House, Rabun County's most famous restaurant enterprise, serves thousands of tourists "family-style" at tables groaning with platters of fried chicken, green beans, country ham, and homemade rolls. This yearly event has historical underpinnings which date back perhaps a century. Bolstered by the coming of the railroad, boardinghouses sprang up all over Rabun County, inviting people to visit, rest, and eat. The second section of this volume includes stories by people who worked in and ran boardinghouses in our community. We chose to feature the stories of a few that have long since disappeared—places like the Glenbrook Hotel at Tallulah Falls, now a ruin—and we include stories and recipes from the Dickerson House which, as recently as the 1970s, entertained guests in Wolffork Valley.

One of the major sections of this book we call "Economic Revolution." It's a ground-level story about the corporate and governmental intrusions into our community between the turn of the century and World War II. We begin with several narratives which illustrate how power companies affected the lives of some of our contacts in North Georgia and western North Carolina. Sixty-five families sold or relocated their farms on the Tallulah River in deals with Georgia Power Company, as it built a system of hydroelectric dams on the waterway, completed in 1927. With the dams and power plants, came construction and logging jobs and today a building industry that primarily constructs vacation homes. During World War II, the Tennessee Valley Authority (TVA) built dams in the watershed of surrounding counties, bringing more jobs and creating lifelong memories for some of our contacts. The "Economic Revolution" section begins with narratives that focus on the inundation of Burton community to create Lake Burton; it continues with narratives by men who worked in the timber and construction businesses connected with both the Burton Dam and Fontana Dam, a TVA project in western North Carolina. Next, we take a look at the Depression through the eyes of several who lived through it. A well-established system of subsistence farming and barter economy tempered somewhat the economic devastation of the Depression; nonetheless, people lived hard, and their stories illustrate their remarkable endurance. Considerable change took place in the community as a result of the intervention of federal programs to rejuvenate the economy. During these years, the U.S. Government established the Civilian Conservation Corps (CCC), which operated in conjunction with the U.S. Forest Service and the Works Progress Administration (WPA). We interviewed a number of people in our county who were employed on these government jobs, and whose lives were substantially affected.

Three powerful personality portraits of Ellene Gowder, Walker Word, and Lyndall "Granny" Toothman comprise a fourth section. They are exceptional people and good storytellers whose lives reflect many of the same experiences chronicled in the Tallulah Falls Railway and the Economic Revolution sections.

The final section of *Foxfire 10* features the subject of folk art and crafts, always popular with our readers. Deeply respectful of the traditions that nurtured them, the more conservative artisans we interviewed were delighted to talk about the issues of persistence and change in their work. Others of a less conventional persuasion break the molds of convention and have no qualms about it; they are not conscious tradition bearers, though their work carries the marks of the culture from which they emerged. All are influenced by some agent of change in our society, whether it be the economy, the crafts guild, the folk art dealers, or Elvis.

Looking back, it appears that many people in our corner of Appalachia, accustomed to living off the land, exchanged their land and its resources for money and jobs. Some survived with their dignity and little else; some thrived and became prosperous as agents in the extraction of wealth. Others farmed the old homeplace and followed the old ways, dubious of modern pretensions that the new way is best. Today, their children and grandchildren are inheriting family farms and shouldering sobering responsibilities for land they perhaps cannot afford to keep but cannot bear to sell.

In our continuing effort to make a living, we are called on to make compromises, and land stewardship is but one issue. There is also the quality of our work and, ultimately, the content of our character, which we must consider as we face new challenges. Perhaps if we continue to examine the process by which others have interacted with a changing world, we can exercise some wisdom in our current decision making. I hope so.

Chris Nix
George P. Reynolds   Rabun County, 1992

Foxfire 10

TRANSPORTATION

STUDENT EDITOR, TIM MARTIN

Nearly two decades ago, when we were Foxfire students, Myra Queen and I co-edited *Memories of a Mountain Shortline,* the story of the Tallulah Falls Railway. Our book was a combined effort by many students who contributed interviews and photographs, and it was overseen by Foxfire staff members Suzy Angier and Pat Rogers. It was the first book published by The Foxfire Press (1976).

A lot has changed since then. Myra is married, has two children, and raises and trains horses. I've married, have one child, and I'm back where the book began. I returned to Foxfire two years ago to work with the alumni and the community programs.

When Wig asked me to help Tim Martin, a tenth-grader at Rabun County High School, work on a new version of the Tallulah Falls Railway, my first response was, "Well, what's wrong with the original version?" But as I have become reengaged in the saga of "the old TF," I've grown to appreciate the fact that while the original story was good, there definitely was room for improvement.

For example, Tim has done a worthy job of broadening the history of the railroad. His facts and figures give the reader a much better sense of what the TF was and what it could have been. The history is still not as detailed as some railroad historians would like, but we feel that what the people served by the train have to say is just as important. For those of you who are interested in pursuing the history of the Tallulah Falls Railway in greater depth, we have provided at the end of the "History" section a bibliography of sources we used in compiling our historical account.

Flatly stated, the Tallulah Falls Railway provided jobs and transportation for people and goods. But its impact on North Georgia's economy and society was immeasurably greater than that. For fifty-four years, the TF ran from Cornelia, Georgia, to Franklin, North Carolina, a distance of fifty-eight miles. When the line was completed in 1907, it was *the* major link to the outside world. A state highway ran parallel with the tracks, but in bad weather it was muddy and impassable.

Before the railroad came, Macon, Rabun, and Habersham counties were isolated, essentially self-sufficient, agricultural communities. Clarkesville was the big resort in northeast Georgia. People went there by stagecoach to vacation, and made side trips to places like Tallulah Falls. When the railway reached Tallulah Falls in 1882, tourists came by trainloads to spend their summers at the hotels that sprang up around the gorge and, soon, further north in the Clayton area.

The train immediately changed this area's way of life. It did more than give people railway job opportunities and provide a way for goods to be shipped to and from this mountainous region. It also helped in the creation of new industries, such as timber and tourism. It provided safe, fast transportation for people who previously had had to ride in a wagon for three days just to get from Clayton to Cornelia. The depots became places for people to meet and socialize. In short, either directly or indirectly, there were few aspects of life that the train did not affect.

In the introduction to the original book, Myra and I said, "Our intentions while compiling this book were twofold: recount from an historical perspective the operation of this particular shortline railroad, and at the same time attempt to capture the 'personality' of the line as reflected by those whose lives it touched. Perhaps the term 'personality' is a romanticized fabrication in reference to a railroad. Or maybe it isn't. For we came to know the TF as a unique mixture of people and machinery—almost as a living being, complete with its own birth, life, and death. We hope you enjoy these memories of a mountain shortline."

—*Kaye Carver Collins*

Tallulah Falls Railway

HISTORY

By the mid-1800s, the Tallulah Gorge in south Rabun County became famed as "the Grand Canyon of the East." The city of Tallulah Falls, located right on the edge of the gorge, became a popular tourist attraction. People poured into the city as fast as they could get there—but "getting there" was quite a problem. In *Sketches of Rabun County History,* Andrew J. Ritchie tells of how much trouble it was to get to Rabun County back in the 1800s:

> Go one day by railroad, the next day by horse and buggy, a third day on horseback, a fourth day on foot and then on all fours until you climbed a tree, and when you fell out, you'd be in Rabun County.

Actually, the real reason for the Tallulah Falls Railway was not to accommodate the masses heading for Tallulah Falls. Nor was it because of any other attraction in this area. The reason for the Tallulah Falls Railway started many miles from here and many railroad companies ago.

You can trace the Tallulah Falls Railway all the way back to the early 1800s. It all started with John C. Calhoun. After serving two terms as Vice President of the United States, Calhoun returned home to his plantation in South Carolina, where Clemson University

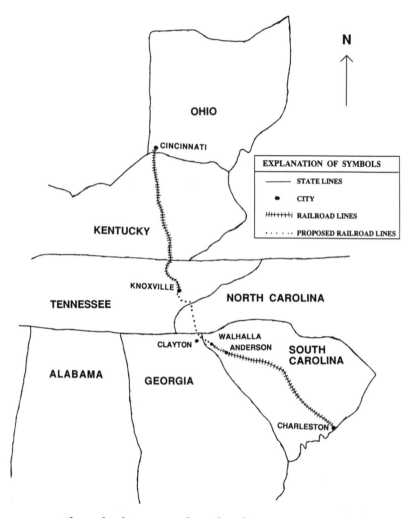

BLUE RIDGE RAILROAD LINE

EXPLANATION OF SYMBOLS
— STATE LINES
• CITY
⊩⊩⊩⊩ RAILROAD LINES
· · · · · PROPOSED RAILROAD LINES

sits now. There he began work on his dream, a major east-to-west railroad line. It would run from Charleston, South Carolina, to Cincinnati, Ohio. Lines were already in existence from Anderson, South Carolina, to Charleston and from Cincinnati to Knoxville. It is believed that the line he envisioned was to have run, originally, through South Carolina and North Carolina and on to Tennessee.

That changed, however, in 1838. In 1838, two coincidences suggest that because of the first, the second took place. The first coincidence was that 1838 was the year of the Georgia gold rush. The second coincidence was that the Rabun County Inferior Court gave permission to the Blue Ridge Railroad Company to build a line through Rabun County in 1838. Although it isn't known for

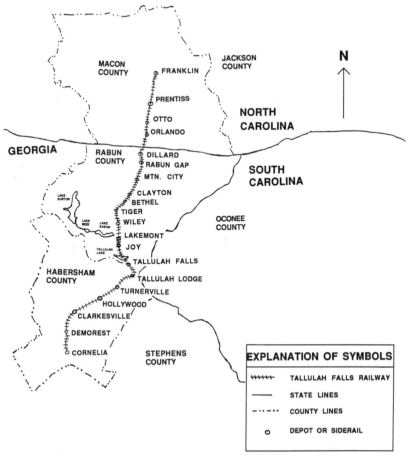

sure, it is assumed that the route of the line was changed because gold was discovered in Dahlonega, Georgia.

The gold rush soon died out, but the line's route was never changed from Georgia. It is believed that Calhoun thought the 1838 railroad attempt premature. When Calhoun died in 1850, others began to make the line a reality, and in 1853, construction finally began on the line.

News of the first major east-to-west line spread through the country quickly. Feeder lines were planned all up and down the new line, including several through Georgia. In 1854, the North Eastern Railroad Company was chartered to build a line from Athens, Georgia, to Clayton to connect with the Blue Ridge line at that point. There were at least two other known lines planned to connect with the Blue Ridge line at Rabun Gap. Nothing, it seemed, would stop the railroads now.

Unfortunately, trouble hit in the late 1850s. With the threat of war closing in, the Southern economy tightened up. In 1858, with the track reaching Walhalla, South Carolina, work had to be stopped on most of the Blue Ridge line. In 1859, the rest of the work came to a halt. When the war hit, work hadn't even started on the North Eastern line.

From 1861, with the firing on Fort Sumter, to 1865, one of the bloodiest wars in our country's history was fought. At the end of the war, the South was crushed. After five years of recovering and rebuilding, the Southern economy began flowing again. Money soon became available for expansion, and the railroads began to rebuild.

In 1869, work resumed on the Blue Ridge line—only to fail again, because stockholders did not want to buy bonds in still uncertain conditions. Several attempts were made from 1869 to 1940 to finish the line. The most successful was made by the Black Diamond Railroad Company, but it, too, failed when construction on the railway grade was 80 percent completed.

The North Eastern started construction on its line in 1871, with a greater ambition than that of just connecting up to the Blue Ridge line. Since the line had stalled with 80 percent of the work completed, it would be easy for the North Eastern to build on to Knoxville after reaching Clayton. By 1873, the line had reached Lula, Georgia, and the Atlanta & Richmond Air Line (A&RAL). The A&RAL had been built earlier that year and ran from Charlotte, North Carolina, to Atlanta, Georgia. Along the A&RAL route were Lula and Cornelia, Georgia.

The scant information that exists makes the sequence of events and acquisitions impossible to untangle with any certainty. What is known follows: The North Eastern *did* use the A&RAL line from Lula to Cornelia as a major component of their line, thereby saving time and money. The capital stock of the North Eastern was acquired by the Richmond & Danville System (R&D) before 1882. The R&D also acquired capital stock of the A&RAL before 1894. These three facts can be combined to form many theories about who bought whom when, but no one knows for sure.

In 1882, the railroad reached the town of Clarkesville, as this excerpt from the January 4, 1882, edition of the *Tri-County Advertiser* reveals:

Look Out For the Engine! On and after Thursday, 5th inst., Trains will arrive at and depart from Clarkesville as follows: Leave Clarkesville 8:00 a.m., arrive Rabun Gap Junction [Cornelia] 8:45 a.m. connecting with trains from Athens and Atlanta, and all points North. Leave Rabun Gap Junction 11:15 a.m., arrive Clarkesville 12 noon. Freights will be received and delivered at Clarkesville on and after the 10th instant.

G. J. Foreacre, President NERR

The train did more than just enhance towns along the route; it created a few. In 1887, the city of Demorest was established as a vacation spot. For some reason, though, the attraction never caught on. Nevertheless, Demorest is now a thriving community with a population of over 1,100.

On June 22, 1882, the North Eastern Railroad reached Tallulah Falls and in doing so fueled a forty-year-long tourist boom in the North Georgia mountains. That is as far north as it would go for twenty more years.

In 1885 or 1886, the Richmond and Danville System acquired a line that ran from Atlanta to Knoxville, thus completing their own east to west line. It then became obvious that the North Eastern Line from Cornelia northward would never make it. Because the R&D already had another east to west line, the line into Tallulah Falls was useless to the company.

In 1887, the R&D sold the line to the Blue Ridge and Atlantic Railroad Company (BR&A), which wanted to build a line from Savannah, Georgia, to Knoxville. But in 1892, the BR&A went into receivership and in 1897 was given permission to sell the line. The BR&A never began any work on the Savannah–Knoxville line.

After five years of receivership, the BR&A just couldn't afford to maintain the huge trestles. Work on the Panther Creek trestle had lapsed and the timbers had grown rotten. On June 14, 1898, a TF passenger train was heading across the Panther Creek trestle when its timbers gave way, and the train plummeted ninety-eight feet. Of the six people on the train, only one was killed, Clinton Ivy, the fireman on the train. Others on the train were the engineer, Henry Johnson, the conductor, John C. Faulkner, the brakeman, Charlie Askea, the baggage master, Doc Shirley, and one passenger, whose name is unknown.

Wood burner in "downtown" Mountain City,
between 1907 and 1914. (Photograph courtesy of Tom Hunnicutt)

In 1898, the Tallulah Falls Railway Company purchased the twenty-one-mile line from Cornelia to Tallulah Falls. Now officially known as the Tallulah Falls Railway (TF), the company was ready to push on. Plans now were to reach Clayton by their own route, follow the Blue Ridge roadbed to Franklin, North Carolina, next, follow the Little Tennessee River to Almond, North Carolina, and connect with the Western North Carolina Railroad.

The year that work on the line restarted is unknown, but by 1901, the TF had reached Wiley, Georgia. In June of 1904, sixty-six years after talk of a railroad through Rabun County began, the TF finally reached Clayton.

Just north of Clayton, at mile 37.4 on the TF line, the TF ran into the Blue Ridge roadbed. By 1905, the line had reached the North Carolina state line. At this point the Richmond & Danville System, now incorporated into the Southern, saw potential for the TF line. So, in 1905, the Southern Railway Company acquired capital stock of the Tallulah Falls Railway.

While further work was being done, the TF needed an immediate source of income. Finances were becoming slim, and the outlook for new investors was not favorable. Then timber became a major industry in Rabun County. Logging was the perfect money-maker for its time. There was a seemingly unlimited supply of timber, and the railroad was a cheap way to export it.

Unfortunately, in 1906, the TF ran into severe financial problems. Work was stopped on the line just south of Otto, North Carolina, at a depot named Prentiss, the name of the man who had pushed the railroad from Tallulah Falls northward.

The people of Macon County, North Carolina, weren't happy with the terminal point of the railway. They wanted the railroad to run all the way in to Franklin, the main commercial town in the area. As a result, in 1906, Macon County voted for a bond issue to pay for the completion of the TF to Franklin. This was as far as the line would ever go.

At this point, the TF had overcome all of the steep grades, rocky cuts, and rough terrain that had made its construction so challenging. It would have been an easy ride all the way to Almond where it would have connected with the Western North Carolina Railroad. If the connection had been made, the TF line would have had much revenue from through freight between the Western North Carolina Railroad and the Southern Railway. This extra revenue would have helped to keep the TF in business longer—perhaps even until today.

Regardless of what *could* have been, the TF never made it past Franklin. In 1908, the TFRR again had financial problems and went into receivership for one year. The property and buildings of the railroad began to be administered by a court-appointed receiver.

In spite of its problems, the TF remained a very worthy asset to Rabun County, as is best demonstrated by its importance to the Georgia Railway and Power Company.

Georgia Power had no way of hauling materials to its dam sites in North Georgia except by using the TF. But since the TF was miles from some of the sites, Georgia Power built five rail spurs from the TF line and purchased several small locomotives to enable the company to reach sites the TF didn't already serve.

For the next several years, the business from the dam-building projects helped generate new revenue for the Tallulah Falls Railway. In 1917, the United States entered World War I, and the government took control of the railroads in 1919. According to Hoyt Tench (a fireman with the TF from 1942 to 1944), "they [the government] seized the railroads and other transportation that they needed for their own benefit. If they needed to haul soldiers, they would get us. When the government has to move a lot of things,

This spur was built off the Tallulah Falls track to facilitate the building of Burton Dam (which created Lake Burton) by the Georgia Power Company. (Photograph courtesy of Tom Moss)

they do it by rail. They just seize them. They seize the employees and the railroad." The government replaced the set-salary payroll with mandated hourly wages, which greatly increased the TF's payroll. By 1919, the TF had lost $919,731.

Though its holdings varied over the life of the TF, a 1922 Interstate Commerce Commission (ICC) report gives a snapshot of the TF's assets. In 1922 the rolling stock of the TF included five steam locomotives, forty-five freight cars, nine passenger cars, and six work equipment cars. According to an ICC report, the railway line consisted of thirty-two miles of straight track and twenty-five and two-tenths miles of curves (with up to twelve degrees in curvature). Ninety-five percent of the line was on native earth. There were forty-three open-deck timber trestles and bridges, ranging in height from eight to eighty-three feet. The longest trestle was nine hundred and thirty-nine feet long and had a maximum height of forty-six feet.

In 1923, the TF went back into receivership for the remainder of its existence. From then on, it lost a little more money each year. To reduce its outgo, in 1929, the Tallulah Falls Railway quit paying government taxes, and never paid taxes again. By 1933, the TF had a cumulative deficit of $2,137,274. Receiver J. F. Gray petitioned the ICC to abandon the line. The ICC granted permission, but action was never taken on this petition to abandon.

Wrecks also contributed to the financial worries of the shortline. On August 23, 1920, eighty-five girls rode train No. 3, returning home from summer camp. Just north of Wiley, the train derailed and turned over. None of the children was injured, but the engineer, John Harvey, was killed and the fireman, Caloway Gibby, was severely burned. Then in 1927, the Hazel Creek trestle collapsed with a passenger train on it. Ernest Hogsed, the "news butcher," and Don Merritt, the baggage master, were killed, and fourteen others were injured. The rear coach, with thirteen passengers on board, stayed on the tracks.

Wiley passenger train wreck of 1920.

In 1938, H. L. Brewer, who had worked on the railroad since he was a boy, was appointed receiver, and would hold this position until the train was abandoned. The TF's problems were the same ones faced by other railroads. Brewer cut expenses everywhere possible. He reduced the number of employees in all departments, delayed replacing timber in cross ties and trestles, and took on extra duties himself.

While it was obvious that, from this point on, the railroad was headed for abandonment, it was decided to let it run as long as it could. On Saturday, May 11, 1946, passenger service ended when Engine No. 73 wrecked, leaving the last passenger coach damaged beyond repair.

In 1948, Brewer replaced four steam engines with two diesel electrics. They reduced the cost of running the engines from ninety to twenty dollars a day. But revenues continued to drop.

Indirectly, the highway ruined the TF's business. Before the paved highway was built, the railroad was the only direct link between Franklin and Cornelia. After the highway opened the area to trucks and cars, trucks began hauling freight and mail, and tourists started traveling in their own vehicles. It was clear that the railroad would eventually die.

There was a brief resurgence in activity along the line in the early 1950s. In 1951, the movie *I'd Climb the Highest Mountain* was filmed on the TF line. Then in 1955, Walt Disney began to film *The Great Locomotive Chase*. The Tallulah Falls Railway was chosen as the location for the depiction of the famous Andrew's Raid, in which Union troops tried to destroy the Western & Atlantic Railroad between Atlanta and Chattanooga, Tennessee. Carl Rogers, the depot agent at Clayton, recalls: "The film prolonged the life of the TF for a little while. The TF got *some* money out of it. Walt Disney gave them around $10,000 to make the movie. Plus, the TF got all the revenue off of those trains coming in, and they furnished Walt Disney with rail cars. It gave the Tallulah Falls Railway a considerable boost in revenue."

By 1960, the rolling stock of the TF had diminished significantly from its earlier holdings. The stock consisted of two diesel locomotives, three flat cars, two caboose cars, one baggage express (nonpassenger carrying) car, one self-propelled car, and four company service equipment cars. That same year, the TF had operating revenues of $155,052, operating expenses of $226,471, and the railway tax accrual of $19,336. So, for that one year the TF operated at a loss of $90,755.

By 1961, the TF had a cumulative deficit of $5,067,586.

Finally, on March 26, 1961, the Tallulah Falls Railway line was abandoned. Soon after, the Rabun Industrial Development Company (RIDC) was formed by citizens of Macon, Rabun, and Habersham counties who wanted to raise enough money to buy back the line. On May 4, 1961, the railroad was auctioned off to the RIDC. The following announcement appeared in the magazine *Trains* in August 1961:

The recently abandoned Tallulah Falls Railway may run again if property sale plans are consummated. Rabun Industrial Development Company, formed by local businessmen, had offered $266,000.00 for the 54 miles of the line, from Clarkesville, Ga., to Franklin, N.C., and hopes to resume operations. Representatives of Southern Railway have made a bid of $36,000.00 for the four mile stretch from Clarkesville to the Southern connection at Cornelia, Ga.

Local businessman Woodrow Reeves remembered: "There were representatives [in the RIDC] from Franklin, Prentiss, Otto, Dillard, and Clayton. There were also some from Tallulah Falls and Clarkesville. The line was purchased for us by our attorneys, Knox Bynum and J. Horner Stockton. The bid was $266,000—but we never had that much money on hand. We had raised approximately $100,000 by the time of the bid.

"Southern Railroad was the first mortgage holder. Mr. D. W. Bronson, who was president of Southern Railway at that time, agreed in substance that if we could get the other claims settled, he would sell us the Southern's TF mortgage for one dollar. The largest claim, other than Southern's, was one held by the National Railroad Employees Retirement Board. They claimed that the TF owed them the sum of $300,000 for back taxes, such as Social Security. [The TF] was in bankruptcy, and the federal courts had allowed it to go on and operate at a loss. They could operate by not paying their taxes. [The TF's revenue wasn't enough to pay any taxes after salary and maintenance costs were met.]

"We made the Railroad Retirement Board a cash offer of $50,000 to settle their claim. They thought that since it had been bid in at $266,000, they would have the first lien against it. They refused the $50,000 offer. Well, as it turned out in the end, they wound up getting only about $17,000 [after a salvage company eventually assumed the bid].

"The main obstacle was lack of sufficient funds. While trying to compromise [on] the Railroad Retirement Board's claim, we visited the Justice Department and spoke briefly to Robert Kennedy, who was then Attorney General, and then the rest of the time we appealed to one of his aides. I don't think we impressed Robert Kennedy very much with our cause."

Businessman Lewis Reeves told us what the Rabun Industrial Development Company planned to do with the railroad when they purchased it: "We didn't think it was necessary for the railroad to lose all that money. We were trying to save it more for the counties that it ran through than anything else. We intended to operate the railroad. I guess it would have wound up as a scenic railroad. I guess we would have hauled freight and had a scenic railroad, too. We had both in mind. But we didn't make any actual plans because we got stopped."

Woodrow Reeves recalled: "Judge Sloan told us to have our money in by 30 days or forfeit our deposit. Well, the only thing to do then was to allow the Midwest Steel Company from Charleston, West Virginia, to come in and take over our bid, which we did. We didn't sell it to the steel company—they just assumed our bid.

"Some folks may blame the Southern Railroad for allowing the TF to go under, but I don't. The Southern needs all the feeder lines it can keep. Anything shipped over the TF also produced revenue for the Southern. Officials of the Southern were very receptive to our committee and really wanted the TF to continue operating."

As Mr. Reeves said, the railroad was sold to the Midwest Steel Company. They took up the track during 1961–62 and scrapped many of the cars. The TF's long struggle was over.

Sources

Acts of the General Assembly of the State of Georgia, 1853–54, No. 375, p. 451.

Acts of the General Assembly of the State of Georgia, 1855, No. 117, p. 178.

Adams, Allison, et al. "You Can Still See the Roadbed in the Winter." *Foxfire,* Vol. 25–26, No. 3 & 4 (Fall–Winter 1990), pp. 131–40.

"Build Rabun Gap Extension." *Franklin (N.C.) Press,* June 28, 1905.

Dunn, Michael, "Little Railroad: Heart of Steel." *North Carolina Daily News,* February 5, 1961.

"Federal Courts Decision in TFRR Hearing Seen as Victory for Public." *Franklin (N.C.) Press,* January 26, 1933.

Financial Packet 20781. Interstate Commerce Commission. November 27, 1960.

Harshaw, Lou. *Trains, Trestles, Tunnels.* Asheville Chapter, National Railway Historical Society, Inc., pp. 58–59.

Interstate Commerce Commission Reports. Vol. 4. November 1923–January 1925 Financial Reports, pp. 537–62.

Interstate Commerce Commission Reports. Vol. 193. April–December 1933 Financial Reports, pp. 689–96.

"Mountain Train Crosses 42 Trestles in 58 Miles." *Atlanta Journal and Constitution Magazine,* August 2, 1959.

Peoples, E. A. "End of Old Seventy-Three." *Atlanta Journal,* June 23, 1946.

"The Railroad Bonds." *Franklin (N.C.) Press,* September 13, 1905.

Ritchie, Andrew. *Sketches of Rabun County History.* Clayton, Ga.: Foote and Davis, 1948, pp. 253–57.

Sharen, Luther. "Tallulah Falls Railway May Be on Its Last Crossties." *Asheville Citizen-Times,* n.d.

"Tallulah Falls Railway Is Just a Memory." *Franklin (N.C.) Press.* February 8, 1973.

"Train Makes Last Trip on Tallulah Falls Railway." *Anderson Independent,* March 26, 1961.

Trains, August 1961.

Tri-County Advertiser, May 4, 1961.

A PIPELINE TO THE WORLD BEYOND

The Tallulah Falls Railway was completed to Franklin in 1907, nearly twenty years before the muddy track of a "highway" that it paralleled was finally paved. Ross Davis, a lifetime employee of the railroad, explained: "I started on the railroad September 3, 1918, and I worked on it almost fifty years. I was there when it closed down. Before the railroad, there wasn't any way of getting up in that country unless you walked or rode a mule. It was rough—especially in the wintertime. There wasn't any automobiles. They usually had oxen or mules pulling wagons. There was no concrete on the highways anywhere, and the road crossed every branch, you know, on the water. There were no bridges—or there might have been one or two. They even crossed the Tallulah Falls River without any bridge before the TF was built. If they had to go across the river, they would go across on the rocks."

The railroad immediately became, in other words, *the* pathway to the outside world. The impact was instantaneous and dramatic.

In part, the railroad's value came through the fact that it was a dead-end line: It served only the communities that lined the fifty-eight miles of track. It went nowhere else but to them. The railway gave the residents jobs, bought things from them, took them places, brought visitors to see them, shipped out their farm produce, brought in things they couldn't raise or make, provided depots to

Ross Davis, dispatcher for the Tallulah Falls Railway.

gather in, kept them company, provided excitement, and even supposedly helped some people forecast the weather by the sound of the whistle. It seems there was hardly a facet of life which the railway did not touch.

In an area with so many forest resources, naturally a substantial portion of the freight carried was timber. With the railroad completed, major logging companies like the Blue Ridge Lumber Company and Morse Brothers moved into the area, set up logging camps back in the woods served by their own narrow-gauge railroads (see the interview with Ellene Gowder on p. 305), and hauled the logs out of the woods to the sawmills that sprang up along the railroad right-of-way. As Carl Rogers said, "They hauled out mainly timber. They hauled an enormous amount of telephone poles, cross ties, lumber, tanbark, and telegraph poles."

Jobs were hard to find in Rabun County, and when the railroad came through it provided many people with work. Lon Harkins told us about jobs cutting lumber and hauling it to the railroad: "Long time ago, when they had that railroad over there, they shipped pulpwood [logs too small to be sawed into lumber]. Millard Grist run a pulpwood yard, and all the people cut pulpwood. They took it over to Dillard and loaded the boxcars. Back then people didn't have much to do, and they'd hire you. I worked over there; they give me about 50 cents or a dollar to help load them cars."

Ellen Alley recalled how they loaded lumber on the cars: "The train would usually park on a flat place. They used what they called a flat car. They measured it [lumber] and put it on the train. After the railroad came there was lots of logging, and lots of logs were shipped out. That was one great asset to the community."

Some of the timber went to the Singer Sewing Machine Company. R. M. Dickerson remembered: "They got yellow poplar to use as a base for oak-veneered sewing machine tables. It made a lighter top than solid oak. They did quite a business here, and they depended on the railroad to get the yellow poplar to them."

A small factory even sprang up in Mountain City which man-ufactured shuttles out of dogwood for the textile industry.

Homer Deal discussed how the combination of the railway and the lumber mills helped the local economy prosper: "When they first put in the railroad, they brought a lot of big sawmills in here and began cutting the virgin timber into lumber and shipping it out. There was a lot of chestnut here, and they cut a lot of telephone and power poles. They shipped out thousands of carloads of them out of here. The people around here definitely prospered on ac-count of the railroad. Franklin grew a lot when the train came in—it was as isolated as Rabun County. It was a great thing back in them days."

Mildred Story's father ran a hotel in downtown Clayton and a general store. She remembered: "When my daddy bought tanbark, people in the community would skin oak trees. He shipped [the bark] to Sylva, North Carolina, where they had a tannery. They used it to take the hair off of the skins of animals and make them into leather."

The railroad also shipped hides that people would tan and sell to companies. Ellen Alley recalled: "I remember one thing that the train did for us. At one time, people tanned leather to sell, and they would tan them and ship them out on the train [to companies that bought them]."

Many people in the area raised livestock for a living. The railroad was the easiest way to transport the animals to livestock yards. Ethel Corn remembered: "A lot of people shipped cattle. Before the railroad they used to drive them [on foot] to Athens or Atlanta, to market. They drove everything that way. I've heard my mother talk of it. They drove ducks, geese, and hogs. After the railroad came in, they went to shipping it, and it helped a lot."

Esco Pitts worked for years as a farm manager at the Rabun Gap-Nacoochee School, in part raising cattle for market. He says: "Then the [Rabun Gap-Nacoochee] school had a big cattle barn down there. They fattened 75 to 100 head of cattle and shipped them on the railroad. They would get sales from off some place, and they rode them in them cattle cars—put them cattle in there and shipped them. That's one way the school made its money."

The train would occasionally bring a special car, called the "chicken car," through the three counties the TF served. People would bring chickens to sell, and others would come to buy chickens. Carl Rogers said: "I can remember when the chicken car used to come. They would take it to Franklin for a day, and the farmers would come in. There would be a representative there from a meat packing company. The poultry cars had little compartments for chickens. They were slatted to give them ventilation. The farmers would bring in the ones they wanted to sell. They'd have scales there, and the representative would weigh them out and pay cash per the weight. Then they'd go to Otto, Dillard, and right on down the line."

Asbestos mines and mica mines were opened. Roy Shope said: "They used to ship asbestos out of here. There was a place on down below the state line [in North Carolina] way up on top of that mountain and the Indians had worked it way back when they was here. I've mined for asbestos up there. (I got a really good stone pot made by the Indians out of that mine up there and I used it

Roy Shope worked on the bridge and section crews of the TF.

for years.) I forget how many carloads we shipped out of that place but it was a lot of 'em!

"There was also a saddle factory in Demorest. The saddle shop did a lot of business. They'd make the skins into saddles and ship them out by train. That factory is still down there, making saddles."

Ross Davis remembers another Demorest factory that used the TF: "There was a large cotton mill—textiles—there called Habersham Mills, and they brought all of their stuff up to a little depot at the side of the railroad tracks. They built them a depot on purpose. They could put two or three carloads of manufactured cotton yarn in that depot, and when we didn't have boxcars enough to put empty cars in there for 'em, they would load it in that station. When we got a boxcar ready, our section man would go up there and load the boxcar for them."

People also shipped produce. Carl Rogers recalled: "Apples were shipped on the train as well as garden produce. The Express used to handle a lot of gift products, and we used to ship hundreds of bushels of apples in the fall. We had a real cheap rate. One day I counted seventy boxes of gift fruit."

Not only did the TF export several items, it imported a few also. It brought things to this area that were unimaginable to the people living here at that time—some of them simple things. This newspaper clipping from the *Tri-County Advertiser* (February 15, 1882) demonstrates this:

The first two bales of cotton that were ever brought to Clarkesville came in last Monday morning. This is some of the good effects of the railroad.

The TF belonged to the people it served. The more integrated the TF became with the lives of the people, the more it changed the society and economy. Most of all, it brought to North Georgia what nothing else could bring: unity. It unified three counties that had been totally independent areas.

The way it did this, in part, was through the jobs it created. Here Carl Rogers tells of the TF's connection to postal communication: "They had a special mail car. Freight trains didn't handle anything but freight, and the passenger trains handled the mail, passengers, and express. Just about every passenger train carried mail—had a U.S. Mail Post Office on the train. The postal clerk had to bag mail for the post offices along the line. He'd just dispatch [the mail] and sort out things for the post offices."

"The way that we got our mail," recalled Jo Brewer, "was on the passenger train. The reason it came on the passenger train was because the passenger train had a regular schedule. [The freight train did not.] It would have been too bad if it came on the freight train because nobody would have ever known when to come down to the depot and get the mail."

Carl Rogers remembered: "The U.S. Postal Service hired a mail carrier for every post office all up and down the line. They were hired on a contract basis for, I believe it was, thirty dollars a month. Their job was to carry the mail between the train depot and the post office. They had a special place fixed for him to park. He'd go to the post office first and pick up all the mail that was going north and bring it to the depot in a bag. Then whenever the train came by, why he would throw his bag into the mail car and they would throw out a bag for his post office. Then [later in the day] he'd pick up the southbound mail at the post office and bring it down and put it on the southbound train and pick up the mail for his post office that had accumulated north of it and carry that back to the post office.

"At Rabun Gap, the [Rabun Gap-Nacoochee School] had the contract, and every time a new family would come in to live on one of the school farms [while their children went to school there], if they didn't have a team of mules, Dr. Ritchie, the president, would let them have the mail on a school wagon [with mules owned by the school]. It was almost three quarters of a mile from the railroad depot to the Rabun Gap Post Office, and he would delegate that job to the new family long enough to where they could buy them a pair of mules. I've heard him tell it many times—he called that 'the mule buy.'

"So the railroad really amounted to a lot of employment for the people along the line. There'd be a mail carrier to every post office—a little bit of income for everybody all along the line."

The railroad also provided telegraph service. Carl Rogers said, "The railroad had a contract with Western Union. I believe they had it from the beginning. When I came to work, we had two telegraph wires. One was for Western Union, and the other was for railroad use only."

Taken in 1904, this photograph is of an excursion train from Cornelia to Tiger. Often people from Atlanta would take the Southern Railroad to Cornelia, then board the TF excursion for an outing.

And, of course, there were the passengers. It can be argued that the existence of the train was the catalyst for the development of North Georgia's tourist industry. Before the turn of the century, the railroad was completed to Tallulah Falls and visitors were filling the hotels that were built there to provide them some relief from the South Georgia summer heat (see the section on tourism beginning on page 89).

There were also excursion trains that Jo Brewer remembers: "A lot of times [there would be] excursion trains on Sunday, just in the summertime. I guess they would usually start about May and probably go into October. The excursion trains came from Atlanta. If they had big crowds, which they did often-times, I guess there would be five cars or more, a lot of passenger cars hooked up together."

WORKING ON THE RAILROAD

When the TF arrived in Rabun, Macon, and Habersham counties, it brought a host of jobs with it that were directly connected to the railroad itself.

This section focuses on these jobs: the daily routines, the techniques, hassles, and dangers of "working on the railroad" from the men who know them best, the men who held them.

The Roadbed

To start off, crews were responsible for preparing the bed for the tracks in the initial building of the road. Through some areas they had to build fills, or long mounds wide enough to take the track over low ground which might be boggy, and to build up small dips in the terrain where they didn't need trestles. The fills were usually made with rock and soil from cuts through hills or mountains.

It was basically handwork, with mules and slip pans, picks and shovels, scratching a route across the landscape. At regular intervals, "cuts" had to be drilled and blasted through solid rock obstacles.

Oftentimes, no notice would be given where a cut had been made. Because people sometimes did not know or forgot about the railroad grading, serious injuries or death would result. The January 11, 1882, *Tri-County Advertiser* reported such an event six days after the railroad reached Clarkesville:

On Saturday night last, in Center Hill Dist., this county, a man by the name of Whitfield W. Berry, a well-known and highly respected citizen of this county, fell into a railroad cut just opposite Lacell's Camp which resulted in his death.

Will Seagle, who helped build the railroad between the Georgia state line and Franklin, North Carolina, told us of another unfortunate death, this time while building the railroad: "I was drillin' my holes and loading down under with powder—what they used was dynamite—and they was drilling to pour that powder in. It was awful deep. They went to pourin' the powder in before that fuse went out there and sprung it. When they poured that keg of powder in, why, it caught down there. They went t'pour it in too quick—the fuse wasn't out—and it catched the powder

Will Seagle helped to drill the cuts and lay track to make way for the railroad.

when they poured it in. That's what caused it. I started up there, and I looked to see the men a-goin' in the air. And they hollered, 'There's a man in the river.' I seed him a-goin' up but I didn't know [who it was]. I had an uncle working there, and I thought it was him. But I'd'a went anyhow, made no difference who it was. I run and jumped in the river and got him out.

"It nearly killed him dead then. It was Mr. Will Talley. I led him to the store over here. [It was] a house on the side of the road—used to be a little store—and it had a bed in it. I told my uncle to get a sheet up at Molly Cabe's and to run as fast as he could. Mr. Talley didn't have a rag nor a shoe on him. Flesh was a-dropping off of him. Boy, he was pitiful. He lived till midnight, then died. I set up there with him till he died that night.

"I worked more than three years on the railroad and never missed a day. I lived on the Taylor Gap up here. The going and coming [to work] was twenty miles—ten miles each way. Had to make the twenty miles a day. I did that every day—I never lost a day.

"I drove steel [made holes for the dynamite]. There was two of us. There should be a right-hand man and a left-hand man. There was a colored man there, and he was a left-hand man, and the boss asked me, 'Mr. Seagle, do you care t'drive with a colored man?'

"I said I didn't care. Well, he come out there. I'd been a-striking steel all the time with Will Talley, and then he got killed, y'know, and they had t'get me another hand. I never will forget it. I was hitting faster'n him. He said, 'Who-o-o-oa, I'm a-gettin' the same money you are. Son, you cut out. You hit soon as I hit.' I never will forget it. I drove with him for a long time."

The Cross Ties

With the roadbed prepared, the next step was to obtain the wooden cross ties to which the rails would be spiked. Many people in our area still remember cutting timber and hewing it into cross ties by hand. John Crane and Chad Bedingfield persuaded their grandfather, Dan Crane, Sr., to hew one and show us the process.

Dan Crane: "A lot of people hewed. They had to. That's the only way they had to make a few dollars to buy groceries with.

"The railroad company had to have the ties for the railroads. They never got too many ties because when one would rot, they'd have to replace it. They was all the time working on the railroad track.

"[The cross ties were made out of] white oak, red oak, and all different kinds of oak for a long time. After several years, then, we started hewing them out of pine, too. After they creosoted the heart pine, they would last a pretty good while. And a lot of times, we would get trees that would have three or four cross ties in them. The hewed cross ties came from the heart of the tree, and they

Dan Crane, Sr., demonstrates part of the process
of hewing a cross tie.

would last longer than the sawed ones that were cut out of any part of the tree, so the railroad would pay more for a hewed one than a sawed one.

"[We mostly used tools like] a crosscut saw, timber wedges, hammers, and a double-bitted ax. The crosscut saw was used to cut the tree down and also to cut the log into sections when we got the log hewed. The little flat timber wedges were mainly wooden wedges made out of locust. We used those to help cut the tree down and fall it the way we wanted it to fall. Sometimes we used [the side of] a single-bitted ax or a hammer to hit the wedge with. And all we ever used to hew with was a three-and-a-half pound Sager double-bitted ax. We never used a broadax.

"We'd hew the cross ties mostly in the fall of the year after the sap went down. You had to hew them green. You used the main body of the tree. The limbs wasn't big enough. [We mostly got the timber] from the government land. Old man Roscoe Nicholson was the Forest Service ranger then. He'd go mark you up a boundary of timber in certain areas around close to your house. You just had to go out to the office and buy a permit. Then he would go with you in the woods where you wanted the timber marked up, and would mark up the trees that were good for cross ties. He had a little ax with an ax blade on one side and a head with 'US' on the other side. He'd hew a little place off with the ax, and then hit it and put a 'US' stamp on it.

"We hewed on Lake Burton. We also hewed across from Homer Parker's [in the Scott's Creek community], at the waterfall branch. We would drag the cross ties out to the top of the waterfalls and then ballhoot 'em off over there. A lot of times, one would bust when you threw it off over there, and you would just have to cull it and use it for firewood.

"My daddy could hew ten [a day]. Eight was a good, easy day's work. He'd hew ten a lot of times. I could hew six or seven myself, and I was just a boy then sixteen or seventeen years old. It was just me and my daddy working mostly. A lot of times, if my uncle, Bill Butler, was here, he'd help us some.

"If we were going to haul them on a mule and wagon, we'd just hew two or three days 'cause the old mule couldn't pull but just so many on a wagon. It would take two good men to lift one and put it up on a wagon. Sometimes we would cut skid poles and roll them or slide them up. They weighed between 300 and 400 pounds apiece. The oak cross ties were heavier than the pine, but the pine cross ties were easier to hew than the oak.

"When we would hew over on the lake, we'd get somebody with a truck to haul the ties from over there. You just hauled 'em when you got a load. A lot of times it would take us about a week to get a load for a truck—we'd hew thirty-five or forty maybe.

"We sold what we got to old man Claude Henson. He was in charge of the cross-tie buying at that time in Clayton. He paid by check when you took him the cross ties. There were first- and second-class ties. The first-class ties would be anywhere from forty-five to fifty-five cents, and the second class would be from twenty-five to forty-five cents."

Roosevelt Burrell was also a cross-tie cutter: "I hewed a many a tie, many. [My wife] had an uncle who lived down there in the edge of North Carolina, and he could hew forty a day. Boys, he was one of the best men I ever seen with an ax. He made every

Dan Crane, Sr., with a finished, hand-hewn cross tie.

lick count. But about ten is all I could do. It'll work you. They say you've got to have a weak mind and strong back to do that.

"This was back there in that Depression. We were about starving to death, I know that. And when I started making them, they [brought] forty cents apiece, and that was a number-five tie: that was eight foot and six inches long and seven inches thick and a nine-inch face. Approximately seven inches thick was [acceptable]; they'd allow you a half inch. And they didn't care if the face of it was twelve, fourteen inches—whatever. But later they got to where they wouldn't take them unless they was worked down to seven by nine or seven by eight [hewed on all four sides]. Seven by six was the least they'd take, and they wouldn't take many of them. Ones that little you wouldn't get nothing for them.

"We'd go to the woods with a good old crosscut saw and an ax.

There weren't no power saws. Then you'd take two chunks [of wood] about eighteen or twenty inches long and cut a little notch in [the top of each] where your log will lay in it. Then you roll your log up on them two blocks [so your ax] wouldn't go in the ground [while you were hewing]. Then you get up on that log with your feet—stand up on it—and score it first and then start busting [the chips] out. Get right up on top of her and go to chopping—just chop one end to the other, and then turn that around and hit the other side. Usually I'd cut a tree down and maybe hew the whole thing plumb to the top and then cut it up into ties eight foot six inches long. You'd hew it off [some at the end of the process] to get it right—take your rule and measure it or take an ax and eyeball it."

Local resident Numerous Marcus remembered: "Usually we'd peel the bark off of the cross ties and tan with it. We used what we called spuds to peel the trees with. I'd get started at the top of the tree and come down, peel the whole tree, everything that had a piece of bark on it, right on out to the limbs. Chestnut oak is what you want to peel tanning bark off of. The new moon in June is the best time to peel tan bark. The sap would have been in free flow. That way it would peel pretty good. After the bark was peeled off, we'd load it on a sled and drag it out to the truck with horses. We used to have many a hard time digging out roads around the sides of mountains for the sled to be pulled on. Every once in a while, the dang sled would turn over with us and spill our bark, or the horse would get in a yellow jackets' nest and run off out of the road and tear up our sled."

Mary Cabe tells of how she used to cut cross ties and how she and her family would go into the woods and get them: "Why, I've helped cut many a cross tie; we'd go to the woods and get a white oak or a black or Spanish oak, whichever. We'd saw them off at eight foot and a half long, and had to hew that to eight inches thick and as wide as the log was. We'd get the bark off all of them and then haul them down here to the railroad station, lay them there. [The railroad] took them up, graded them and paid us a little for them, about fifty cents. Anybody who could hew good could hew one in an hour, after they got it sawed down."

In addition to hewing cross ties, in the very early years of the train, when the engine burned wood, many people cut firewood to

fuel the trains, and stacked it at designated places along the side
of the track. The railroad would then measure the wood, load it,
and pay the person accordingly.

The Section Crews

Once the line was built, and trains were running over it, it became
a maintenance challenge of considerable proportion. Two types of
crews were constantly at work: the section crews, which maintained
the roadbeds and track, and the bridge crew, which attended to
the bridges and trestles. Section crews were usually assigned to an
eight- to ten-mile section of track, and many of them were hired
from the area surrounding their section and lived at home. Bridge
crews, on the other hand, roved the line, usually living in railroad-
supplied shanty cars unless the trestle they were working on was
close to home.

   In an attempt to understand more fully the job of the section
crews, we interviewed Donald Anderson and J. B. Waldrop, section
foremen on the then still-operating Graham County Railroad—a
line almost identical to the TF in terms of the size of the rails used,
the types of ties, etc. Donald Anderson explained some of the basics:
"We have to keep the ties in, keep the joints (the point where two
rails come together) smooth, and raise the low joints up level with

A section crewman tamps dirt around a tie.

the rest of the track. To keep the rail tops even, you raise the rails up and pack dirt and gravel and tamp it in under the ties to hold them up.

"When ties have to be replaced, we have to jack up the rail to put the new ties in. We use a regular railroad jack. It raises both sides of the track. We take the old tie out; then we dig [under to put] the new tie in. I'd say it takes one man a day to put in about six to eight ties. That is to dig his ties and put them in himself.

"Sometimes you have a rail that will wear out and has to be changed, or it will break. These rails are sixty pounds—sixty pounds to the yard. If you have to change the rails, you have to gauge the rails when you put them down. They've got to be fifty-six and a half inches apart. You could let the gauge come off as much as half an inch and you're okay. On a curve, you should have wider gauge than you would have on a straight rail. That gives it room to keep it from turning your rails over. Every time you put a tie in, you use your gauge to gauge it in.

"Now you've got what are called rail dogs. Two men get hold of the rail dogs and catch the rail, one on each side, and lift it with them. We can put down about fifteen rails, or four hundred feet, a day."

J. B. Waldrop said: "I'm a section foreman. I look after the track, see that it's put on gauge. I put in ties, raise track, and align

A rail dog is used to grab the rail when lifting it.

it. Sometimes the track isn't parallel—it wavers. That's got to be redone. We have to go back over it and align it and lay it. We have an aligning bar to align the track, and men pry it over by hand. The spikes hold the rails and the ballast holds the ties in place. They just lay the ties flat on the ground, and the dirt and gravel in between them hold them and keep them from sliding. Gravel raises the track up out of the water, and when it rains, the gravel keeps the track dry. The water runs right on through the gravel. It keeps the ties from rotting, too. Your track will hold up a lot better on gravel because in the wintertime and rainy weather, dirt will give way while gravel holds up.

"You can replace a tie in about forty minutes. It takes three men. We have some that are made of pine that are reused ties from other railroads. All I've ever used on this road are oak, pine, and locust. Locust was what they used twenty-five years ago—locust makes good ties. There aren't any new locust ties, though. The only locust left are those that have been here for the last twenty-five years. They're better than oak, a lot better. A good creosoted oak tie will last fifteen or twenty years. Untreated ones don't last but four or five years. They get to where they won't hold the spike.

"The rails expand and contract, depending on the weather. The joints fill back in in hot weather, and in cold weather they open up. In the heat of the summer, the rails will all tighten—the joints will be all tight. The rails will buckle sometimes. When they do that, sometimes you have to cut out a piece and line the rail back. The joints are like laying bricks—you've got one joint down there and then on the other side, the joint is not opposite. This way the two joints will not be as likely to come out of line—if they are opposite each other, the track will get out of line faster.

"If you have to replace a rail because it breaks or wears out, it takes a long time to take the rail out. Each of these rails is thirty feet long. You've got to take the bolts out—you've got eight bolts—and all the spikes on about sixteen ties to pull on one side. To lay your old rail out and lay the new one in, and to put your bolts back and then spike it back in, will take an hour."

Jim Bingham worked on both the TF section and bridge crews: "I worked on the railroad thirty-one years. I started around 1909 and I quit the railroad in 1940. First job I ever worked on I got a dollar a day when I first started—the day was ten hours long. Worked six days a week.

"The first thing I did—I went to work on 'the section,' we called it, where you put ties and smoothed up the track. I lived at Dillard, and we had a little car we went in and out on. When I first started we had a lever car, but after several years they got us a little gasoline motor car. Took us to where we had t'work. We repaired the track— had t'keep the ties under it and keep it smoothed up. It was hard work, but you got tough with it.

"Laying track, some days you'd boot a quarter of a mile, de- pendin' on how many men you had working with you. That doesn't include the grading. If the grade started t'wash, we'd have t'haul dirt and fill it in. They didn't sow any grass; they just built up their fills and let the bushes take over. They followed on right after the grading with the track—put it down as soon as the place was graded out.

"We had t'keep the track up, and long about August, we'd have t'cut the right-of-way. Bushes and growth—that was a big job. One time I was starting through and I run into a yeller jackets' nest. I cut out pretty fast t'get ahead of 'em, and the other boys come on behind me, and the yeller jackets was stirred up good for them. They got it all!"

Lawton Brooks recalled: "Well, down in Clayton the train come around a big curve and two cars wrecked off the road out there. One of them was loaded with cement and one of them with lumber, I believe. That man didn't have many hands, and he come out there and wanted to know if I'd come to work awhile on the railroad. I didn't have a job and told him, 'God, yeah, be glad to.' So I came on out and went to work. See, if they had wrecks or anything they'd call in other men to help take up wrecks. So we worked there one night all night long, and two days, and got it back together—got the stuff cleaned back up so the train could run. God, I got tired of carrying them old bags of cement. They was a lot of them. We had to carry those things up a bank, back up out of the way. We had to go down in the hole [where the wrecked car was and get a bag of cement] and go up on the bank and lay it down. Got that one car moved out to where a train could pull another one by, and had to load that cement back in the car. God, I thought I would

Lawton Brooks, section crewman.

never make it. We did. Boy, it was rough on me 'cause I hadn't done none of that in a long time till that day. That was my first day.

"After that, I worked up and down the railroad—all the way up and down it—for five years, nine months, and five days. I had to work ten hours for a pitiful dollar. Ten cents a hour is all they'd give you. You had to work, too. I mean you *worked* ten hours. You worked from the time it got light enough to see till it got so dark you couldn't see.

"[It was] the hardest work you've ever done, but I loved it better than any work I've ever done in my life. I just got used to it. I knew exactly what to do and what had to be done, and every day, you knew exactly what was gonna be done before you went the next day. It wasn't no changing around in it. You knowed how to put in ties. You knowed how to catch up a track. You knowed how to line the track, and after I got that in my mind, I'd rather do it than anything in the book. I got so good on it that I got sub-boss. If my main man went off, he'd turn it over to me. He'd be gone a week or two at a time and I'd run it myself. I got just as good as anybody could laying ties and everything. I just stayed with 'em.

"I could walk up and down the track and stand out here and I could see a place [that needed fixing]. And then you go to where a rotten tie broke or something, and we had to jack it up and take that tie out and put another one in. I've drove in many a spike—now you might think that was easy drove. You start that in an old hard white oak [tie] with an eight-pound hammer—that's what you drove with. Come over that hammer and hit the spike, you straddling that hot rail, the sun a-boiling down on you; man, you talk about sweating. Me and my wife's brother—the foreman—put it in every day. When we wasn't putting in ties, they'd say, 'All right, Lawton, you two go and spike up track today.' We'd go along and check the rails—we'd gauge them—sometimes the rail would play and lean the spikes back and the rail would get to playing worse. We'd go along and put our gauge on it, and we'd have to pull the tracks into a tight gauge and respike them. It was shore a job—I'd rather do anything than spike up track all day. It hurts your old back stooping over all day. With two people working together hitting a spike, taking turns, with him on one side and me on the other, it still takes a good little bit of time to pound a spike in.

"Or in a place where the truck would go down, we'd have dirt to put in there and catch all them ties up and let our track down on it. Get you a big old jack there and jack the rail up where you want it. Catch up the head of the tie with the shovel and put your dirt in there. Them old jacks weighed almost eighty pounds, and they had to carry them up and down the darn road where you were putting in ties.

"Then, in the summertime, the railroad track would run and we'd have to get on those curves and line that thing in and saw off about that much of the rail [holds his hands apart] and then put it back together and smack it down. In the wintertime, that blame thing would draw up and shear the bolts and we'd have to put that piece back in. You didn't think steel would run, but it does. Railroad track will run—draws out and draws up. You've got to line it up.

"But nothing new come up unless they had a wreck. [After that] you never would use the old rails. You couldn't straighten them. You'd be afraid the train would climb out on them. We'd have to go get the new ones. We went to way over in North Carolina to get them. We'd go over there and load 'em on a flat car over there. Then they'd bring 'em in on our line and we'd have to unload that stuff. Now that's some work picking up them rails. They got them old hand things—you over here, me over here, and a hook there in the middle. Boy, when you come up with your end, if you let that man get an inch on you, you can't get up. I liked to killed my poor old self, but I learnt what to do—take advantage of him every time. I'd watch and about the time I seen him tighten his hands, I tightened up on mine just a little bit. That made him have to come with all he had to get his end up. After you get up, you are all right, but when you go to pick it up, you're straining 'cause it's heavy. They'd have about six men to the rail, you know. Two out here in the front, two about the middle, two at the back.

"One time, the whole mountain slid off. Slid the railroad off down into the dirt roads. We had to take that up and build a railroad back. They even sent the convicts to help us that time. They had the durn woods full of convicts there helping us put that railroad back up there. I forget how many days and nights. It was three nights, I know, before I went home. Worked all night 'cause they wanted them trains to move. They was a-hollering all the time, 'Get it fixed, boys. Got to move.'

"It come an ice storm one time, and that ice began to break loose and washed some trestles out. Good God, then we had to build all them trestles back. You get in that water, stay in there five minutes, and get out and stand by the fire five and jump back in and stay five more minutes. Your legs get so numb you couldn't stay but four or five minutes. Your legs would get numb, froze. I went to the house a many of a time when I laid down on the bed and my wife would have to pull my overalls off, and she'd set them against the wall and they'd stand there. After a while, you'd see them go down. Yeah, froze. Get on that motor car and hit that wind going home. Just made 'em freeze three times worser, you know, but we made it just the same.

"Why I liked this, I don't know, when there is lots of easier jobs. It's a whole lot easier to farm, but I'd still rather railroad as to farm.

"And I always did want to work on the train, but I never did. A man let me drive one a little piece one time. I wanted to drive one just to see how it was. I always wished I was on these main lines where they would just go, like a faster train, just head off from one big town to another somewhere. Go through the country and see the country. Never did get to do that, but I'd sure love to."

Minyard Conner worked on the section crew that covered the line from the Georgia-North Carolina state line to Franklin, North Carolina. He said: "I worked on the railroad twenty-four years, four weeks, and fourteen days. I started working on the railroad in '36. See, I moved here in '36 and bought this place. They wanted somebody to work on the railroad, and I went to work.

"Never was sick. Never missed a two-week payday. I put in cross ties—took out the old and rotten ones and put in new ones. Then they'd be a derailment, tear up a half a mile of track, and we'd have to fix it back.

"When I commenced to workin' on th' railroad, I got twenty-one cents an hour. I'd draw twenty-five dollars or thirty dollars every two weeks, forty-eight hours a week. It didn't go far, but it was a living."

J. C. Stubblefield recalled: "I worked two years, '39 till '41, and then I went in the service, and then when I come back, I worked another eleven months. I was on the section crew from Wiley to Tallulah Falls—seven miles. There was three of us there. [But] they only had two regulars.

"Part of the time we cut right-of-way. That's cutting bushes and things back, you know, to keep 'em from growing out on the tracks. Had bush axes. Back then you didn't have no kind of machine running out there to do that. You would get into yellow jackets' nests and hornets' nests and wasps' nests, snakes, and everything else.

"The foreman on the section was Andrew Watts, and if we had the track jacked up when a train was coming—well the foreman knows right when that train is coming because they keep him informed, and he'll tell you when it gets so close, 'All right, boys, take your jack out.' You would have to take the jack out and just wait for the train to go by then and then start over.

"And on curves, now, the ties was replaced pretty often. Some of 'em would [last] two or three years or something like that. On curves, the train would run against the outside rail all of the time and it would spread the track, and you've got to gauge that back to the right gauge. That's how far apart the two rails are. It was four foot and eight inches, I think. We had an iron gauge that would measure the track. And when you get that tie with too many spike holes in it, you have to take that tie out because, you see, you hadn't got nothing to hold the rail. You've got to take that tie out and put a new one in. Sometimes you take plumb sound ties that's just been gauged up so much you've got too many holes in it. And if the track was to spread out the train would just fall on the inside of it. It happens."

For Leo Ramey, working on the railroad still provided a comparatively good living: "I worked with Andrew Watts when I started. He begged me for a long, long time to work there before I decided maybe I'd better. It looked like I was gonna run out of a job. I'd work a day for fifty cents, just hoeing corn or doing anything else. I finally decided to work a few days [for the railroad] and I never did quit! I started in 1928 and quit in 1960. That's thirty-two years! Wasn't long before I was top man of the whole bunch. I got to be foreman after I was a laborer. Then I got to be roadmaster over the whole business—tracks, trestles, over everything.

"When I started, I was making $1.55 a day, not an hour. It was a whole lot better, but we still wasn't making nothing. I lived pretty good then. Course I'm living better now than I ever did all the time I was working. When I quit, I was at the top, doing $250 a month. Make that much in a week now. But when I have more money, I spend more money. I don't save more money. I just spend more money."

Jess Page said: "I started in '54 and worked on the railroad till it went dead in '61. We worked on the maintenance—take out ties, put in new ties, put in new rail where it needed it. There were four of us plus the boss, and we'd travel along the track in a pittypat, a gas-powered vehicle with iron wheels, just like the railroad car. Sometimes we'd pull a push car behind—just a flat thing, about eight-foot square. We'd lay cross ties on that and haul it to the job behind the pittypat.

"We had a wreck one time on a pittypat, but there wasn't but three of us on it. It was time to quit work. We were coming around the curve on it and it jumped the track. Boy, you can't tell nothing at all when it gets off the track, all them ties and jacks [loaded on the pittypat] flying ever' which a way!"

A. J. Gudger remembers the time two section crews collided on the track: "The superintendent told my foreman to bring his crew down to help the Demorest section crew. He failed to notify the Demorest crew that we was coming. While the Turnerville crew was going down to Demorest, the other crew was going on up the line to do some work. Well, they hit a sharp curve, and [the foreman] come out of that cut right into this other man and his crew. None of them was hurt too bad."

For any number of reasons, a train might derail, at which time all the men were called to the scene.

"Several things could cause a derailment," recalls engineer Goldman Kimbrell. "Could be a broke rail, or a track spread, or running too fast and jumping the track on a curve—plus, the condition of the bed has a lot to do with it."

Minyard Conner said: "We'd have to fix a temporary track to the derailed train to get it back on the track. We didn't have no lift—just generally pull 'em back with the engine. Hook on to 'em just like if you got stuck in a mud hole, and somebody come along with a car and got on solid ground and pulled you up."

Goldman Kimbrell: "The passenger engine wrecked right out here at Clayton. The switch into a side track must have gotten a little open and throwed the engine off. We call that 'splitting a switch.' The engine stopped right at the end of the trestle in the dirt, still standing. It never did turn over. We worked from five one evening to about three the next morning, and quit till daylight. Then we went back to work, and along late in the afternoon, we got it back on track. It just shut everything down until we got [that engine] back on the tracks."

Trestles

Aside from that portion of the ride that took the passengers along the very top lip of the 1,000-foot-deep gorge, the most spectacular feature of the line was its huge trestles. They were made entirely from wood and bolts. There were forty-two trestles over the fifty-eight-mile route—the most per mile of any shortline in the country. All were wooden except the one across Tallulah Lake. The longest was Wiley trestle, and the highest was Big Panther Creek trestle at 98 feet. It's surprising that a totally wooden structure could hold up a seventy-ton train. To find out how they could stand the pressure, we went to talk to Roy Shope, a former bridge crew foreman

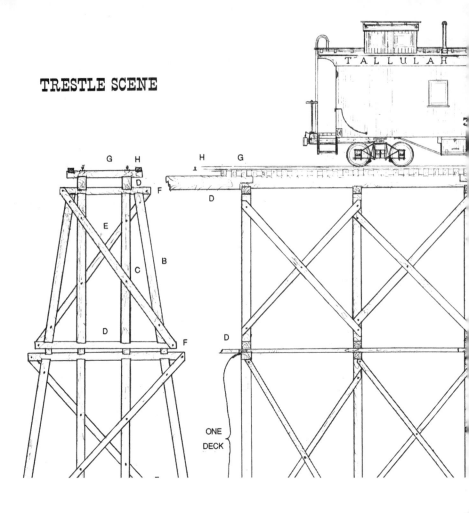

on the TF line, and Dess Oliver, a railroad historian who has studied the TF. Their comments are keyed to the accompanying diagram.

Roy Shope: "[Starting from the bottom upward] right here under every one of these posts is a 4 foot long, 12 × 12 wooden block. This was underground about four foot."

Dess Oliver: "On top of those were these posts here [B&C]."

Roy Shope: "We call this a batter post [B]. On the outside, these would lean. [These were 12 × 12s.]"

Dess Oliver: "These were to keep the trestle from swaying back and forth."

Roy Shope: "And this here's a plumb post [C]. [They were also 12 × 12s.]"

Dess Oliver: "This was called the plumb post, I suppose, 'cause in older days when the trestles were built they'd hang a plumb or a weight or something on a string by the stringer [D] to see if [the

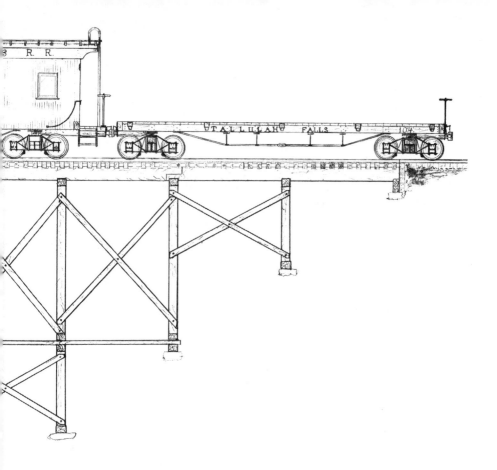

post] was straight up and down. I imagine that may have been where the stringer got its name too."

Roy Shope: "Now that's got an X-brace [E] that way on it. These were 3 × 10s. They'd get [these] braces on it."

Dess Oliver: "These were to keep the plumb and batter posts from slipping away from each other."

Roy Shope: "Then this right here was called a cap [F]"

Dess Oliver: "There were notches in these for the posts to fit into them."

Roy Shope: "Every one of these [notches] was [cut] right down to eleven inches. [The caps were 12 × 12s.] The [stringers] are laying across the top of these. [They were] 8 inches × 16 inches × 24 inches long. They'd be eighteen inches for [the cross ties] to lay on."

Dess Oliver: "The cross ties [G] [were 7 inches × 9 inches.

They] would be set on their [7-inch] side across a trestle. [Usually they were on their 9-inch side.] They were notched out to sit on top of the stringers to keep them from shifting from side to side. The rail [H] was [spiked to] those."

Roy Shope: "One set of blocks, a lower cap, two plumb parts, two batter posts, a set of X-braces and a cap made one layer or one deck of a trestle. On top of the cap would be a stringer. Over the stringer would either be the cross ties and rail or another deck.

"[The bolts used to hold the wooden trestles together were] 3/4-inch bolts, and they were 15 inches long. Some of 'em we had to use was 20 inches, 18s and 20s, 15s to 18s and 20s.

"There are one, two, and three [deck trestles]. We had some three decks high. The Big Panther down there was 98 feet high. [It was made of] all wood except the rail."

Oftentimes, railroad jobs could be very dangerous. An article in the *Tri-County Advertiser* (January 4, 1882) tells of a man getting killed while building one of the trestles on the TF line:

On Tuesday of last week, Jack Harris, a colored man working on the Railroad between this place [Clarkesville] and Mt. Airy, fell from the trestle, a clear fall of about 42 feet, plunging his head into the ground to his shoulders and breaking his shoulder and taking his scalp. His condition is a critical one.

The Bridge Crew

Carl Rogers remembers: "[The bridge crew] did the repairwork on all the stations and trestles. I guess you would have to call the trestle crews professionals. They would just swing down right under the trestles. They had ropes, and they had a hoist mounted on that flatcar, and they'd secure that flatcar to the rails and let the lumber down. And they would climb those trestles—I don't mean to compare them to monkeys, but they were very agile. They were used to doing that kind of work so it was no problem with them whatsoever."

J. C. Stubblefield remembered working on the bridge crew: "They had an inspector, and he'd come around and inspect every so often, and if it was a little rotten there, he'd have [the timbers] replaced. They would change the bad ones out and put in new,

*These men most likely were on the bridge crew, as evidenced
by the shanty car and cook.*

and all that was bolted together. You've got to get it up here and
you got to swing the timber down on ropes to get it where you
want it, you know, and you've got to have somebody that knows
what they're doing or they'll get hurt. They's a few got hurt once
in a while—just carelessness really. They'd let a piece of timber
fall and hit 'em, or maybe their foot slipped and they fell.

"The bridge crew had about six or eight men on it [instead of
the three the section crews had] because the bridge work is a lot
slower than the section part, and they had to have enough men
when they had something to do to carry the job along as fast as
they could because there was going to be a train a-coming."

Fred Williams traveled with the bridge crew: "On the bridge
crew we had shanty cars. There we cooked, ate, and slept. We had
one car to cook and eat in, the other to sleep in. The shanty cars
pulled us from one place to another to repair the trestles. We had
to work from here to Franklin."

A. J. Gudger once became a cook by default on the bridge crew:
"On the bridge force, they couldn't keep a cook—it only paid

This picture of the Panther Creek trestle being taken down in 1962 shows the possible devastation of a collapsing trestle.

twenty-five dollars a month and board, and a week or two was as long as they could keep a cook. I wasn't a cook by no means, but when the cook quit, I had to go in the kitchen and do the cookin' until they could get another cook."

Roy Shope recalled that the bridge crew was better paid than the section crew: "When I left section to go to bridge gang, I was making twenty cents an hour. The bridge gang was paid good money, and I think I went to work there for thirty-seven cents an hour. That was good pay."

He had a close call with a freight train: "When I was on the bridge gang, [we were down at the lookout] on a motor car. We was pushin' a push car in front of us. I was sittin' in front. We went around that curve and met the freight train! Well, I left it. I jumped off! Rest of them boys jumped off and went over the bank, [too]! We made it though. The freight train, he was kinda lookin' out for us."

Despite their sturdy design, the trestles did not always hold as they should. Two of the three fatal train accidents that happened on the TF line occurred when a trestle collapsed under a train. Florence Brooks remembered another instance where the trestle did not hold: "We'd started somewhere one night to a dance—we'd walk the railroad track ever'where we went—an' boy it 'uz a-rainin', an' th' creek was up, and just as we got across th' trestle, here come some big logs an' away went the trestle. We did just get off of it."

Hoyt Tench recalled an incident that demonstrated the fine line between safety and disaster while working on the railroad: "It happened on the trestle just north of Dillard. It was plowing time, about March or April. I was standing on the deck watching this fellow plow as we left Dillard. There was a trestle after Dillard [that was] about twenty foot high and fifty feet long that went over a ravine. When it rained, water would run in it.

"Jim Brown and I were on Engine No. 75 going to Franklin, and just as the engine went over the trestle, one of the eight-foot-long [beams of the trestle] just come falling out from under it. There were four people riding in the cab—the conductor, a flagman, a brakeman, and a swing brakeman. [We all just watched that beam fall.] We went on across by letting it roll to the other side. [We never slowed down. Thankfully] we didn't have ten or twelve cars and the cab. They had to rebuild that trestle before we could come back."

There are also stories in which a trestle *did* hold its weight as it should. Leo Ramey told one: "Camp Dixie Dam busted one time. There was this little old bridge down there this side of Lakemont School. There was a trestle there, and the bridge was pushing against the trestle. The trestle crew was there with their jacks and moved [the bridge]. They put the jack on a sill and put a block on that, then put a chain around it on a pole and pulled the bridge away from the trestle."

Dispatchers

Without the dispatcher, who was based in Cornelia, the Tallulah Falls Railway would have been simply a collection of equipment, frozen in place, unable to move. He was literally the brains of the

Carl Rogers, depot agent at Clayton, Georgia.

entire operation. He had to know the contents and the weight of each freight car, as well as when the freight each carried was needed by the customer, so that he could make up the composition of each train—and make sure that it wasn't too heavy for the engine to pull over the line's grades. And he had to know where each train on the line was at every moment to avoid collisions. It was a heavy responsibility.

Carl Rogers said: "The dispatcher was the boss of all the trains going and coming. He gave the order for them to go out, and he told them what to take and told them how far to go. He made up the consist of the train—[a list of] what to pull that day and how far to go and where to [leave] it and so on—and gave it to the conductor of the freight train. A lot of times, maybe they would have more cars than they could pull in one day, so the dispatcher would check with the agent along the line [and if] someone [was getting] a carload of something they wouldn't need [right away], they would put it on the sidetrack and haul the cars that [the customers] needed the most."

For part of his career with the TF, Ross Davis was a dispatcher: "The dispatcher had to protect all of his trains, know where every one was at and which way it was headed to. Anything that had to move on the tracks, I had to know where it was and plan it that way. For instance, if I had a train going to Clayton on its way to Dillard, and one at Clayton coming back this way, I would have to call the agent at Lakemont and give him an order for that train above him there to meet this other train at Joy sidetrack [between Lakemont and Tallulah Falls].

"I also kept a record of all the cars in and out. As the cars came into Cornelia, the Southern Railway delivered them to the TF, and then the tonnage had to be figured out for the freight trains as to how much they could pull from one point to the other. You see, for those little engines we could just haul so much tonnage. For instance, they could only pull three cars of rock to Clarkesville, [because of the steep grades], but they could take six cars of rock from there [north]. So we'd have to take three cars from Demorest to Clarkesville, and come back and get the other three. Lots of times I'd have fifteen cars going up to Clayton, and everybody wanted them up there at the same time, so I'd have to divide those cars up all along. Set part of them off at Demorest, get part of them to Clarkesville, then get the rest of them on up the line. And sometimes we would get enough cars until we could run two freight trains—usually to Dillard—and if we run an extra train, I had to get an extra crew rounded up to run that train."

Carl Rogers recalled: "A first-class train is a passenger train, and it has priority over a freight train, so the freight train would be the one that had to go onto the siding. [When they discontinued passenger service and had a] mail train, we just had a little diesel for the mail train, so it was easier for it to go onto the sidetrack than it was to push the whole freight train onto it.

"And if they had special orders, why, the dispatcher would tell them. If they were working on the track somewhere and they had to slow the train down, they'd get the word to the dispatcher, and he'd dispatch it out to the agent, and they would give it to the train to watch out.

"We had scheduled runs, and then we also had extras where they had trains [besides] our regular scheduled ones. He had to schedule those. And if the freight train was delayed, the dispatcher had to find out how much the train was delayed and tell [it and the others] where to meet. Those dispatchers would wire those orders to the agents along the line, and the agents would show the red stop sign on the signal board to alert the engineer to stop the

W. G. McADOO, Director General of Railroads

TALLULAH FALLS RAILROAD

TIME TABLE NO. 17

Effective Sunday, Oct. 20th, 1918, 6:00 A. M., Eastern Time.

SOUTHBOUND			Eastern Standard Time.		NORTH BOUND		
5	**11**				**12**	**6**	Capacity of Track in Cars
2d class	1st class			STATIONS.	1st class	2d class	
Tuesday Thu. Sat.	Daily	Mi			Daily	Monday Wed. Fri	
A. M.	P. M.		Lv.	Ar.	P. M.	P. M.	
8 00	2 10	58	..........Franklin..........		1 55	3 30	71
8 40	s 2 23	53	............Prentiss............		s 1 39	3 00	19
9 05	s 2 38	48	.... Otto		s 1 24	2 38	23
....	f 2 50	43	...... Orlando, N. C.		f 1 10	....	
9 40	s 2 56	42	..........Dillard, Ga..........		s 1 05	1 50	17
9 45	s 3 00	41	.... Rabun Gap		s 1 00	1 35	52
10 05	s 3 09	38	.......Mountain City.......		s 12 50	1 15	16
10 30	s 3 19	35	.... Clayton............		s 12 20	12 55	28
....	f 3 24	33	..............Bethel.............		f 12 10		
10 50	s 3 29	32	..............Tiger.............		s 12 12	12 12	17
10 10	s 3 43	28	...............Wiley...............		s 12 00	11 40	9
10 20	s 3 48	27	...........Lakemont...........		s 11 54	11 35	8
11 48	f 3 52	25	................Joy................		f 11 48	11 25	19
12 15	s 4 06	21	......Tallulah Falls.......		s 11 36	11 00	21
12 20	s 4 11	20	..... Tallulah Lodge		s 11 31	11 00	18
....	f 4 16	19	....Tallulah Park......		f 11 28	....	3
12 40	s 4 26	16	.... Turnerville		s 11 19	10 20	15
12 55	s 4 34	13	.... Hollywood		s 11 10	10 00	8
....	f 4 39	11	.... Anandale		f 11 04	....	4
....	f 4 44	9	.... Hills		f 10 59	....	5
1 30	4 52	8	.... Clarksville		s 10 56	9 33	42
....	f 4 56	6	.... Habersham		f 10 48	....	5
1 50	s 5 03	5	.... Demorest..........		s 10 44	8 30	25
2 25	5 18	0	............Cornelia		10 30	8 00	126
A.M.	P. M.		Ar.	Lv.	A. M.	A. M	
5	**11**				**12**	**6**	

All Northbound trains have right of track over trains of same class in opposite direction.

S—Regular stop. F—Stops only when flagged.

Riverside M. P. 50, Norton M. P. 45, York M. P. 40, Parkers M P 34 1-2, Bovard M. P. 30, Burton Jct., M. P. 28 1-2 not shown on Time Card, are Flag stops for trains 11 and 12.

Nos. 5 and 6 do not carry passengers.

11 12 stops 20 minutes at Clayton for dinner.   D. W. NEWELL, Supt.

A Tallulah Falls Railway schedule was published weekly in the local papers. This one was taken from the Clarkesville Advertiser.

train. The conductor would go into the depot station to receive the special orders before the train would move on. The conductor signed and received two written copies of the orders, one which he kept and one which he carried back to the engineer. A third signed copy was held in the station by the agent as a permanent record of the fact that the conductor had been notified of the special orders. Very complicated, but a very safe way to operate. They don't do it that way anymore. They do it by computer, I think. Back then we did it manually."

The Running Crew

Engineers

The lives of many people depended on the reliability of the track. Those who trusted their lives to it every day were the running crew—the men responsible for the safe delivery of the train between depots—and the passengers.

The running crew of a freight train consisted of the engineer, fireman, brakeman, and flagman. On the passenger train there would also be a conductor, and often, a postmaster, and "the news butcher," someone who sold newspapers and refreshments during the trip.

Goldman Kimbrell was an engineer on the railroad for many years. He tells of some things that the engineer was responsible for: "The engineer was responsible for the train between stations— how fast to run, where to run, where he couldn't run, all that. They had timetables to go by—the only way you could figure your speed was from one mile post to another. The passenger train made a round trip a day, and they had one regular scheduled freight train. Then they run an extra if they had enough freight to run another train. Most of the time they had two freight trains out. They'd have meet orders, where to meet at—one train going north, one going south. If they didn't have meet orders, they had to go by this timetable—a freight train would have a certain time to be at a certain place; so would the passenger train. If you were delayed, you had to report it to the agent at the nearest depot; they had telephone and telegraph back then, so they would report it to the station nearest the train you were to meet. You could usually flag down an automobile to go to the nearest station. Course if you broke down or derailed, and they was somebody coming behind you, then a flagman had to go back to flag him to keep him from crashing into you."

The relationship the running crews had with the communities the train served is legendary here. Kimbrell illustrates the fact: "We had all the children spoilt—we got to buying a little chewing gum and pitching it off. When they heared the whistle blow, they got to where they was coming out of the woods and everywhere else a-looking for chewing gum. They was a family lived just this side of Franklin, and there come a snow; we'd been throwing the kids chewing gum all along as they lived pretty close to the road. The kids were always barefoot, no coats, nothing. So we thought we'd get them something afore Christmas. We got the section foreman to work on the track right in front of their house and give them a little candy. We decided we'd get them kids some socks and shoes. He got the kids over there with some candy and measured their feet with a stick. So all the train crew went in together and got 'em all a pair of shoes, and maybe half a dozen pair of socks apiece. We was hoping the next time we went up through there, we'd see 'em with them shoes on. A week or so afterward there was another snow, and they were out barefooted just like always, right in the snow."

Fireman Hoyt Tench told us about how friendly and helpful the people along the line were to the railroad men: "One day we had the work train down at Tallulah Falls—right on the end of the big trestle. [The bridge crew] were working on the trestle with big timber and we were there with the engine. All the ladies brought us a big shoe box full of fried chicken and cat-head biscuits. I told the superintendent I didn't care if they do have a few derailments every once in a while [if we could eat like that]. They would do that all up and down the road. People all up through here was real neighborly people."

Often, in the case of injuries and deaths, the engineer would blame himself for the accident, as Leo Ramey related in this story: "One night it was raining and thundering, couldn't hardly see anything. Jim Brown, who was the engineer, was taking a train down the track, and he hit and killed a man that was walking on the tracks. It broke him up so bad that he quit right after that."

Firemen

Dan Ranger, the engineer for the Graham County Railroad, explained the operation of that line's coal-powered, Shay-geared locomotive. Built in 1925, it had three trucks (sets of wheels), three vertical cylinders, and weighed seventy to eighty tons. It was still used until the Graham County line went out of business in 1975. Though a different type of steam engine from those operated by the TF, the process of operating the engine was similar, and Dan's description of that process brings into clear focus the critical role of the fireman on mountain lines:

"From dead cold, it takes four hours to bring the engine up to operating temperature. If you were to bring it up any faster, you'd put a racking strain on the boiler—that's a lot of steam! To bring it up from cold to operating temperatures in less than three hours is putting a lot of torture on the boiler. We like to take between three and four hours to bring it up to where we can get a nice, slow, easygoing process. The locomotive, under normal operating conditions, is hot most of the time. [At the end of the day] you put a bank in it; pile a lot of coal up against the back of the firebox, and it just sits there and burns away slowly and keeps the engine relatively hot and keeps steam on it. We fill it up with water and it just sits there at anywhere between one hundred pounds down to thirty or forty pounds of steam, which is enough to work with to get it fired up again. If you drop the fire out of it and kill it, then you have to start up with wood. When you get up to steam on wood, you go to coal. There's an artificial draft on the locomotive while you're firing up and starting to move. Once the engine is moving, you turn the blower off because the exhaust steam from the cylinders goes out a pipe and in underneath the stack, and out what they call the nozzle. It then goes up what's called the petticoat pipe, which induces the draft, feeds the vacuum in the front end of the engine, and sucks the air through the fire and the fire tubes in the boiler to heat the water, and finally out the stack. To get it ready [if the boiler is hot] is maybe a forty-five-minute or hour job. It depends on where you are—if you've got a high steam pressure, it takes a shorter time; if you have a low steam pressure, it takes longer.

It takes twenty-five or thirty shovelfuls of coal—a couple of wheelbarrow loads—to fire up the boiler. Going from Robbinsville to Topton [twelve miles] and back again on an average freight run, the duration of which is probably two to two and a half hours, figuring your switching time and all the air-brake tests that you have to go through, we burn a little less than a ton of coal. We can operate here all day with our four passenger trips, which would be about a twenty-mile round trip all told; go from maybe eleven in the morning till four or five in the evening, and we would use about

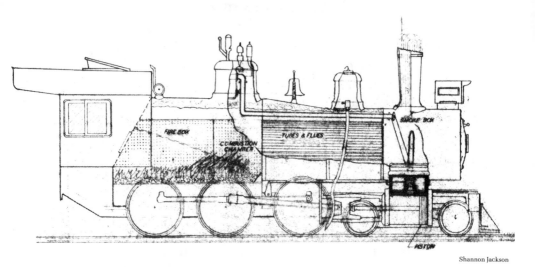

Drawing of a TF wood-burning engine.

a ton of good grade coal, same as on a freight run. If you get bad coal, it's going to take you more.

"The little back part of the cab holds the coal; the rest is water. It holds 5 tons of coal and 3,000 gallons of water. The amount of water used depends on what you're pulling, how hard the grades are, and how well the engine is maintained. If we go over on a freight run and come back, we'll use anywhere from a half to three quarters of a tank of water—between 1,500 and 2,000 gallons.

"There are two domes up on top of the boiler. One holds sand and the sand is dropped on the rail under slippery conditions—oily track, wet track, icy track, anything like that. It causes your wheels to adhere to the rail and will give traction. The second is the steam dome. It's there because as the water boils in the boiler and gives off steam, the molecules of the steam break the surface of the water and come up dragging water with them. The water is called saturated, or very wet, water close to the water surface. The higher up you go the drier it is, so steam from the cylinders is taken off through a pipe out of the dome. The throttle, the valve that admits the steam to the cylinders, is up high in this dome—as high as it'll go, so that you get the driest possible steam. You want dry steam, because steam is a gas that will compress, but the more water, the less it can compress. Water is not compressible, so if you have your cylinders full of water and you start to move the engine, you run a great danger of blowing the end of the cylinder right off.

"The forward portion of the boiler is called the smoke box.

From there back into the cab, about even with the window edge, is the boiler proper. The boiler is broken down into different sections called courses. The first is a tapered, or conical course; then there's the second course; then the roof sheet course over the firebox. From the metal band in the front where the smoke box starts, back to about the band right above the first cylinder, is the part that has the flues. Flues are pipes with water around them that the fire and hot gases go through, then on out the stack. This heats the water and boils it.

"From that area back there's a rectangular section that sits down low that's called the firebox—where the fire is carried on the grates. In the front of the firebox is the flue sheet that holds all the pipes together on that end. The top part of the firebox is called the crown sheet. The firebox sheets are made out of sheet steel at about 55,000 pounds tensile strength, and held together with stay bolts from the inside to the outside. Between these two pieces of metal is water, and over the top of it is water. If the water gets down below the crown sheet, you have a firebox failure—in other words, a boiler explosion. So you have to be very careful about where your water level is. On a mountain railroad like this one, you've really got to be with it. You let it get away from you, and you're in serious trouble. It's a demanding job.

"As you back up, the position of the boiler on the grade will tend to lower the water level in the back part of the boiler—the firebox end. As you are going uphill, it will raise the level because all the water is in the back. The difference between a good fireman and a bad fireman is that a good fireman knows when to feed water into the boiler to keep the water level up, and how much, and he knows at all times on any portion of the railroad where that water level is supposed to be. That is a trick, a real trick."

Hoyt Tench, a fireman on the TF, explained some of the preparations made to get the engines ready to run: "Before we would do anything of the morning, [we'd] get up enough air—start the air pump, grease it and all so it would run—then we would blow all of these, about 100, flues out in that engine. When you'd put the air to 'em—seventy-five pounds of air—it would blow the cinders, dirt, and accumulation in those flues out the stack. We had done that where it would heat better because the fire went through these flues and then circled all of the water. That's how that we could keep the steam up. Nobody that didn't fool with them couldn't hardly believe how powerful the steam was because the little cylinders were only about twenty inches in diameter. It was hard [to keep enough water] because you were using steam and water so fast. You had to have many water tanks. We used to have to leave Cornelia with a full tank, and we'd have to get another tank before we got to Tallulah Lodge, less than ten miles away."

Roy Mize told us about his job as fireman on the TF Railway: "I started late in the fall in 1917 as a fireman. I quit in March of 1919. I was on the passenger car run part of the time and the freight car run part of the time.

"The fireman kept the engine hot to make the steam that pulled the engine. It was a lot of hard work. When I started, the engineer taught me how to do it—get down off his seat and help me, showing me how to fire it. The fireman had to keep the steam up. The actual coal box was about three and a half feet by six feet. On a passenger run, I'd use four tons of coal for a round trip. On the freight run, they'd burn six and eight or more, depending on what kind of load they had. There's skill to it. You've got to know how to throw your shovel in, spread your coal. If your coal is not good, or if you put too much in at one time, then you get the white smoke. Then you've got to get your rake and rake it up a little, shake down your grate in order to get a dark black smoke. That's when it's steaming, when you get a black smoke, not a white smoke—I always watched my smokestack."

Ernest Anderson recalled his days on the TF: "I was fireman. I shoveled coal. Everything on the left-hand side of the engine cab the fireman was responsible for. The engineer was on the right, and he was responsible for things there. You had to learn the road,

Roy Mize, fireman for the TF.

shovel your coal. When you went around a curve where the engineer couldn't see, the fireman had to watch—if anything happened on that side, the fireman was responsible.

"I went to working in '42, about March 15. [My] first trip out was with Frank Bardon. I fired for Frank Bardon for several years—the last run I made was January 20, 1960, because I got sick, but the railroad shut down about a year later. Mr. Bardon, he was a fine ol' man.

"The fireman had to watch out for his water pump. If you've got heavy tonnage like going up through Mountain City, why maybe you'd have to put on both pumps—the one on your side and the engineer's. Whether you worked on the passenger or freight trains depended on the length of time you've worked on the railroad. Working the passenger train didn't pay near as much. You see, you never did get over eight hours on it unless there was a wreck on the passenger train. On the freight train, after you worked eight hours you got time and a half, and it was a normal thing to put in twelve to sixteen hours on the freight train, depending on how much freight you had to let off and pick up. If you didn't get in before sixteen hours was up, somebody else had to take your place. Sixteen hours, you stop right then.

"A lot of firemen quit because it took a lot of work shoveling coal. Some young feller once wanted to work on the railroad. He asked me about being a fireman, and I told him there was no trouble to it—all it took was a weak mind and a strong back to shovel coal. Well, he got him a job. He just made one trip with us on the freight train [and quit]. If you shovel coal sixteen hours, why, when you wake up the next morning, you turn out of the bed and hit the floor, and it'll jar you loose."

Hoyt Tench maintained that shoveling coal also required a degree of finesse: "There was quite a knack to [shoveling coal]. But one of the greatest things that you had to do—and if you weren't a good ballet dancer you couldn't have done it—was you had to put your right foot on the tender and your left foot right up here next to the fire door [inside the engine]. You had to sort of spread out to do this. There was a split [between the cars] and a cover keeping you from falling down between. It had to be loose where it would work because one of them would go one way and one the other and that little old road was sinking a lot of times. You'd start

Hoyt Tench began as a fireman for the TF, and later became an engineer for Southern Railway.

to throw a scoop of coal into the firebox and might end up throwing it up in the engineer's lap. He didn't like that much.

"All the steam engines were made like that. You hit your left foot on an air button and the doors [on the firebox] flew open. You took your right hand and got whatever coal you could in the scoop, mashed that button, and throwed [the coal] in the firebox, made it scatter, released the button, and [went] back [to the tender with the shovel]. In the meantime while you were firing, you couldn't hold to a thing. You didn't have nothing in your hands but a shovel. So you had to go with the rocking back and forth. After a while you could learn to do that and never miss a lick."

Brakemen

Walter Williams describes his job as brakeman: "I went to Cornelia and started in as a brakeman. This was 1919. Then when the war was over and these men in the Army came back [who had worked on] the railroad, I got laid off. So I went to Gainesville and went to work on the railroad out of there.

"As a brakeman, your job is to throw switches on the sidetrack that goes in to where they set out cars to be loaded and unloaded. You gotta go and unlock the switch, throw the switch, and put the cars in there. [You] cut the air on the brake to cut the train so whatever car you want to set off [can be set free]. Then you set it in there so they can load it or unload it. The conductor would tell you what he wanted done, and then you would do it. So you would go and set these cars in wherever they want them, and then you'd come and couple the train back up. And you [hook up] your air brake, and then you'd go on to another station."

Roy Shope was also a TF brakeman: "One time we was down in Clayton getting a car off here on the sidetrack, and I was up there to tie up the brakes. They kicked the car loose, and it started running on its own. The main train was coming down, and I thought I'd run off the top of this car when I got the brakes tied up and jump onto the main train. It was too far gone, and the main train was still coming, so I went down between the tracks. A boxcar and a half went over me before they got stopped. It didn't hit me. I was laying against one rail, and the brakes has got a crosspiece on it. I just had room to lay between that and the wheel. The train pushed me down because it was still moving. I landed on one heel on a cross tie, and I was off on crutches for about thirty days. That thing made a scar up my leg and I thought it was pretty close.

"A cow would get killed every once in a while. If a cow was on the track, we didn't stop to push it off. It was very hard to stop a train on that short notice. Most of the time, we'd just go on and hit it. You could lock every wheel down, but that engine still just kept sliding. Usually, if something was hit the railroad paid for it."

According to Hoyt Tench, animals were sometimes spared a fatal end: "[There was] another instance that included a big old bull. Right before you got to the depot at Lakemont coming north, they had a cut [for the train to go through]. There was generally always water running in it. It was higher than the boxcars. [The train would] get to rocking in there and it'd hit the sides. Rocks and dirt would fall [on the train] because it was such a high cut.

"It was a good cool place for cattle to be. Right the other side was the water tank at Sandy Flats. We had stopped to get water and weren't running very fast. We were just getting started off pretty good. We went into the cut and there was a big old bull. Some of [the cattle] got away, but he just stood there. We knocked him down with the cow catcher. By the time [the train] got stopped, he was [under the train]—between the step on the fireman's side and the cow catcher. He couldn't get out from the cow catcher because it was too high and the step would have tore him up if we'd went on. So we had a bull on our hands.

"We didn't know what to do. But being young, I said, 'Hey, I'll get him out of there.' I just stuck my shovel in the firebox and got a whole shovelful of hot coals and I just sprinkled them on his back. Boy, you began to smell hair and meat in a little bit. You never heard such a roar he give. He went out over top of the cotton-picking cow catcher. He got them feet over it and he pulled the rest of himself and over it he went. He got away from there. We laughed about that a lot of times. Of course, they said, 'Shame on you for putting fire coals on him.' [But] that was the only way to get him to move. I saved his life by doing it. We never did see him in that cut anymore."

Ernest Anderson said: "There was a second brakeman, called the head-end brakeman. You see, if you had twenty freight cars, there had to be several on the ground to give signals about backing in, pulling out, and all that. There wasn't no play job on the railroad."

Joe Snyder worked in several capacities on the railroad: "[The first job I had was as a brakeman.] I tied brakes up on cars when they were set off on the sidetrack to keep them from rolling out. I also unloaded freight cars, along with just a little bit of everything else.

"The number of cars we had on a train depended on [the merchandise and the size of the load]. Sometimes we would have ten or fifteen cars, some more than that. We would just pull so many up the grade to Mountain City or in Clayton. Can't take but so much [up the grade]. We'd have to cut off half of the cars and go back and get the balance of the train. We had what we called 'doubling.' When we'd reach Clayton, we'd stop and cut off part of the train and take part up to Mountain City and set them out, then go back and get the balance. I have doubled like that, letting the engineer think that I had set out [the cars] on the sidetrack, when

Joe Snyder.

I hadn't. [He laughs.] [He would] pull the whole train at once. That was kind of dirty to do. Have done it though.

"I remember when we set a car off in the sidetracks that didn't have but one switch in it, and the guy that worked there told me that if I stopped it on the money he would give me a pint [of moonshine]. I stopped it in the right place, and he said, 'Come and get it.' I said that I didn't need to do that but he said, 'Yeah, you're gonna take it.'

"One time we went into Clayton, the third trestle had grown up [in weeds and undergrowth] pretty bad. We saw this little girl standing out there in the middle of the trestle, and we stopped. I told her just to stand still and wait on me till I got there and not to move. I went out and took her by the hand and led her off. She was shaking so, I couldn't carry the little thing. I wonder how she got out there.

"[One thing that I didn't like about the railroad] was working in all kinds of weather. When ice got on the handrails going up the side of the car, there'd be icicles that big around [gesturing the size with his arms]. You'd have to break them off before you could climb up there. Pretty dangerous in a way.

"I have walked across cars a lot of times when there'd be some-body standing between the cars and on the coupling just a 'hoboing' it. Then I'd step over them to another car and you looked down again and you'd see them just a-hanging on. We had quite a few. Along towards the last we had a lot of them. They were just riding, you know. [One time] I was sitting in the cab filling out my reports, and I heard somebody coming up from the other end. I went to open the door and looked out, and there was three or four boys standing on the back of the cab. It was dark, so I told them not to jump—they might get killed—but they did anyway.

"I really loved the railroad work. I looked forward to doing it every day."

Flagmen

Carl Rogers recalled the responsibilities of the flagmen: "What the flagman did whenever you went into a siding when you met another train, he'd get off and turn the switch so you could go onto the siding, and then he'd turn it back for the other train to go by.

"The flagman also had to couple and uncouple the cars, and it was fascinating to see them work—they'd get out there and wave their arms and move their hands in a special way to get the cars coupled just right. If it was around a turn, the conductor'd relay [the signals] to the engineer. About the time the cars made contact, the flagman would drop his arms, and the engineer would stop the engine, and the [momentum] in the other cars would [force the couplers to lock].

"The flagman also checked out behind the train. If it had to stop on the main track, and there was another train coming, he'd jump off the train [and run up the track to flag the other train down] to stop it."

Ernest Anderson remembered: "If you were to pull in a switch here for another train to pass, he'll run up there in case the train comes on before you get in. After you get in, he signals to the other train that everything is clear. If you're not ready for him to pass, as soon as he comes into sight the flagman'll flag him down. He's also got to help unload freight, along with the brakeman."

Ernest Anderson.

Depot Agents

For all the towns up and down the line, the depot was a center of community life. Though most people immediately think of arriving and departing passengers when they think of depots, that was only part of their function. As Jo Brewer remembers: "Everything in the world [came through the depot]. The furniture that people wanted, the lamps, tables, chairs, beds, anything that anybody wanted they had to order them."

At the center of all this activity was the railroad agent.

Roy Beshears was depot agent in Franklin, North Carolina: "In the beginning a depot agent worked until way into the night—sometimes the freight train would be waylaid, and I have sat up all night waitin' for the freight train. You didn't have any hours.

A large crowd gathers at the Franklin, North Carolina, depot.

You worked all the time, paid by salary, and it was very low. Worked every day.

"One time a man brought a dog to the depot to be shipped. Now, I was responsible for accepting or rejecting anything to be shipped. If it wasn't crated or packaged right so it'd make the trip safely, I had to turn it down. If I accepted it and the crate tore up and something got lost or broken, it was my fault. So this man brought this big dog to be shipped to Cornelia. I was doubtful that the crate was all right, but he really wanted to ship that dog, so I finally accepted it. I asked him how much he wanted to value it for. Well he hemmed and hawed and finally decided on $50. Well, just a few miles down the road that dog got out somehow; the crate wasn't good enough to hold him. I should have known it. When I notified the man, he said that dog was worth $300! Well, they hunted for that dog and finally located him and returned him to the man. I never was so glad of anything in my life.

"The boy who worked with me stayed in the freight room and handled the freight. I handled the books, and the telegraphing. During World War I when there was all the government telegraphing to do, that kept me busy most of the time, so my wife sold tickets for me, but they didn't pay her any salary. She just worked

Roy Beshears, Franklin, North Carolina, depot agent.

with me to help me out. I would try to get most of my bookkeeping done after work and sometimes I'd work till midnight."

Ross Davis was depot agent in Prentiss: "I started before the sixteen-hour law became effective, and we had to stay on duty until the last trains come in and were handled and went on their way. For instance, I went to work one morning at six-thirty up at Prentiss, and they had a wreck down this way somewhere, and I remained on duty until four the following morning. I think that was the longest day I ever put in. The government sort of took over the railroads during the First World War, and it wasn't long until the sixteen-hour law was passed, that we couldn't be constantly on duty over sixteen hours. The northbound freight train very often got to Prentiss between 9 P.M. and 1 A.M. Then it left out of Franklin in the morning. I waited many a night till one, and they always had a big load for the warehouse, and would just about fill it up with freight. Sometimes they would check out five and six cars. They'd fill the platform full. When they got it full, they'd go on into the warehouse with it. My job next morning was to get all this freight inside and sorted so I could tell who it belonged to, and get it ready for delivery. Now, we worked seven days a week; not many people would be interested in that kind of job!

"Before the government stepped in during the war, we got $1.50 a day, but after that, all stations was moved up to a standard rate of 48 cents an hour. I believe in the year 1919 I made nearly $1,400. The government soon gave the railroads back to their rightful owners after the war, and it wasn't long after that till the Tallulah Falls Railroad went into the hands of a receiver. The telegraphing was discontinued at Prentiss, and the job was put on a $50 a month basis, which reduced my income quite a bit."

Carl Rogers, the depot agent in Clayton, recalls: "I was agent from 1954 to 1961, when the railroad went out. The agent was responsible for everything that went in and out of the depot. You were responsible for keeping books on all your cars, and carload lots. You had to enter the time that the cars were set in place for unloading, then when they were available to be returned.

"The first thing I did whenever I came in, I checked in, and then I had to make a 'yard book.' In this yard book, I had every car listed on my yard. The first thing I had to do was to go all the way up and down the yard and check these cars to see if any of them were empty or how many empty ones there were. If they were empty, then I had to report [for them] to be picked up. I had to make a yard check every day.

"Then, of course, freight came in and you had to help unload the cars. As an agent, the usual thing was I checked the freight, and the train crew unloaded it into the warehouse, and I had to make expense bills. The expense bills were just two bills. One of them was a receipt for the customer, and the other one was a receipt for the railroad.

"Now that was for the LCL—the less than carload lot—freight. That's small shipments like bags of nails and feed and pieces of furniture and all kinds of hardware and electrical appliances such as stoves and refrigerators and washing machines that used to come in. On the upper side of the warehouse, we had two big doors there where the trucks could back in to load up the freight that had come in, or haul in the freight that they were shipping out.

"The other kind of freight we had to deal with was whole car lots [when a customer was receiving or shipping an entire freight car load of merchandise].

"You had to make expense bills on it, too, and collect from the customer for the carload lot. All of this money that you collected, you had to deposit it in the bank for the railroad, and you had to keep records on how much you collected and how much was uncollected, and you had to give a report on how much was on hand at the end of the month. It was really a detailed bookkeeping job.

"Cars that came in that were going to one customer were put out in the car lot for them to come and unload. You had to know what was in those cars because you were responsible for it. If it was a carload of cattle, you had to count the cattle because you were responsible for the count. If the car got to its destination and there wasn't the proper number of cattle in there, well, the railroad was responsible because the agents had counted them [at the point where they were shipped, and at the point they were delivered to].

"It was the depot agent's job to keep track of all these cars. Then we had a demurrage bureau that audited us on it—came in and audited our books. We had a big book that was made for all this. It showed the date of arrival for a car, the date it was placed. That book must have been eighteen by twenty-four inches. The depot agent had to go out every morning and check every car to see what its status was. And you'd give the consignee two days, commencing at 7 A.M., to unload his car. He had forty-eight hours to unload that car without paying any demurrage on it. That was one reason you had to keep tabs on the cars. Now that was excluding Saturdays and Sundays and holidays, and rainy days. If the car wasn't unloaded in two days, why, you had to charge him demurrage on it whenever you made your yard check.

"The longer it took a person to unload a car, the longer the railroad had to pay the rent on it. That's where the TF was hurting so bad because on weekends, holidays, or rain, the per diem might run more than the railroad made on the freight. The longer it stayed, the higher the demurrage got.

"We had the big books for years and years. [Then one year] they had the section crew to haul 'em off and dump 'em in a big hole south of Clayton and cover 'em with dirt. Now those that we had on hand when the railroad deactivated, why, they had to send them to Cornelia, Georgia. They stayed at Cornelia, and then later on they were transferred somewhere else, and I don't know where to find them. Last time I ever asked, they told me they had moved these records to Greenville, South Carolina, and didn't know whatever happened to them. You see the TF was on the Southern

Railroad Company, and these records were turned over to the Southern Railroad. I guess they destroyed them. I don't see what use they would ever have for them, so I imagine they destroyed them."

Homer Deal, relief depot agent for the TF, tells about his job: "I was a relief depot agent, which included Morse telegraphing, Western Union telegraphing, freight agent, express agent, and baggage agent. Those were the jobs of the depot agent. I did relief work at depots all up and down. I started doing some relief work by the time I was twelve or thirteen years old—I was raised up in it. My stepfather was a station agent, and I worked under him. By the time I was twelve I was doing commercial telegraphing, and railway telegraphing. I worked with them till I was about seventeen years old. I did a little relief work after that, but I started in the pharmacy business in 1915. But Morse telegraphing operators were always scarce, and [even after] I first started my drugstore at Dillard, I did some emergency work for the regular agent."

When he was a boy, Homer Deal was almost killed on the railroad: "I was crazy about the 'road. When I was about twelve years old, I was as sure that I'd be a railroad engineer as I'm setting here. They'd send me from one small station to another small station, being I was just a young boy, and they'd send the regular agent to the heavy job. I rode the train back and forth. Some of the best times I ever had in my life was riding that train. The engineer would let me pull the throttle, let me pull the whistle, and ring the bell. In other words, they all let me do as I pleased. That's why I was sure they were gonna let me be a locomotive engineer. One time I was riding the cow hook on the front of the engine. We were running into a cut, and this great big old cow was in there, and there wasn't room for it and the train to pass, and she jumped on the track. There wasn't time to stop the train. I guess that is the fastest I ever moved in my life! I slammed myself back and under that boiler. Just about the time I got under it, the train hit the cow, and it come up the cow hook and slammed into the boiler. If that cow had hit me, it would have been the end. That broke me from riding the cow hook—I never rode it no more."

Jo Brewer, a public health nurse in Rabun County for most of her professional career, was the daughter of a depot agent for the TF. She gave us her perspective on the job. "My father, Jim Kinman,

Passengers purchased tickets at the depots to ride the train.

was a relief agent on the TF. I was fourteen when he died, in 1924, and people have told me that he knew more about this work on the railroad, and the history of the railroad, than any other person on the road.

"He went to Mercer University in Macon, and he moved to the mountains—Cornelia—in September 1911, for his health. I was just a baby. My brother, Donald, was older, and later he was also a TF agent—the youngest agent on the road.

"My father started on the TF March 22, 1912, and he was a relief agent at Prentiss, North Carolina. We stayed up there until September 1912, and moved to Hollywood, Georgia. We were there just a few weeks, then we moved to Tallulah Falls. That was a two-story station, and we lived up above it on the top floor. The depot was right across from the Cliff House, a great big old hotel. And then the depot burned. We were upstairs, and there were some boxcars on the siding right there by the depot that had dynamite in them because they were building the dam at Tallulah Falls. The men in the town were just worried to death because they were afraid with the station burning down that those boxcars would catch on fire. They knew how to undo the brakes on the ends of the cars, so they moved the cars on down a little further away from the station south so that they wouldn't catch on fire because it would have burned up all of Tallulah Falls if they had. That was May 13, 1913.

"May 16, 1913, we moved to Clarkesville; June 1, 1913, we moved to Turnerville; September 13, 1913, we moved to Clayton and my father was assistant agent, doing the bookkeeping. We were there until 1918 when he got the flu. He never was well after that. So he asked the railway company if he could have a smaller station because work was just too much here because he was not well. The reason he couldn't remain the agent here is because everything in this world that came to Clayton came on the train, and it was heavy work. So they let him go back to Turnerville. So in 1921 we moved back to Turnerville because it was a smaller station. My mother continued to help him and he also had helpers to do the rolling of the big barrels and the lifting of the feed sacks, because the agents weren't supposed to do that. He was just supposed to do the phoning and the telegraphing. Back in those days the phone system wasn't very good, and you had to holler your head off, and, frankly, I think you could have heard somebody from Clayton to Cornelia almost."

THE HUMAN SIDE

Practically everyone over forty years of age who lives in the counties served by the TF has some special memories of it: derailments, wrecks, going to the station to meet the train, hearing the whistle blow at a certain time of day, seeing the train for the first time, riding the train for the first time, hitching free rides, etc.

The train was an indifferent machine, but the people endowed the TF with a life and personality all its own because of its qualities, which transcended the more obvious and practical functions of bringing in money and transporting people and goods from point A to point B. The train was a noisy, dirty, sometimes unreliable, and probably cantankerous creature, which provided much excitement and was regarded with love and awe. Thus as each leg of the line was completed, inevitably there would be a community celebration. Kenny Runion recalled one of them: "They wasn't no cars then, and that train was a new thing. The first time the train went south they had a big dinner up here in Mountain City, and everybody came. That was the first time I ever seen any loaf bread. I was just a kid then. I reckon I was five or six years old. That train was full. I wish you could of seen it. The cars was full, and people was standing on the steps. It was a new thing."

Aunt Arie Carpenter remembered another such celebration: "I remember the train coming in here as well as if it was yesterday.

"[The first train to Otto, North Carolina] came in just a-rollin', and there was a celebration. Everybody was as proud as they could be 'cause it was a good asset to the community. We was proud t'death of it. I never will forget it. You know, it come in and went

Aunt Arie Carpenter.

backward down to Franklin [North Carolina]. For years and years it went backward and turned there. I been on it."

Some people were frightened of it when they first saw it. Harry Brown recalled his first sight of the TF: "I can remember when it [the train] turned around at Rabun Gap. I was about nine, and I come with my mother to get a load of stuff for my father's little country grocery store up at Scaly [Mountain, North Carolina]. The train backed up there and turned around. The best I can remember, they said I got scared and started to run away."

Mrs. Con Mitchell remembers a time when a train was such an intimidating sight: "At that time, I was just a teenage girl, but I knew two girls that lived back over on Lake Burton. They was older than I was, and they'd never seen a train. They come over one Sunday; they was singers, and they come to Clayton to sing. We brought them and come to the depot with them to see the train go by, and they was scared of it and left. They seen it and heard it coming, and they got back up the street! They could see it go by, but they wouldn't get close to it."

Afraid or not, though, people were drawn to the depot like magnets. Jo Brewer said: "When I was little the most fun in this whole town was going to the depot and seeing the people come in.

They'd get off the train and walk out maybe a minute, and we'd look out and see the clothes—you know, they were so different from the way we looked up here. On Sundays, it was really something. I bet the whole town turned out to go to the [depot] in the summertime because they'd have excursion trains. On Sundays, it was really something to see these people come up here and get off at Tallulah Falls and go down to the gorge and look at all these mountains and look at us mountain folks and then get back on the trains. I guess they thought we were some sight because back in those days we didn't—well, we didn't have a place to buy good clothes much."

Lelia Gibson recalled: "All the recreation we had was going to the depots on Sunday. All of us young girls and boys would go to the depot to see who was on the train! We'd generally only go to the depot on Sunday afternoon, and we'd go to the 'Y' [turnaround at Franklin] and get on the train and ride down. That was a free ride." Lelia also told us about the time her husband was delayed because of a bad storm: "My husband was on the night passenger once—they had a complete rainstorm. While they were going through a cut here at Dillard, the storm had washed the banks, and the train couldn't cross. My husband had to spend the night there. They didn't have the machinery like they do now to clear tracks so soon. They had to work about eighteen hours clearing the track for the train to go over."

Ellen Alley: "People would go out to meet the train. Then, of course, they had a big waiting room, and especially on rainy days, people would gather in there, and one great thing that the young lakeshore people would do was sing. I remember how they'd gather down there and just sing up a storm. The men 'loafed.' They would sit in the depot. That was one place to meet. There and the post office were the places to meet to see each other."

R. M. Dickerson said: "When it got train time, everybody just left the store—just closed up the store and went down to meet the train. They went to see if they got express and freight or anything, and would go down to see who got on and off. It was a real community thing."

Raleigh Hopper remembers one man who was a fixture at the depot: "There was a man named Uncle Bob. He met the train every time it come in. Well, one night it come in there late with a big load of freight, and it was going real slow, just barely moving it was so heavy. Well, Uncle Bob run out and he yelled at the crew, 'How come you don't get out and push?' "

Many local people have vivid memories not only of watching the train, but also riding on it. For many of them, the train meant the difference between an exhausting two- or three-day wagon ride to see a relative, and a quick trip in comparative comfort protected from the elements. For others, it meant the difference between being able to go to school or not. Mary Pitts rode it from her home to the Rabun Gap-Nacoochee School where she was a boarding student: "I used the train when I came up here to school in 1921. I rode the train from Cornelia up to the Gap. That was the only way for me to get to school. There wasn't many cars. There was a lot of passengers then. I knew the engineers. They were real friendly and nice. Lots of times we would go down on Sunday evening and watch the excursions go by."

Mary Cabe remembered: "It cost a dime to go the ten or twelve miles from Otto to Franklin, but I didn't ride it very often—dimes were hard to get back then. But people would get on it and ride to Franklin and back or ride down to Clayton. I took my first ride on the train to Prentiss, down this side of Franklin. Got on at Otto, went to Prentiss, and it came right back to Otto—it didn't go up to Franklin at that point. Why, I really enjoyed that!"

Leona Carver recalled: "I was about nine or ten years old, I guess, the first time I rode the train. I was going to Clayton with my daddy to get a pair of shoes. We walked to Dillard and caught the train to Clayton and got my shoes and come back.

"People didn't have cars back then like they do now, and when we had to go somewhere, why we would go to the depot and catch the train. It cost twenty-five cents to go from Clayton to Dillard and back. That was cheap transportation. When me and my husband first married, we lived at Clayton and his mother lived the other side of Dillard. We'd catch the train there in Clayton, and we could ride to the crossing beyond the Dillard depot [and walk from there]. Anywhere you wanted to get off, why they'd let you off. The train would stop and let you off just like you was riding with anybody in a car. Just let 'em know where you wanted to get off, and they'd stop and let you off."

Jim Taylor said: "I rode the TF every time I could—whenever

I had a dime and wanted to go from Dillard to Clayton. I'd hear the train blow for the Highlands Road Crossing [north of Dillard], and I'd sort of put myself in high gear, and I would get into Dillard in time to catch it by the time it had made its stop and delivered the mail and before it got gone. Didn't have but a few minutes [to get there because] it'd be chugging on up the road, but I would catch it. I would make it. It didn't run too fast nohow—I guess about like a good dog trotting."

The train opened up other opportunities along the route— Harry Brown remembers: "The first time I rode a passenger train, we walked to Otto and rode the train to Franklin to see the Ringling Brothers' circus."

R.M. Dickerson remembers letting his children ride the train by themselves: "Everyone went for a ride on the train. We used to have four trains. We could ride down to Clayton at noon and then ride back. We had three kids—two boys and a girl. When they were little fellers and big enough to sorta mind, they'd go down and buy them a ticket. The conductor always looked after them, the little boys and girls, just like you would look after them if you was a teacher."

Florence Brooks told a story about an excursion from Nantahala, North Carolina: "We went up there one day to a picnic, and started back, and th' brakeman, and th' engineer, and everybody got drunk. And you talk about coming back down that track, well it was the awfullest thing in the world. 'Fraid it was gonna wreck and kill every one of us. A wonder it hadn't. It was several miles, twelve, fifteen, or twenty, a long ways up there. Somebody ought to have whipped them trainmen when we got it stopped. It would have killed a pile! Well, everybody over there would've been killed. There wouldn't have been any people on Nantahala left 'cause everybody went. We didn't leave nobody at home."

Aunt Arie Carpenter remembered the TF "just like it was yesterday": "The trains was all strange to me, and I didn't care to ride 'em. I don't know why that is, but I didn't. But I helped everybody in the world I could help—now, that's the truth—and they was an old woman that lived on the head of Coweeta, name of Sanders. And she come asking me to go with her—she wouldn't go by herself—to get on the train and go down to Franklin and stay all night, then come back on the train the next day. We went down there and turned around backward, then got off the train and walked maybe a mile to where she wanted to stay all night.

"I'll never forget the day they had an explosion of some kind. It blowed up this man and killed 'im. That's been many a year ago. I never thought about remembering it.

"Last time I got on the train, I cried all the way home. I don't know what his name was. He was a conductor on the railroad. I think I had a box or something to put on and 'course I couldn't lift it and do like I love to. He thought I could, I reckon. He didn't treat me right. Anybody don't treat me right, I'm bad for that. I just cry and never can get over it. So they tried to get me to report him, and I said, 'No, sir. I just hope I never see him again as long as I live.'

"He didn't do me no harm, but he acted hateful. He didn't do a thing to me; he just didn't treat me right. That's the last time I ever got on the train. I said I'd never ride that train again as long as I lived and I never have. It's been about forty-five years ago, I guess. I said I'd walk before I'd get on that train anymore, and I never have been on it no more.

"But that old train was a good help to Macon County with all the cross ties and all. It was a lot of help to Macon County. Seems like just the other day they removed the railroad."

Some Rabun County folks remembered stealing the small push cars. Jo Brewer recalled: "[Nan Hamby Short] and I used to play together a lot. So one Sunday, Nan and I and a bunch of kids, we got this little old push car. It is a square kind of a car with wheels on it that you push on the track. So we pushed it to Mountain City, and my daddy, the Clayton depot agent, just came down to the depot to see how things were, and he saw that little push car was gone. He said, 'Where did that push car go?' Somebody standing around that depot said, 'Your daughter and Nan Hamby and a bunch of kids pushed it up to Mountain City.' I imagine my daddy just about had a fit. You see, we didn't know anything about grades, and from Mountain City it's a lot higher elevation than it is at Clayton. So what he did was get my brother and some more boys to get buckets of sand and go running up the track toward Mountain City and put sand on the track so that we wouldn't just fly off the track. If we'd been coming down from Mountain City without any brakes on that little old push car or anything, we could have just shot out over them trestles, and some of them were higher than this house. [There were] at least two big ones between Clayton and Mountain City. I don't remember getting a whippin' about that but I bet you I did."

Stealing a push car ended Florence Brooks's school career: "The time we stole the lever car, we just got it. We was riding down the track in front of the schoolhouse, and liked t' killed the teacher! He tried to stop us, and got in the middle of the track and waved his arms. I was sitting where you put the brakes on, and all the kids a-saying, 'Florence, don't stop, don't stop!' We went through there as fast as we could [go]. We just barely missed him. He shouldn't have got in the middle of the track if he didn't want to be run over. Now, let me tell you, if we'd hit him, we would have jumped the track, gone into the river, and killed him and us too. I never went back to school after that."

Some folks, Esco Pitts said, used the push cars to date: "The section hands had one of these old handcars for the train. We'd have dates at Mountain City and we'd go get that handcar and crank it up and pile on it and ride down to the dance and come back in at midnight. We had lots of fun doing that."

Lon Harkins told us about hoboing: "I've hoboed this old TF freight train, from here [Dillard] to Cornelia. That was back in 1935—I just got in a boxcar and stayed with it. Me and Lester Thomas would go over there to Dillard and see if we could get in the boxcar."

Frank A. Smith remembers a wreck that involved girls from Camp Laurel Falls: "I remember the girls getting on the train, on their way home. And I remember getting the report. It was one of the greatest shocks I've ever had in my life because the report was that they had had a wreck, the engineer was killed, and the fireman almost killed, and that camp girls were lying on either side of the railroad. Well, I never had such a shock, really. I got down there and found that not a single child had been injured. My feeling was one of immense relief."

Jim Bingham remembers this about the wreck: "I was on the passenger train one morning and down yonder below Tiger it jumped th' track—the engine went way over in a field. Th' car I was in, it turned over on its side. Well, quick as everything got still, I went out the winder, underneath of [the car]. It didn't go plumb flat to th' ground—caught something and I had room enough to git out from under there. Now I was scared. I went to hunting for th' engineer and th' fireman—we got [the fireman] out, he liked to a died [though], but he's still living yet. I was looking for th' engineer—and I jumped off the corner of the coal tender, and I jumped right off on him. He was covered up with dirt. I hated that so bad, but I couldn't help it. I didn't know he was there."

The August 26, 1920, edition of the *Tri-County Advertiser* announced the death of John Harvey:

On last Monday morning, about eight thirty o'clock, Mr. John Harvey was killed in a wreck on train No. 3 just about one mile south of Tiger, Georgia. The fireman, Mr. Caloway Gibby, was severely bruised and scalded.

A story about the TF in the February 14, 1960, *Atlanta Journal and Constitution* commented:

John Harvey could have saved himself by jumping from the train. Instead, he stayed to put on the brake as long as he could. If he had jumped, many more people would have been hurt and several more killed. John Harvey did a noble thing for the people on Engine no. 3. His last noble efforts were appreciated by many.

A. J. Gudger tells of a wreck that he heard stories about: "The train went through Panther Creek [trestle] in 1898 and a fellow named Ivy was killed. That was the highest [trestle]—I believe it was ninety-eight feet high."

In 1927, another major disaster occurred on the line. Ross Davis remembered: "The Demorest wreck happened in the twenties at the trestle over Hazel Creek. The trestle crew had been working on it. The crew quit about five that afternoon, and they were all on their way home.

"Whenever the evening train come, the trestle just split out. Mr. Miller was the engineer on it and I believe he was killed in that wreck. That was the wreck that Mr. Miller went down with his engine. The mail carrier and his car went down and he was killed. The baggage master was Don Merritt and he was killed.

The Hazel Creek trestle collapsed under the weight of a passenger train.
This photograph shows how many of the supporting beams are gone
from under the passenger car that remained on the tracks.

Everything went down except one coach right on the rear end. The wheels happened to lock, and it hung up there right on the end of the rails. I don't know what caused it. The pictures showed that the tracks just split apart."

Hoyt Tench related this humorous tale of an incident on his train while waiting for a derailment to be cleaned up: "You had a lot of derailments. It was nothing just to be going along minding your own business, and all of a sudden you would look back and one [wheel] would be running on the cross ties.

"They had a derailment up here at Otto, North Carolina, one day. We got caught behind it and couldn't get by. So the engineer and I was sitting there biding our time, keeping the engine warm—it was in the wintertime.

"Mr. Brewer, the general manager, came crawling up on that engine and told the engineer, 'Man, I'm glad you still got some coffee. I need some coffee.'

"The engineer told him, 'Mr. Brewer, you can have anything I got. You can have the old lady; you can have *anything* I got, but you can't have my coffee.' [The engineer] reached up and got that coffee off of the jacket of the engine where he kept it and drank it. I thought that man wasn't very hospitable to do something like that with the big boss getting up on the engine.

"Mr. Brewer said, 'I'll go hunt me some.' He got down off that engine and I thought, 'Now I know what it is,' because you could smell it. The engineer would take a pint of white whiskey—rheumatism medicine—and put black coffee enough to turn it black and put it up on the jacket of the engine and it would keep it warm. He drank a pint to two pints a day. I never did see him drunk [though]. He just sipped on it all day. I thought it was just warm old strong coffee but it was just some of this good Rabun County booze."

Jess Page told us about wrecking a train on purpose for the Walt Disney production *The Great Locomotive Chase*. "One train, we wrecked it a-purpose, when Walt Disney was making that picture. It was down below Clayton. We had a train pushing a boxcar up and we had a switch there. The train stopped, and we threw that switch and the car went off the main line. It went off and turned over down in Tom Roane's field. Sometimes we had to take out a rail, fix it where a push cart jumped the track."

The "Texas" was one of the engines used during the filming of "The Great Locomotive Chase."

John Kollock had a small part in the movie: "Anytime anybody came to town to make a movie we all went down and tried out for it. Since my voice is kind of North Georgian, I got a part as one of the engineers, and so I came up to Clayton in October for the shooting.

"Since there were no tunnels on the TF, they built a fake entrance to the tunnel just below the Lakemont station in a little gap down there. For one of the hotels, they just built the first floor and faked the upper part of it.

"The station that I worked in was just above Otto, North Carolina. They built a siding and the station right out in the middle of nowhere. We would get up in the morning and go down to the train station in Clayton where they had the makeup people. They put the makeup on and we got our costumes, and then we'd get in the bus and ride up to Otto.

"At that time of year there's a deep fog up in that valley, so we would get up there and sit around by the fire and wait until the fog lifted. It was nine or ten o'clock in the morning before we would even start work, and then we would work the rest of the day. I was up there for a week or so waiting around. Finally the day came that I got to play an engineer on a train coming south out of Chattanooga and had a little scene with Fess Parker. When we finally got around to shooting it, we shot the whole thing in about an hour and then I was through.

"I was supposed to be the engineer, so I hung out the window but I didn't drive the train. They had a man laying on the floor between my feet and he was driving the train laying down. All I got to do was blow the whistle as I came in."

Ernest Anderson remembers Walt Disney as a generous man. "Walt Disney sure was a fellow. He hired a whole lot of people from around here to work on the film. You ought to have been around when Walt Disney was making that picture up there. He really paid you something. He gave you fifty dollars a week extra, just to buy your Coca-Colas with, outside of your salary; then you got your dinner and supper made. [The movie] was made in 1955. The women and girls in the pictures dressed just the way they used to seventy or eighty years ago: long sleeves, collars way up around, the skirts a-dragging. Disney hired a lot of people for the movie—and when you signed up, your pay started when you stuck your name down. I got paid two weeks before they got up there to work. Me [the fireman], and the engineer and the brakeman wore the regular clothes they worked on the railroad in all the time."

Carl Rogers told us how Disney brought the old steam engines up to Rabun County. "They pulled those trains up here by the Tallulah Falls Railroad. The TF furnished the engineers and conductors. They brought the trains from California, shipped them by regular freight. One of them came out of the museum in St. Louis, I believe. The others were shipped from California. They were shipped to Cornelia by railroad. Then our railroad crew took them over at Cornelia and brought them on up. We had about three locomotives and one regular TF diesel up here that was used. They had dining cars and passenger cars. They operated on diesel fuel, but it looked like they were operating on wood. They could make them smoke, just like they were operated on wood.

"The regular scheduled trains, the ones carrying freight, operated at night. They gave this picture industry the daytime operating. Most of the picture was made on the north end of the track, from right here in the Clayton vicinity up to Franklin. Those trains that operated under Walt Disney Productions had to be regulated under the ICC just like a regular train."

Roy Shope recalls that it wasn't always a breeze going down the line. Local folks would occasionally play pranks on the TF, and natural obstacles would also slow them down: "There were people who used to get Octagon soap and soap up the rails between Mountain City and Clayton! When the train came through there, it'd just sit and spin until it burned that soap off, and then it'd come on through. Boy, I can tell you that thing'll just nearly jump the track when all them wheels go to spinning. The railroad crew kept buckets of sand on them engines, and if they could ever get sand on the rails, they could pick up and go. People would pick up old spikes and put 'em on the rails to make the train jump. They'd put all kinds of stuff on 'em—rocks, bolts, spikes, anything! That soap's what give us trouble. They did it for fun to see if the train would spin. We've got out and run the sand out and put it on the rails with our hands."

Buck Carver told us about a game he used to play at the railroad track: "When I was a kid, we lived by the side of the tracks for five years. We'd take straight pins down to the track and cross them and lay them on the track and the train would run over them and it'd press them together. It looked like a tiny pair of scissors. Lord knows the times I laid pennies on the track and let it flatten them out."

Joe Hopper remembers the sound of the TF as the train went down the line: "The train would just go backward and forward, backward and forward, and blow that whistle. I've been over where Nell Thomas lives, and you could hear it blow for the Highlands Road crossing, and I've caught it in Dillard before it got away. It run pretty fast—it run about twenty miles per hour. I wish it was still going."

"AND THEN IT WAS GONE"

Thirty years have passed since the TF finally closed down. One of the most moving stories we've heard about its passing Lelia Gibson told us: "They was a Mr. Bob Donaldson who worked with the construction crew as a section foreman. He rode the first train into Franklin. The last time the train came to Franklin, Bob Donaldson was on [it]. He didn't live very long after that. He died with grief over the loss of the train."

Jess Page was the only man we interviewed who worked on the railroad after it was abandoned in 1961. He helped take up the tracks to be loaded on trucks and taken to different places. He tells us here what happened to the tracks and the cross ties and the rest of the equipment: "I started working there in '54 and worked till it went out in 1961. And I helped tear the track up. We took up all the rails, loaded them on trucks, and hauled them off, picked up all the spikes—and a junk man bought it. I think the rails were shipped someplace to these sugarcane factories, make a little railroad to haul that sugarcane out with. The old spikes and bolts, they just sold them for junk—they were iron. They saved some of the ties, took them over to Maggie Valley and used them. But the rest of them they'd give to people for wood.

"They came in here from Chicago to do it. They had machinery. I guess it took them about two months to take the track up. It didn't take long."

People in the area still speculate about why the Southern Railway closed the TF. Esco Pitts said: "I was sort of sorry to see it discontinued, but they claimed it was running in the red all the time. They had in applications to discontinue it a long time before they ever committed to abandon it. They was losing money, and people didn't have too much to ship on it like they did when it first come here. Fewer and fewer people would patronize it. People had automobiles. Finally, they wound up bringing the mail; that's about all they done. So it just had to be discontinued. I was sorry to see it go. But it couldn't continue losing money all the time."

According to the February 8, 1973, *Franklin Press*, "The old Tallulah Falls helped dig its own grave by hauling materials to build the roads. . . ." Many of our contacts agree with this statement, among them Ross Davis: "The highways are so much more convenient for everybody. Everyone got their own transportation, and of course, they used that. Wasn't necessary to run a passenger train. Then they got to hauling their own freight. Then came the motor lines, and competition, and the railroad just couldn't survive with all that competition."

Roy Mize blames the Southern Railway for the closing of the TF: "It certainly was a hard blow to this area to lose that railroad. People was all heartbroken to lose the train. It was the main way of transportation, as well as transporting all the products that came from this area at that time because there was very few trucks. I think the biggest reason for the train going out was that the Southern Railroad had controlling stock, and it got to where it was a losing proposition, so they just didn't want to keep it up. When they closed it, it was a great blow to Rabun County."

Other people blame the receiver, H. L. Brewer, for the railroad's demise. Roy Shope said: "They claimed it wasn't makin' any money, but I kinda believe it was when it went down. To tell you the truth, old man Henry Brewer, the receiver of the railroad, he [was] going to retire. He wanted to take it out with him, and he did."

Carl Rogers defended Brewer against this allegation: "He wasn't a popular man because the railroad was in receivership, and things that were beyond his control were blamed on him. They claimed he sold out to the Southern. He was supposed to be working for the TF, but he was working against the train, they said, and for Southern. They said Southern put him in there to kill the train. That's not true. The shortline railroads were *all* going out. It was just the change of the times."

The majority of the people we interviewed still miss the train, for it held a special place in many hearts. When asked how he felt when the train went out, Homer Deal said: "I had a sister that lived in Portland, Oregon, and when they junked the TF, I wrote her a letter and told her about it. I told her that I felt like I had lost my best friend."

Leona Carver: "We depended on the train, and the last run that it was going to make, I don't know how many of us who lived up there on Kelly's Creek walked to Dillard to the depot to see it make its last run. It was just like losing a friend, or seeing a friend leave. Then after the train quit running, why it was so sad. They'd blow their whistle every day before they got to the depot, and after they quit running, why it was just so sad in the morning, you know. When it come time for the whistle to blow, why you'd be so sad."

Lon Harkins said: "I wish they'd put the train back and get these old trucks off the highway. You could hear that old thing go, 'Wo-o-o wo-o-o wo-o-o-o-o-o.' And you'd hear 'em let the steam out: 'Phew phew phew phew phew.' Every day you'd hear that whistle and you'd know what time it was."

According to Fred Grist, many people could see the end of the TF coming, even before it ceased: "We knew before long it would be gone. The messenger service went out [and] then later the freight went out. I hated to see it go. I would like to see the railroad come back, but I don't think it would have any business."

Lex Wilburn said: "We just had to do the best we could when the railroad went out. I felt like we was ruint—it hurt us all when they junked it. When they had that train, people could travel for a long ways, and go to work for the railroad. They's just lots of people that wanted to keep it, but they just junked it."

Ernest Anderson felt the loss was greatest in the northernmost counties served by the TF: "I'd done retired when the railroad went out, but I hated to see it go. I was fond of the TF Railroad, as was everybody who worked on it. There was lots of people that didn't work on it that lived along it and done business with it. They hated to see it quit. It wasn't as great a loss to the people around Cornelia as it was to the people in Macon and Rabun counties, because they still had the Southern in Cornelia."

A number of the people we interviewed gave reasons for why the railway should have stayed. Two of our contacts felt that the railway should come back because of the energy crisis. Esco Pitts said: "Sometime there may be a need for it, and they may bring it back and put it through. It could be mighty handy to haul coal from up in Virginia and up in there down here. This energy crisis is going to call for more coal than they have been using in years. And that's one cheap way of getting it from up there down here, get it on that train. Them trucks is finding it harder to get fuel, and run their trucks. The railroad is the cheapest transportation we got. They may put it through again. I'd like to see it take place. It would give people jobs and it would bring new industry and the country would be benefited if it went through."

A. J. Gudger agreed that an energy crisis might make another railway possible: "If we keep having problems with the gasoline, which we will, in my opinion, the railroads, I believe, will come back, because trucks and cars may have to come off the highways, unless they come up with something or other else to pull the trucks with. We'll have to go back to the old steam engines."

Lex Wilburn thought that a new TF would fill a gap in public transportation in the area: "Lots of people would like the train back now. I would, too! A lot of people could go places where they can't get t'go now—lot of old people could ride it. It was real nice riding it."

Jess Rickman commented: "I believe there's just a lot of people that would like to see it back, because it was cheaper operated than trucking, and shipping [by train] is cheaper than trucking will ever be. We miss it a lot because you could have stuff shipped out of Franklin back up here lots cheaper than trucking."

The argument Lawton Brooks gave us for the railroad staying was based on emotion, and it probably reflects the feelings of many: "I'd like to have the old railroad back, and I bet the other people does now, the way things is a-going, buddy. It'd be used more than it used to be, because the way stuff's a-getting, and as high as gas is getting to be. I think it was good for the county. I never did see no need of doing away with the railroad. I've always thought the railroad still ought to be a-going. I still think it would'a paid off. That's the worst mistake they ever made in Rabun County. If I had it just for a month, to get what I could make off that train and two cars for a month, I would never ask for nothing else. You'd get rich. They could get rich off all these tourists coming in here now if they just had that thing to run around them old falls where you could sit there and look straight down and them old cars just a-rocking. Good God, it'd take somebody standing there with a sack carrying the money off as fast as they could take it in.

"If they had it now, Lord have mercy, they couldn't keep the folks out of there. These tourists would've filled that thing full. A man could've went from daylight to dark running that blasted thing. Sure could, and all the money a man could've made. That's the moneyest thing I've ever seen torn down in my life.

"I miss hearing the old bells—it'd come around the same time, and it'd blow for all the train crossings. You could hear it coming before you could ever see it."

Carl Rogers summarized how the railroad affected the community: "It was a great boon to this section of the country. It give this country a good many years of business long before the buses and trucks came. If we'd waited till the buses and trucks came, this would have been a dull section for a good many years."

WHAT'S LEFT

The TF has been gone for thirty years. It was sold to a steel company for scrap. It seems that not much would be left of the railway, but throughout the years, a lot has survived.

When the TF was scrapped, George Welch purchased two cars and three trestles. "I give $3,000 for the three trestles. But I got a lot more than that out of them, and if one hadn't been out over a lake [one of the Georgia Power lakes at Tallulah Falls] I wouldn't never got it. You see, I stayed overseas a lot and I knew how to rig a lot of cranes and a lot of anything else. So I knew how I could take it up before I bought it. I bought one section in Dillard, one in Clarkesville [both wooden], and that 585-foot one [metal] down there across the lake. That trestle was 100 foot up over the lake."

Coyle Hollifield bought the rail car that was used to carry mail along the TF route from Cornelia to Franklin. Here, he tells what he planned to do with it: "When I bought that car, I was gonna make a diner out of it. The highway went right along here. That was before the bypass, you know. This was the main highway then. When they built the bypass, there wasn't enough traffic to open a diner for. We graded out a place, but we didn't make it into a

The old rail car owned by Coyle Hollifield is now a residence.

diner. We've been renting it to people that wanted it [to live in]. I think we get thirty dollars a month for it. It has three rooms."

Other cars still in this area include one that was owned by Claude Giles. It was used as a residence for a while and is now vacant. It was a wooden coach turned into a maintenance car B-2.

Another is the wooden-sided TF caboose X-5. X-5 was discovered by Gene Cannon of Yancey Railroad, who purchased it. Re-

TF caboose X-5.

*This stretch of track just north of Mountain City where this train ran
in the 1920s is now maintained by Wallace Scruggs. Jim Taylor
commented: "Wallace Scruggs ain't even tore the railroad bed down. He
ain't wanted to let it go down. He said there might be another [train]
come through sometime and they wouldn't have to build it back."*

cently it was donated to the Atlanta Chapter of the National
Historical Railroad Society. In August of 1991, it was brought to
Cornelia for renovation, where it had been built ninety-one years
before.

Some of the depots of the TF remain. In Tallulah Falls the
depot is now used as a craft shop. In Demorest the depot is also
intact. The depot in Otto was torn down, but then a shed was built
in its place using the wood from the original depot.

A section of roadbed in Mountain City is still maintained by
Wallace Scruggs.

Georgia Power Company is considering opening a section of
roadbed in the Tallulah Falls area to hikers and joggers.

Railroad historian Dess Oliver collects Tallulah Falls Railway
memorabilia. He has built a "railroad depot" in Wolffork Valley,
Rabun County, for his collection.

The *Franklin Press* in Macon County, North Carolina, ran an
article about the TF on February 8, 1973, from which the following
excerpt was taken:

Today, there's not much left except traces along the Little Tennessee River, and many memories in the hearts of Maconians.

Dess Oliver's "depot."

Maconians who helped build the TF, patronized her, and shed a sentimental tear when she died.

What's left of the Tallulah Falls Railway? We have a few tangible things—some pictures, some wood, some steel—and one very important intangible thing—our memories: memories of good times and laughter, sad times and tears, memories of sounds and smells and sights—things that exist only in our minds. But we hope that by sharing some of our memories of the TF, we are helping to keep them alive.

The Cliff House porch, ca. 1906. (Courtesy Georgia Department of Archives and History)

TOURISM

STUDENT EDITOR, JULIE DICKENS

Tallulah Falls is a small town located in the northeast Georgia mountains on the border of Rabun and Habersham counties. Since the early 1800s, the area has been famous for its natural wonders. People visited Tallulah Falls to see the gorge and waterfalls created by the rushing Tallulah River, drink from the mineral springs, and breathe the fresh mountain air.

If you had been a traveler passing through Tallulah Falls during the early 1900s, one of the first things you would have noticed would have been the fancy Victorian hotels and boardinghouses with their neat white trim decorating the windows and doors. Stopping at one of these places, you would have seen lined all the way across its inviting front porch anywhere from twenty to a hundred rocking chairs. Just imagine all the fun and good times that took place on these front porches! If you then opened the front door and went inside one—the Cliff House, for example—laughter from chattering vacationers would fill your ears, along with, perhaps, the sounds of an orchestra tuning up for the evening's entertainment. Walking through the lobby and into the main wing, you might be surprised at the more than comfortable accommodations available in the middle of the North Georgia "wilderness."

Travelers passing through Tallulah Falls today will find that hardly a trace remains of this bygone time. Even many of the natural wonders—the romantically named falls, cataracts, and rock formations that once drew vacationing crowds—have been hidden or altered by the construction of a hydroelectric plant on the Tallulah River. Now, it might seem curious that people used to make a difficult trip of sometimes hundreds of miles to visit this place. What did the people in those hotels do for entertainment? What were the daily living arrangements? What sort of food did they serve in those vast dining rooms? How did all those people get there—and *why* did they come in the first place?

Much of the town was destroyed by fire in 1921. In *The Life and Times of Tallulah*, John Saye describes the cold December night the town went up in flames:

> . . . [A] terrible wind whipped through the streets of Tallulah. Residents awakened to find the town burning around them. The wind picked up chunks of burning wood and hurled them into nearby buildings. Soon every building on both sides of River Street, the town's main thoroughfare, was blazing. There was no fire department for miles, there was nothing to do but watch it burn. It burned for several days destroying stores, hotels, and residences. Very little that was destroyed was ever rebuilt.[1]

With photographs, reminiscences of the folks we could locate who were connected with those places, and the few published sources on Tallulah Falls, we hope we can help you imaginatively re-create a grand and largely forgotten era, when a small town in the northeast Georgia mountains became, for a time, a very well-known vacation spot.

—Julie Dickens
Article and photos by Brooks Adams, Suzanne Nixon, Darren Volk, Julie Dickens, Von Watts, Donna Turpin, Georgeann Lanich, John Crane, and Chad Bedingfield.

The Tallulah Falls Hotel Era

"People mostly sat on the porches and rocked."
—Pete Franklin

No one knows who first laid eyes on the Tallulah River area. It is known that as early as 1725 the Cherokee Indians had settled in the Tallulah Falls area in a small village called Turura—a variation of "Tallulah."[2]

The Cherokee "Tallulah" and "Terrora" are the variants now used, but it isn't certain what the words mean. Some sources have translated the terms as "terrible," "cry of the frog," or "unfinished," while other authorities say that they are not translatable.[3] The Cherokees called the falls themselves not "Tallulah," but "Ugunyl."[4] The Cherokees developed myths and legends about this impressive area, some of them about "a race of little people who lived all about in that region, but especially had their homes in the nooks and crannies of the great gorge overlooking the Falls."[5] Another legend concerned "a cave in the side of [a] cliff wall [which] was the entrance to the Happy Hunting Ground. Indians who entered the cave never returned."[6]

The first white visitors to the area were probably South Carolina Indian traders. The Cherokees controlled the region until 1817, when they began to cede the lands, first one side of the river and then the other. Two years after that, Habersham and Rabun counties were established, with the dividing line the Tallulah River and gorge.[7] By 1820, the land was surveyed for a land lottery system to open up this rugged, beautiful area to white settlers.[8] (The limitations of this land survey were later to provide a glimmer of hope for those who were fighting to save the falls from a hydroelectric dam.)

In 1819, the falls became known to visitors outside the Tallulah area, and soon they were a popular spot, even though they were not easy to get to. The earliest published description of Tallulah Falls, in the September 1819 *Georgia Journal*, called it "one of the greatest known curiosities in the United States."[9] Georgians came to see the falls by whatever means available: horseback, carriage, or wagons. Their visits were occasionally part of a more ambitious trip that included Toccoa Falls, Nacoochee Valley, and Currahee Mountain.[10] Because the area was virgin wilderness and the trip rough, sometimes guides were necessary, especially in the early years.

Although today's traveler has to use some imagination to envision how the freely flowing river cascading down rocky precipices must have appeared before the 1913 damming, early visitors undertook the hazardous journey there because Tallulah Falls and the gorge were truly spellbinding. Engravings of the falls appeared in the illustrated magazines of the times, and quite a few writers captured their impressions of the falls in prose or verse.

Many visitors compared the falls at Tallulah to those at Niagara or Yosemite. In fact, the Tallulah Falls were not as high as those at Yosemite, nor was the volume of water as great as that of Niagara; but the setting of the falls within the wild and craggy gorge created a strong impression on visitors. Sometimes referred to as "the Grand Canyon of the East," the gorge walls at the Grand Chasm near Horseshoe Bend were estimated to be 1,000 feet high. The impression began well before arriving at the gorge, because the falls were so immense that visitors could hear them for over a mile away.[11]

Early visitors began, like Adam, to name the natural surroundings of the falls, as well as the falls themselves. Indian Arrow Rapids was the swift current where the riverbed suddenly narrowed and sped on to a succession of falls, pools, and rapids for two miles below. Ladore, Tempesta, Hurricane, and Oceana were the major falls; the minor ones were Bridal Veil and Sweet Sixteen.[12] The

*Stereopticon view of one of the major falls at Tallulah,
before the dam's 1913 construction. (Courtesy Georgia
Department of Archives and History)*

*Members of the Glover family pose for a photograph while
on an outing in the gorge around 1906. Witch's Head
(in profile) is at the upper right. (Courtesy Georgia
Department of Archives and History)*

highest waterfall was Tempesta, at eighty-nine feet. Hurricane Falls,
at seventy-six feet, was the second highest. (One source says people
estimated this falls to be ninety-six feet.) Sweet Sixteen was, as you
might guess, just sixteen feet high.

Natural rock formations along the gorge were popular spots
with visitors, who gave them fanciful names. A couple of the best
known were the Devil's Pulpit and Witch's Head.

When the Tallulah Falls area first began to grow, people had
no choice of what hotel, motel, or boardinghouse at which to stop.
A visit at that time meant either camping out or staying at a pioneer's
cabin. The closest comfortable stopping place was Clarkesville,
some thirteen miles away. By about 1835 to the late 1850s, Tallulah

Falls had become so popular that people who lived within the area started announcing that they would take in travelers, and a couple of "rough and ready" hotels were established.[13] Apparently, the Civil War put a halt to Tallulah Falls' development, because around 1868, there is no report of these or any other places within five miles of the gorge.[14]

But in the 1870s, the area began a growth spurt, with hotels springing up and tourists again seeking out the sights. Some of this growth was a direct result of improved transportation. As John Saye notes in *The Life and Times of Tallulah*: "Vital to the growing popularity of Tallulah Falls was the Tallulah Falls Railroad. Reaching Tallulah in 1882, the railroad opened this rugged region to many more tourists than the hardy individuals who had made the trek over the rough mountain path. Beds were blasted from granite mountainsides; high wooden trestles were erected to span the deep hollows; as the train puffed into town, it hugged the very rim of the gorge."[15]

The railway made access to the area both easy and cheap, and its daily schedule and Saturday special train eventually brought visitors from Athens to Tallulah Falls in little more than an hour. Special excursions ran during the busy summer season with connections to New Orleans. Coulter says, "In the early 1900's special week-end rates from Atlanta and return were $3.35 and from Athens, $2.50 . . . [bringing] people . . . by the thousands, some to spend a week-end, others to stay a week, and some to spend the whole summer."[16]

Leo Ramey, a former Tallulah Falls Railway worker, told us: "A big excursion train from Atlanta came up here on Saturday or Sunday. They'd bring just tons and tons of people out and around the gorge looking off there. I used to go down there every Monday morning. There'd be people down there cleaning up [after the tourists]."

John Saye describes the festive air that surrounded the arrival of visitors to the falls: "The arrival of the train was greeted each day with an elaborate reception as bands welcomed the guests at the station, and buggies whisked them off to their hotels. Once settled in, there were ample ways for guests to spend their time."[17]

The coming of the railroad began the era of the grand Victorian hotels and boardinghouses. At one time there were as many as

*The old Moss House is one of two original Tallulah Falls guest houses still
standing, and the only one still in use, though not as a boardinghouse.
Owned by the Tallulah Falls School, it was operated for years as the
Tallulah Tea Room and now houses an adult education center.*

seventeen of them. Some of the smaller, quieter cottages, accommodating about thirty guests, were The Pines, Oak Haven, Chasm
Brink, the Maplewood Inn, Riverside, Arcadia, Willard House,
Young House, and the Moss House. The largest establishments
were the Cliff House, the Grand View, the Robinson House, and
the Tallulah Lodge, which offered lodging for up to 300 guests.
The dining rooms of the Grand View and the Robinson House
could both seat up to 250 guests. Not only were these hotels large,
they were also comfortable. Both the Cliff House and Tallulah
Lodge were given a star of commendation in the well-known Bae-
deker travel guide to the United States.[18]

Many of the visitors who were from South Carolina, Alabama,
and the lower parts of Georgia came to Tallulah Falls for the cool
summer climate—especially planters and others living in low-lying
coastal regions infested with malaria-carrying mosquitoes. The climate and air of this region were also considered healthy for people

with respiratory ailments, and its amenities and romantic setting soon made Tallulah Falls a popular spot for honeymooners.

Although many early visitors probably were just as interested in sitting and enjoying the view, Saye mentions the more active pursuits available: "Activity . . . centered on the natural wonders of the gorge. Whatever one did the crash of the falls provided a constant backdrop. Local men blazed trails to the floor of the gorge, kept them clear, and hired themselves out as guides. Stairways and walks took tourists to all points of interest, both in the gorge and on the rim. An eighty-foot observation tower was built at the foot of Tempesta Falls which could be climbed to the top of the waterfall."[19]

Guests could also drink from the well-advertised mineral springs. The Grand View Hotel clearly considered the mineral spring on its grounds a real drawing card and published an advertisement to that effect in the July 1, 1897, *Tallulah Falls Spray*, with the mineral content certified by a well-respected local physician. Guests could obtain bottles of the water during their stay, or it could be shipped to them after they left.

Not only did local proprietors promote the healthful and scenic aspects of Tallulah Falls, they also tried to draw even larger crowds with sensational reports of "a mysterious monster which had been washed out of the Tallulah River below the Falls, by the great freshet of 1891." The monster supposedly was forty feet long, had a head like an alligator's, a body like a rattlesnake's, a row of short legs or paddles on either side of its body, and, to top it all off, a series of large fins. The story went that it was eventually killed by a shot in the eyes.[20]

Still others tried to stage spectacular—but real—events to draw the curious. In 1886, when the proprietor of the Grand View, Colonel Frank Young, saw a tightrope walker make an aerial crossing of Atlanta's Peachtree Street, he decided that a similar feat would be an irresistible advertisement for the Tallulah Falls area in general, and his hotel in particular. He immediately engaged "Professor Leon" (J. A. St. John) to perform "the greatest feat of rope walking on record."[21] His trip across the Tallulah Gorge would be "not only the longest walk (1,449 ft.), but the highest walk ever accomplished by a human being."[22] Professor Leon's walk a thousand feet above the Tallulah River that July 24 required 20,000 pounds of rope stretched across the gorge, anchored by fourteen guy wires. The crowd was estimated at anywhere from 3,500 to 6,000, and tradition has it that the curious came in a dozen excursion trains from South Carolina, Georgia, Florida, and Alabama. [23] While in Tallulah Falls, Professor Leon stayed, of course, at the Grand View.

The comparison of Tallulah Falls to Niagara was apt for a couple of reasons. America had always seemed a bottomless bag of resources for a restless, growing population. In the last decades of the nineteenth century, industrialization, expansion, and just plain greed or ignorance fueled a tremendous exploitation of the nation's timber and mineral resources. The Southern Appalachian mountain area particularly felt the effects of this increasing consumption.

The desire for cheap hydroelectric power for expanding cities, factories, and modern comforts meant that water resources would also be harnessed to produce power to feed the nation's growth and development. Around the turn of the century, a national fight to save the magnificent Niagara Falls from a hydroelectric dam spurred Georgians to look in their own backyards. Developers were also eyeing the crashing waters of Tallulah as a never-ending source of cheap power. The state's first major environmental movement began as a groundswell of support to protect the falls before they could be developed. A state senator from Rabun County, Robert E. A. Hamby, introduced a resolution calling for a committee to explore the feasibility of buying enough of the surrounding land to make a state park. Newspapers around the state generally supported the drive to save Tallulah. The *Savannah Morning News*, for example, said, "To commercialism there is nothing beautiful except a machine that grinds out dollars, unless it possibly be the power that actuates the machine. Imagine Bridal Veil falls sawing logs, or majestic Tempesta ginning cotton!"[24]

While the state was not able to find the $100,000 the committee estimated it would take to buy up enough land to protect the falls and make a park, a new power company was. Organized in 1908 by C. Elmer Smith of York, Pennsylvania, and Eugene L. Ashley of Glens Falls, New York, and joined by two other industrialists, George G. Moore of Detroit, and Elliott G. Stevenson of Detroit and Toronto, Canada, the partnership that would eventually become

Georgia Power Company pooled its resources "to purchase a strategic tract of land [in Tallulah Falls], costing $108,960."[25]

The original Georgia Power Company purchased and merged with other smaller power companies such as the North Georgia Electric Company, the Etowah Power, and Blue Ridge Electric. Then, in 1911, having contracted out the construction work, they began the job of building the dam and power lines to feed electricity to Atlanta. Although the dam went up, it did not go up without a fight.

While assorted individuals and newspapers had been protesting the sacrifice of the scenic beauty of the falls for power, one person stands out in the movement to save them: Gainesville resident Helen Dortch Longstreet, widow of Confederate general James Longstreet. Under the banner of her newly organized Tallulah Falls Conservation Association, she waged a spirited battle against the destruction of the falls, which had already begun. Helen Longstreet wrote letters, hired lawyers, and brought together quite a number of supporters to fight the construction. She wrote about one of her

Tallulah Dam during construction. (Courtesy Georgia Department of Archives and History)

more ingenious ideas to save the area in a May 25, 1912, news release entitled "Tallulah Falls Dixie's Garden of the Gods to Furnish Summer Home for President":

[The Tallulah Falls Conservation Association plans to] purchase Tallulah Lodge hotel and surrounding lands for conversion into a summer home for the president of the United States, where, it is hoped, that the executive head of our nation can spend at least a few weeks each year, and in the surge of Tallulah's waters hear the voice of God who, through a mighty nation of awakened patriots, has decreed that his fairest handiwork shall be saved from the destroying touch of commercial vandalism.

Helen Longstreet was tireless in her efforts, enlisting the help of the legislature and the public and calling on the patriotism of the "war-worn heroes of the sixties." Her final challenge to the utility was the claim that, since the lines for the original survey conducted for the 1820 land lottery had extended only to the rim of the gorge, the power company's land holdings did not, in fact, include the Tallulah River and the gorge, which were still actually

This photo was taken from the rim of the Tallulah Falls Gorge today.

owned by the state. In 1913, when the question of land ownership finally came to the test in Rabun County Superior Court, the jury decided against the state. The state appealed the decision to the state Supreme Court but lost again. Meanwhile, construction on the 116-foot-high dam had continued.

In September of that year, a natural wonder gave way to a man-made wonder as the Tallulah River was dammed at Indian Arrow Rapids for a Georgia Power hydroelectric plant, and "18,000 horse-power of electricity went streaming out of defunct Tallulah Falls over the wires to Atlanta."[26] Many of the spectacular cascades were covered by the impoundment of water behind the dam, and the water going into the lower parts of the gorge slowed to a mere trickle compared to the original volumes.

Although hotel manager F. D. Handy bravely advertised some-time between 1913 and 1916 (when Tallulah Lodge burned):

Tallulah Falls Still Untouched
Tallulah Lodge Open for Guests

at the bottom of the ad for the hotel he noted: "The famous Lodge is located on the brink of the gorge, near the great power house and incline railway of the Hydro-Electric Company."[27]

While one printed source commented that "the damming of the falls greatly accelerated the flow of tourists from Tallulah Falls," there is no clear evidence that this was so, or to what extent it was so. Along with the extension of the railway and improved roads that drew vacationers further north into the higher mountains, it is probable that the dam did change the nature and extent of the area's tourism; and it is certain that the fire of 1921 finished most of it off.

Ollie Dyer was a teenager when she moved to Tallulah Falls with her family in 1916, shortly after the river was dammed. Living in Tallulah Falls from that time, she witnessed its decline from a booming tourist town to a small community with a post office and a general store, serving a population of 162 residents. For recreation, when she was growing up, she remembered: "People did a lot of walking. They'd walk around the lake, or they'd walk to the post office and pick up their mail." Mrs. Dyer told us there were trails all around the falls area and down into the gorge. She said: "People hiked, climbed the mountains, and went to see things.

"One of the popular things for younger people to do would be to get up before or by daylight and climb Hickory Nut Mountain to see the sunrise. Rock Mountain was a popular place to go to watch the sunset. It was beautiful."

Mrs. Dyer remembers that people came to Tallulah Falls to drink from the mineral springs: "The only one that I know much about is just off the old railroad bed, just [south of] the depot," she said. "It had been drilled out of a rock into a round basin, and the water flowed in it. They called it 'Iron Springs.' There was so much iron in it that it would get sort of fuzzy-looking around the edges. Someone was always cleaning it out.

"Then they say the one that was out below the Indian Springs Trading Post was a mineral spring, but it was not as popular because people didn't know about it as much as they did the Iron Springs." Tallulah Falls native Mary Franklin explained her views of the springs: "I've never drank any water from the mineral springs, I don't think. I think people just wanted something different when they'd come up here. I believe—now I don't *know*—that the people who owned the resort hotels sort of made those things up. You know, it was an attraction. Their guests wanted something different, and they'd fall for it."

"All of these springs in these mountains are mineral springs," Mary's husband, Pete Franklin, said, "because there are minerals in all of 'em. And it's the healthiest water there is in the world."

Ollie Dyer recalled that hayrides were popular with visitors, too: "There was a place between Tallulah Falls and the South Carolina state line that people liked to go to. They'd put hay in the wagons and take hayrides over there to Aunt Fannie Smith's. Everybody called her Aunt Fannie. She had a home over there, and she served noonday meals. That was the thing to do—wagon rides to Aunt Fannie's to eat."

Fannie Picklesimer Smith and her cabin became well known locally during the late 1800s when the mountains opened up to tourism. This was because of the cabin's location and Aunt Fannie's enterprising nature. Oma Gipson was one of Aunt Fannie's grandchildren. She related that the mountain, at the base of which sat

Aunt Fannie Smith at her spinning wheel.

Aunt Fannie's cabin, began to sink into "nowhere" at the rate of about two and one half inches per year. This was quite apparent because only *half* the mountain was slipping down. Standing at the site of this phenomenon, visitors could see that trees which had once stood side by side were moving apart. By the 1940s, a viewer standing on the high side of the crevasse that had been formed could look down on the tops of trees. The mountain became known as Sinking Mountain.

The strange sight drew many people to see it, and the mountain had become quite an attraction by the 1890s. The tourists came on the excursion train to Tallulah Falls and hired buggies to Sinking Mountain. Aunt Fannie, who was known for her good cooking, decided to serve meals to those who traveled by her house on their way to the mountain. By serving fried chicken, fresh garden vegetables that she raised, and milk and butter from her cows, in the summertime she daily fed scores of people who were always delighted with her home-cooked meals. She was reputed to serve some of the best fried chicken in Georgia.

After a noonday meal at Aunt Fannie's, travelers continued on up the mountain to see this unusual natural phenomenon. They sometimes stopped by later in the day for a cold glass of milk from Aunt Fannie's springhouse before returning to Tallulah Falls to catch their train home or to catch up on gossip at the boardinghouse where they were spending a week or two. This tradition continued for many years, supplying lots of people with a happy afternoon and Fannie Smith with a much-needed income.

With the help of her children, and, later, grandchildren, Aunt Fannie continued serving dinner to tourists until her death in 1914. By then, people might have come as much for her home-cooked meals as to see the mountains. The tradition died with her, and there aren't many people who visit Sinking Mountain anymore. In fact, there are many people even here in Rabun County who have never heard of it.

The Cliff House

The largest of the Tallulah Falls hotels was the Cliff House, named for a famous hotel in San Francisco, and noted, its proprietor W. L. Bain announced in 1903, "for its very home-like surroundings and the congenial feeling that is promoted among its guests." Built in 1882, and probably enlarged later, it had space in its main building and cottages for 300 guests and a dining room that would seat 250. The Cliff House was situated between the Tallulah Falls Railway and the Tallulah Falls Gorge. The back side of the hotel abutted the edge of the gorge, so that, one source said, anyone wishing to do so might have jumped from one of the many windows on the back side of the hotel directly into the yawning chasm below.

As its 1903 advertising brochure modestly announced, its forty-acre park offered "the only approach to the Falls."[28] Those forty acres included good stables, and room enough for the governor's Horse Guard to camp there for a few weeks in the summer of 1899.[29]

Although the hotel was large, the rooms themselves evidently were neither large nor fancy. Pete Franklin visited the Cliff House while it was in operation: "I had a friend who boarded there. He

The Cliff House Hotel.

worked for the Tallulah Falls Railway. I went with him to his room a time or two, and that's the only time that I was in the Cliff House. [I remember that] they had guest rooms underneath the ground level and three levels above that."

Since Bob Edwards opened his photography studio in Clayton in 1935, he has learned a lot about the county. In conversations with longtime Tallulah Falls resident Tom Moss, he heard some things about the Cliff House, which he shared with us: "Tom said the Cliff House had 140 rooms, and the rooms were about ten by ten feet. There was a double bed in each that took up most of the room, and a chair. These were the only [furnishings] in the hotel rooms."

A 1904 promotional brochure assured prospective guests that "AN ORCHESTRA has been engaged for the entire Season." That season would run from June 1 to October 1, and the Cliff House would offer all of that for "$2.00 to $2.50 per day, $8.00 to $14.00 per Week, $30 to $45.00 per Month." Ollie Dyer remembered that in her day the Cliff House always had an orchestra come and stay for the summer. At night, they would spread a big canvas awning over the yard for dancing. She also recalled: "There was a tennis

THE CLIFF HOUSE
TALLULAH FALLS, GA.

SEASON 1903   W. L. BAIN,
Open June 1st to Oct. 1st   ✤ ✤   Proprietor

This Cliff House promotional brochure is dated April 12, 1904. (Courtesy of Hargrett Rare Books and Manuscript Library, University of Georgia)

court up on the hill near the Cliff House before the new road was cut down through there, and there was also a swimming pool [nearby]. Those were primarily for the Cliff House guests." The Cliff House offered other amusements to guests, including hunting, fishing, lawn tennis, bowling, billiards, ping-pong, and "card parties galore."

An ad for the Cliff House in the August 1934 *Clayton Tribune* announced: "Round Dances every Saturday night. Music by Hurst Dancing School Orchestra, Atlanta, Ga. Square dances every Wednesday night: Music by Tim Hicks' Tallulah Orchestra."[30] By then, the Cliff House, the Glenbrook, and the Moss House would have been among the few survivors from the heyday of Tallulah Falls tourism.

Three years later, the Cliff House burned in a blaze resulting from the flying sparks of a passing train. Built the same year the railway reached the little village, and fronting the tracks that had brought thousands of guests, the fifty-five-year-old landmark fell victim to the very thing that had made it a thriving business. As any other old wooden structure would have done, it burned down very easily without benefit of the fire department. Much of the town had already done so in the fire of 1921.

The Glenbrook

Mary Franklin grew up in Tallulah Falls and went to Tallulah Falls High School in the 1930s: "The hotels were a big boost to the economy of the area," she recalled. "It took a lot to feed the people when the hotels were going. The farmers from Rabun and Habersham counties could

Ollie Dyer reminisces about the Cliff House.

sell their produce there, so they would grow extra vegetables, hogs, and chickens. It really gave the economy a shot in the arm."

While she was in school, she worked in the dining room at the Glenbrook: "I worked there when I was a teenager. It was being run as a tourist hotel in the late 1930s. I worked in the dining room and in the kitchen, washed dishes, and served meals."

The Glenbrook was smaller than the Cliff House, and popular because of its quiet setting away from the busy main street and train depot. Mrs. Franklin explained what she remembered of the Glenbrook's menu and service: "We served three meals a day. It was country-style food—fresh vegetables, corn bread, biscuits and fried chicken, country ham, and things like that, a little bit like the Dillard House has now. We took the orders and carried the food to the tables. We didn't use much canned and packaged vegetables. We did serve good food.

Mary Franklin worked in the kitchen of the Glenbrook when she was a teenager. "We served three meals a day. It was country-style food . . . We didn't use much canned and packaged vegetables. We did serve good food."

"It cost about thirty-five to forty dollars for three meals a day for one week. I can't remember what it cost to just stop in and buy one meal. Often people would, but mostly [we served] people who would stay for several weeks at a time. Some of the people were construction workers, working on the new bridge, and we would cater to the men working on the bridge.

"The only room service that I remember was [for] one woman [who] stayed [in the Glenbrook] who was writing a book. She was British. We used to carry her breakfast to her room because she liked to sleep late, and breakfast would be over when she would wake up."

Mrs. Franklin explained the layout of the Glenbrook: "The Glenbrook had elaborate scroll-work on the front in the main lobby. The beautiful floor was made of little tiny pieces of wood. Much of the material was brought over here from France.

"As the guests entered the hotel through the main door, they walked into the lobby where they could buy postcards. There was a little window, over to the left, where they registered.

"To the right there was a room called the Blue Room. I guess it may have been because it had the colored glass [in the windows]. It's been broken. I guess people just threw rocks and broke it for no reason, except just to destroy it. It is such a shame.

"Across the lobby from the Blue Room, down a couple of stairs, was a big dining room. There was a big fireplace on the back wall with a mantelpiece high enough to stand up under.

"The kitchen was behind the dining room. It was not in very good repair when I was there." Since Tallulah Falls became a tourist

*A group gathered for a vacation photo in front
of the gazebo that stood in the Glenbrook's yard. (Picture
given by Tom Moss)*

town in the 1870s, the hotels built at that time were not planned
to accommodate wiring and lights. After electricity became available, "The hotels," according to Mrs. Franklin, "installed exposed
wires for lights. In the kitchen [of the Glenbrook], the cooks used
both an electric and a wood stove. Also, the water for the guest
rooms was heated with an electric water heater.

"They had two or three rooms in the old part that they used
for guests. On the other side of the dining room was the exit to
the new part of the building with the guest rooms. When they built
the new wing, it added fourteen more rooms and baths. The new
part had a basement and three other stories. There were two rooms
in the bottom, and three on the rest. Maybe not all of the rooms
were full all of the time, but they had pretty good business.

"The whole hotel was laid out on different little levels. The new
wing was on a different level than the dining room. The dining

One of the most notable features of the hotel are the decorated window frames, nearly every one of which is different. They have even inspired people to make sketches and drawings of them.

room, the lobby, and the Blue Room were all on different levels, too. There were only a couple of steps between each level."

The hotel closed for the first time in the early forties. J. D. Crowe opened it back up in the fifties, but unfortunately, he did not do well and had to shut the hotel back down. Mr. Crowe told us that one room that really stood out from the rest was the belltower room, and he told us a "ghost story" about it. Not long after the hotel had been closed down, a count from England hung himself in the belltower room. Mr. Crowe told us that when he went to the hotel in 1957 to try to start it back up, he found bloodstains still in the belltower room. He mentioned that all the windows were

The hotel has nearly been engulfed by surrounding vegetation.

imported stained glass. He also said there was a bridal suite in the big middle room, where people could get married.

There was a little pool in front of the Glenbrook. There used to be fish in it, but when Mary Franklin worked there, it was used as a swimming pool. It was square with a semicircle arch on the side facing away from the hotel. It was about four and a half feet deep with about three feet of water being held by a rock wall.

Ollie Dyer remembers: "There used to be a beautiful spring [near the Glenbrook] that had been walled around with rock. There were also places for people to sit or have picnics at the spring. A lot of people, when the railroad brought in an excursion train every Sunday, would just swarm out to that spring and picnic spots."

Mr. and Mrs. Franklin had much to tell about the original owner of the Glenbrook, who is locally regarded as something of a mystery man: "It was built by Mr. Duboeay, or Norcop, as he was called in those days," Mrs. Franklin said. "He was a French count. He had two names because he was born English—I think Norcop was his family name—and I think that Duboeay was the title that the French bestowed on him."

Dr. Percy Trant Hickson Norcop (1833–1922) was an English-

The wading pool in front of the Glenbrook was a place where guests could spend time, cool off, and relax.

man who had a French uncle named Count Edouard Saint-Algier Duboeay. Mr. Norcop's uncle offered to make him his heir if he would change his name to Duboeay.

After he changed his name, Duboeay and his mother, Margaret Hickson Norcop, came to America and settled in Tallulah Falls about 1888. There he built Glenbrook (as a residence, not a hotel), evidently sparing little expense, from the descriptions of the interior. When his invalid mother finally died and was buried nearby, Dr. Duboeay "built a small chapel where a priest, Father Louis Bazin, held services once a month."[31]

Duboeay married Sarah Leicester Hunnicutt (1873–1954) of Tallulah Falls, and they had one daughter. When Duboeay's English relatives offered him yet another inheritance to change his daughter's name to Norcop, he changed the family's name back to the original. Dr. Duboeay/Norcop eventually sold the Glenbrook and had his mother's body moved to Rock Mountain Cemetery, on the other side of the gorge.[32]

Mary Franklin said: "My daddy always thought that there was a little mystery to [Dr. Duboeay's] leaving [England to come here]. The old folks used to tell—now, I don't know whether this is true or not—that he was shipped out in a barrel—that he was in some trouble in Europe—like he had to leave in a hurry. That's how the old people used to declare it was. I guess Tallulah Falls just looked good to him when he got here. When he came over here, evidently he brought money with him, because he was able to have the Glenbrook built. He came here with his mother, and he married a girl from Tallulah Falls. They had one daughter, Margaret. He was considered one of the best medical doctors in Rabun County, in this area, during his time."

Ollie Dyer also knew of Dr. Duboeay: "A lot of local doctors around would consult with him and kept up [that way]. He knew things to help them with. He was a good doctor."

Pete Franklin has been familiar with Tallulah Falls since his childhood visits to the area.

Mrs. Franklin has fond memories of the Tallulah Falls Railway coming into town, bringing visitors and excitement: "The train was entertaining because the people were moving. Just a little dirt road was all we had anywhere. At that time, 'long back in the early days of Tallulah Falls, there were no cars. [It was] all horse traffic.

"People that would come and stay at the hotels would gather up sometimes and go on what they called a hayride. A lot of the men out in the country had horses or mules. They would pile a lot of hay and straw in the wagon, and then these vacationers loaded on the wagon." Mrs. Franklin told us a story that Tom Moss had told her. Mr. Moss grew up in Tallulah Falls, eventually buying a house that was built in the late 1800s by friends of the Moss family. He could "remember many times that his mother fixed them lunch or supper and took them as children to walk up to the top of Rock Mountain." Mrs. Franklin said: "They'd have their picnic supper and view the sunset from there. That was the thing to do."

Mary's husband, Pete Franklin, used to visit Tallulah Falls regularly when he was young. He told us: "At that time [the hotels] had guides to carry parties into the gorge [before the dam was built], and that was part of their pastime—walking from one end of the gorge to the other." He also recalled another popular pastime for the tourists: "People mostly sat on the porches and rocked. They enjoyed that. I suppose it was a change. Most every hotel had porches, because they didn't have air-conditioning then. They had porches, and the people enjoyed sitting out."

After all these years, not much is known about the Tallulah Falls hotels and the people who stayed in them. Although it still stands, the Glenbrook's frame is now in ruins, and the white paint is so faded that it matches the trees and vines surrounding it. The vines have grown up so much that it is almost impossible to see from across the spring at the end of Spring Street. Now, only it and the Moss House (owned by Tallulah Falls School) live on as reminders of the resort hotel era.

The Glenbrook in its prime. Pete and Mary Franklin said, "The Glenbrook was a beautiful building. It's a shame it was allowed to just deteriorate. The main part of it could be restored if someone had the money and the time to put into it."

We do know, however, that the hotels played a major role in the economic development of Tallulah Falls. We also know that once the river was dammed and the gorge flooded, and the automobile began to make transportation to vacation spots farther north easier, the area began to lose much of its original appeal and its economic vigor. Like the Tallulah Falls Railway, the hotels have long since gone, but through the presentation of this article we hope this grand era will not be forgotten.

NOTES

1. Saye, John, *The Life and Times of Tallulah . . . The Falls, the Gorge, the Town.* Toccoa, Ga.: Commercial Printing Co., 1986, p. 25.
2. Coulter, E. Merton, "Tallulah Falls, Georgia's Natural Wonder from Creation to Destruction," *Georgia Historical Quarterly*, Vol. 47, No. 2 (June 1963), p. 124.
3. Ibid.
4. Ibid.
5. Ibid., p. 125.
6. Ibid., p. 126.
7. Ibid., p. 128.
8. Ibid.
9. Ibid., p. 137.
10. Ibid., p. 3.
11. Sherman, David, *Tallulah Falls: A History*, n.p., n.d., p. 4.
12. Ibid., p. 4.
13. Coulter, E. Merton, "Tallulah Falls, Georgia's Natural Wonder, from Creation to Destruction," *Georgia Historical Quarterly*, Vol. 47, No. 3 (September 1963), p. 250.
14. Saye, p. 9.
15. Ibid., p. 11.
16. Coulter, September 1963, p. 255.
17. Saye, p. 13.
18. Coulter, September 1963, p. 251.
19. Saye, p. 13.
20. Coulter, September 1963, p. 252.
21. Ibid., p. 253.
22. Ibid.
23. Ibid.
24. Ibid., p. 257.
25. Ibid., p. 260.
26. Ibid., p. 261.
27. Saye, p. 12.
28. The Cliff House, brochure, Hargrett Rare Books and Ms. Library, University of Georgia.
29. Coulter, September 1963, p. 251.
30. *Clayton Tribune*, August 9, 1934.
31. Coulter, September 1963, p. 272.
32. Ibid., p. 273.

Clayton
Boardinghouses

"Nearly every family . . . had rooms for boarders."
—Fred Derrick

Once the railway opened up Tallulah Falls to crowds of visitors, the rest of the county soon found itself in the middle of a tourist boom. In an article on tourism in the *Atlanta Journal & Constitution Magazine*, Fred Derrick explains why: " 'A lot of folks didn't care for the crowds and the higher prices at Tallulah Falls, and came on up here,' he said. 'Men who had to stay in Atlanta, Savannah, Brunswick, and Jacksonville sent their wives and children for two or three months. Nearly every family in Clayton had rooms for boarders, and a lot of summer visitors stayed on farms.' "[1]

A glance through notices and advertisements in back issues of the *Clayton Tribune* reveals that over the years Rabun County had almost sixty inns and boarding establishments, usually named for the people who owned them: the Nicholson House, the Bleckley House, the Bynum House, the Dickerson House, the York House, the Dillard House, the Earl House, and many more. These brimmed with summer visitors who came to enjoy the relaxed pace, temperate climate, and mountain scenery.

Hotel and boardinghouse events were always newsworthy, partly because of their impact on the local economy and partly because they were a visible, vital strand in the social fabric. Not only were the visitors a lively, interesting addition to the local population, but their vacations would provide many jobs for inn owners, their em-

HOTELS AND BOARDING HOUSES

Private Boarding House
On Chechero Drive
Home of Mr. and Mrs. J. L. Smith

Baord and Private Home
East Clayton
Mr. and Mrs. J. R. Stonecypher

Mountain View House
East Clayton
T. C. JUSTUS, Proprietor.

GREEN HOUSE
On Main Street
V. A. Green, Proprietor

McQUEST LODGE
East Clayton
Col. J. T. Davis, Proprietor

DERRICK HOUSE
Near Baptist Church
J. H. Derrick, Proprietor

Blue Ridge Hotel
Has Been Serving the Public
Over an Hundred Years
Mrs. J. H. Cannon, Proprietress

Dickson House
North Clayton
W. P. Dickson, Manager

Woodland Lodge
On Chechero Road
Rev. C. W. Smith, Manager

HOTEL LAMAR
THE BEST BEDS IN TOWN
Mrs. Fannie Green, Manager

Forest Hill Inn
On Shady Side
B. T. Dockins, Manager

BLECKLEY HOUSE
Across Railroad from Depot
L. M. Bleckley, Manager

BEECHWOOD INN
On Checero Drive
Mrs. L. E. Buchholtz, Prop.

Black Rock Lodge
Opposite Court House
J. W. Derrick, Proprietor

Twin Maples Inn
Centrally Located
Mrs. Susie McJunkin, Prop.

NICHOLSON HOUSE
Private Board
On Main Street
Mr. and Mrs. R. C. Nicholson.

HAMBY HOTEL
Newest and best in Northeast
Georgia.
On Main Street.
Col. and Mrs. R. E. A. Hamby

Summer Camps

Laurel Falls Camp
For Girls
Rev. C. W. Smith, Prop.

Restaurants and Cafes

JABE'S CAFE
"Pleased to serve and serve to please'
Corner of Main and Court House St.
JABE CANNON, Proprietor

CLAYTON BAKERY & CAFE
Bread, Pies and Cakes
Wholesale and Retail
Confections
On Main Street
MATHESON BROS., Proprietors.

Garage

Derrick Motor Co.
Main Street
The best equipped filling station
north of Atlanta
Authorized Ford Service Station

Stores

General Merchandise
Dry Goods, Notions, and
General Merchandise
. M. L. Keener
On Main Street

Dry Goods, Notions, and
General Merchandise
Bryant Hill
On Main Street

Dry Goods, Merchandise, Furniture
and Funeral Supplies
J. H. Cannon Co.

Dry Goods, Notions, General
Merchandise and Furniture
C. E. Cannon
Cannon-Roan Building

Boy's and Girl's Shop
Dry Goods, Notions, Millinery
Books and Novelties
Cannon-Roan Building

Staple and Fancy Groceries

Staple and Fancy Groceries
Fresh Fruits and Vegetables
W. S. Long
On Main Street

Staple and Fancy Groceries
Cold Drinks and Confections
Leon Bleckley
Across Railroad from Depot

PHILYAW & LONG
GROCERIES
Coffee a Specialty
Masonic Building, Main St.

Feeds and Heavy Groceries

WHOLESALE and RETAIL
Groceries and Feedstuffs
Clayton Grocery Store
On Main Street

Heavy Groceries, Dairy and
Poultry Feeds, Staple
Groceries
W. S. BEARDEN
Near Depot, Savannah Street

Meat Markets

The newspaper directory of June 24, 1926, lists quite a few places for tourists to stay.

ployees, and tradespeople. The *Tribune* frequently ran announcements of new hotel constructions or improvements to the old ones, of an old landmark that had gone up in flames, of who was staying where and where they were from, of prospects for the current season.

Frank Smith was county ordinary from 1937 to 1951. In a brief "Description of Rabun County" for a 1943 report, he wrote: "The summer-tourist business began to develop about 1908–1910, and continued to increase until 1925 which was probably its best year. The reaction from the Florida boom and the failure of the Manly system of banks had a decidedly bad effect on this business for several years. Revival was getting under way when the Great Depression came along."[2]

An article that appeared in the *Tribune* a month before the stock market crash spelled out just how important tourist dollars were to the local economy:

> Most all of us know that the summer tourists business is the greatest asset that we have but few of us have taken time to gauge a fair estimate of just what it means.
>
> . . . We asked [local businesses, including drugstores, hotels, barbershops, filling stations, postal and telegraph clerks, etc.] for an estimate of the increased receipts from the 15th of June to the 15th of September—three months of business. . . . The folks interested . . . have conservatively estimated their increased receipts . . . and the amount given for the three months of the businesses named [in the Clayton city limits only] amount to $117,000.[3]

Because receipts for taxis, saddle horses and ponies, cottage rentals, local summer camps, and general stores were not included (the latter because hotels spent much of their money with local merchants and thus the figure they reported would have included that amount), the editors of the *Tribune* estimated that the actual figure for the Clayton area was probably more like $125,000. The estimates of "several good business men" indicated that "the balance of the county would amount to as much as the receipts for Clayton." Thus, the *Tribune*'s informal poll revealed that summer tourism was worth a quarter of a million dollars to the county's economy—and those are 1929 dollars.

How many tourists does that figure represent? A few months after discussing the county's tourist receipts, the *Tribune* announced in its January 23, 1930 issue that "The Government wants to know how many visitors were here last year and how many tourists passed through the county last year." Neither the county nor local businesses kept records of the number of tourists either passing through or stopping over in the county; because U.S. Forest Ranger Roscoe Nicholson ("Ranger Nick") was a local government official and a man well known and liked in the area, the Forest Service asked him to conduct an informal poll and come up with an estimated number. That number would include guests of hotels, anyone who stopped even for an hour to eat a meal at a local café, or someone passing through who paused long enough to eat a picnic lunch at one of the springs. Ranger Nick concluded that there were "something like 50,000 guests in the county" in 1929. (Incidentally, Ranger Nick's wife, Emma, would have offered their hospitality to some of those guests at their boardinghouse, the Nicholson House.)

Visitors to the Clayton area were met there with as much enthusiasm as they would have been at the more tourist-oriented Tallulah Falls, especially if they arrived on the train. Fred Derrick recalled: "In summer we had an excursion train every day. It went up in the evening, spent the night at Franklin and came back next morning. The Clayton Brass Band was always down at the depot to play for the excursion. I never did learn much about music, but to me it sounded mighty good, especially Fletch Hollifield's part. He blowed the big horn."[4] Local people turned out in great numbers to get a look at the visitors, particularly those who arrived on the Sunday excursion trains.

People who came for more than a meal and a day of sightseeing tended to stay for several weeks and then would often return year after year, for a month or two, often requesting to stay in their old rooms, becoming a part of an extended family with a family's eccentricities and pleasures. While visitors are still welcomed to motels in the area that are now open year round, they are here only briefly, and no longer does the *Clayton Tribune* say about them, as it did in August 1927: "Many of them have been coming here so long that we want to consider them a part of us and those who have been coming longest seem to be the happiest when they come."[5]

That era of passenger trains and extended visits to the big wooden hotels with their huge porches has vanished along with nearly all of those hotels, although tourism is still a crucial part of the area economy, generating about a third of its annual revenue. Now, folks who want to stay longer than a few days generally stay in their own second homes or those of friends, on one of the man-made lakes or in other resort areas. No longer are there the same kinds of opportunities for visitors and local people to mix at dances, concerts, or other events, or to spend long evenings talking and rocking on porches.

Because there were far more boardinghouses during the early tourist boom than we have space to cover, we have selected a few representative ones to focus on. Most of these no longer operate or even exist. But the stories of these establishments create an unforgettable and charming picture of the ideal of recreation in a more leisurely time.

—*Julie Dickens, Mandy Cox, and Allison Adams*

NOTES

1. Neal, Willard, "First Train to Tiger." *Atlanta Journal & Constitution Magazine*, February 14, 1960.
2. Smith, Frank A., "Brief Description of Rabun County." April 6, 1943.
3. *Clayton Tribune*, September 26, 1929.
4. Neal, p. 9
5. *Clayton Tribune*, August 18, 1927.

The Blue Ridge Hotel
"Home of the traveling man"

Many tourists and even local people who drive down Clayton's Main Street every day to go to work, get something to eat, or even drag town, probably never think about what used to sit where the furniture store, clothes store, craft store, or hardware store do now. Imagine a hotel where some of the downtown businesses are now, on a Main Street that was just a dirt road. Mrs. Mildred Cannon Story remembers when the Blue Ridge Hotel, the oldest hotel in town, sat on Main Street and was known as the "home of the traveling man." The Blue Ridge was also one of the few hotels in Clayton—Mrs. Story could remember only one other—that was open year round. Originally owned by the Duncan family, who operated it as a trading post in the 1800s, near the turn of the century it was sold to H. Raleigh Cannon and his son, Cecil. They turned it into a hotel.

Mildred Story's mother and father, John Henry Cannon and Celia Ann Dovilla Philips Cannon, opened Cannon's Store on Main Street in Clayton in 1909. The store sat adjacent to the Blue Ridge Hotel. Around 1915 or 1916, they purchased the Blue Ridge from Henry's uncle Raleigh and his son, Cecil. After John Henry Cannon died in 1924, his wife and children carried on both businesses. Mildred Story lived at the Blue Ridge during her early childhood, until her mother retired in 1945 or 1946 and the hotel was torn down. Then she moved to Needy Creek along with her brothers and sisters.

Mildred Story taught school for forty years before she retired. A gifted storyteller and frequent substitute teacher, she and her stories are still in demand at local elementary schools. Mrs. Story has been interviewed by Foxfire many times, but never specifically about the hotel her family ran. When we interviewed her in her home, she greeted us all with a smile and made us feel very welcome. As we walked from the kitchen into the living room, I asked her about the little white notepad she carried. She told us she had written down some notes the night before. She began by telling us some of her childhood stories and special things she remembered among all the events that took place at the hotel.

—Julie Dickens

Interview and photographs by Julie Dickens, April Shirley, Celena Rogers, and Jewell Murray. Historical photos courtesy of Barbara Duncan, J. H. Cannon, and Mildred Story.

An early view of the Blue Ridge Hotel.

Now, Uncle Raleigh Cannon was a great hotel man. Cecil was his son. They left here and took the Princeton Hotel in Atlanta, which was across from the railroad station, where people would come in and spend the night. Later, Cecil had the Henry Grady Hotel, which was very exclusive at that time. When they left here [around 1915], my father bought the hotel.

Originally, the building was built as a trading post back when the first settlers came into this area. It was made of logs. Then later it was made to take in boarders and things like that. The hotel was open all year long. It was our home, and we lived there in the hotel year round. We lived and ate with the boarders.

There were twenty-six guest rooms. Later there were about eight fixed up above my daddy's store [which was next door to the hotel], and there was a stairway by my daddy's store that went up to those rooms. There were two rooms that had a double bed in them, one room that had four beds, and the other rooms had two wide beds. We had three bathrooms—one for each of the floors, one upstairs and one downstairs. In each room, we had a washstand.

In the washstand there was a glass bowl and a pitcher. The pitcher was always full of water for washing. On the side of the washstand was what we called a "slop jar," where they put their waste water. That was our job—to clean that up the next morning.

In the dining room, which was on the right-hand side of the main lobby, there were three long tables that would seat twelve people each. We had white damask tablecloths and napkins that went with them. We also had two other tables that would sit six people. Now sometimes the dining room would be full, and sometimes it wouldn't, but we always tried to [be prepared] in case people came in.

On the other side of the hotel, the front room was what we called the parlor. In there was the piano and two or three settees. In the front room there was also a large office. In the office was a desk and a sitting room where card tables were. I still have the bell that was in the hotel office. If you came in the office and no one was there, then you'd tap that bell, and wherever we were, we could hear it and come. [There was also a large dinner bell used at the Blue Ridge to alert the guests that meals were being served. This bell was also used to sound alarms. People in town knew that if they heard that bell ringing at night that there was a fire, and they immediately got up to go to it.]

The hotel sat on what is now the front part of the sidewalk [in Clayton]. The hotel was built before the sidewalk was ever made. We just had half of a sidewalk going up to the Blue Ridge Hotel. Later my brothers and my mother had it jacked up, put props under it, put it on logs, hitched chains to the back of the hotel and with several trucks pulled it back enough to be on line so that the sidewalk could be made solid in front of it like it is today. At that time we put brick veneer in front of it. That [was] the third time it had been veneered. First it was the logs, and then the planks trimmed in blue [and then brick veneered].

After my mother had [the hotel] pulled back, she had a big porch put in front. She always had rocking chairs, and anybody could come in and sit and talk. She always enjoyed when people came to visit. Women who came with their husbands to trade [at Cannon's Store] and got tired came up to the hotel and sat on the porch. Anybody was free and welcome to come in and sit anytime they wanted to.

With twenty-six rooms, I would guess as many as fifty to sixty people [could stay there]. We were not full all the time. In the wintertime we didn't have a great many people except those people that made their living selling things to the store. The hotels in the area were mostly summertime hotels. The Earl House, the Smith House, and the Bynum House would have more guests than we would in the summertime, with a hundred to a hundred and fifty. There was one other hotel that was opened for twelve months a year [as we were], and that was the Clayton Hotel.

At the foot of the hill where the rock house is now is where we had a barn. When a carnival or a circus would come to town, my daddy would rent [the lot to them]. People would go down there to the circus. On the other side of the road was a high bank of dirt. In the wintertime you couldn't get across the road because of the ruts and mud. You couldn't walk across the street except down at the corner. The marshall—what we called the police—would put planks down there so you could walk across the street. If you wanted to walk across to the other side of the street, you had to go down to where the drugstore is now and go across.

We had four trains a day [that came through Clayton]. When the Tallulah Falls Railroad came through the people would come off the train and eat lunch. The conductor on the train would call my mother somewhere down the road to tell her how many people to prepare for. An old black man called Uncle Charlie—Uncle Charlie Westmoreland—[worked for us]. Uncle Charlie would put on his white starched coat and his white trousers and go down to the depot station. He would ring the dinner bell and call [to] the people and tell them that he was taking people to the Blue Ridge Hotel for whoever wanted to eat. The price for a meal at that time was seventy-five cents for a midday meal, which included two desserts, two meat choices, and five vegetables and fruit.

We always felt the main reason people came [to the Blue Ridge] was the good eats. They weren't embarrassed [to eat their fill] since they could reach and get what they wanted. Chicken and ham were the favorite dishes, and as soon as the bowls were half-emptied they were taken back to the kitchen and replenished. That was one of the things that we advertised: "All you could eat for seventy-five cents." I think, looking back now, that that was the main reason people came, because they knew they would get plenty to eat and a good variety of things at a good price. Of course, they enjoyed the fireplace and the fellowship with the people that came there. They would always find someone that was a friend to them.

Outside of town was my daddy's farm. There was an apple orchard up here. There was a barn on top of the hill where we raised pigs and cattle. We also had a tract of land over in South Carolina where they would take the cattle and let them run wild. They would make their own way part of the year by eating acorns, plants, and roots. Then in the fall of the year, he would bring them in and fatten them up. That was where a lot of the meat came from. He was also in the produce business. He would sell those to people [in the store]. In the case of things like apples, oranges, beans, and particularly tomatoes, they could be used at the hotel [if they did not get sold].

Mother was a great canner. She could cut out the bad parts of tomatoes or apples and can much of the leftover store produce to be used at the hotel dining room. Sometimes we canned as many as 500 half-gallons of vegetables in a season. We always canned 500 half-gallons of both peaches and apples and things like that. She also used cabbage to make kraut and pickled some of the beans. She made hominy from corn grains. Very little went to waste. I never saw my mother idle. When she sat to rest, she was either crocheting or stringing beans. It took a lot of beans to feed people then.

It is funny to me that chicken wings are a delicacy now. Back then the guests ate the thigh, the leg, and the white meat. [Our family] got what was left—now, it doesn't mean we didn't get some of the good pieces, too—a lot of backs and wings! You couldn't buy chickens already dressed. My daddy bought chickens by the coop. We killed the chickens, plucked them, and cut them up. Behind the hotel there was a shack called the wash place where the washing was done with two great big iron pots. We had to kill the chickens by the wash place. I guess we did about twenty-five at a time.

We couldn't kill those chickens very long ahead, because they wouldn't keep with no electric refrigerators or freezers. [Instead of] electrical refrigerators like we have now, we had a great big icebox. The icebox was homemade. Somebody made it out of wood and put sawdust in the inside as an insulation. They lined it somehow

"This is my father, Mr. J. H. Cannon, standing in front of the hotel in 1921," Mildred Story said.

with some kind of metal and painted it. [It had] block ice in it to keep it cold. It was paneled off so that the sawdust didn't get into [the food or ice]. That's where we kept things that wouldn't keep for too long. Mr. Ritchie had an ice plant down there across from Kramway [grocery store]. He sold coal in the wintertime and ice in the summertime. He had a deliveryman who had those great big ice tongs which were used to carry the ice blocks. Every morning, they loaded the ice on the wagons and delivered it to different people. There were certain homes and boardinghouses that would get ice every day. The hotel would usually get 500 pounds of ice every day. We could run down there and get ice all the time if we ran out, particularly for iced tea and things like that. If people wanted a soft drink, we had orange drinks and Coca-Colas. Those were the bottled drinks, and they were kept in that great big old icebox.

The fuel for the whole place—the cookstove and all—was wood. Even in each of the guest rooms there were stoves. We had a wood box in each room, which we had to keep full of wood. We had to keep a great big box in the kitchen behind the stove full of stove wood. So it took a heap of stove wood to be able to have fuel.

The lights were not owned by the Georgia Power Company. A local man, Mr. Tom Roane, owned the light and the telephone company. When you went up to pay your light bill, Mr. Tom would never come out and check your meter. He would always ask how many light fixtures you had in your house. He charged you by the number of lights in your house. We didn't have light all the time. We would have been in a fix if we'd had an electric refrigerator like we have now. Any time of the day or night you could expect the lights to go off. Sometimes they would stay off as long as two weeks. So in each one of those rooms we had to keep a lamp. They had to be washed, the wicks had to be trimmed, and the kerosene [kept] full. In case the lights went off, you would just strike a match and light the wick.

When the Georgia Power Company bought the light franchise from Mr. Tom Roane, sixteen boys came and stayed at the Blue Ridge Hotel while they were working on reconstructing the new lines for the county. The power company paid for them to stay with us, and every morning we would fix lunches for them to take with them. My mother bought a mangle iron at this time for us to do the ironing. We had a lot of things that had to be ironed, with sixteen boys there. She gave it to me when my boys got older and told me that I would need it.

There were eleven children in our family, so we all had our jobs. The boys mostly worked in the store. My two older sisters worked in the store, too. And the girls worked at the hotel. We waited tables and washed dishes. We did not have dishwashers like we do now. We had three cows that had to be milked twice a day. Somebody had to do that, and the churning had to be done. We all learned to do our part of the work because we couldn't ever have made a living if we'd hired everything done.

We did hire some people [to help in the hotel]. My father and mother both loved people. They liked all races. We depended a great deal on black help to help us. We had some very lovely people that we felt dear to. Lizzy Dubois was about my age. I always felt like she was my sister, because she was so close to my age. She would come with her mother to work. We depended on her to do the laundry, because it took a lot of sheets, pillowcases, and things like that. We had to wash and change the sheets daily. When the boarders would move out, we would then have to take those sheets off and wash them. The sheets were washed in a great big galvanized tub out there in the back and then put in a big iron pot and were boiled. This would boil all the dirt out and sterilize them. We then rinsed them and put them on the clothesline in the back to dry. Then they had to be ironed before they were put back on the beds.

[To make the washing soap] my mother would take the grease that accumulated from frying all of that chicken, let the dregs settle to the bottom, and take that grease and boil it. She put lye in it to make homemade soap. We would pour the hot liquid soap into wooden boxes, then slice it into blocks after it cooled and hardened. That soap would ruin your hands, but it would really make your clothes come good and clean. It would bleach them just like Clorox does now.

We depended on white people and black people to help us as waiters and waitresses. We had a cook and usually a maid, though she didn't wait on us. Uncle Charlie was our butler. He lived with us for quite a while, but he had a family living in Atlanta. They lived at No. 9 Auburn Place. I remember that. He couldn't read or write, and I would write letters for him, and then I would read letters for him when they came back.

I remember [one story in particular about] Uncle Charlie. There was a boarder who was very particular, and his coffee was never hot enough. Uncle Charlie would say, "I bet you I will get his coffee hot enough today." So he put the man's coffee in one of those thick cups and set it in the oven and heated it. When the man came for breakfast that morning, Uncle Charlie had to handle that coffee with a stove lifter to take it in there. The man looked up at him, and Uncle Charlie said, "Dag jammit if that man didn't drink that coffee and it a-boiling."

Some of the guests came on the train, and some came in their cars. We used to have colder weather then than we do now. The weather was so bad that you couldn't leave water in your radiator overnight. You had to drain those radiators every night. The next morning it was Uncle Charlie's job to go out and close up those radiators. He would take warm water and put it in each one of those radiators so that the cars would start and people would go on their way.

We didn't have reservations at that time. We just knew to expect so and so. There was an old man who lived at Tallulah Falls, and his wife had died. He also had only one child, who had also died. So he came and boarded with us full time. We knew he would be there.

[During the Depression, we had] a right good many guests. The hotel business went on pretty much about the same. A good many people who worked in town came in to eat lunch. At night we had a lot of traveling people. We had traveling salesmen who came from as far away as Atlanta who would make a whole week's trip coming up the road, up through Cornelia, and all the stops through the way. More of them came out of Gainesville than any place else. The salesmen would often leave Gainesville on Monday morning, coming up this way. They would usually stay all night in Cornelia, and they came to our house usually on Tuesday nights. Salesmen were called "drummers" then. There were certain drummers came on Monday night, and they always had a special room that they wanted. We saved the room for them. They would come here and go out to [sell their merchandise at] what is now La Prade's Camp [on Lake Burton], and they would go to these smaller stores around, and then they would go on up as far as Franklin and spend the night again. They would come back and spend the night again, then would go back home. That was their route for sales. [One such salesman was Bill Chambers.] Mr. Chambers traveled for Carter Grocery Company, I believe, and we always expected him on Monday night. Then, he went on to Franklin and spent the night. We expected him again on Wednesday night. He was always there. [We came to know him as] "Uncle Bill."

Of course, we had more people in the summer. During the summertime, we had certain people who would come from Florida, Tampa particularly, for a week or two weeks. During their stay here, they liked to hike and sit on the front porch, listen and rock. Nobody came much that didn't like to hike up to Black Rock. If you couldn't hike very much, you hiked as far as the reservoir here. We didn't have any picnic tables, but you thought nothing much of taking your lunch and sitting on the ground and having a nice picnic. There were more springs then. Places [where] I used to find springs have dried up. I don't know what it is, but one thing, I think, is that we have cut too much of our forest so that the leaves do not fall to hold the water in. Another reason is I have seen the population of Clayton grow from around 500 to what it is today [about 1,613].

At night, some of them went off riding, or some of them dated. We tried to have things to do for those who didn't. One of their things for amusement was to play set-back. It was a game that you would play with cards. It is a real fun game, and sometimes I remember there would be three tables set up with twelve people playing.

My brother Gervace played the piano [in the parlor]. It was a usual thing nearly every night to have what we called singings. These were for anybody who wanted to, and everybody was welcomed.

There was a huge fireplace that was probably almost the size of that wall over there. One tree would make two or three logs. Uncle Charlie would bring those logs in and keep a fire. The fire never went out in the wintertime. They roasted chestnuts in the coals of the fire and popped popcorn. My daddy always had a big barrel of cider. So that was the thing they had for refreshments.

Court week was always a busy time. We had court two times a year. The Blue Ridge Hotel was the headquarters for the people who came. They would come and stay all night or the whole week in town. If the court was trying a case like a murder case that lasted two or three nights, they always brought the jury to the hotel. My daddy had furniture in his store, and they would get mattresses and cots to put in this big room that had four beds. They put enough in there to take care of twelve people, because they had to keep them safe and so nobody got to them. There were two bailiffs that stayed outside the room so that nobody would come. They would eat three meals a day as long as the jury was in session.

Now that was a social time, as well as a time of trial. People would come out from the country and bring their horses. My daddy had hitching posts behind the store where they were always welcomed to hitch their horse. He also had a place where they could camp back there sometimes for a whole week. The hotel was a gathering place. One of the social things they did during that week was they had an old-time fiddlers' convention. People from all over the county and around would come and bring their fiddles. Usually, it was held at the courthouse. That was the meeting place of people. They had fiddlers' conventions there, and they had the box suppers and singings, community singings.

Another thing they tried to plan sometimes—the Odd Fellows Organization, particularly—was a womanless wedding, a wedding in which the men were dressed like the women, the bridesmaid, the bride, and all of that. They were all dressed as women, except the preacher, of course. That was usually a lot of fun.

Another thing they used to try to do were benefit box suppers. A girl would take a pretty good-sized box and decorate it beautifully with crepe paper, flowers, and things like that. Sometimes when she had a little tinsel, she'd put some on it to make it real pretty, because the prettiest ones always got the most money. Then she prepared a lunch of sandwiches, cakes, and things enough for two people [and put it in the box]. They had a big table, and she brought it and put it on the table. There would be piles of boxes there. Mr. Luther Rickman used to auction off each one of the boxes. He'd take it up and say, "Look at this pretty thing! Mmmm! Smells like fried chicken! I think there's chocolate cake, too!" And he went along like that about what things people could maybe find inside that box. And, "What do I hear bid on this?" And they would tell how much they would bid for them. And he would say, "Ahhh, you can do better than that! Let me have another bid." Somebody else would bid. And if two boys were liking the same girl (and sometimes they'd do it on purpose), they would run it up ten cents or five cents or what, till they'd keep running it on up until finally, he would say, when it looked like the bidding was all gone, he'd say, "Eight dollars once, eight dollars twice, eight dollars three times and *sold* to so-and-so." So, he got to eat that lunch with the lady or the girl who had made the box.

Sometimes a box would go up as far as twelve dollars, and that was a lot back then. Then that money was taken and given to worthy causes. Sometimes, it was a project of the school that the state did not pay for. [The state] only paid for teachers' salaries then. Sometimes, it was for people who had had their house to burn down. Sometimes, it might be somebody that was in the hospital and was not able to pay their hospital bill. Sometimes, there were children who had lost both parents. It was donated to worthy causes, but it also made a lot of fun and amusement for us young people, and even the grown people, the old ladies and the old men, would do that. It was quite an enjoyable thing.

At that time we had a town band. People would volunteer to play. My brother played the trombone, another played the French [horn], and somebody else played the drum. Lamar Green played the trombone. Mr. Bill Long, who had a fancy grocery store up the street where one of the Reeves buildings are now, played the cornet. For entertainment they would go over to the public square where the fountain is now and play all together. There was no building there. There were sycamore trees all up the aisle. They put up rope swings where children could go and swing. People would gather there to hear the band playing.

The Blue Ridge was usually headquarters for the politicians, and my mother would often be campaign manager for various candidates for state, district, and national offices. Richard B. Russell, who was later United States senator from Winder, Georgia, would come. A man by the name of Mr. Hardman was from Commerce, Georgia. He ran for governor and was the governor of Georgia at one time.

We celebrated Christmas [at the hotel with] a big Christmas dinner, and we hung up our stockings. Usually the things we got were toys, because my daddy stocked them in his store. Mostly, though, we got things to wear.

Daddy also sold fireworks. Always on New Year's night, the community knew that Henry Cannon would shoot all of the fireworks he didn't sell. He loved to take all the little tots or children that didn't have any money, go down the line, and give them a Roman candle. He wouldn't let them have skyrockets, because they were too dangerous. He would light them up. Those penny fireworks went to the little children, because they could handle them. They would light them and throw them in the street. The older boys would set off the bigger skyrockets, and there was nothing on the other side [of the street] so they wouldn't catch anything on fire. The bigger firecrackers went to the older children. He would always empty his store of firecrackers. If he had a bad year and there were a lot of fireworks, then he would put them out there, and people knew that they were welcome to come and take part in it. I don't think you could do a thing like that today. I am afraid you couldn't. People liked to have fun in a good safe way, and they liked to watch out for all the children. People loved children— seems like more than they do now.

I had a home wedding in 1933, and I was married in what was the office at the Blue Ridge Hotel. There was a winding staircase, and I came down those steps. Roses were in bloom that time of year, and I remember going to Duggan's Hill and getting white roses that just hung over the banks all the way down. We used baskets filled full of home-grown roses for decoration, and my wedding dress was homemade white crepe. [Because] my father had died by that time, I came down the steps with my oldest brother escorting me. We had some chairs in there, and my family was in the background. After the ceremony, we went to Cornelia to eat. The Depression [economy] was so bad, that was our honeymoon.

In the late 1930s, Mrs. Story's brother, Horace Cannon, and his wife became owners of the store. Her mother, Mrs. Celia Cannon, continued running the Blue Ridge Hotel until about 1945 or 1946 when she retired and the hotel was closed.

My mother had hoped, after she reared her children, to get out of the hotel business. She had a yearning desire to build a house on top of this hill up here. All the time, if she could she would put a little extra money aside. During World War II she couldn't build at all, because all the supplies were used for our military personnel. After the war she had started to build it, but building materials had gone up so high that she didn't think she could afford to build it like she wanted to. My brother Gervace was in service and didn't ever marry. He told her that he would help her build it. The two of them built the house, and when she moved up there they tore the hotel down and put in store buildings on Main Street.

You hate to see your old home place go [but] I was really happier, because my mother was going to have a place she was not going to have to constantly spend on. When your plumbing fixtures get old, there is never a week that passes that you don't have a plumber in. And the house was so big to heat. I was real happy that she could come up here and have steam heat. From my father's farm she gave me a lot where my home is built. The one next to me went to my brother Gervace, and he didn't have a wife so he rented it. To my brother Horace she gave about three acres adjoining. All up Needy Creek she gave all the children a house place.

The Dickerson House
"I just kept adding a bedroom or two"

I have lived in a community called Wolffork Valley near Rabun Gap, Georgia, and attended Wolffork Baptist Church going on four years now. At church I have seen an elderly man with a smile that radiates from a joyful heart. He sings in the choir and is a very active participant in the church. I never knew his name until I started collecting the previous Foxfire *magazine articles he has appeared in. His name is Isaac Terry Dickerson, and his family operated a boardinghouse in Wolffork Valley for more than fifty years.*

We were not able to call and schedule an interview with him about his family's boardinghouse because Terry, who is in his nineties, does not hear very well. We just went to the Dickerson House, and standing at the front door was Terry—very surprised and happy to see us. After I told him who we were, he put his arm around me and smiled from ear to ear.

Terry invited us onto the porch and took us on a tour inside and outside the Dickerson House. The house is a maze of sixteen bedrooms fitted together like a puzzle and what seems like a hundred doors. Many of the rooms are not much larger than the beds they hold, and their walls are narrow, horizontal tongue-and-groove boards. It's obvious that the guests spent most of their time on the upstairs and downstairs porches, rocking and talking and, as Terry told us, telling jokes. From the porches, we could look out over a narrow creek toward the fenced cornfield and barn and hill beyond. From the Dickerson House front yard, Wolffork Valley looked like one big farm. During our tour, Terry showed us postcards, things he had made, and items he had collected through the years. He also talked about his experience of running a boardinghouse with his mother and sisters for more than half a century.

The Dickerson House in Wolffork Valley, Rabun Gap, Georgia, was a resort hotel from the early 1920s until 1973, when the Dick-

ersons retired. *After their retirement, Miss Mimi Dickerson (Rabun Gap's former postmistress), Miss Arizona Dickerson, and their bachelor brother, Terry, lived together in the long, rambling house. For many years, their other sister, Mrs. Lucy York, owned and operated the Cold Springs Inn, another resort hotel in the valley.*

Miss Mimi died in 1989, Miss Arizona in 1987. Mrs. Lucy lives in Clayton at the Mountain View Convalescent Center. Now, in 1991, Terry Dickerson, aged ninety-two, divides his time between a local retirement home and his family's place, where he still goes on warm afternoons to mow his grass. He still gets his own groceries, runs errands, and visits with a few other people, driving his truck wherever he needs to go. Terry has never married, and now that most of his immediate family has died, he gets lonely. He told us that it wasn't easy living by himself: "It's not a complete life one by himself. We're here to mix and mingle, and one's life is not complete without it."

Now, every time I see Terry, he is always as warm and friendly as the first time I formally met him on the porch of the Dickerson House. Writing this chapter has made me reflect that all the people we see every day walking down the street or even sitting in our church choirs have a story to tell. Without Foxfire, I might never have known Terry Dickerson's story of the Dickerson House, and I also would not have made a new friend.

Over the years, Foxfire students have interviewed all of the Dickersons, most frequently Terry and Miss Arizona Dickerson. Miss Arizona did the Dickerson House cooking and was an invaluable informant when we were preparing Foxfire's Book of Wood Stove Cookery *(1981) and* The Foxfire Book of Appalachian Cookery *(1984; rpt. 1992). This article is composed of several interviews conducted some years apart with Terry and Arizona Dickerson, interviews originally gathered for a Foxfire class, then expanded and used in* Foxfire's Book of Wood Stove Cookery. *The last part of this article is devoted to Miss Arizona's recipes that were featured in* Wood Stove Cookery *and* The Foxfire Book of Appalachian Cookery.

—*Julie Dickens*

Interviews and photos by Kim Hamilton, Dana Holcomb, Rosanne Chastain, Tammy Hicks Whitmire, Kim Foster, Matt Alexander, Hope Loudermilk, Heather Scull, Scott Dick, Tammy Henderson, Al Edwards, Julie Dickens.

My daddy was born over at the foot of the Blue Ridge Gap on the Persimmon side. My mother was born right over here [Wolffork Road]. She was a Keener.

I was born here [in Rabun County] and I've stayed in the same house all my life. I was born in 1899. There were nine of us [children] in my family, but just six of us lived to adulthood: [Melton, Miriam (Mimi), Lucy, Jim, Arizona, and me].

The Dickerson family lived in a small log cabin near the site of the present Dickerson House when the six children were small. Their father, a carpenter, decided to build a larger house for them, but he had not the intention at that time of making their new home into a hotel. The lumber for this house came from trees grown on their land. Mr. Dickerson and his sons, Terry, Melton, and Jim, cut them and had them sawed into boards at the nearby Sylvan Lake sawmill. Terry told us, "We started with a thirty-foot span," which includes the present kitchen, dining room, pantry, and hallway. Terry added sections through the years and made it the large place it is now.

My father was a carpenter and helped build some of these houses around here in Wolffork Valley. He worked for a dollar a day! When my dad was alive—that was before 1912—he would get Mother up at four every morning. He was a worker! Had to work to live. She'd come in the kitchen and start her breakfast, and Dad would come up to the barn, feed his cattle, horse, and sheep, and he'd come back and wake all of us kids up to eat breakfast with them. We'd all eat together.

He started this house some time before 1910. He had just got that thirty-foot span in the middle of the house [finished], and he went across the Blue Ridge Gap to haul logs and get lumber off the land to finish the rest of our house. He got sick one evening, so he stopped over at some relatives' home and went to bed. He died that night from a ruptured appendix. That was February 11, 1912.

When we first moved in, we didn't have any [indoor] bathrooms. We had no electricity until about 1948. Nobody in this valley did because the power line wasn't run up here till then. We used candles and kerosene oil lamps. We've still got a few of them left.

We operated this house here without a refrigerator for all those years. We had a mountain spring way up on the hill there, and I built a concrete trough in our milk room [a porchlike room behind the kitchen]. That trough's about two feet wide and eight or nine feet long. It's about an inch and a half deep and fifteen inches wide over where they kept the butter, cream pitcher, and little small things in the cold water. That water stayed around forty-three degrees all the time. Then we'd set small jars in a section that's a little deeper, and on down further we had big crocks—two- to three-gallon churns with buttermilk, pickled beans, kraut, and sweet milk. That kept our stuff, and we did without refrigerators.

Finally we got electricity and bought a deep freeze and a refrigerator, but this old boy here is still used to that cold water! It'll keep stuff just as good as a refrigerator. The water comes in here and pours out a little pipe I've got for an overflow. There's never been any ice in that water. All through the wintertime, this water comes in and goes out twenty-four hours a day; so there's never any ice accumulated here. That was cheap refrigeration, wasn't it? I built that trough when I was probably fifteen or sixteen years old.

We were curious to know how the Dickersons got into the hotel business. Terry related the story:

Mimi's [former] schoolmate at Rabun Gap Industrial School [Rabun Gap-Nacoochee School now], Carrie Kay, started our business. When she was still in school, she and eight or ten of her friends would come up here in a two-horse wagon with tubs and buckets. They'd pick blackberries on that hill up yonder and haul them back to the school.

Carrie finished school and went to teaching, but her nerves went bad. The doctors said, "You're gonna have to quit and take a rest," and Carrie wanted to come back here to rest. We let her come, and before she got her rest period over, her father and mother was up here and maybe two or three of the neighbors, and that started our business.

Melton, Miriam, and Lucy finished high school at Rabun Gap-Nacoochee School. Jim and Arizona finished seventh grade at Wolffork and didn't go any further. Jim went to farming. I attended Bleckley Memorial Institute in Clayton for several years. The school there burned and was not rebuilt. [The students had to find other schools.] I heard about a new school down near middle Georgia, Monroe A&M School in Walton County, and I transferred down there.

It was a boarding school, and there were about as many boys as there were girls there. The University of Georgia sponsored a lot of that program over there at A&M. We specialized in growing some crops just to test. I also remember we did some work with carpentry and building. [Since then] I've put roofs on houses and I've repaired things. I finished there in 1924. [About then, we started our business.]

Arizona stayed home and helped Mother with the cooking [for the Dickerson House].

Arizona Dickerson: Rooms were about twelve dollars and fifty cents a week. I know it wasn't much, but things were cheap back then. We had some people who stayed two weeks, some two months, and a very few would stay three months. We would open about the first of June and close the middle of September—be open about three and a half to four months a year. In October, we'd sometimes let them come back for the weekend to see the leaves turning.

We cooked and served three meals a day to all the guests staying here—breakfast at seven-thirty, dinner at twelve noon, and supper at six. And we didn't miss them hours by many minutes at any time. I always tried to cook things and make 'em look pretty. I knew they'd eat it. Folks eat with their eyes anyhow.

Terry: We raised most of the food we served—vegetables, meat, milk, eggs, and butter. We grew a flock of chickens, and me and two young girls we hired to help us each summer would get out and kill and clean about three fryers every day.

Arizona: We milked three or four cows and got a lot of milk. We had to churn every day. I'd get up at the break of day and get out in the garden and hoe until time to start breakfast. Then I'd go after supper and hoe until the gnats run me out of the garden. You know, you can grow a lot of carrots and beets in a little row.

Terry: We just served out through this serving window. The girls in the kitchen would set the big bowls [of food] up there, and they were served on the table family-style.

They got the system started that whenever anyone got up from a table after a meal, he would bring his plate, his cup, and his

"We all had responsibilities every day, morning, and night. Brother Jim was a little older than I, and he would go to the barn and help over there. I had to look after the stovewood box, and night never caught me behind but a very few times. You know, kids are afraid of the dark, and I had to go out in the dark and feel around for some wood a time or two. Nowadays you just have to turn a knob for cooking or heating, but I still like to burn wood and cut wood."

dishes and set them on the ledge. We could get the dishes when we wanted to. Everybody got into that habit. That was a awful helpful habit. That was a blessing for us. The guests didn't mind. They just fell in line—lived like a family.

Lord, it's a job, cooking. One can't do it all. I have a time of cleaning pots. I cook vegetables, and it takes a long while, you know. And then I get them on [the stove] and get busy. I don't know any more about them, because [I am doing something else. Then they are] burnt and already dry, and I have to run and clean the pot. A cook needs to be around the stove, but when you're doing everything like mowing grass, cutting wood, visiting with people, it's hard to do. A cook has got to stay pretty close around.

Many of the rooms in the Dickerson House have been closed off now. The beds are covered with handmade quilts or spreads and look ready for the next season's guests. Terry showed us through the house, pointing out things he had made.

*Terry remembered, "When Dad and us boys used to go cut wood, Dad
would say, 'Boys, don't you hack on this good timber. If you want
to hack, get over there on that rough stuff.'" Terry soon learned how
to make things out of both "good timber" and "rough stuff," including
this chair and bench of mountain laurel—a particularly ornery and
strong-willed type of wood.*

Terry: I made quite a lot of the furniture in the house. I built
the shelves and chairs and two single beds. I also designed the bins
where we keep all the silver and glasses. J. H. Smith [former principal of Bass High and Tech High in Atlanta] helped me make
those five cabinets up there during the thirties.

When the tornado came through here in '32, it blew down those
big trees on the side of the mountain. We hauled those logs down
almost to Clayton and sawed them and brought the wood back.
That's what those flour bins are made of—that white oak lumber.

A man who knew one of our guests printed up some postcards
for us. That's the only advertisement we ever had, because the
people [who stayed here] done that for us. It was all done by lip
service and them using their tongue. They would advertise our
place, and I just kept adding a bedroom or two.

People would come up here to Rabun County on the Tallulah
Falls train and get a taxi from the train station to our place. While
they were staying here they didn't go off much. They didn't even
go as far as Mountain City to the square dance. They just wanted

This Dickerson House postcard was the only advertisement they had besides word of mouth. Terry told us when he was very busy he'd send these to let people know if he "had accommodations."

to eat and talk and walk. One of the ladies [a Mrs. Wilhide from South Carolina], who came for about ten or twelve years until her death, would get up every morning and walk about three or four miles around the loop of this valley down by our brother Jim's place and back by the church and come in here for seven-thirty breakfast. She'd whistle for the dog, get her stick, and go off by herself. She didn't want anyone with her that she'd have to wait on.

We had an old bachelor from Atlanta who came up here. He was planning to marry a little Scottish lady. They came up here—before they were married—when they had to have a chaperone and stayed for about a month, I guess. Then they were married. That couple came up here for twenty-seven years for July and August on their vacations. He finally died, and I don't know if little Betty went back to Scotland or not.

We had [as a guest] a Canadian lady who had moved down just below Tampa, Florida. She had lost her husband real early in life, and she never did marry again. Somebody took her the news down there about this place. She wrote for a reservation one time, and we accepted her. She chose a little single room up here next to the back, right in the corner. So she come up here and stayed about two months every year on that one reservation. She'd get here about six-thirty or seven in the evening. The last time she came, I was in the bed and I heard a car drive up and stop. She got out. She had on hard heel shoes—not high heels—and you could hear her little short steps on that concrete. She pecked on the door. [It was late enough that] I had to have the light to see to get dressed to go out.

[She said,] "Aren't you going to let me in?" I said, "Just a minute, Mrs. Hodge." When I got to the screen door, she said, "Where are you going to put me this time?" I said, "Well, you're early. You can have the same place." "Well, that's just good enough."

And she stayed in that little room as long as she came here—twelve or fourteen years. She never did write and tell us she was coming. She knew when we opened, and when the first of June come she was right here. She was the nicest person you ever met.

We had a few little incidents when we had to call down some guests. We had three or four young ladies—I imagine they were teenage girls about eighteen or nineteen years old—one time from South Carolina that were staying in the bedroom above the dining room. They had finished school, and they might have come up on their own, or their family may have sent them up. They acted like eight- or ten-year-old girls, jumping from one bed to the other. They were having fun over there, but some of the guests that were staying back there couldn't sleep. So we had to get onto that bunch.

We had three tables in there [in the dining room]. We had two ladies here from South Carolina. They brought cigarettes with them. They would finish their meal and sit there till they'd smoked two cigarettes. They would shake the ashes in a plate, cup, or whatever they had. We couldn't clean the tables up and do our work with them sitting around and them puffing on two cigarettes right after their meal. We had to wait in the kitchen until they got through in the dining hall, and they would puff away and tell a joke and laugh. It took ten or fifteen minutes to use up a cigarette. They didn't realize what they was a-doing. J. H. Smith, he stayed up on the second floor upstairs. He come the first of May until school started. So, we talked it over with him and he said, "Let me handle it as a neighborly deed." So we just said, "Mr. Smith, if you have an idea, go to it. You are living at home here."

So he wrote a sign and hung it up there right up against that wall for us: "NO SMOKING IN THE DINING ROOM." Those ladies noticed it the first time they went by there. They came to the

The dining room, with the serving window to the kitchen on the right.

service ledge in there where the people sat their things up on this ledge for the lady in the dining hall. Those ladies came in there one day after they finished their meal and put their elbows up on the ledge. You never heard such a pitiful noise, both of them apologizing, almost crying. They never thought what they was a-doing to our system.

Lord, I don't see how people smoke two packs of cigarettes a day. That's two or three dollars a day in and out of your mouth. That is extravagant and harmful, too. Lots of business places are loaded up with butts around the door, so they must obey the rule.

Then along later on, we had a fellow by the name of Coleman and his wife. They were up in their years—about sixty or so. They brought a radio along with them, and they got in the habit of wanting to hear the eleven o'clock news at night. We had our house already trained that ten o'clock was time to pull the light out. I heard the radio down the hallway at eleven, and I got up and went to the switch [fusebox] in there and pulled the switch on them. I left it off maybe just a few seconds; then I pushed it back in and everything was quiet. I never said a word, and then I heard that man say, "Something's wrong with that radio. Keep it going. Keep it going." I pulled the switch again. The next morning they were just about

*One of the guest bedrooms. Note the tongue-and groove walls, and the
size of the room.*

ready to leave. They came for two weeks, and they did finish out
their vacation, though. But they were disturbing all of this house
by waiting for the eleven o'clock news to come on. When he went
to bed after he heard the news, he probably couldn't sleep; so he
would be better off to have went to bed at ten.

I have gone to bed a lot of times [after sitting a while] out there
on the front porch. There would be a crowd sitting there talking
and laughing, and they would see me go in there and pull my light
out. I would turn in pretty early—as soon as we got the kitchen
cleaned up—and I guess I was in bed by about eight-thirty. And
when ten could come, they'd say, "Ten o'clock. Mr. Terry wants
to sleep." You would hear them going upstairs like squirrels.

*Although they have been closed for years, Terry told us he still
gets requests for reservations:*

I had a letter from a lady who wanted to come up here for her
vacation. She was last here in '55, which would be over twenty-five
years ago. She's from some place around central Florida. She said

*Leaning against a homemade crocheted rag rug, Terry reminisces
with Julie Dickens.*

(vegetables)

Arizona, Mimi, and Terry always gave their guests a good send-off.

it gets so hot down there and she was by herself, so she wanted to come up and spend some time this summer if she could get away up here. She says she can't drive—she's quite old now—but some friends will bring her. We had to write and tell her that we quit the business. You can't keep up with the clock when you get your three score and ten, plus some more.

Even after his retirement, Terry still enjoys visiting and joking with people:

There is this lady that I know. I don't know if she's an old maid or lost her husband, but she's above a middle-aged lady. Every time

I go out to the Clayton convalescent home to visit my sister Lucy, this lady sees me a-coming and she gets close to the door and shakes hands with me. Then she says, "You ever got married yet?" I said, "No, I just love them all and patch them up!!"

Menus and Recipes

Relaxing and eating were two of the main pursuits of guests in Rabun County boardinghouses. Visitors enjoyed food that was fresh and locally grown, eating heartily and well out of the establishment's garden. Often even the poultry and meats had been raised and preserved on the premises. Though the menus might vary with the inclinations of the proprietor, boardinghouse fare was abundant, often consisting of at least two meats (very often chicken, with ham or pork or beef), several dishes of good garden vegetables (many of them cooked with a streak of lean bacon or other meat seasoning), bread, dessert, relishes, and jellies. *Foxfire's Book of Woodstove Cookery* included the following sample menus gathered from some of the best cooks in Rabun County. These menus were designed for families, not boardinghouses, and therefore have fewer items than guests would find in boardinghouses. A daily boardinghouse dinner or supper would probably have come closer to the special menu that families would serve on Sunday or holidays. The different dishes on these menus can be combined in many ways to produce any number of good meals.

Breakfast

Eggs
Sausage or ham
Grits and gravy
Biscuits, butter, and jelly

Egg omelet
Fried ham or sausage or bacon
Corn bread or biscuits or fritters or biscuit pone
Honey, sorghum syrup, blackberry jam, or other jellies or jams
Applesauce
Milk and coffee

Other foods served for breakfast include:
Cornmeal mush
Baked fruit
Fresh creamed corn
Berries and cream

Noonday and Evening Meals

Pork tenderloin
Rice or dressing or fried potatoes
Green beans or turnips and greens
Sauerkraut
Blackberry pie

Cured ham, sliced
Squash
Boiled okra
Sweet peppers and onions
Mashed potatoes
Fried apples

Cured ham and red-eye gravy
Baked sweet potatoes and butter
Chicken and broccoli casserole
Rice and gravy
Peas
Applesauce

Fried chicken
Stewed or fried apples
Green beans or peas or greens
Corn
Corn bread or biscuits and gravy

Pork chops, fried or baked
Fried green tomatoes
Potatoes
Biscuits and gravy
Peaches

Sunday dinner has always been a special time for families in this part of the country. The cooks would have one or two menus that they would generally follow for the Sunday meal or for special occasions such as holidays. A special dinner menu might consist of:

Fried chicken and gravy, ham, or turkey
Stewed or mashed Irish potatoes or sweet potatoes, if available
Boiled corn, on or off the cob
Green beans or lima beans or white half-runner beans
Other vegetables from the garden, as available
Cooked apples or applesauce
Corn bread and/or biscuits
Pie, cobbler, or a special layer cake

Miss Arizona shared with us many of the following recipes and menus she used to serve to the twenty or more guests three times a day from late spring through early September when "cold weather would run them off."

Pepper Relish

1 gallon red sweet peppers	*2 cups sugar*
1 gallon green sweet peppers	*2 cups vinegar*
1 cup chopped celery	*3 tablespoons salt*
1 cup diced sweet apples	*Spices, if desired*
1 cup diced onions	

Dice the peppers. Pour boiling water over the peppers, celery, apples, and onions, and let stand for a few minutes. Drain off. Add sugar, vinegar, salt, and spices and cook until apples, peppers, and celery are tender. Stir often and blend well. Seal in canning jars. Process 10 minutes in boiling water bath.

White House Relish

12 green sweet peppers
12 red sweet peppers
12 onions
1 cabbage, ground fine

2 cups vinegar
2 cups sugar
3 tablespoons salt

Chop peppers and onions up into small pieces. Add cabbage and cover with boiling water. Let stand 5 minutes. Drain. Add vinegar, sugar, and salt. Boil 5 minutes. Seal in canning jars. Process 10 minutes in boiling water bath.

Chicken and Dumplings

1 chicken
¼ cup rendered chicken fat

3 to 6 tablespoons flour
Salt and pepper to taste

Stew the chicken in water to cover, then remove from the broth; cut it up and keep warm. Mix other ingredients together and pour into 3 or 4 cups of broth, stirring constantly over heat until it thickens slightly, and begins to boil.

¾ cup sifted flour
2½ teaspoons baking powder
½ teaspoon salt

1 egg
⅓ cup milk

To make the dumplings, mix dry ingredients. Add egg and milk and beat. Drop by small spoonfuls into the boiling chicken gravy. Cover pot tightly and cook 15 minutes. Do not remove lid while dumplings are cooking. The steam is necessary for them to be light. To serve, spoon out dumplings and gravy together with chicken into dish.

"Riz" Biscuits

1 package dry yeast
1 cup warm buttermilk
½ teaspoon baking soda
½ cup lard

2½ cups flour
1 teaspoon salt
2 tablespoons sugar or more, if
    desired

Preheat oven to 425° F. Mix yeast in warm buttermilk. Add soda. Cut the lard into the dry ingredients. Slowly mix liquid mixture into dry ingredients. Roll out on dough board. Cut out biscuits. Let stand long enough to rise (or until a lightly pressed fingertip leaves a slight impression in biscuits). Then bake about 12 minutes (until lightly browned) in preheated oven. YIELD: 24 biscuits.

Sweet Potato Soufflé

1 cup sweet milk
1 tablespoon butter or margarine
2 tablespoons sugar
½ teaspoon salt
2 cups mashed cooked sweet
    potatoes

2 eggs, separated
1 teaspoon nutmeg
¼ cup raisins
¼ cup chopped nuts
5 marshmallows, if desired

Preheat oven to 350° F. Scald milk. Add butter, sugar, and salt. Stir until butter is melted. Add to sweet potatoes. Stir until smooth. Beat yolks and whites of eggs separately. Stir yolks into potato mixture, and then add nutmeg, raisins, and nuts. Fold in stiffly beaten whites and pour into buttered baking dish.

If desired and obtainable, arrange 5 marshmallows over the top. Bake in preheated oven for 20 to 25 minutes or until set. Use as main course or dessert. YIELD: 6 servings.

Applesauce Cake

2 teaspoons baking soda
2 cups applesauce
2 cups sugar
1½ sticks butter
2 eggs
3 cups plain flour
1 teaspoon baking powder

1 teaspoon ground cloves
½ teaspoon salt
1½ teaspoons nutmeg
1 tablespoon cinnamon
1 cup chopped pecans
1 cup raisins

Preheat oven to 300° F. Add soda to applesauce and set aside. Combine sugar, butter, and eggs and mix well. Beat in dry ingredients except the nuts and raisins. Add applesauce, nuts, and raisins and mix well. Pour into a greased and floured tube pan and bake in preheated oven for an hour and a half. Cool before removing from pan.

No-Fail Coconut Pound Cake

This cake may be prepared and frozen for a later date. Freezing gives it a moist texture.

3 cups flour
1 teaspoon baking powder
½ teaspoon salt
1½ cups shortening
2½ cups sugar

5 or 6 eggs
1 cup milk
1 cup grated coconut
1 tablespoon coconut flavoring

Preheat oven to 325° F. Sift together flour, baking powder, and salt twice and set aside. Cream together the shortening and sugar; add eggs, one at a time, beating well after each addition. Add flour mixture and milk alternately to creamed mixture, beating continuously. Mix in coconut and coconut flavoring last. Pour batter into a greased and floured tube pan and bake in preheated oven for 1 hour and twenty-five minutes.

Scotch Cake

2 cups flour
2 cups sugar
½ cup butter
½ cup vegetable oil
4 tablespoons cocoa
1 cup water

½ cup buttermilk
2 eggs
1 teaspoon baking soda
1 teaspoon cinnamon
1 teaspoon vanilla

Icing for Scotch Cake (recipe follows)

Preheat oven to 350° F. Combine flour and sugar. Mix butter, oil, cocoa, and water in a saucepan; bring to a rapid boil and pour into flour and sugar mixture. Mix well. Add buttermilk, eggs (one at a time), soda, cinnamon, and vanilla. Mix well. Pour batter into two greased and floured 9-inch layer pans or a greased and floured 13 x 9-inch sheet cake pan. Bake in preheated oven for 30 minutes. When cool, frost.

ICING FOR SCOTCH CAKE

½ cup margarine
¼ cup cocoa
6 tablespoons milk
1 teaspoon vanilla

1 box confectioners' sugar
1 cup chopped pecans
1 cup flaked coconut

Cream together margarine and cocoa. Add milk and vanilla. Stir in confectioners' sugar and mix thoroughly. Last, add pecans and coconut.

Quick Gingerbread

2½ cups flour
2 teaspoons baking soda
½ teaspoon salt
1 teaspoon cinnamon
1 teaspoon ginger
½ teaspoon ground cloves

2 eggs, well beaten
½ cup sugar
1 cup molasses
½ cup vegetable oil
1 cup boiling water

Preheat oven to 350° F. Sift flour, soda, salt, cinnamon, ginger, and cloves together twice. Set aside. Combine beaten eggs, sugar, molasses, and oil. Mix well. Add to dry ingredients and blend. Add boiling water and stir until smooth. Pour into oiled shallow baking pan. Bake in preheated oven for 40 minutes.

Top-of-the-Stove Cookies

4 tablespoons cocoa
2 cups white sugar
1 stick margarine
½ cup milk

½ cup peanut butter
3 cups quick-cooking oatmeal
Pinch salt
1 teaspoon vanilla

Put cocoa, sugar, margarine, and milk into pan on top of stove. Heat 2 minutes. Add peanut butter, oatmeal, salt, and vanilla. Lay a sheet of waxed paper on the counter and drop the cookie mix by spoonfuls onto the paper. As the mixture cools, the cookies will harden and be ready to eat.

Layered Cheese and Apple Salad

1 small package lemon gelatin
2 cups boiling water
1½ tablespoons lemon juice
1 teaspoon salt
1 medium red apple, cut into
   ¼-inch dice

1 teaspoon sugar
3 ounces cream cheese, softened
½ cup broken walnut meats
Lettuce
Mayonnaise

Dissolve gelatin in boiling water. Add 1 tablespoon lemon juice and the salt. Chill until slightly thickened.

Combine apple, sugar, and remaining lemon juice. When gelatin mixture is slightly thickened, fold diced apple into half of it. Turn into mold. Chill until firm.

Beat remaining gelatin with rotary beater until it is the consistency of whipped cream. Fold in cheese and nuts. Pour over firm first layer. Chill until firm. Serve in squares on crisp lettuce. Garnish with mayonnaise. YIELD: 8 servings.

Survivors

While the Rabun County boardinghouse boom is over, each year thousands of tourists stay in local motels and parks. And several special establishments still serve as links to times gone by.

Glen-Ella Springs
Glen-Ella Springs was constructed in 1875 as a homeplace for Glen and Ella Davidson on a 600-acre tract of land near Tallulah Falls. In 1890, and later in 1905, they expanded their home to take in paying guests. Guests visited the inn because of the mineral springs there and the Davidsons' home-grown food.
With the decline in tourism in the 1920s, Glen-Ella ceased operation as an inn. The building remained in the Davidson family until the 1950s, after which it passed through the hands of several owners. The inn and seventeen acres of land were purchased in 1985 by Barrie and Bobby Aycock, who restored and reopened Glen-Ella Springs for guests in 1987. The sixteen-room inn, now listed on the National Register of Historic Places, draws guests from around the country with its charm and quiet, secluded setting.

The Dillard House
Though the Dillard family has been in the business of providing boarding
facilities for much longer, the present Dillard House was started in 1910
by Arthur and Carrie Edwards Dillard. The Dillard House, located
in Dillard, Georgia, was first known as "Oak Lawn."
The Dillards' first boarder was Methodist minister Henry Byrd, who
intended to stay with them for three weeks but remained for three years.
From its beginning as a two-bedroom boardinghouse to the present
eighty-room hotel and cottage facility, the Dillard House has hosted
people from all walks of life who enjoy the beauty of the mountains, good
food, and friendly people.

The York House Inn
Beginning as a two-story log cabin built in the early 1840s in Rabun Gap, Georgia, the York House later became the home of William Terrell York and Mollie Gibson York. They established the York House as an inn in 1896. With a Tallulah Falls Railroad siding only four hundred yards away, early visitors were delivered almost to the York House door, and the inn flourished with the tourist trade.

The York House Inn has been in continuous operation since that time and is now listed on the National Register of Historic Places as one of the oldest mountain inns. Even though its thirteen guest rooms have modern conveniences, the York House Inn has maintained an atmosphere of timelessness with its large verandas, majestic trees, and unobstructed view of the mountains.

ECONOMIC
REVOLUTION

STUDENT EDITORS, CELENA ROGERS, APRIL SHIRLEY

The Appalachian Mountains are a source of great wealth. Investors and industrialists have recognized the value of the region's natural resources for well over a century, and vast individual fortunes have been won and lost in the exploitation of timber, hard minerals, and water. Government has played its part as well: though millions of tax dollars have been channeled into Appalachia for public aid, government has blessed the conduits through which billions in commerce have been channeled out of the region. In the process of redistributing the wealth, populations have been displaced and replaced and local economies virtually revolutionized.

In North Georgia on the southeastern skirt of the Appalachians, the 1820s gold rush at Dahlonega precipitated the Trail of Tears when the Cherokees were driven out of the region. As the Cherokees streamed out and the white settlers streamed in, the state of Georgia parceled out the land by lottery. During the nation's Industrial Revolution in the latter part of the nineteenth century, the region's natural resources were again the focus of attention. As outside speculators acquired land and its wealth, many of the next generation of white settlers were bought out or relocated. Unlike the Cherokees, they were allowed to participate to some degree in the economic process, primarily as laborers in the various industries. Today, a substantial second-home industry in parts of southern

Appalachia is bringing another wave of settlers who are slowly but surely displacing another generation of "natives."

There is just concern that with all its natural wealth, Appalachia has historically been plagued by economic depression and by substandard public services. Education, health care, and transportation have gradually improved throughout the region, but the economy is still driven largely by industries that extract the wealth, or offer low-level service employment. Especially in areas of finite resources like coal, the future holds some big question marks.

Businesses such as textile and appliance manufacturers contribute to local economies in southern Appalachia, but they characteristically are attracted by low taxes, and a nonunion work force, providing a relatively low income for both the workers and the local municipal governments. Currently, in some communities workers are fearful that some businesses will relocate to find even cheaper labor forces.

In Rabun County, Georgia, where the Foxfire program is located, there is little debate as to who owns the land: the United States Forest Service and Georgia Power Company are its largest holders. Most of the timber in Rabun County was logged in the first half of the century, leaving only the big trees high up on inaccessible ridges. As our interviews indicate, a good bit of the logging was done by local residents, family farmers who cleared land for pasture and sold off the timber in the form of cross ties, tanbark, acid wood, and lumber. But far more of the timber was logged by big outfits like Ritter and Morse Brothers.

The environmental impact of the timber companies in the early days would indeed be considered criminal by today's standards. One interview published in *Foxfire 4*, for example, described a sawmill built over a creek so that the sawdust would be carried away by the current. As the big logging companies moved on to other locations, the United States Forest Service began to purchase logged-over timber tracts for the sake of conservation.

Land acquisition began in 1912 and continues to this day. Today, 63 percent of the land in Rabun County is owned and managed by the Forest Service with the multiple goals of producing timber, protecting watersheds and wildlife, and providing recreation. It contributes to the county tax base, employs dozens of people in the county, and contracts jobs to a good many others in the logging business; its influence is also felt in large measure by the tourist industry and outdoor sportsmen.

Between 1911 and 1920, Georgia Power Company acquired the necessary land (5.6 percent of the total land in Rabun County) to build four hydroelectric power projects in Rabun County. While continuing to generate power, the lakes impounded by the dams provide recreation and draw a significant number of tourists and second-home buyers into the community. The lakes are surrounded by homes built on land leased from the power company (some of them are magnificent), and the building trades or associated tourism provide the livelihoods of many local residents.

When the acreage assigned to state parks, schools, and public rights-of-way is added to the total, it is evident that a lion's share of Rabun County is owned by public entities. The land remaining is scarce and valuable. The beauty of the landscape and the agreeable climate have spawned a booming real estate business that targets retirees and summer visitors. As indicated in the tourism section, tourism in Rabun County has a long history, inexorably connected to the peaceful beauty of the landscape, recreational opportunities, and travel accessibility. Rabun County is indeed a wonderful place to live, but as the Broadway play (and television movie) *Foxfire* dramatizes, the sharply rising price tag on land spurred by second-home development makes it increasingly difficult for local blue-collar workers to own their own property. Small family farms and timberlands, split up in inheritance disputes, are often subdivided and sold as housing lots which local folks can rarely afford to buy.

By and large, depending on the current national economy, the year-round population in Rabun County makes a reasonable living. In the recession of the nineties, times are very tight, but local people do not live in economic depression and poverty. But from the beginning of the Depression through World War II the community went through very rough times. Because local families had small subsistence farms, they could at least raise their own food, but there was little money and no jobs and people suffered. The federal government then intervened as it did in thousands of other communities, to bolster the economy through the Civilian Conservation Corps and the Works Progress Administration. Federal programs provided jobs and public services and made a positive impact on the community. The federal government came again during World War II. As soldiers left the county for the war effort, in adjoining counties in Georgia and North Carolina, the Tennessee Valley Authority built hydroelectric dams, providing jobs for people throughout the region. Because of public jobs and federal development initiatives, mouths were fed—but the impact went further. It was more personal. The local folks who went out on the construction jobs worked with others from different parts of the country, learned new job skills, traveled to places they would have never seen otherwise, ate store-bought light bread, played league baseball. Their stories are full of anecdotes recounting memorable moments, both sweet and sour.

This section is made up of eight chapters. The first four feature narratives by people affected by the impact of hydroelectric projects in Rabun County and surrounding communities, and include a few examples of the oral folklore related to the rivers, lakes, and power dams.

The fifth chapter, "Hard Times," chronicles the experiences of people who lived through the Great Depression.

Sixth is a piece that focuses on the role of the U.S. Forest Service in Rabun County, featuring the legendary Mr. Roscoe Nicholson (Ranger Nick), the county's first forest ranger.

A seventh chapter is devoted to the story of the local residents involved in the CCC camps, or the Civilian Conservation Corps.

The final chapter examines the impact of the Works Progress Administration (WPA) on the community. While the CCC was designed for young single males only, the WPA hired both men and women who were more experienced, most of whom had families to support and little means of making a cash wage. The phenomenon led to greatly improved social services, in addition to lasting brick and mortar improvements in the community.

As the words of our contacts will demonstrate, the economic impact of the outside world on communities like Rabun County is not divorced from personal, cultural, and political realities. And it is hard to separate the long-term effect of outside economic intrusions from the changes wrought by home-grown entrepreneurs, politicians, and culture bearers.

Burton

Formerly a field general in the Union Army, General A. J. Warner was looking for mining properties in North Georgia when his eye was attracted to its swiftly flowing streams. He observed the potential for creating hydroelectric power, the market for which would be Atlanta.[1] In the years between 1902 and 1905, he and his associates optimistically bought up several water power properties.[2]

But Warner was ahead of his time. The market for electric power was as yet immature: "He came up against the stark reality that all pioneers in the field of hydroelectric development sooner or later had to face: namely, that electricity is of no economic value in the absence of a market. . . . Markets had to be created and developed. Electrical appliances and equipment had to be invented and manufactured; and the people—still skeptical about the future of electricity—had to be sold on the economy and conveniences of these devices."[3] General Warner died a broken man, but it was not many years later that the market caught up with his vision.

The company that bought Warner's property was first in the railroad business. Why the connection between railroads and electric power? They were in the *electric* railway business in Atlanta, the equivalent of today's MARTA (Atlanta's Metropolitan Area Rapid Transit Authority). The business became Georgia Power Company.

Even when the Georgia Power Company contracted with the

Northern Contracting Company, the New York corporation, to build the first of four hydroelectric power dams on the Tallulah River in Rabun County in 1911, the market for consumer electricity was as yet green. But by that time, there was growing potential, and Rabun County was made a member of a larger electric power grid that extended into northeastern Georgia.

Reverend James E. Turpen, Sr.

Reverend Turpen is a veteran member of Foxfire's Community Board and an ardent Foxfire supporter. His grandfather, J. E. Harvey, was a local entrepreneur who made land purchases for the Georgia Power Company preceding the building of hydroelectric dams in Rabun County. In the interview Reverend Turpen first commented on Mr. Harvey's custom of swapping real estate, and then he filled us in on what kind of man his grandfather was.

Whenever the land acquisition was going on, not all the land was bought. Some land was actually traded for. If a family said they didn't want to sell because they needed land to farm on, Mr. Harvey would do his best to find a piece of land that would suit them that they could trade for. I think it were common for people to swap land for land. That way they was guaranteed a place to live. I can see how it would be tough to sell out and not know where you were going, not have some other place already in mind. But if somebody had a piece of land you agreed to swap for, there was a little more security in that than having the money.

Well, [my grandfather] was just an ol' mountain boy that grew up in the Wolf Creek community on the farm, a self-made individual. He probably had a second-grade education, if that much— he could read and write—but [he was a] very industrious person. He had a lot of native ability, I guess you'd call it. He had a knack for getting along with people, and he was really a man of his times. He was a big man—about six-six, barrel-chested, just a big fellow. He wore a black coat, black pants, a blue shirt, and a big black hat like a ten-gallon hat, and about everywhere he went, people knew who he was.

Prior to when Georgia Power came into the area, he'd made most of his living by farming and sawmilling. Then when Georgia

Power came along, and they needed timbers to be sawed, why he was already in business. As a matter of fact, when [Georgia Power] bought land to back the water over, they cut a lot of the trees to make lumber to form the dams, and he sawed all that. I guess he sawed most of the timber that they needed. He had commissaries on the jobs at various plants, various dam sites. He did a little of everything to keep the jobs going. He had theaters there. It was silent movies, but somebody played the piano. There used to be an old theater there in Tallulah Falls.

But he was a fellow that had sawmills, carpenter crews, dairies; he had a boathouse on Lake Rabun (after the lake was built, of course). It stayed in business for years. He had tourist cabins up there. He had Tallulah Point, the gorge overlook in Tallulah Falls; he was a T-Model Ford dealer at one time; he trafficked and traded in mules and steers and cattle and whatever was necessary to keep folks going. He liked to turn a nickel. He was a good horse trader— not just horses, but anything that come along he'd trade with people on.

But he was a quiet man. He never liked for his picture to be made. He never liked to be in the limelight; he just liked to do for people. Mr. Andrew Ritchie and other people had an appreciation for J. E. Harvey because, as Mr. Ritchie says in his book [*Sketches of Rabun County History*], he could have been a very wealthy man, but that wasn't his style. During the Depression years he looked after his men and their families. A lot of the time there was nothing really to do, and he would let the men come in and they'd go out and whitewash trees around in the little town down there or other places just to give them something to do so he could pay them. There are still some families around that will tell you that because of J. E. Harvey, they had something to eat during the Depression, that their dad worked for him and he looked after 'em. He used to own a lot of houses that he just let people live in—folks that worked for him.

People used to always be taking tools, and he sort of had a sayin', "Well, if they need it that bad, let 'em have it, 'cause if they can live with it, I can live without it." It didn't bother him if somebody would pick up stuff and take it off.

After his death, why mercy, there was a big ol' box down there full of books where people had charged stuff in the commissaries in the general store that he never got paid for. If you'd have taken that one box of books and all the stuff that was charged in there and collected on it, you and I probably could retire today.

When he died in 1950 [he had] just gotten to the place where he was converting from steam to diesel to run sawmills and beginning to modernize. He'd seen a lot of changes in the Tallulah Falls area from the time of the tourists—hotels, boardinghouses, eating places, excursions coming to town [by] train—till the industrial part with the power company coming in.

The following three interviews were conducted with people who had lived in the communities of Burton and Powell Gap until the property was acquired and flooded by Georgia Power Company. The first two were edited from transcriptions of interviews conducted in 1982 by Mary Elizabeth Etheridge, a researcher who eventually wrote a fictional children's story based on the town of Burton.

Dr. John C. Blalock

I guess I'm the oldest man living that's from Burton. [I was born] June 24, 1894. My father was born just above Burton, in what we call Persimmon. Dad had eight children, six girls and two boys— a big family. Everybody had big families back then.

[My sister, Willie Blalock Elliott] is the baby of the family, and I'm the oldest boy. [There was] one boy older than me but he died in infancy. You know, a lot of children would die in infancy, people not knowing what to do for 'em. If one of us lived, I guess, they kind of lucked us out. I had four or five friends die of typhoid fever.

We lived a mile above Burton. We had a boardinghouse up there. We kept all the drummers then. I don't know if you've ever heard of that word or not. That was the people that came through and sold stuff. And they carried a pretty good stock.

Where we made our living, my father was the merchant in a store about a mile above the Burton post office. His store was as big as the other two [Burton stores] combined with one more in Clayton. We had the biggest store in the county. I've driven to Clayton to meet the train when I was a teenager. You had to load your merchandise you brought back with you, you know. I couldn't

OUR HOME, 1908.

A Burton family in front of their home.

even pick up a sack of salt. We bought coffee, green coffee always, in five-bushel bags, and then we'd sell the green coffee to [our customers]. People'd take the coffee and parch it in their ovens and grind it in coffee mills.

Dad had the syrup mill, and we made syrup. I think we had the only syrup mill there. Have you ever seen one of those where the horse goes round and round? We had one of those. If you were a farmer there, you'd haul [your sorghum or cane] in, and then we'd take it [and process it] and when the syrup was finally gotten out, if you had thirty gallons, we'd [take] three of it for making it for you.

[Until I was twelve], I went to school in Burton. We had the largest school in the county for a while. [There were] about seventy-five students, and two teachers.

We had singing conventions there. That was a big day. A singing convention lasts all day! You start about ten, and go to about three or three-thirty or so. We'd sing all kind of [gospel songs]. We had the King family and the Gastons, and the Philyaws, they were all

Gospel Singing Convention at Powell Gap Church/School, August 11,
1907. (Kastner Collection)

singers. They just enjoyed getting up there and singing, you know.
We had a singing school there every year for two weeks, and they'd
come where they'd teach. [The singing schools] were easy; you
either could sing or not sing, that's what you could do. The teacher
would call on you to see if you could sing, and he found right quick
I couldn't even carry a note to the post office.

Just before [the town of Burton was bought up to make the
lake], we went in and bought an organ. We had one girl who could
play it, so that was all [the musical instruments we had]. That's the
only [organ there was in the community, and other folks would]
borrow that and take it to the other little churches. Persimmon was
in the circuit we call Burton, and then we had Timpson Creek and
the other creeks. It was kind of in sections.

They surveyed out there, and some lumber people came out
there and [bought] a lot of timber. George W. Beebe, an old bachelor who boarded at our house a long time, went through there
and bought all the poplar trees, just put a "B" on each tree. He
figured someday they may come to him. He bought those about
the time I was born, and I think he got the pleasure of selling it
before he died. He lived there with us for a long time, till he went
into Clayton, and then he lived in the Blue Ridge Hotel.

My father gave away a fortune [in land], not knowing that they would ever get a railroad in there. He sold one mountain which is called Big Bald Mountain up there. It's about three or four miles north of Burton. [It was] 480 acres, and he sold it for eighty-one dollars and thought he gypped the guy! [Laughs.] That guy kept it for ten or twelve years till they finally got the [railroad through, which made the land much more valuable]. You know, they were four years building that railroad from Clarkesville till they got to Tallulah Falls.

There was no railroad at all in Burton. Burton's about ten or twelve miles from Tallulah Falls. You've got to cross that mountain to get there.

We owned some property, and we had two tenants that stayed with us for thirty years at Burton—had one on each side of the river. Well, you see the Tallulah River came down like this [from north to south]. We must have had about 2,500 acres across there and up across the river and to the top of old Charlie Mountain. Dad sold 2,200 acres at one time, and [today] that would be glory, you know, but I think he got $1,500 for it, or something like that.

[He got more than that for the store and the parcel of land it was on when the town was bought up to make Lake Burton.] We didn't know anything about [them buying up the land for a hydroelectric project]. I'll give you the exact way it was bought, every bit of it. The power company first sent up three surveyors, all graduates of Tech, and surveyed all this. The surveyors stayed at our [boarding] house two or three months, all the time they were doing it. They were that long surveying from Tallulah Falls to Mountain City, above Clayton. They said they were surveying for the government. The government was having it surveyed on account of the waterworks, and so on and so forth, [having to do with] the river. That's all they ever told anybody. We never did know any different about that. I saw two or three of them often after I started practicing [in Atlanta some years later]. They came to me as patients. They said, "Well, they just informed us what to do and [we were told to] just say that."

[J. E. Harvey was one of the major land agents for the power company. After the survey] old man Harvey went to Clayton and [checked the] county digest and found out what everybody paid taxes on. This was about 1910 or '11. I never will forget when he come riding in. Old man Harvey just walked in and said, "Mr. Blalock, I want to buy you out." He told Dad that he was working for the government, and they wanted to buy the property up for some kind of utility. [They] had gotten the railroad, you know, by Tallulah Falls and they bought out [there]. He said, "You can live here the rest of this year." Said, "We want your property next year."

And Dad said, "Well," he said—he'd gotten a little wise to it—"I don't want to sell; I'm not going to give you the place." And then Dad told him, "I'll take $9,000 for it." Didn't think he'd buy it at all. I never will forget. I was just standing there listening at it. I was thirteen, and I [could] see what was going on.

And Harvey says, "That includes both sides of the river and your store." Dad said, "I won't sell you the material in the store."

Dad thought he got rich when he got $9,000. He had $4,000 in it. He just thought he'd make a price that would bluff him, but if he'd just known what he was doing, he could have got $25,000 easy, a lot more out of him.

Harvey went to every house in Burton District that day and made every one of them an offer. He had two good horses with a buggy, and it didn't take long to go around to those houses. He just said [they were buying] it up for the government. And then he said they wanted to get some lumber up and so forth. Made an offer and gave them some money. And he got nearly all of 'em.

Everybody was pretty well satisfied [for] this reason. Nearly every one of 'em got a pretty good profit on what they thought the land was worth. I mean by that, they weren't tricked. But there wasn't much [choice. And some of them] found out they got gypped. They even made some of them go back and give some of them a little bit more money. See, if that was to do over, that wouldn't work at all. But, then, nobody ever said that.

We didn't move until the next year. Nearly all of us back there left in the same year. We had to haul all our merchandise to Clarkesville [to the train]. We drove down there with a pair of mules or horses. And then we'd camp out that night. They had a campground in Clarkesville. Next morning we'd go and load [it] at the depot.

[As a child, it wasn't that hard for me to leave Burton.] You see, I had already gone to Clarkesville to school a year. I went to Clarkesville A&M school down there. Agricultural Mechanical School, they call it.

My grandfather lived in Tiger, Georgia. That was my mother's father, and they had about 2,000 acres over there, so we got that. Half of it was inheritance. We moved to Tiger and built a big old white two-story house, down right next to Tiger Mountain. It's got a porch that goes all the way around it. When the family moved into Tiger, I went up and stayed for two summers [during vacations from Clarkesville A&M], and I'd work in my daddy's store while I was up there.

I went on to Emory [University]. I took two years literary and four years medical and then two years intern. I stayed five years in a hospital after that. I came to Atlanta when I was seventeen, and I'm still here. Can't get away.

Mrs. Willie Elliott

Mrs. Elliott is Dr. John Blalock's youngest sister.

We children did have to do chores at home. There was always something to do. My mother saw to that. She liked to keep me busy. There was four of us children, and all of us shucked corn, fed the cattle and put them up, and got in the wood. I always fed the sheep in the bottomland. We had a whole big flock. We sheared the wool and sold it.

We had an old horse, but she didn't do anything but have colts. She was wind broke. I don't know what that was, but she coughed. They never give her any dry food. Every afternoon I'd take a big ole bundle of fodder and put it in the [watering trough] and then take it and give it to her. They didn't work her, but we'd ride her four or five deep—just as many as could get on. We would ride her around the farm 'cause there wasn't any automobiles or anything. And if one [of the children] fell off, she wouldn't move a foot. She'd just stand till that kid got up. [Frequently] we'd have to go back to crawl upon something to get back on her.

We had a waterfall above the house. This has been seventy years ago. It come on down through under a bridge and went into a springhouse. The water was so close to coming out of the mountain, it was the same temperature year around; it never changed. There was a trough built in the waterline through, and we had churns and everything in there. It kept the milk cool. We would kill a sheep

Willie Elliott.

in August, and of course there was no refrigeration, but I can remember my mother and all the older girls cooking all that night, and packing it down in churns and covering it and settling it in the springhouse. It was just as good a month later as it was then. That was the only way we could keep it, you know. And we fixed apples somehow and put them down in that churn, and kraut, and pickled beans, and it wouldn't freeze or get hot either. In the summertime when it got hot, we'd run up there and get cool. Big trees and flowery bushes grew all around that springhouse. It was beautiful.

There was a bridge across the river, and there were two stores down there. We lived between three quarters and a mile from the post office. It wasn't a big trip to go get the mail, we did it everyday. [This was because the school was just past the post office.] Sometimes we school kids didn't go, so they'd get somebody to go on a mule or walk.

I remember going to school. There were several [rooms in the schoolhouse], several. It was up on a hill, and then the big playground and then the road and then the river. Nothing [was in the playground]; it was just an open area to play in. We did [play kickball, and other games. I was there until] fourth grade, I think. [I] started at six and moved away at Christmas, and I was in the fourth [grade].

The store was about one mile above Burton bridge on the Tallulah River. They sold general merchandise, sold a little of everything—horse collars, bridles, saddles, sugar, coffee, spice, cloth. And a little of everything [else].

[There was] no doubt that [moonshining] was one of the chief

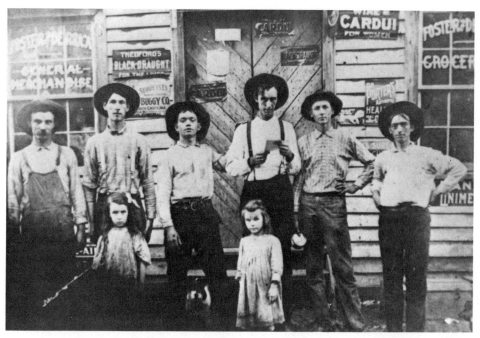

Burton General Store run by Foster and Derrick in the Burton Community. (Kastner Collection)

means of cash income. The moonshine business in those days was considered an honorable profession. It was just a matter of evading the federal law. In those days they called the federal law the revenuers. Long as they could evade the revenuers, why, they didn't have much problem with the local sheriff, I don't think. And nearly every family had something to do with moonshine, I'd say, in those days. They traded on stuff, and the store would take it in, barter it. An old farmer would bring in a few jugs of moonshine, and he'd get his staple groceries and grade flour and coffee, sugar, or whatever else he had to have. And the owner of the store would take it and trade it right along.

All I remember [about the flooding after the dam was constructed was that] they didn't tear down the house, it was left standing. We took all the belongings, of course. I remember my father making the remark that they moved out the last load of furniture just before it got high enough to flood what he had in the wagon.

[No one refused to move.] There wasn't no such thing. It was covered in water, and there wasn't no way to help it. There was no way to make a living, even if they'd left the houses on the side of the ridge somewhere, if all their land was covered. There was no way out of it. I don't know about [getting good money for the land]. I don't think we got anything [like] what it was worth for what it did to the community. My mother didn't live long, but as far as I know, I reckon my daddy was fairly well satisfied, but hundreds of them never were. It just ruined their lives. They never were satisfied.

Virgil Craig

I have been hearing about Powell Gap, one of the communities that was covered up by Lake Burton, all of my life. I do not remember the first time I heard about it, but it must have been from my father. I thought, as most little kids do, that there might be some ghosts under the lake, maybe in the old graveyard. As I got older, I found that there are no such things as ghosts.

Even though I no longer think there are ghosts under the lake, I was still very interested in the history of the Burton area. I went to talk to Virgil Craig, a ninety-one-year-old man who lived in Powell Gap around the time Burton Dam was built. When I was small, I would see my daddy wave at Mr. Craig when we would go by his house and Mr. Craig would wave back. I thought somehow that was great, but though I have known Mr. Craig all my life, I had never gone and talked to him before.

Mr. Craig is a small, soft-spoken man. I think he's just plain out proud of who he is. He has lived to ninety-one years of age, and maybe the main reason he has lived so long is that he doesn't seem to worry about getting older. My parents say he looks seventy years old. I don't know about that, but he acts very young. His house is right on the road, so I often see him mowing his lawn during the summer. That has always given me the impression that he is a hard worker. When I went to interview him, he told me that he has been working ever since he quit school in the fourth grade.

Mr. Craig worked on the dam, so he told me how the dam was built and how this led to his community being covered by Lake Burton.   —Kim Wood

Virgil Craig at his home.

Dad had a little farm down there. I don't remember how much land my family had then; the lake covered it up. That's what they done, you know. Water came to about eight feet over where we lived on a high place about a quarter of a mile right down there [from where I live now]. [My dad] took the money [that the power company gave him for his land] and went to Chechero [east of Clayton] and bought another homestead. All the rest of the people in the community done the same—one here and one yonder, to and fro. They just took up their beds and walked.

In the Burton settlement there was big farmland, [but the power company] scared them out, just big-talked them. People thought they was getting a good price, but I say they didn't get a third of what it would bring. Ol' man J. E. Harvey bought all that land for the company. He was a big talker, yes sir. Of course, after they got so far, the rest of the [landowners] had to sell anyhow. All the rest of them sold out. They just about cleaned this place out; they wasn't nobody left much. That was it.

My daddy's name is Isaac. [My daddy] was born here, but his daddy and mother, I think they came from North Carolina. The [first Craig to come into the county] was Ellis Craig. He and his wife, Hilda, had a bunch of boys right in the time of the [Civil] War. You know what a time that was. They come out of North Carolina, and it was just days [before my grandpa was going to be drafted] so they left out there and went way back in to the head of Crow Creek, and they never caught up with him. Then the war

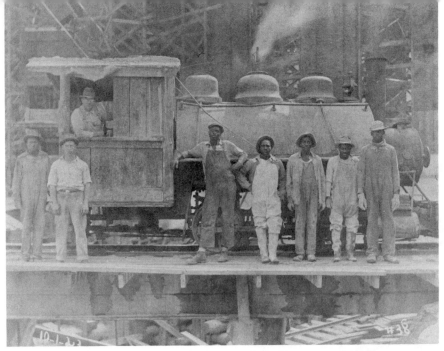

*Construction workers pose with a typical small steam railroad engine,
1923. (Dyer Photo Collection)*

was over. I heard my grandpa talking about it. He's the one that
told me all this.

They just had a little log house on the banks of the road, so
they went down the road and built another one just like it. [Then
the power company] bought all the farming land, so people had to
move out, you know. We didn't have enough [people] to have no
[church] service. It is altogether different now. I was thinking that
it looks different—it looked more old homey than it does now.

I guess y'all seen the picture of that old church school that was
in the [*Clayton Tribune*], didn't you? That's where I started school
at. [In the fall] there was the Rabun County Singing Convention.
It come every year. It's over a hundred years old. [After I quit
school], I'd hoe corn or pull fodder. Anything I could get to. I'd
[earn] about twenty-five to thirty cents a day doing something like
that. We had to live.

[The buying of the land and the drilling] all started about the
same time. I started [working on the dam] in 1916. I worked in
the rock quarry a long time. First they started drilling. That took
a long time. They drilled both sides of the river to see what kind
of foundation they had. It was rock bottom. They went in and drilled
and drilled, filled the rock full of powder and blew it up, and we
had to get in there and clean it up and get that rock out. It was

dangerous [working], brother. We dug up some caps and powder in there that hadn't ever been blown. It was me and [an older fellow named Lovell].

We walked out and never did go back. Then I wasn't ever worried about myself; I just quit the quarry and went to work in the sawmill. It wasn't as dangerous. Old man J. E. Harvey, he owned the sawmill [and] he sawed all the lumber they used in the dam and building the shacks and things. They put up a lot of houses over there, the power company did, for their helpers. [After they finished the dam], they tore the houses down and moved them.

NOTES

1. Wright, Wade H., *History of the Georgia Power Company, 1855–1956.* Atlanta, Ga.: Georgia Power Co., 1957, p. 110.
2. Ibid., p. 111.
3. Ibid., pp. 115–16.

Tallulah Falls Dam and tunnel intakes, which diverted water several thousand feet downstream to Tugalo hydroelectric plant and dam. Put into service in 1913, it was the highest head hydroelectric plant in the East and generated 72,000 kilowatts. (Courtesy of Georgia Power)

Clearing the Land

Bennie Eller

When Al Story chose the history of the town of Burton as a research topic in Wig's senior English class, he sought out a person who could recount the clearing of the land for Lake Burton. That person turned out to be Bennie Eller. Like many of our Foxfire contacts, Mr. Eller's grandchildren and great-grandchildren have been students in the program at Rabun County High School, and other students were delighted to get to know him. Several years after Al's work, while we were compiling the materials for Foxfire 10, *it was interesting to discover that Bennie had worked in the same lumber camp where Ellene Gowder taught school (See "Personality Portraits," p. 303). The path of Mr. Eller's life's work also converged with other contacts whose interviews tell about the construction of Fontana Dam.*

I couldn't tell you the logging jobs I've been on. Just about spent my life on jobs thataway. I been everywhere, nearly, and worked. After I quit goin' I'd get so homesick.

I was just a little better than sixteen when I started. Back then you didn't have to have a work permit, and they'd take you on any kind of job. It ain't like it is now where you've got to be a certain age before you can work on something.

I helped clean off the Burton reservoir over there. It took us somewhere about a year and a half, cuttin' all the timber, clearing it off before they turned the water on to fill it up. We just went ahead an' cut that timber. They was a cleanup bunch come behind us and got all the brush and burned it right on the land. What was fit for anything they took out for lumber, and what wasn't fit for nothing, they just rolled it in big log piles and burned it. It was the only way they had of getting rid of 'em.

I was with Morse Brothers eight years. [Morse Brothers Lumber Company logged the timber all around Lake Burton.] I commenced with 'em on the head of Goshen—that's back at the head of Soquee River, and we got all that timber through Wildcat Creek, moved the camp up to Moccasin Creek, Plum Orchard, Charlie's Creek, up to the head of Tate City, and that's where we finished up at.

[When I was with Morse Brothers] I built railroad most of the time. My first two years I helped subgrade. We would level up the old railroad bed with mules and slip pads, haul that dirt away, and then they'd lay the track on it. I worked six years with a steam shovel, and I did grease-monkeyin'—all the oilin' and greasin'—whatever they had to do to build them trestles and cribs and things. Where we had to cross the river, we'd hang tongs on that dipper of the shovel, and [the operator would] swing me across the river and I'd hook 'em to the logs and they'd bring 'em back to build [trestles and cribs]. You know, they's lots of places where there was a rock cliff, and we had to build a big crib plumb along the rock cliffs and then take and fill in behind it with dirt to get the road where they could lay the track down.

[A crew of] about six or eight [Negro laborers] done the laying of the steel—the railroad steel and things. We'd get it graded off and fixed, and they'd come behind and lay the steel in. Sometimes we'd be two or three mile ahead of them with the road we were building.

Where we cleared the right-of-way off for the road, we had to shoot them big stumps with dynamite so the shovel could get 'em out. That's what I done the most of when I worked with the shovel. I'd commence off to the side and just take a big ole long crowbar and go down into the tap root and fill that with dynamite, then just blow the stumps out of there. By quitting time Saturday I'd have about forty or fifty stumps up where we could blow 'em up so we could start in with the shovel on Monday morning. By the time I got the last one lit, the first ones would be a-blowin' out. [Laughs.]

Back then we got thirty cents an hour. We'd start at seven and work straight through ten hours a day for three dollars. Sometimes after we'd quit work of an evening, we'd go in after we eat supper and load a load or two of acid wood (old chestnut timber) on them old flatcars. It would take us about two hours for a load or two of it, and they'd give us time and a half.

[At most, Morse Brothers had about fifty or seventy-five people working for them at one time.] They gave you your board free. They sure did feed, too. In the camps that I was in they generally had a woman cook—maybe two or three women would cook. They'd give you good food, anything you wanted if they had it, and just as much of it as you wanted. They had a dining room where we'd go to eat.

We'd sleep sometimes in car boxes, and part of the time we had camps built to sleep in. If we didn't have to stay too long, why, they'd just park them boxcars. They had plenty of 'em. They were as big as a freight box on a freight train, or there about it. Had beds and everything in 'em.

We'd go in and out to work of a mornin' on the old train. They had several awful train wrecks. Those old log trains would run right off the track. They'd wreck and break some of 'em all to pieces.

I had a lot of work and a lot of fun, too. [Laughs.] Old man Claude Day—he was the main supervisor over the whole job—me and him coon-hunted the biggest part of the time, two nights a week anyhow. I had three awful good coon dogs, and I'd take my coon dogs and keep 'em over there. We would go hunting around Moccasin, Wildcat, Popcorn, Plum Orchard, Tate City. Sometimes it would be twelve the next day before we got in, but my time would stay the same as if I was a-workin'. [Laughs.] I enjoyed myself what time I worked there.

The shovel man I worked [directly under] was a great big man; he used to weigh three hundred and some pounds. We had a lot of fun. If we'd go to cross a creek or anywhere, we'd get to planning how to get across it, and he'd catch two or three of us up pretty close to the water a-standing in a row and, first thing you know, he'd knock us every one in! [Laughs.] If you done him thataway he didn't laugh about it. When I'd swing that cable across the river to get them logs, lots of times I'd get out about midways in the river, and he'd let his brake off and dip me in. [Laughs.] We had a good time. We was always playing tricks on one another.

At Tate City, we had this [camp doctor]. He watched us as close as a hawk. We throwed him in the river lots of times. He'd push us in the river if he'd get a chance. We'd lay two-by-fours or two-by-sixes to walk across on rocks across the river, and he'd come out on that makin' his rounds, and he watched to see if any of us were a-standin' close, and then he'd run across, and then he'd sort of get around and jerk it out from under us and throw us in. [Laughs.] We acted a fool about as much as workin'. But it was a good company to work with.

I got one man out of the river one day up there while we were building trestle. He fell in, and he couldn't swim nor nothin', so it scared him. He grabbed a log down on the bottom. I jumped in that river, and they slipped me down, and I grabbed around him and fetched him out. He brought the log up out of the water in his arms. [Chuckles.] He'd 'a drowned right in there. It scared him. He couldn't swim nor nothin'.

I was bad to drink back then. [Laughs.] One time when I was about eighteen or nineteen years old, I came in one Monday after being drunk and thought to myself, "I am going to do something to make them fire me." [Laughs.] I went on out to work that morning and just sat on the bank while they worked. The foreman was an awful good feller, thought a lot of me. He would pass by me and say, "Hello" and keep going. Dinnertime came, and I went and ate dinner and came back and crawled back up on the bank. I never struck a lick.

After a while he came down through there again and started a-grinning and said to me, "Ben, you're wanting me to fire you. You're wanting off a few days. Sit right there all week if you want to; I ain't a-goin' to fire you. You're the best hand I have got." I got ashamed and got up and went to work.

That night he came to the camp and said, "Now, Ben, anytime you want to take two or three days, just tell me and when you come back here, your job will be here for you." [Laughs.]

When we didn't have a load of acid wood to load up, we'd get out of an evening and ride them lever cars. Go down to the commissary. They had a commissary we'd go to, and there was a little store near Moccasin, down there right before you get to LaPrade's Camp. We could get nearly anything you wanted there. Burton was just a little town with a store, and a few houses, and post office. There were about six or eight families that lived there. They called it "Old Burton." The store sold just about everything and anything that you could want.

I got into sort of a bad accident one night. The cook [who had just moved in] had one of the prettiest girls you'd ever see—that was before I was married. They was livin' in one of them old car boxes, and I met her one evening and said to her, "What about comin' down to see you tonight?"

"Come ahead," she said.

I went down there all friskied up. [I thought I was] real big, and I stumped my toe on one side when I was comin' in—car boxes are only about eight foot wide—pitched on across, and butted my head against the wall on the other side. [Laughs.]

I got married about two year before the job was over. I met my wife near where I lived, and she was thirteen when I married her. We [eventually had] nine children, six girls and three boys.

After [Morse Brothers] finished up at Tate City, we didn't move the camp no more. They tried to get me to go on with 'em to [the next job in] El Paso, Texas, but I wouldn't go. [From then on] I worked all the logging jobs, Buck Creek and Nantahala, and everywhere else. I worked four years over there at the TVA at Nottely and Hiawassee cleaning off them reservoirs. I just stayed on them about all the time.

Pulling an old crosscut saw was about the hardest job I ever done. I done that on Buck Creek for about three years. We had saws anywhere from five to eight foot long, and you had a man on each end. When me and another boy went to work at Nottely over there, they [first] put us to work with a bushhook. They come around directly and asked the boy with me, says, "Can you use a crosscut saw?"

He said, "Yeah."

He says, "Pick you a buddy."

He motioned for me just as soon as they done that. We cut timber over there all the time. We'd go ahead and cut all that timber off of the creek banks. They had a climber, he'd climb a way up in the top [of the trees] and tie [a cable], and they'd get a way off out yonder with a tractor, and we'd saw it down, and they'd pull it over. Some of it was down so far they'd have to let it go down into the water. I've stood there a half a day at a time in the water and sawed with a crosscut saw. One time we cut a big old holler maple. There was a limb over the creek, and we were down in a-cuttin' it off where they could get ahold of it with that winch to pull it out, and I kept feeling something tickling me on the side of the head. I thought it was a leaf. I'd shake my head thataway. Directly it got a little worse, and I turned around and there was a little young possum sitting there almost on my shoulder! [The tree] was holler and there was about eight or ten of them in there.

We had five saw crews with two to a saw, and we done the logging with horses or mules. All we did was drop the tree and saw it off as far as it would make lumber. We'd cut all kinds of trees, anything from pine, oak, hemlock—anything that come along. The best timber was shipped out for bridges and forms and things like that. We would go ahead and cut the timber, and the cleanup bunch would come behind us and get all the brush up in piles and burn it right on the spot.

[When I worked at Nottely, I lived at Hiawassee.] I had five miles to walk and then sixty miles to ride to the job. I'd get in at eleven o'clock of a night and leave at three [in the morning]. There was a year when I never seen my young'uns all week in daylight. Then I got a transfer from there back to Hiawassee. [The logging company] was movin' on, and they wanted me to go on with 'em, but I went down to Murphy to sign off. I wouldn't move. The head man on the job asked me. He says, "Would you like to work on?"

I said, "Yes, if I could get anything to do I would."

He says, "Come with me." He took me up to the personnel office, and says, "Give this fella a card that says to be at the bridge on Monday mornin'."

They transferred me back to Hiawassee so I'd be close to home. I helped build all them bridges through Hiawassee there then. I put in nearly two years with them. I night-watched most of the time at the bridgin' down there. Go down at three of the evening and then stay till one, and then the other feller'd come in and take my place. I didn't have nothin' to do only through the wintertime except I had lanterns, the big kind that hang up. We'd pour a form and then just had to keep them lanterns a-goin' so they was burnin' good to keep that [concrete] warm, keep it from freezin'.

I was the night watchman one time when we were putting a tunnel through a mountain. I had to go every hour through the night and punch the clocks. I could sleep the rest of the time. [But I didn't have a clock to wake me up.] There was a big spring coming out right above the little camp, and they had a water spout run into where I stayed, and I got me a can and I worked about a month gauging the can—a-getting it gauged and emptying out. I hung it up right over my face, and every hour that would run over and go to dripping out on my face and wake me up. I'd get up and go around and punch the clocks and things and come back and I'd empty it and hang it back up and lay back down and sleep an hour. [Laughs.]

I worked up there for about a year and a half, and then I quit that and I come to Ritter Saw Mill up here. I put in eight year and eight months up there, stackin' lumber up there. About ever' day we'd load two or three car boxes. We stacked it and it had to season out, and they shipped that. They had a company somewhere that took ever' bit of that lumber. We worked there rain or snow or shine; it didn't differ which it was. When the mill run, we worked. When it was snowing or raining we had an overcoat we put on but it run down the sleeves of them. I've had my clothes to freeze and break on me. And your hands—you couldn't tell you had ahold of a piece of lumber, only just by the weight of it, your hands would be so cold.

And at Sunburst, North Carolina, I worked up there on a logging job for a long time. I recollect two creeks come together, big creeks, and they had camps there. There was a little young'un got missing, and we hunted everywhere. They called in five camps, and they called every man in from every camp. Where the creeks come together—not far from where they lived—we hunted them creeks for miles and miles and miles, and we couldn't find him nowhere. And his mammy, she just rubbed all the skin off her hands, wringing them. We come back in, and they had a big old long wood heater, and it was in the fall of the year and they hadn't put no fire in it that night; they'd had papers put in it. We come in, and I happened to walk through the house, and I heard little papers a-rattling in that heater, and I looked, and the door wasn't latched. I pulled the

door open, and he was sitting in there rubbing his eyes. [Laughs.]
I grabbed him out and hollered, and mammy, she run and she
grabbed me, and she beat my face with a broom! And I never heard
so foul ever spoke in my life out of a woman!

Loggers pause in the midst of loading cut timber onto flat cars.

The Fontana Dam

In January of 1942, construction began on one of America's tallest dams. The Fontana Dam, as it was called, is located on the Little Tennessee River near the small village of Fontana, North Carolina. The site of the dam had been surveyed many years before by Aluminum Company of America (ALCOA) for generating power to refine aluminum, but government regulations regarding the dam's construction caused Alcoa to back away from the project. Later, the demand for aluminum during World War II resulted in a joint effort between Alcoa and the Tennessee Valley Authority: the government would build the dam and Alcoa would operate it.

Once the negotiations had ended, TVA went into Fontana and literally carved a town out of the woods. A hospital, school, dining hall, jailhouse, drugstore, community building, dormitories, cottages, tents, recreation center, etc., were all built in the small village of Fontana to make the dam workers feel at home while working out in the "middle of nowhere."

TVA worked between 5,000 and 7,000 people on the Fontana project. If they weren't working on the dam's construction itself, they were working a job in the village in the cafeteria or in one of the stores or offices. TVA worked three shifts twenty-four hours a day seven days a week until the construction work was finished in 1945. The overall cost of this project was $70,420,688.48. The height

*Fontana, one of America's tallest dams, is
480 feet high and 2,365 feet long.*

of the dam is 480 feet and its length is 2,365 feet. The 29-mile lake has 248 miles of shoreline and covers 10,640 acres. The dam, which is composed of 2,815,300 cubic yards of concrete and 760,000 cubic yards of earth and rock fill, has a generating capacity of 225,000 kilowatts.

The village of Fontana is still somewhat like it was when the workers lived there. Although some of the original buildings have been torn down and new buildings are in their places, many of the cottages are still there and are available to be rented as vacation quarters. The Fontana Village is now a resort with a movie theater, swimming pool, tennis courts, golf courses, and many other activities found in resorts.

The reservoir is still surrounded by a wilderness with the Great Smoky Mountains National Park bordering much of the lake and TVA owning the remaining land. Very little is available for private ownership.

Students Allyn Stockton, Stanley Prince, and Rance Gillespie went with Wig to Fontana to interview Stanley's grandfather, Jack

Fontana Village, built as a construction workers' housing project, still provides accommodations for modern visitors.

Prince, Sr. Of the many things Mr. Prince talked about, they found the part about his role in the surveying and construction of the Fontana Dam very interesting and followed it up with interviews with other people who live in Rabun County who had been involved with Fontana.

—Allyn Stockton

Interviews by Allyn Stockton, Stanley Prince, and Rance Gillespie.

Jack Prince, Sr.

Fontana was first surveyed in 1922 and '23. There's one dam site now that they call Needmore, and we surveyed that in 1927 and '28, and that survey for Needmore showed that it backed straight up the Little Tennessee [River] into Franklin, North Carolina. They've got a little dam way back in the mountains the other side of Franklin. It's what they call the Glenville Dam. That's the least dam there [on the Little Tennessee]. Then they come on down, and there's another one or two on Tuckaseegee [River]. The power

Jack Prince, Sr., still lives in Fontana.

company [TVA] bought all the land up and down the [Little Tennessee] River. They owned the biggest part of it.

[Fontana Dam] has been in good condition up till about eight or ten years ago. They had an earthquake that was pretty severe and shook things up pretty bad. It's had cracks in it, and they brought all kinds of different machinery in there and drilled holes in it. They've got it in pretty good shape now.

I worked on Fontana Dam about fourteen years. I was the first man ever sounded the [Little] Tennessee River for the dam. [Sounding] is when a cable is stretched across the river and [somebody on the shore] takes a transit, while somebody in a boat sticks a rod down [in the river]. If they hit sand, they'd wave their hand [to signal] it was sandy. If they hit rock, they did nothing. They wanted to see if it was hard—a lot of rock in it—to know if it would stand up, you know.

There were about thirty to thirty-five people up in the maps and surveying division. It was interesting work and a wonderful place to work in. They didn't do a thing in the world but put signal flags on these high tops when we were surveying the land. We'd go over to the courthouse [in Bryson City] and get the callings of all deeds for certain property. Some of them were big properties of thousands of acres. A feller would figure that to survey out a bunch of land like that would take years and years. In fact, they figured four years on it, but I'd been surveying for the power company for a lot of that land, and I knew where a lot of the corners were and where a lot of the roads that they planned on building [would be located]. We got started in there, and it took us about eighteen months to get that all done. And they were figuring that to be a three- or four-year-job!

We had about twenty-five to thirty [signal flags] between here and Bryson City. We'd just get up on the high peaks and get a good clear spot where we could get our bearings. Then someone would make aerial photographs. They called him a reconnaissance man. Someone on the ground would go to certain corner trees, paint them and make a mark [so the pilot could spot them and make photographs from the air].

I could actually take a compass and map, and walk up to most of the corners. They didn't know what in the world to think about me. It was kind of a gift to me. I'd done so much of it, I'd look at [the map] and get my bearing and direction, and I'd just take off. I'd look around a few minutes, and I knew that they were all marked. After a while, I'd holler at them and stick my rod in the air and boost'er up. They didn't want to have to read one over fourteen, fifteen, sixteen hundred feet.

[Later on] I got transferred out of maps and surveying and water control from Bryson City [where I used to work] to construction here [at Fontana].

Mary Ann Hollifield

I graduated from Rabun County High School in May of 1943. I went to work [at Fontana] soon after that, and I worked until October of that year. When I graduated from high school, my brother that lived at Fontana thought I could get a job. I went over and applied, and they put me right to work. All I had to have was my birth certificate.

We stayed in a dorm. They furnished us a place to live. It wasn't bad at all. There were two people to a room with two bunk beds in them. There was a waiting room [like a reception room]. There

Mary Ann Hollifield worked at the Fontana Dam site in her youth. Her son, Parker, is a teacher at Rabun County High School and her granddaughter Leigh Ann Smith is an active student in the Foxfire Program.

must have been a bathroom for every two rooms, and they had a laundry room. They also had a den mother or housemother for each dorm. I can't remember what we called her.

I think my wages at Fontana were something like twenty-three dollars a week. We thought it was fantastic pay because while I was going to high school, I worked at the Bynum [boarding] House and different places like that, and made maybe six or eight dollars a week, plus tips. That's all I made.

My hours at Fontana were from 3 till 11 P.M., the swing shift, they called it. We didn't work but forty hours a week, because I remember we'd get to come home occasionally. That twenty-three dollars was for forty hours of work.

At the beginning of my shift, I had to always make the coffee. I was responsible for it. After that time, the men who went to work at eleven would come in for breakfast, and that was around 10 P.M. We would take orders from the workers for how they wanted their eggs cooked and so forth.

We also had three shifts a day that did nothing but make sandwiches, and we had to pack lunches [for the workers]. I believe we would give them three sandwiches and a piece of fruit for their packed lunch, which they would eat in the middle of their shift.

The dining hall was really the largest place there. It had to seat probably 300 people a shift.

I never did go see the dam while they were building it, but after it was finished, I went back over there.

Bob Vickers

We poured a million yards of concrete up at Fontana Dam in four months. You know how high it is—480 feet. We worked all the time and never did stop. [We worked around the clock] Saturday and Sunday and all, twenty-four hours a day. The only time we would stop is if something would break down, and then, by God, everybody went to fix it!

I poured that—where that emergency tunnel is. We built that emergency tunnel in case it got too much water. That's the emergency spillway. When I helped build that, that was the first time I ever poured concrete over my head.

One time they dumped concrete on me 135 feet under the ground, right up to my nose. What happened was we called up

Bob Vickers served for many years as Rabun County ordinary or probate judge. He served as a concrete-pouring foreman at various dam sites, including Fontana.

there to the person dumping the concrete and told him to hold it, and he didn't. The way they got me out was they pulled me out with a rope. When I got up to where I could climb a ladder, I went on out the top. I don't think [anybody ever got covered up all the way, but there have been people killed up there]. I never worked in a tunnel [again] after I got covered up.

Over there, you had to do what you had to do. They didn't beg you to do it. They just told you to do it or go home, whichever you wanted to do. [Now] they beg you to work, but they didn't beg you to do it back then. If you didn't want to work, there was always someone waiting to take your place.

Claude Kelly

I poured the first and last bucket of concrete on Fontana Dam. We poured a million yards of concrete in one hundred days' time. That was when the dam was at the height of construction. At that time, about 4,000 people were working just on the dam.

There were usually about ten people in my crew, but when I went in the tunnels, I had about twenty. You had operators [in the tunnels] to operate the air gun. You also had tunnel mechanics, a couple of iron workers, a couple of carpenters, and a couple of pump operators.

The day shift was my regular shift, but anytime there was concrete poured in those tunnels, I was there no matter what time it was. I supervised the pouring of all the concrete in all the tunnels. Superintendent told me, "Whenever that concrete is being poured in that tunnel, you be there!" and I was. The only time you got off time was when you said, "I've got to be off," and then you had to find someone to work for you. The job I had, if a man didn't come in [at the end of the shift to relieve you] you stayed there till he did. I worked a lot of extra hours while Bob [Vickers] and them was coming home [to Rabun County] 'cause I was living over there [at Fontana]. I went to work lots of times and didn't come home for forty or fifty hours. We worked when it snowed and rained, seven days a week, twenty-four hours a day. Didn't make no difference. Didn't have no fire to stand by, either. We spent Christmas pouring concrete. The last two Christmases we were there, we took off but the ones before that, we didn't.

Claude Kelly served as a supervisor of the concrete pouring at Fontana Dam. For many years he ran a rock quarry business in Rabun County.

We had a tunnel over there where a railroad had to come through, and we had these tunnels where we switched the water back and forth according to where we poured concrete.

[To make the concrete] we had a rock crushing plant, and we had our big primary rock crushers over there. We manufactured our own sand and our own stone. We had a conveyor that took the rocks across the river into a big pile over there. It come out of that pile and went through all the secondary units and different screens [and sifted out] all the different sizes of stone. We conveyed from there to a concrete plant where we mixed it up. The only thing we brought in was cement. There we had five five-yard mixers sitting in a big circle, and each one of them would dump into the same hopper. Then we had a train with four buckets that came under there and picked up [the concrete]. It went out on the bridge where four cranes would set the buckets on [and off] them. Then the train switched tracks, and here he come back. There was two or three other trains on the track. It was a big circle.

We tried to pour concrete at sixty-five degrees winter and summer. In the summer, we had to use ice. We had a big ice plant there. Lots of times, we had to put tarps over the concrete for twenty-four hours till the concrete got set.

You pour the bottom of the tunnel so high, then put your track on it. It's like an ol' railroad track. A big, archlike, sixty-foot-long steel form goes on the track and it moves. The form has jacks on it where you can jack it up or pull the sides in. You fill the form full of concrete. Then the next day, pull the sides in and move [the form] ahead sixty feet. Jack it up tight against the end of what you've already poured and jack the other end up where it ought to be. Pour that section. Then the next day, get it up and get started on the next pour.

The overhead work [in the tunnels] was done with an air gun

The first bucket of concrete poured at Fontana Dam.

running right behind the forms, that you shot your concrete overhead with. It had a one-yard hopper that you put the concrete in, with the air gun under it. You'd open a door [on the hopper] and let your concrete fill it up; then shut the door. The gun had a pipe that went up and over into your form. You shot your concrete through it. You shot one cubic yard at a time. The gun used 125 pounds of air pressure going through a six-inch line. Why, it'd cut an 8 × 8 in half! I mean it was in there in a hurry! [The six-inch line from the gun] would float around [when shooting concrete] until it got buried in concrete. As the form filled up with concrete, you'd back up [the air gun] a little till you come out [of the form] with it. We'd get about two yards a minute. All you'd do is pull them big levers [that open the hopper doors], fill it up with concrete, push the door to put the air to it, and wham, it was gone! Just like that.

In certain places where you can't get to, to pour concrete, you take your cement and just barely dampen it just enough to where you can pack it. You'd just get in there and dry-pack it and tamp it in there good. You had an air tamper you'd use if you was in a space that you could use it. If you wasn't, you done it by hand.

Honeycomb is where you pour concrete and don't vibrate it in good like you ought to, and so it leaves a big ol' void. When you stripped the forms off of it, [the honeycomb] would stare you in the face and you had to dig it out and redo it.

At the height of construction, I'd say 6,000 or 7,000 people were over there [at Fontana construction village]. Very few people from Clayton had a house over there. Some of them stayed in places over there called Slab Town or Bee Cove. It was for people who couldn't get houses. It was where you could park your individual trailer [or] some of 'em built little shacks, using slabs or any kind of lumber they could get ahold of, just as long as they could eat and sleep there.

They started building houses the day they started building the dam. When I first went to work there, I lived in a tent furnished by the TVA, and when they got a dormitory built, why I had a good enough job to get a room. They charged us about two dollars a week for room and board. They got a half dozen houses finished one Friday afternoon, and I moved into one of them on Saturday. I had a three-bedroom house, and I paid about four or five dollars a month rent.

They had a post office, a grocery store, and a schoolhouse. They had a school set up for any kids that lived there. A lot of people taught two classes during the day [for extra money] and worked on the dam at night.

They also had little play areas for the children, and a ball field. There was lots of ball-playing in the summertime by different people on different shifts. Some played in the morning, some in the evening, and some at night.

It was a big village with people working 'round the clock, stirring at all hours, and in and out at all times. After a while, [the noise] didn't bother you. It was a city. They had buses [that took the workers back and forth from the village to the dam]. Some had company trucks. I had one. It depended on the job you had.

TVA was a good job, best any of us had ever had when we went to it. We was getting 10 cents an hour around here [in Rabun County] and they started us out over there at 45 cents an hour. That wouldn't be no money today, but we thought it was pretty good then. Supervisors were getting around $1.37 per hour, and I worked in a tunnel, so that gave me about 25 cents [an hour] extra for working underground. We got paid twice a month. They didn't have insurance and things like they got today. Of course, if you got hurt on the job, they'd look after you.

TVA was the best jobs around for a long time. Lord! I've seen 400 or 500 people stand out there waiting [for a job]. TVA tried to give so many people jobs out of each area [of the Tennessee River Valley]. They came to Clayton and took applications at the courthouse. They let you fill out a form, and then they called a half a dozen of us to go to work. Of course, afterward, they called several others [to work]. Very few of the people that came to the dam hoping to get a job got on that way.

[Every worker at Fontana Dam was required to wear an identification badge which was simply a circular badge with an identification number on it. Each worker also had a tab.] It was a little piece of brass about an inch wide and two inches long with the same number on it as your badge. When you went to work, you had to pick up your tab at the time office. Then you had to turn it in that afternoon so they'd know you'd been there. Folks had to wear the badges on the job, and there was a time checker that come around and checked your number off. Then he'd go back to the time office and they had two checks on you. They checked you out on the job to be sure you hadn't slipped off somewhere. If you were a supervisor, you filled out a time card on everybody under your supervision. All you did was just their names down on the card and the hours they worked and what they done—took about ten minutes to fill the cards out. You had a white card for regular time and a different color for overtime. When the job was over, we were supposed to turn in our badges, but I kept mine as a souvenir.

There's some steps going up on the dam there at the overlook building where you look off in them spillways. The last pour of concrete was on those steps. You can see some little round places on top of that little parapet wall going up the steps. I had took what change I had in my pocket and finished [the coins] in that pour. Somebody took the coins out but you can still see right where every piece of it was.

John Lee Patterson

I started working at Fontana Dam in 1943. I helped build the dam from the foundation all the way up to the top. I worked [there] thirteen months, seven days a week, excepting one day off every two weeks.

There were a lot of key men from Rabun County that was on that dam, lots of laborers. I could call you off a whole lot from all over the county. There was 2,800 people worked on that project at the time I went in there, and there was about the same force till sometime around September 1944, I guess. They were organized just like Uncle Sam's army.

When I first went there, I run a wagon drill, shooting out the loose rock over in the east keyway. A wagon drill is a drill on wheels. It's like a jackhammer, but bigger; it's all hydraulic-operated, and you drill a hole back in the wall with a drill. They had five that worked in there then, four from the Forest Service. I already knew how to drill [because of work I had done] in the rock quarries in Rabun County. I was called the troubleshooter because if anything went wrong with the drills, I fixed them.

I worked on that job for the first three months, then one of the men quit or got fired at the mixing plant, the same shift I was on. So they looked at my application and saw that I'd signed up for different jobs, so the superintendent of personnel came up to me and asked me if I wanted to have a little raise at a different job in a nice warm place. And I said I sure would. Who wouldn't? So he carried me and showed me about it, and I started to work mixing the cement then.

They had just poured the foundation on that dam and on the place where the powerhouse would be. We poured one day in February of 1944 over 1,000 yards an hour—8,270 yards that day. That was written up on the bulletin board, and nobody ever capped it. See, we never stopped. If something went wrong, we had those troubleshooters that would fix it. Five minutes' loss would lose us about 15 to 20 yards of pouring. For fifteen minutes, you'd lose about 100 yards of pouring concrete. That was some rough job. I made good money at it, though.

I operated the mixer on the "graveyard" shift for thirteen long months. They poured concrete for twenty-four hours a day, but I

John Lee Patterson in the Foxfire classroom.

poured on the graveyard shift from eleven to seven in the morning. We got thirty minutes off at four in the morning to get a little dinner if we wanted to, but the mixer kept running.

I had a dispatcher to tell me what type of concrete was [to be] poured. Now when you was pouring "mass concrete," that was for the big forms of the solid dam. That was big rock, sand, small gravel, and cement mixed. The "grout" [sand and cement] was for when they finished it. They'd pour so many yards of grout mixing when they finished. I got my order from the dispatcher to do that. All I done was operate the machinery that mixed it, and saw that [the machines] were running all the time. We had a machinist, an electrician, a welder, and a troubleshooter at all times. If anything broke down, they'd jump right on it and fix it and get it back into operation.

They'd pour one section, then skip one, then pour another— each section twenty foot long. Then they would leave them overnight and then take out the forms and make more sections. There was a two-inch pipe running through them forms to keep the concrete hot. I've seen them pour concrete no matter what, whether it was five degrees or eight degrees or raining—no matter what. It might slow them down a little, but they wouldn't stop.

Every bit of concrete that went into that dam was weighed on scales. Everything was electric- or hydraulic-powered, and almost everything was automatic. I just dumped concrete into the mixer from the dispatcher. It would mix for three to five minutes, and I'd be dumping one every three to five minutes.

There was a big hopper that the concrete went through. If you don't believe some concrete went through that thing, it was a half-inch of solid steel, and every once in a while where that concrete hit that hopper, it would wear holes in it, and they'd have to patch it. They'd do all the repairs on the swing shift once every week. They had people that fixed just about anything there.

I was lucky. I was inside a good warm place, just looking at a chart and watching my machines running [but sometimes the work was dangerous]. I knew a lot of them who got killed there. They had a slide in there in the winter of '43, a cave-in in what is called the eastern keyway, where they were cutting back into the mountain to get to the solid rock foundation for the dam. They had a slide in there and had some laborers in there mucking out—that's cleaning up dirt and stuff like that. Slip pans was what they loaded it onto, so a crane could carry it out. The slide slid in on them and killed one and covered two up, and it took eight hours to get them out.

Then, one time, there was a foreman that fell off the top of the dam. He went to sleep and fell off the side and landed into a big pile of lumber about 150 feet [below].

And there was a colored fellow who was helping in the quarry where they crushed all the rocks into gravel, and they was pulling a shot of dynamite, and they had a barricade up around the gas tanks made out of big logs. They told everybody to move out, so he tried to hide behind them to keep from having to go so far, and a big rock went between a crack in the logs and cut his head slap off. I mean cut it off.

I guess after the whole thing was finished, about twenty-eight people got killed. You take a construction job like that, somebody's gonna get hurt every once in a while or get careless and not watch themselves, and something falls on them or something. Different things happen. Trucks turn over. Machinery turns over. Like I saw a gas [powered] shovel fall over that mountain, and it went 300 feet down that mountain turning over like a car, and it didn't even kill the fellow. I think it just broke one of the bones in his arm just above the wrist. He stayed in the cab of that thing all the way down the mountain. It looked like a beer can mashed up when they started salvaging it. I mean it tore that thing all to pieces.

That was one more job. All of it was dangerous. Any construction job was dangerous. We had safety men there, but they couldn't be everywhere. They had security officers, and we had to wear certain safety gear and a safety hat and shoes. Some would pull them off and didn't use them.

Then they poured one man in the dam. A colored man. He was cutting with a straight spade around the form. When they poured two or three feet of concrete, the men would get in there and use big vibrators to get in and settle the concrete down. Then a bunch of men would go around smoothing it so it would have a smooth surface when it hardened. When they started to pour, they would pour five yards at a time, and they had a concrete bucket that swung out over the form and would dump five yards at a time. And when the crane got ready to dump it, the foreman would use signals and get all of his men out of the form, and then the crane would automatically drop the concrete into the form, and they would keep dumping until it got up to about six or eight feet in a twenty-foot by twenty-foot form, and they would do it in sections. There was this fellow in there working and he didn't hear the foreman tell him to get out. Course there was a lot of racket with the steelwork going on and the cranes running. He was working in there facing toward the form, and when the concrete hit him, it slapped him up against the side of the form. It didn't kill him right then, but when they stripped the form, there he stood, set up in the concrete. They never could trace him down to where he was until they stripped the form, and there he was a-standing there with a hoe in his hand, and they just slipped him out.

SOURCES

Brewer, Alberta and Carson Brewer. *Valley So Wild: A Folk History*. Knoxville, Tenn.: East Tennessee Historical Society, 1975.

The Fontana Project: A Comprehensive Report on the Planning, Design, Construction, and Initial Operation of the Fontana Project. Washington, D.C. Government Printing Office: Technical Report No. 12, 1950.

Folklore

Over the years, Foxfire students have collected folk beliefs and legends of the area. We have selected a few narratives that focus on or come from communities mentioned in this volume: Burton, Tallulah Falls, Fontana Village. Some of the stories are preceded or followed by commentary from Barbara Duncan, a folklorist and Foxfire Teachers Network Coordinator. (Not only folklore but also fiction has sprung from local communities. Burton is the source for Stuart Woods's novel *Under the Lake.*)

The Witch's Grave

A student in our school told the folklore class about a witch's grave. See the interview with Don Patterson.

Where Lake Burton is now, there used to be the town of Burton, and to build the lake they had to move the whole town. There was churches and graveyards and things, so they had to dig up the graveyards and move all the bodies to another graveyard. A lot of people who knew people that were buried there and had kinfolks there really protested, and they left some of the graves. And they say there's a witch there and everytime you go you'll find new flowers on the grave 'cause somebody keeps putting new flowers on the grave. But nobody knows who it is. And they say you can go up there anytime and there'll be flowers on the grave and that weird things grew on it. Somebody went up there and tried to make it stop growing, whatever it was, but they just say that the woman that's buried there is a witch.

Monster Catfish at Burton

Tombo Ramey heard this legend from some men who went scuba diving at Burton Dam.

Some boys went down scuba diving at Burton Dam to just look around. They were all down there, and they saw some catfish as big as they were. They got scared and came up and said they were never going back down there again.

Another student tells us about the catfish in Burton Dam.

Divers have been down salvaging things and stuff, and they come up and swear they'll never go down again, and say they saw a catfish big as people. The divers at Anchorage and La Prade's [boat docks], when they come in, you know, they'll be there just swearing that they'll never go back down again. The catfish are so big they're scared of 'em and they're bigger than they are. Big as a grown man. But I won't believe it till I see it.

Historical legends are important not so much as factual historical accounts, but as accounts that satisfy the human need for drama and intrigue. The following legends represent an important link between people and places in our community. There have been many documented deaths in Tallulah Gorge. Some committed suicide, some fell, and many were killed in mishaps on the river. Though the average visitor need not fear Tallulah Gorge, it is not a place to be foolhardy. Moviegoers might be interested to know that scenes from Deliverance *were filmed there.*

Lover's Leap at Tallulah

We collected this Tallulah Falls legend from Ollie Dyer, who works at the Tallulah Falls Park. She referred us to a postcard inscribed with the legend.

I asked the man who owns this place if the Lover's Leap story that's on the card was true, and he says, if it's not true, it must have some truth in it because the story was told to his grandfather when he bought the land here just a few years after the Indians were driven out from here. So it's possible. There's a drop of about 900 feet from that ledge of the rock to the riverbed that's known as Lover's Leap, and it would've been quite a place to get rid of somebody, because the river, then, went on through here, until Georgia Power Company bought and dammed it.

They say that Indians threw the white man off—he was one of the first men that came into, or settled this area. He and the Indian girl [Tallulah] fell in love, and the Indians didn't want him in the tribe, and they didn't want her to leave. So they took him out to Lover's Leap Point and tossed him off into the river, and she jumped after him. That's the story.

Dennis Dodgins heard this version of Lover's Leap.

Lover's Leap is in Tallulah Falls Gorge. This is where an Indian fell off one time. This Indian was a great lover to another Indian mate. So when this Indian fell off, the woman just jumped off after him.

Clarence Bramblett tells us the version that he heard about Lover's Leap.

Well, one time there was this little boy and his sister, and his mama and daddy got killed in a car wreck. They wouldn't put the kids in the same orphanage, so they separated them. When they got out of the orphanage, they were about eighteen years old. They met each other and they fell in love, and about a year after they were going together, they got married. When they found out that they were brother and sister, they went to the Tallulah Falls Gorge, and they jumped off and killed theirselves.

Lover's leap legends are common throughout the United States, often as stories told to tourists. In many cases, they are told as legends of Native American lovers, which seem doubly appealing to tourists but half as likely to have happened.

The Hermit That Lived in Tallulah Gorge

Mrs. Dyer tells us this story about an old man who used to live in Tallulah Gorge.

There was an old hermit that lived in a cave down here, but he has been gone for years. There was a man, I believe his name was Ledford, that used to live down below what used to be the Lodge, down there below the Power Company Village. He had been married, and his wife had died, and it upset him so much he just didn't want to be around with people. That's why they say he went off in there. He stayed down in there for a time and slept in a cave that's down in the gorge. And he just didn't want to be where people were.

I've seen him. He used to bring old little bundles of kindling he'd cut, and bring out and sell it and get whatever he needed, like salt and maybe a little bacon, and things from the store that was out there. And then World War II came on, and he came out. He said that he had stayed long enough, that he'd come out and help win that war.

Man Buried in Foundation

Mrs. Dyer shared this account with us about the Tallulah Dam.

I have heard that there were one or two black people that were working on the Tallulah Dam. They had no relatives, nobody knew where they came from or anything. From the things that I was told, they fell in while they were pouring, and they just were never fished out. It was purely accidental. Of course, there was not any of the machinery like you have now, that was used in building that. So much of it was hand work that would be [done with] machinery now.

Stories of people being buried alive in foundations can be traced back thousands of years among the Celtic and Finnish people, and even in India. The Romans, when they invaded Britain in the early first century, wrote about the pagan customs of the Celtic people (ancestors of the Scots, Irish, and Welsh) including burying a sacrifice in the foundation of buildings. These stories have become part of the Arthur and Merlin legends.

Folklorists have turned their attention to modern legends, which include: the accidental entombment of people in the foundations of big buildings in the cities; workers falling into vats of molten metal or molten chocolate, their bodies never to be recovered; the inclusion of workers' bodies in the concrete of the Hoover Dam, and the big dams out West; workers buried alive in the foundations of bridges and canals. These legends have been collected in Ohio, Indiana, Nevada, Missouri, North Carolina, and Georgia.

Often the person entombed is a poor person, or a minority person, with the implication that he or she isn't important enough to stop work to recover the body. Perhaps this legend expresses one of our fears in the industrial age: that "the work" has a life of its own, more important than our own life and death.

Thanks to Jan H. Brunvand (University of Utah) for sharing similar stories from his files; thanks also to Kenny Goldstein (University of Pennsylvania) and Marilyn Motz (Bowling Green State University).

Witches at Burton—Don Patterson

As one will observe, Don is a gifted talker with a good memory for detail. He is from a big family who once lived in the Burton community. John Lee Patterson, who talked to us about Fontana Dam, is Don's brother.

My grandaddy, Lee Frady, told me several stories that took place where Burton Lake is now. That was his fields down in there below Burton Bridge. He told me he bought that from the government in the 1800s and gave fifty cents an acre for a hundred acres of it.

He said that Hiley Bullard lived across Tallulah River from him on Bullard Mountain, her and her daddy. They forded the rivers then with wagons and things like that—no bridges were across it or anything. Back then it rained more than it does now, and that river'd get level with the banks. She could cross that river when it was level with the banks.

She'd come over to his house to buy milk and eggs and stuff like that from him. He said one time it had been raining for a week and the river was out of the banks, and she come across that river. As she came up, she was wanting some milk. He didn't hardly know what was going on. But he said he knew that she was a witch when she came up there with that river out of the banks—they wouldn't let her have anything but buttermilk after they found out that: if they'd let her have sweet milk, just plain milk, as long as she could keep [her milk] from spoiling, they never could get any milk from their cows. After a few minutes, she went on in to get her buttermilk. He said, "How in the world did she get across that river?" When she came out, he said, "Hiley, how in the world did you come across that river?"

She said, "Oh, I made me a horse."

He just let it go at that.

The next day, after the river went down, my granddaddy said, he was down looking to see how bad [the flood had] damaged his fields down there. This Philyaw fellow that joined my daddy's land across the river was also checking his fields. They run into each other and got to talking, and this Philyaw fellow said to my grand-daddy, "I got up this morning and I was never in such a fix in my life." He said, "I want you to look at my hands."

He said he looked at his hands and they looked like they'd been drug across rocks and things.

He said, "My knees is the same way. I feel just like I been rode to death."

That was who she made a horse out of to come across that river. They know pretty well that's what took place.

Stories of witches spoiling cows' milk are common in Appalachian traditions, from New England through Pennsylvania Dutch country and in the South. The belief is also common that if you give a witch something, she (or he) has power over you. Stories of witches "riding" someone, usually in a nightmare, appear in many European traditions and have been documented by David Hufford in The Terror That Comes in the Night.

Then one time, his sow, you know his hog, had ten pigs. They was nice pigs. Hiley Bullard seen 'em and told him, "I want two of those."

He said, "Hiley, I can't let you have them."

"I got to have them."

Back then they had to have stuff for their winter food, back in the 1800s. They couldn't just let it all go like they do now, sell all their hogs and everything. He said, "I got to keep them for my own meat to go through till next year."

She said, "If you don't let me have them, they won't do you any good."

Sure enough, he said, he went out the next morning and every one of those pigs were just running around the edge of the pen with their backs bowed up. He said it went on for several hours and every one of them dropped dead. She killed them all, see. She didn't have to be there.

Just like I was telling you before, if you ever let a witch have milk, as long as they keep it sweet, they can get all your milk. You can't get any milk. If he had let her have them two hogs, he'd never have had any meat. He could have went ahead and killed the ones he kept and cured it and everything [but it would have] disappeared. See, that's the way a witch operates. If they got something that you let them have or sold to 'em or whatever, as long as that's intact and good, they can clean your plow on other stuff. As long as you have it, they can clean you out.

The belief that giving a witch something gives him or her power over you reflects the idea of transference: that a part can represent the whole. (In poetry we call it metonymy.) This is common in Appalachian traditions of healing and witchcraft. In witchcraft beliefs, the idea is that if a witch has something of yours, he or she can act on that object and those acts will affect you. This is a universal belief—from ancient traditional beliefs in Africa (ste-

*reotyped as "voodoo dolls") to modern "psychics" doing readings
or finding lost persons by holding an object that once was theirs.*

*Witches are also believed, in Appalachian tradition, to be able
to act on a person at a distance.*

Then this other feller by the name of Teems was a witch. If
you're familiar with that area this side of Burton Bridge, I believe
they call that Devil's Race Path. Back then it was natural for deer
and bear and stuff to be in there. People hunted them for meat.
The dogs would run 'em up on a high ridge and they'd shoot 'em—
that's against the law now. They catch you doggin' a deer and you're
gone. Anyway, this feller went up one afternoon to get him a deer.
He said his dogs struck one down in the cover over there and he
was up on the high ridge waitin' on him. He had a muzzle-loader,
and all of a sudden this great big buck come right down toward
him. He waited till he got pretty close, and he throwed that rifle
up and bam! He knowed he hit him right between the eyes, and
he didn't run off. He just kicked up his heels and turned around
and snorted like he was saying, "Come on, buddy, come on again."
He said he loaded that muzzle-loader again right quick and pulled
down and bam! He said he knowed he hit it right between the eyes.
He said [the deer would] just kick up his heels and snort and
wouldn't pay him any attention.

Those people was up on things like that witch stuff. Silver would
kill one, you know. He reached in his pocket, took out a dime like
that, and said, "I will get you."

He just scraped that silver off that dime with his knife like that,
put it down in the barrel, loaded it, throwed it up [against his
shoulder to shoot that deer] like that, and said when he did, here
was this man standing there saying, "You wouldn't shoot me, would
you?" He said, "I was just teasing with you."

I believe I'd've shot 'im.

Now, he didn't shoot him, though. He knew 'im. Yeah, he said
he knew he was a witch then. He was just kiddin' with him. That's
the way your witches were.

BIBLIOGRAPHIC RESOURCES
COMPILED BY BARBARA R. DUNCAN

For anyone interested in urban legends:
Brunvand, Jan H. *The Vanishing Hitchhiker.* New York: W. W. Norton, 1981,
    and others by Brunvand: *The Mexican Pet, The Choking Doberman,* and
    Curses! Broiled Again.
Brunvand has established the "urban legend" as a familiar genre through his
    books and columns.

On occupational folklore among steelworkers:
Dorson, Richard. *Land of the Mill Rats.* Cambridge: Harvard University Press,
    1981.
A collection of occupational folklore from steelworkers in Calumet, Illinois.

About folklore and how to collect it:
The American Folklife Center's pamphlet *Folklife and Fieldwork.* Washing-
    ton, D.C.: American Folklife Center, 1990.
To obtain a copy, write The American Folklife Center, Library of Congress,
    Washington, D.C. 20540.
The best brief introduction to the field of folklore and its methods.

Ives, Edward D. *The Tape-recorded Interview: A Manual for Field Workers
    in Folklore and Oral History.* Knoxville, Tenn.: University of Tennessee
    Press, 1980.
A more in-depth introduction to doing fieldwork.

Introduction to the field of folklore:
Brunvand, Jan H. *The Study of American Folklore: An Introduction.* New
    York: W. W. Norton, 1968, 3d ed., 1986.

Dorson, Richard M., ed. *Handbook of American Folklore.* Bloomington, Ind.:
    University of Indiana Press, 1983.

Toelken, Barre. *The Dynamics of Folklore.* Boston: Houghton Mifflin, 1979.
All are excellent introductions to the field of folklore, on the level of a high
    school/college textbook.

Folk Arts and Crafts:
Eaton, Allen H. *Handicrafts of the Southern Highlands.* New York: Russell
    Sage Foundation, 1937; rpt. New York: Dover, 1973.
The classic collection of Appalachian folk arts and crafts.

Jones, Michael Owen. *Exploring Folk Art: Twenty Years of Thought on Craft, Work, and Aesthetics.* Ann Arbor, Mich.: UMI Research Press, 1987.
The most thoughtful work on folk art and its makers.

Vlach, John Michael, and Simon J. Bronner, eds. *Folk Art and Art Worlds.* Ann Arbor: UMI Research Press, 1986.
Distinguishes folk art and fine art and all their interconnections.

Whisnant, David. *All That Is Native and Fine: The Politics of Culture in an American Region.* Chapel Hill and London: University of North Carolina Press, 1983.
Folklore and folk art and how they have been used, misused, and exploited in the South.

Witchcraft and Ghost Stories:
Hand, Wayland D., ed. *The Frank C. Brown Collection of North Carolina Folklore,* vols. 6 and 7. Durham: Duke University Press, 1964.
The classic compilation of beliefs and superstitions of all kinds.

Hufford, David J. *The Terror That Comes in the Night: An Experience Centered Study of Supernatural Assault Traditions.* Philadelphia: University of Pennsylvania Press, Publications of the American Folklore Society, 1982.
The nightmare and the experience of waking up to find ghosts in the room are documented, analyzed, and placed in the context of beliefs and traditions worldwide.

Reimensnyder, Barbara (now Duncan). *Powwowing in Union County: A Study of Pennsylvania German Folk Medicine in Context.* New York: AMS Press, 1989.
Folk healing and its relation to witchcraft in a Pennsylvania County; these methods and stories are related to Appalachian traditions.

Hard Times—

AS TOLD BY THE EXPERIENCED

Melvin Taylor

During the summer and fall, one of the common sights around Clayton, Georgia, is a green Dodge pickup, the tailgate of which is usually loaded with snap beans, sweet corn, or purple-topped turnips, a regular rolling produce market operated by Mr. Melvin "Bean Man" Taylor. Even though he farms tens of acres of vegetable fields in the early morning hours, he always finds time to peddle his produce on the street corners and parking lots of town. A big man with rough tan skin, a deep powerful voice with a strong Southern mountain accent, Melvin loves people and he loves to talk. His jolly face crinkles when he laughs, which is often, and people know they get more than just vegetables when they buy from the "Bean Man."

Part of an extended family of our community supporters, Mr. Taylor was recommended to us by his wife, Janie P. Taylor. She knew he had endured many hardships during his childhood and that he would represent a wealth of information. She was right. He knew firsthand about the Depression, especially about things like school, farming, and how life in the thirties was different than it is today. He is filled with all kinds of stories. Mrs. Taylor also talked eagerly during the interview, reminding him of various points: "Now, Melvin, talk about this," and "Don't forget that!"

Melvin Taylor swings comfortably on his porch.

Interview by Jenny Lincoln and Celena Rogers.

Well, I lived here in Rabun County during the Depression. I can remember times was bad here, and in 1931, before I went to school, my dad went to Claymont, Delaware. He worked in a Ford Motor Company and in a steel factory there. In a few years [work began] to wind down, and they laid 'em all off, and we came back home to Georgia. But, anyway, we just moved. Like my mother always said, we moved thirty-six times! [Laughs.] Just one place to another.

My uncle had a sawmill, and we moved over here on Burton Lake. At that time there wasn't ten houses on Burton Lake. We fished, and lived on fish. Our cow run wild in the woods. She got into still beer, where they made moonshine whiskey, and she'd come home every night loaded with that. We had to tie her to a tree and put hobblers on to milk her.

Anyway, we lived there, and we went from one sawmill camp to another. That was the only business there was in Rabun County—sawmills. My dad made a dollar a day working at the sawmill. You didn't get money. You got to order it [in credit] at the store, and you'd take that and get whatever groceries you needed, or whatever you had to have. And if you needed shoes, it was the same way. So we got one pair a year, and if you wore them out in the win-tertime, you didn't need any in the summer. That was it. I used to tote wood and go with my feet wrapped up with a sack on top of my shoe.

When we moved over here at the head of Timpson Creek, I started to school. I was seven years old. I went to first grade up here at Clayton and made it fine. We rode an old bus—an A Model Ford that had a homemade hickey [carriage] on it. You know, they didn't build 'em then like they do now. That was the hardest riding thing that ever was. The second year, at Christmastime, the teachers in the state of Georgia hadn't been paid in six months, so families had to pay two dollars and a half a month for each student—or go home. I went home.

After that we moved to Germany [Mountain, near Clayton] and farmed. Of course, most people farmed back then. That was about all you could do to keep from starving to death. We lived on Mr. Bynum's farm. He had two old steers, and that was what we made a crop with—animals. And that's "some fun" plowing them things. Me and my daddy hewed cross ties with an ax in the wintertime, and we'd bring 'em [by oxen] to Clayton on Saturday to sell 'em. I guess it's about ten or twelve miles, and it would take us from daylight that morning till ten o'clock that night to take them slow things [steers] to Clayton and back. And we'd sell the cross ties and buy groceries.

When the Depression began coming on, it was harder to get [even] a little money. Dad used to give us a bushel of corn for Christmas, and we'd carry that thing to Clayton. You couldn't get a red cent of money. You had to trade it for whatever was in there. And every store—grocery store and stuff—in Clayton had a pigpen, and a cow lot, and a chicken coop behind the building. So you brought whatever you had into town, and you traded it for whatever you needed in the store.

We had a real hard time, and a lot of people did without food. If you didn't grow it on a farm, then you were in bad trouble. In the section there they started passing out commodities like they do now, and we'd walk all the way from [Germany Mountain] to get 'em. They had some pretty good groceries. I remember they give out white celery, that bleached [celery]. Nobody didn't like it. I did. The rest of the kids wouldn't eat that celery. I'd take care of that.

I'll just be honest with you. It took all of us in the family day and night a-trying to keep food in our mouths. During the Depression days, I guess [the family had] one [child] come on about every two years, but in all they was eight of us. I was the oldest, and my youngest sister was a month and a half old when I went in the service. She was born in October—the baby of the family.

It just took us all scratching around to try to keep from starving to death. We used to go over there in Cathey's orchard, and scratch apples out of the snow. [Laughter.] It was awful good. To live, we [would get] poke salad and the wild greens that grow on the creek bank. Me and my brother would go down Blacks Creek all the way to Dillard with a sack and get it full of poke salad. It would take you all day nearly, by the time you walked back home. But that was food, you know. That went good with corn bread and maybe a little salt meat. And we always had a cow—that saved our life. Refrigerators and all that stuff had never been invented. People, if they had enough money, had an icebox and an iceman come by and put a chunk of ice in there. We kept our milk in a springhouse or in a well or somewheres to keep it cold.

We kept rabbit boxes all the time to catch rabbits, you know. Every morning before school we'd go check them things before daylight to see if we had one. [We'd] cut down a dead tree, a hollow tree, where you could kind of see through on one end, where the rabbit thought he could go through, and then you put a trap door on it, and put something in there to bait him with, an apple or something, and he'd go in it then. When he hit that little ole trigger there, the door'd fall down behind him.

We had a possum dog too. We'd hunt possums at night. People caught a lot of old possums back then; you didn't see 'em on the road like you do now. By grannies, a lot of people around had 'em a pen back there behind their house, and they'd put 'em in there and feed 'em—fatten 'em up just like fattening up a hog till they got 'em good and fat, and then they made supper out of 'em.

[People ate] all kind of wild game, anything. That's the reason the turkeys and deer and everything disappeared from Rabun County. When I was a boy, I don't remember ever seeing a turkey, and I was in my late thirties before I ever saw the first deer. I mean live. Now you'd see a picture, but I'd never seen a *live* deer.

We didn't have many clothes then. They was scarce. Except for some old work clothes, about two or three changes of clothes is all we had. When we come in from school, we took off our best that we wore to school and put them up, and for work we put on our other stuff.

My mama used to make the clothes for the girls out of feed sacks, fertilize sacks, and stuff like that. You know, back then they put feed up in hundred-pound sacks that had prints—cloth, you know. My mother was a pretty good seamstress. She could take some of my dad's old pants he'd wore out and make the children a pair of pants out of them. We were just about two years apart, you know, and just one size would pass on down. [Each younger child] was always one size smaller, and the other'n would grow into 'em right quick—it didn't take long. There was so many of us, there wasn't nothing that was throwed away or wasted.

They didn't have no washing machines; you'd go down to the spring or wherever you got your water and [boil your clothes in] a big ole black wash pot. They had a rub board back then—a thing that had crinkles on it, and you'd rub 'em over it. Had a big old table there, and you'd put 'em on there and beat 'em with a paddle. My job a lot of times was to keep the pot a-boiling the clothes, and beating that paddle, and tending the kids. Usually, your youngest baby, you'd set it up on the clothes, and put a little syrup on its hand, and put a feather in its hand. It would set there half a day at a time just pulling it off one finger, and it would stick to the other'n. Just pull it off of that'n, just back and forth.

We made the toys we had. We made wooden-wheel wagons out of sourwood trees or black gum. We'd just cut down a big ole tree and take an ole crosscut saw and saw 'em up [to make the wheels]. Sometimes we'd try to burn holes through 'em, but lots of times there was somebody in the community that had an ole auger, you know, that had a handle on it, and we'd borrow that. You'd turn that around and bore out all the wheels. We made pine [wagon frames], and that's what we rode. I've carried them things for miles through the mountains, get on top of the mountain and ride her down. Just fly. We made some wagons that had steering wheels, and brakes, and everything on 'em, but most of 'em you'd steer 'em with your feet. You just steered 'em through the woods. We used to haul wood on 'em, too—have trailers behind 'em, pull that thing, and haul our wood.

My daddy had an old T-Model Ford "strip down"—what we called a "strip down." It didn't have nothing but the hood and the motor on it and a wooden bed on it. Everytime he would crank that thing you'd have to jack up the back wheels before you could get the motor started. [Laughs.] See they didn't have no starter. There was a big ole crank on the front end and you'd go around that thing [and turn the crank by hand]. Sometimes that thing would turn and backfire and go the other way. And, boys, you was lucky if you didn't break your arm or something. But it was lot easier to turn it over if you had one of the wheels jacked up, see. You jack that up, and get it cranked, and then get it going good. [T-Models] had three pedals. One of 'em you mashed in and that put it out of gear. When you let that thing out right quick, boys, it took off! That's the way you went off the jack, you know. I believe it changed gear one time. And then you had your brake pedal over here, and the other pedal was your reverse, a middle one. That was all, at that time, that was on the transmission.

If you'd get it going down the grade pretty good, I'd say it would probably make thirty mile a hour, somewhere in that neighborhood. But you couldn't hardly pull a mountain. You'd start up, and that thing would bog. It just didn't have the power. It stalled up on Germany Mountain and run backward down there, and turned over, and pinned my mother and daddy under it and killed my brother. And my other brother was in the back, and it throwed him out, and he went down that mountain. Daddy told him to go to John McCurry's down there where they'd started up the mountain, to get help. He went down there, and they came up there and got the car off of Mama and Dad. It broke Dad's ribs all on one side, and burnt Mama. Boy, that gas run out of that thing. It was up front, and it took the skin off of her and all, bad.

What we did on Sundays for entertainment is go out and climb mountains. There was a lot of chinquapins. There wasn't any chestnuts. They was gone, but there was a lot of chinquapins back then, and we would hunt them things. The woods used to be full of them. We'd take a sack and go all over wherever the chinquapins were and gather them up, and we used to sell 'em sometimes. They was a lot of [them then]; they's not any now. They're gone. The blight and stuff finally killed them out like they did the chestnuts.

A lot of people [would cut] what you called acid wood. These woods was full of big dead chestnut trees. And I want to tell you what, they was three or four saw logs to the first limb on 'em! People sawed them up, and busted 'em up, and hauled the wood, and loaded it on boxcars. They made gunpowder out of 'em during World War II. If they hadn't done that, these woods would be full of them big trees now, but that was their use for 'em. And people peeled tanbark to tan leather with. That's what a lot of 'em made a living at.

Back then, everybody's cattle and hogs run loose. Now you've got a stock law; back then they didn't have no stock law. In them sawmill camps, I tell you what, we were trying to make a garden to keep from starving to death and had fence made out of slabs out around our garden. And I'll be doggone, them hogs and stuff would tear down and eat everything we had. That was a job about day and night, trying to keep them things out of there. I remember one Sunday when we used to live over there at the head of Timpson Creek, a man's hogs was in our garden, and Dad had a twelve-gauge shotgun and Paw was just putting the lead to 'em. That man came down through here and hollered over there and said, "Leamon, I'm going to go get Luther [Rickman, the sheriff]."

Paw said, "Just go on and get 'im." Pow! And that hog would holler and get out of there. But they would eat up your crop. I mean you had a hard time, I tell you. If you was trying to farm anything, and somebody's cattle and hogs would get in there, they'd eat it up.

But I remember when that [stock] law come over in about '36, '37. They had to let 'em vote on it. A lot of them said, "Turn the hogs loose," and a lot of them said, "Put 'em up." Most of 'em said, "Put 'em up," so they passed the stock law. Then if a feller's stock got in there and eat up your stuff, you could take him to court, or he'd pay you for it. Boy, that was a good law, too. I'll tell you that, because that was when a lot of these people got to killing one another in these mountains. They had their hogs and stuff marked, and one would go and say the other'n stole his hog. And they'd fight over it. Yeah, it was bad!

Clyde Runion

Clyde Runion lives in a white house on Electric Avenue in Mountain City. Foxfire students have interviewed Clyde many times, and if you have read other Foxfire *books, then you already know him and his uncle, Kenny Runion. He has been making furniture and toys for years, but he is also a good storyteller.*

This is the first time we have interviewed him about hard times. We learned that the old times were not always really the "good old days." We were amazed at how Clyde's family had to live back then, struggling to make a living.

We left with Wig after school to go on the interview. (This was the first interview for most of us.) When we got to Clyde's house, we sat on his front porch and visited with him as he told us about his youth and about his father's family. He had just finished making a table that had a checkerboard inlaid into the wood. It was so good that Wig decided right then to buy it.

During the conversation, Clyde told us: "They called them the 'good ol' days.' I don't call 'em so good. I remember when Daddy used to work for a bushel of corn a day. You didn't make much but you paid a whole lot."

—Robbie Bailey, Julie Hayman, Keri Gragg, Brooks Adams, Franz Menge, and Shelly Henricks.

In 1925, Gus Runion [my daddy] and my granddaddy came [across Hightower Mountain to Mountain City] from Hiawassee, Georgia. They built a house right over there [within 500 yards of where I live today] and we lived there till '39 where, in the daytime, he shoed horses and mules and made wagons.

At night, he would run a power generator that he had in his shop. He drew that dynamo with a big ol' one-cylinder engine, and

Clyde Runion whittles as he talks.

had the only power plant there was in Mountain City. He worked around [at the blacksmith shop] where he had the motor setting. He made power for the two hotels at that time. He turned the lights on at dark and turned 'em off at eleven o'clock. [The hotels] paid him so much a night to make light for 'em. Then Georgia Power Company come in here and they put him out of business. I don't know what ever happened to his little ol' dynamo. He kept the motor for long years after that. Last time I remember seeing it, he had it pulling a corn mill back in, I guess, '30 or '35.

He made about anything he wanted to make in that shop. He tempered steel. If he had the iron parts, he'd make the rest of a wagon himself. He'd build the wheels and make the axles. On rainy days and at nighttime, Daddy would work in the house making wagon wheels. Yeah, he'd spread 'em out there—the wheels and the spokes—and take a drawing knife or a pocketknife, whittle out those spokes, and get a wagon wheel. He got two dollars and a half to do a wagon wheel.

Gus made his own horseshoes, and he'd make a set of shoes and put 'em on a mule for thirty cents. When I tore down his old house down there, I found his old book where somebody owed him forty cents for shoes. I guess it'd cost twenty-five or thirty dollars nowadays.

When they was building the Black Rock Road, they needed someone to sharpen and temper the steel. Daddy went up there to see about getting a job. When he got up there, he done a good job on steel sharpening and on tempering, so they gave him the job. In order to do the work, he had to have his shop up there, so he carried it about a half a mile all the way to the lower spring right below Black Rock. He carried that shop piece by piece on his back. A 125-pound anvil, all his tools, and everything he had he carried on his back up there. He put that old big anvil in a tow sack across his back and walked up there without stopping or setting it down once. Now he was *stout*.

He'd run that blacksmith shop and sell whiskey [out of the back of the shop]. He used to make it all of the time, and my granddaddy made it, too. I've heard him tell about it. [But] there just wasn't no money to be made. In wintertime, we just about starved to death here—would have if we didn't have no canned stuff to live on. In 1939 and '40, you was lucky if you made over two or three dollars a day. In the spring, things would open up a bit and you could get some money then. Daddy worked for years for fifteen dollars a week, and we thought that was big money.

To make [what money we could] in the winter, we had to hew cross ties and cut pulpwood. There wasn't no factory to work in until the shirt factory came in 1950—somewhere in there. We hewed cross ties and carried them up to a half mile off the mountain on our backs. They paid us forty to ninety cents a cross tie, and you was lucky to get a ninety-cent cross tie. We hauled fifteen or twenty cross ties in a week. We made pretty good money for those cross ties. I think we got about eight dollars a cord for pulpwood, but it'd take you a week to cut and peel it with a drawknife in the wintertime. The only way there was to haul 'em to the railroad was on the Model T, an old A Model, or on a horse and wagon. We'd get a load hewed and then we'd buy the gas and go haul the rest.

WPA [the Works Progress Administration set up during the presidency of Franklin Roosevelt] had a rock quarry up on the Highlands Road, and in '35 or '36, Daddy, Kenny, and several of 'em went up there and got 'em a job at a dollar a day. [Congress] passed the law—in '35, I guess it was—that you had to pay a penny on a dollar for Social Security. One day, [WPA] took a penny out of Daddy's pay for Social Security. And he said he wasn't going to pay the government his money, and he quit. That was the only penny he ever paid in his lifetime for Social Security. [He] never done another job where tax was taken out—he wouldn't work. He wouldn't give the government his money.

Well, back then, taking a penny out of a dollar was something big. Kenny quit, too, and I don't think he ever paid no Social Security. Of course, Kenny never would work on a public job. A public job is one where they take out taxes. He liked to piddle around too much. He had his own living pretty well, and he wouldn't work with nobody a'tall, hardly.

Daddy always made a living, though. His favorite job was peddling. He'd rather peddle than anything. He and L.G. made pretty good. They didn't make no big gain, but it was the only way there was of making any money to amount to something. He used to travel a horse and wagon to Athens. That was before I was born. I've heard him tell about it. He'd drive a horse and wagon all the way to Athens, and take a load of anything he could get—apples or beans or anything. They had a farmers' market down there. He'd buy him a load of apples—on credit—and when he'd get back, he'd have enough to buy another load. After about three or four loads, he'd have him a profit.

I remember my first job. I was nine years old. I helped my uncle Jim with a crosscut saw. I was on one side, and he was on the other. Boy, we pulled that saw. We had to go to work. There wasn't any laying around back in them days. We had to walk to work every day. Nowadays, people walk and run for their health. Back in them days, you had to. We lived, but that was all.

The following series of hard times recollections comes from contacts who experienced Foxfire *book readers might remember from the early years of our project. Unfortunately, many of our old friends like Marinda Brown have passed on. We're thankful that Lawton Brooks and Harriet Echols are still with us.*

Interviews by Roy Dickerson, Holly Fisher, Gary Warfield, Karen Cox, and Tony Burt.

Marinda Brown

I'd hate to go back to the washtub and scrub board, and wash outside in cold weather. I tell you, there was a lot of hard work we had to do, and all the people around us had it to do. Of course, every once in a while people who didn't have children could hire somebody to help them if they could get them. But where there were children, all the children worked, and they all had chores to do. They knew what they had to do, and [did it]. It doesn't seem to me like we ever had any trouble in our home, because we always knew what we had to do. Soon as people got one job done, there'd be something else waiting. We were used to it. We didn't know any difference. No way to get out of it, so it didn't bother us.

I felt like, when I was young and growing up, that I had to work harder than anybody. My daddy was a farmer, and you know on a farm there's always something to do. The boys in our family were the older ones, and when they left home, that left us girls to help Dad farm. I felt like I had a really hard time back in my teens,

Marinda Brown.

'cause I had to feed cattle, milk cows, saw wood, just do everything a boy would do on the farm, even get out and help my dad harrow the land.

After we moved to Franklin, we had a neighbor, and this fellow worked in a lumberyard. They just had a house full of children. They were the easiest, most good-looking kind of family I've ever known. Everybody was so happy, and the children didn't have to work. They didn't do any farming, just a little bit of gardening, and those children—it doesn't seem like they ever did have to work. I would wonder how they could get by. Now my parents just worked all the time, and they kept us working all the time. This woman would get out in the yard and play with her children, and she'd sit on the porch and sing to 'em. And I wondered a lot of times, "Why can't my mother do that?"

I used to say along through the years, "When I grow up, I'm gonna get an education so that I don't have to do this kind of work." I did. I went away and took a business course as a secretary for a number of years.

Harriet Echols

We went through the Depression when my first baby was still living. It was hard; we just didn't have any money, and there was nothing t' make any—there was no work. You couldn't get but just so much flour. Each person was allowed just a few pounds of all these commodities that you'd have to buy.

The people that had a farm and raised their own food could live, but you didn't have anything to buy clothes. My oldest daughter and son were in school. People got together—like someone was larger than you, and she handed down her clothes to you to help out. [My daughter], Mavis, still today won't wear hand-me-downs because she got so tired of other people's old clothes.

My first baby that was born during that time died. My second baby died; then my oldest daughter came along, but we didn't have any money to pay the doctor. I came near dying, and the doctor said, "That's all right. I know how times are, and probably you have things that we don't have." We had plenty of corn, nice fat hogs to kill, and plenty of meat. So we gave him hams and corn in place

Harriet Echols.

of money. We couldn't buy sugar; we had to use our homegrown honey and syrup. We made gingerbread, and sweetened the fruits and things, and lots of times made jam with syrup or honey. It wasn't only us, it wasn't only the country people; our ministers, they didn't have money because we couldn't afford to pay our tithes at church. We shared our food with our ministers, and they were just as happy to get it.

That's the way people got along. They just exchanged with each other. The colored woman that lived close to me helped me [when I was feeling poorly]. She was the sweetest thing; she says, "Mrs. Harriet, I don't have any chickens and eggs." We had plenty of chickens and eggs. And we had a lot of syrup that year, and milk and butter, so I shared these things with her. She'd do my washing to help pay her bills, she'd wash and fold our clothes, and she'd come and hoe the garden. [I wasn't able for a long time, but] when I got able to get up and sew, I'd sew for her. I worked with them and helped them, and they helped me. I'd never have been able to raise my first children if it hadn't been for that good woman. That's the way people lived back then. They shared with each other.

I quilted for people to get money to buy cloth to make clothes for the children and me and shirts for my husband. In times of need, we just helped each other out, 'cause you just didn't have money to hire it done.

My husband's father set up a sawmill, and then my husband worked there at the shingle mill, and then we got to where we could have a little money. The Depression eased up, and then it hit hard times a few years later. My husband had several different jobs, then his father got sick and he moved back to the farm. My son and I worked on the farm and that's how we lived.

Then my oldest son was killed at Pearl Harbor, and my oldest daughter was training for a nurse, and I raised the two next ones by myself. I just moved up here with 'em. I raised them and got my oldest daughter through college, and Leonard worked during the day and went to school at night. They made it on their own.

Of course, it was hard times during the Depression and the World Wars, but it's been hard on me all the way through.

Lawton Brooks

When we was a-growing up, it was hard times. It wasn't like it is nowadays. We all had to walk to school; there wasn't such a thing as a school bus. We had to walk four miles there and then four miles back—that was eight miles a day. We'd go barefoot until the corn was gathered and then sell corn to buy our shoes and things, and that's the way we come up. People helped each other a lot. If anybody ever got sick, we always took care of their stuff and they took care of ours. We'd go in and gather their corn or gather their wood to make sure they had plenty of wood for the winter. That's the way we was always raised. My dad owned a big mill. We ground wheat and made flour. We always had plenty of meat with our hogs and cattle. But I'm telling you we had some hard days back in them times. Work in the fields paid seventy-five cents a day and that's all you got. I've seen my daddy work many a day for seventy-five cents a day. I'd go with him lots of times when he'd be laying off rows or planting corn for a man, and I'd be dropping seed and make fifteen cents a day while he'd make seventy-five cents.

But the hardest times I ever remember seeing was [the time period] when I got married, what they called "Hoover Days." When

Lawton Brooks.

he said a dollar a day and a pair of working overalls was enough for any working man, he made it that way and liked to starved people to death. There wasn't no money. I could get all the work I wanted to do. We had plenty to eat but couldn't get no money for nothing. We grew all our stuff to eat. Sometimes we'd have to work in our garden during the night and work for somebody else during the day. Why, I've put my lantern on my plow and plowed many a time till way after midnight. An old man come down to the field one night and said he had seen a light going back and forth to the bottom and top of the field. Said he couldn't figure out what was down there, and he drove plumb down there to see. He wanted to know what in the dickens I was doing down there at that time of the night, and I said I was just killing a few weeds while it was cool.

The money was scarce for they claimed they didn't have none. Everybody was in the same boat. He had plenty of food, but he didn't have any money to pay with. I could work for a man, and he'd pay me in meat, corn, or anything I wanted. I grew my own stuff. No money though, you couldn't buy anything you needed. Me and Florence [my wife] had to go along and swap a stack of fodder for a cookstove, but we couldn't get enough money to buy two joints of pipe. They wasn't but a dime or a nickel a joint. Me and Florence just cooked over a fireplace for over a year on account of not being able to buy two stovepipe joints. Now a man can call that hard times.

Times won't ever be as rough as they were then. It just wouldn't do, 'cause it'd be too rough. If ever it come again, there would be one of the biggest wars you ever seen, 'cause people would be trying to take it away from one another. People would start killing each other before they'd put up with what we went through, they'd just go out there and kill 'em somebody and take whatever they could get. I have done some hard work and made it honest—what I've got, I worked for and nobody gave it to me. By gosh, I believe them old days were good, 'cause I don't believe hard work would hurt anybody.

Minyard Conner

Minyard Conner has been one of our most generous and venerable contacts for two and a half decades. In his ninety-plus years in the southern mountains, Minyard has been a bear and hog hunter, woodsman, railroad man, and good friend to many. His family was one of those who sold their home places so that the Smoky Mountains National Park could be created, and he moved to Rabun County during the middle of the Depression years.

I bought this place in '33—moved down here in '36—and they'd set up a soup line in Atlanta. You'd see people walking this old highway asking how far it was to that soup line, walking this highway to Atlanta where they could get a bowl of soup once a day. I remember once I was here visiting before I moved here, and a feller come in and said he was starved to death. Wanted to know how far it was to the soup line. I told him about a hundred miles. He said he wanted something to eat. Hadn't had nothing to eat in a day or two. I said, "Run in there in the kitchen." I said, "Ain't got nothing to eat 'cept some meat and some corn bread, and it's cold."

But he said he'd take anything. Said he'd work for it, you know.

And I said, "No," and got him something to eat. Got him a big glass of milk and a big piece of corn bread and a whole dish of fried meat; and gosh, he cleaned her up and eat all that bread, and he said that was the first time that belly'd been stuck out in a long time.

After the CCs, when I moved down here, I had six boys and three girls. That pasture there had one cow on it. Well, I went to working for the Tallulah Falls Railroad for twenty cents an hour, and cut wood off this place here and cleaned up another acre or two, and first thing you know I had five or six cows. We had cows and chickens and hogs—you name it and we had it. And the boys, they'd just go to school and work on the farm, and they didn't want for nothing. We made it all right.

Edith Cannon

Edith Cannon became an acquaintance of Foxfire by way of her husband Robert Cannon. She first helped the students with an article about the community brass band which played around Clayton right after World War I. This past summer when they asked for her recollections about the CCC camps, she offered the following story about hard times.

Well, we didn't know very much about the Depression because it wasn't advertised way out in the country like it was in the cities. The city people hurt worse than the country people. We were farmers, and we had our own milk, and butter, and meat of all kinds, and chickens, and eggs, and vegetables, and we canned and preserved stuff. We didn't really know much about the Depression like other people did.

My parents didn't have any money. They were just farmers. They didn't have any way of making any money, so we'd just sell a little produce every once in a while, maybe, or something like that, but people just didn't have money back then like they do now. Wasn't no Medicare or no Social Security or nothing like that back in those days.

There weren't any school buses back in those days, and I had to go away from home to go to school. We went on a work program to Tallulah Falls School during the Depression. It didn't cost us anything. We just worked our way through for our room and board. Maybe you would have to wash the supper dishes, or you had to clean some part of the school buildings, or you had to sweep the walks, or you had to look after the laundry building, and just different things. We worked, and went to school. The food wasn't much good, of course. It was during the Depression years, and it wasn't too awful good, but we made out, what time we stayed there.

The CCC boys came in about '33 or '34, somewhere along there, while I was away at school, and we would come home in the summertime and see them working on the roads. They would eat dinner along the road close to our house, and they would give us their scraps for our hogs. There would be big loads of [commercially baked] bread in it, and we just wondered what that was. We thought that it was the most wonderful thing to see light bread; we didn't never go to the store and buy bread back in those days. They called it loaf bread, and that was all they had to eat. They didn't have any good homemade biscuits and corn bread like we did.

The Forest Service and "Ranger Nick"

During the nineteenth century, timber interests and coal companies moved into the mountains and began to take out what they wanted. Residents of the area, who were cash poor, sold timber, mineral rights, and often the land itself to those outside developers. As a result, beginning around the 1870s, many people began to be concerned about the overexploitation of these resources. This concern was not limited to the mountain areas. In 1873, New York physician Franklin Hough gave a paper before the American Association for the Advancement of Science (AAAS) which presented evidence suggesting that there were economic reasons to preserve America's woodlands from overexploitation.[1]

With some encouragement from AAAS, Congress eventually acted on this suggestion, passing the Forest Reserve Act in 1891. Through this act, national forest lands were set aside, mainly in the West, from lands already held by the federal government. In 1911, Congressional passage of the Weeks Act brought the federal government and its policies of land management into the Southern Appalachians. This act was designed to set aside lands for the establishment of National Forest Reserves in Eastern regions of the country.

Through this and various other acts, by 1984 over 4 million acres of the Southern Appalachian Mountains had left private hands to become government-owned and -managed. In Rabun County and throughout the region, much land was purchased from large timber companies, which had already stripped the usable timber from tracts bought for as little as one dollar an acre in the 1800s. A great deal of that land resembled a lunar landscape. Soil erosion was a problem as the rains pounded unprotected slopes, washing topsoil into streams. Skidding the cut logs down mountainsides gouged ruts that rain and snow turned into gullies.

The movement to make the Great Smoky Mountains a national park, for example, began in the twenties; before the last of the 6,600 tracts had been purchased from the logging companies and individuals who owned them, some two thirds of its magnificent stands of virgin timber had been logged or burned, or badly eroded.[2] The Smoky Mountains national park movement was spearheaded by groups of private citizens and was not a result of the Weeks Act; but it was related to the nation's alarm at its disappearing resources.

In 1925, the Nantahala National Forest included more than 226,000 acres of timberlands in North Georgia, northwest South Carolina, and North Carolina. (In 1936, the North Georgia and South Carolina regions split off, the North Georgia region becoming the Chattahoochee National Forest.) The first ranger in the old Nantahala district, which included Rabun County, was Roscoe Nicholson—or Ranger Nick, as he affectionately came to be known. As the chief officer of the Forest Service in this area, he, at one time, covered parts of three states on horseback—the roads were just too bad to drive a truck. Beginning in 1911, Ranger Nick oversaw land acquisitions and management for the service until his retirement in 1952. The work included writing plans for management of soil and water, wildlife, and recreation resources. Those plans emphasized reforestation, which was badly needed due to indiscriminate logging.[3]

As the Depression took hold, Ranger Nick and others like him became responsible for helping manage newly allocated government resources to help the unemployed, as well as meet their own goals in the areas of reforestation, soil and water conservation, and wildlife and recreation management. According to a paper prepared by the Tallulah Ranger District, Roscoe Nicholson spent many hours, sometimes in the evening by lantern light, marking timber for cross-tie sales when hewing railroad ties was about the only way some local people had to make any money.

Earlier, the large logging companies had had a virtual monopoly on much of the county's timberland, squeezing out the smaller concerns. As the Forest Service began opening up sections for bids, the smaller outfits had a chance to compete with the larger companies.

On April 5, 1933, President Roosevelt signed Executive Order 6106, Relief of Unemployment through the Performance of Useful Public Works. This created the Emergency Conservation Work Act and mandated an advisory group from the departments of War, Labor, and the Interior. Ten million dollars was set aside for this program, which soon came to be known as the Civilian Conservation Corps (CCC).[4] The CCC hired single, fit men from the ages of eighteen to twenty-five to perform needed tasks for the improvement of public lands, including building bridges and fire towers, building truck and foot trails and minor roads, erosion control, flood control, forest culture and protection, landscape and recreation, range and wildlife, stream improvement, fish stocking, and other conservation jobs.

Ranger Nicholson lost little time. On June 8, 1933, the *Tribune* reported that he, along with "Major Finch, of Fort McPherson . . . selected two sites. . . . One of the camps will be located at the old Lovell place on Lake Rabun and the other on Moccasin Creek on the west side of Lake Burton. . . . With the two camps already in this county which have a man strength of over four hundred and with two others to come, when all have been completed, will give to the county somewhere near a thousand men that will devote their efforts to improving the forest and roads in this county."

Suddenly there was money and lots of muscle available to enact Forest Service programs. Nationwide, the Forest Service supervised 50 percent of the work done by CCC men. Many of the camps were located in the national forests, including the Nantahala National Forest in Rabun County. At the end of the first two years of the CCC program in this area, Roscoe Nicholson reported in the *Clayton Tribune* on the accomplishments of the young men under his jurisdiction. In two years, the young men he supervised in his forest conservation and improvement programs had built almost 150 miles of new roads and maintained 1,120 miles of existing road; strung some 40 miles of telephone lines while maintaining 300; covered some 37,000 acres in their timber stand improvement program; constructed 3 miles of new foot trails and maintained almost 170; surveyed over 129,000 acres of timber; built 28 new bridges; cleaned 18 miles of roadside; planted 50 acres; controlled disease on almost 4,100 acres; controlled erosion on 14,000 feet of roadbanks; maintained 2 lookout towers; constructed a new picnic ground; and built 2 new public campgrounds and 2 fish pools. Road improvement was probably of most immediate and daily benefit to local folks.[5]

As we looked for information about the timber business in our area, we found the name of one man at every turn: Roscoe Nicholson. We wanted to know more about someone who played such an important role in the county, but he is no longer living. We interviewed his daughter, Margaret Nicholson Marchman, who reminisced about her father and shared with us some photographs, clippings, and testimonial letters presented to him in a scrapbook when he retired.

Margaret Marchman: "My father was born in Pine Mountain, Georgia [about twenty miles from Clayton], and lived there on a big, almost self-sufficient farm. He went to North Georgia Military Academy for three years, but caught typhoid fever when he came home for Christmas during his senior year, and never did get to finish. He learned to survey from his father, and that was the first job he had with the Forest Service, surveying the land that they bought. The service started [here] in 1912, but he did not go to work until 1913.

"He bought the house down on Main Street there called the Nicholson House before he and my mother ever married. It was only one story, but he lived there. They were married in 1922.

"He always wore the uniform. It looked like a Royal Canadian Mounted Police uniform. It was that style, only it was solid green. He was always dressed up, you know, in the style of a ranger.

"He was gone every week for several nights at a time. He rode a horse in those days. He said he kept his horse until 1929. The government did not supply any vehicles. He camped out a lot. He had various families that he knew that were fire wardens. Sometimes he stayed with some of them.

"When they fought fires he would be gone sometimes for two or three days at a time. He had to be sure that all of the men had all the equipment they needed. He had to supply food and blankets and be sure all of that was accounted for. He had first-aid stuff. He was responsible for all of that. He was the government authority here in Rabun County for a long time.

"He would go out into the woods, and he would tell Mother that he would be at a particular store at five o'clock and, 'If I don't call you by six o'clock you call them and send somebody to find me.' You know, back then there were a lot of bears and all kinds of things. He could have been hurt. There is no telling what [could have happened].

"Because he was gone a lot, my mother was afraid, and so she started taking boarders. That is how the Nicholson House got started. She kept some elderly people there for the first few years just to have somebody in the house with us.

"He kept a diary every day of everything he did. He had to turn 'em in every month. We can't find them. I guess they threw them away. They said they sent them back to Washington, and they probably threw them away because after he died we couldn't find them.

"He was responsible for building the telephone lines. He put a phone in the home of every man who was called a warden in the various communities. If a fire broke out in a community, why, the warden called it in, and they got up their men to go and fight it. Each warden had a tool house on his property, a little, round corrugated metal house, with tools in it for fighting fires: axes and rakes and saws and everything they needed to fight fires.

"[When the CCC camps came in] the camps were run by the Army. But he had to select the sites for them and see that the site would be suitable for a camp. Then he had to help select the projects that they did like building trails through the woods, and roads. Lots of the main roads, like the Warwoman Road now, were redone by the CCC men. He was in charge of that. They had an engineer that came with the Army to do such as that. But he [Ranger Nick] was the man in *charge* of all of that.

"During World War II, he had a lot of different responsibilities. They had the fire towers. They were supposed to spot for enemy airplanes should any have come over. He got a weather report every day from the military. It was not sent out on the radio like it is today. He got that in code every day. He had a codebook. He was told what page to look on and the code changed every day. He had to tell the spotters so they would know what to expect.

"I know that he was very busy going around to get reports from all of the camps and seeing that they did the jobs they were supposed to do. They built the fire towers. I know that several of them came prefab. They were metal, and they came in parts and had instructions about how to put them together. He was very instrumental in that."

One of the amazing things about Ranger Nick was that he was responsible for doing at least two things that should not have made him very popular. First, he was responsible for buying large tracts of land to add to the national forests, thus taking it out of private ownership, and second, he had to stop people from burning off the forest floor to "green it up" for free-ranging livestock. And yet he was, from all accounts, a very popular and well-respected man. Mrs. Marchman told us that he considered education a big part of his work. Part of that included periodic columns and articles in the *Clayton Tribune* in which he discussed the rationale behind Forest Service practices, warned people against harmful ones like burning or careless fires, and provided information about areas of concern, as in the mysterious death of the chestnut trees which once thickly forested the mountain sides:

Notes from the Forest Ranger's Office
I have been asked the question numbers of times recently why so much chestnut timber is dying. The government has made considerable study of the chestnut timber in the southern states along the Blue Ridge and found it to be a blight and to date no remedy has been found to prevent it spreading, and at the rate now spreading it will only be a few years until all the chestnut timber will be killed by this blight.[6]

(The blight was first noted in 1904; by the middle of the century almost every chestnut tree was gone. See "Memories of the American Chestnut," Foxfire 6—Ed.)

Ranger Nick used movies, in addition to print, to inform audiences about the importance of conservation practices. He scheduled showings of Forest Service films to local schools and community groups, and to the boys at the CCC camps:

Ranger Nicholson brought moving pictures to Camp Rabun last Friday night. There were no films of the flamboyant Bow, or the fascinating and sophisticated Chatterton, nor of the dynamic Gale and handsome March, but an intensely interesting reel depicting the untold value of our fast diminishing forests, and stressing the urgent necessity of rectifying timber slaughter. We are always glad to have Mr. Nicholson at Camp Rabun because he never comes without something interesting.[7]

Margaret Marchman: "He was responsible for all of Rabun County, and when he began he had a big part of Oconee County [South Carolina], and he just eased over into North Carolina— North Carolina mostly was another ranger district—and then over into Towns County. When he retired, they divided it up and made three sections out of what he had.

"One of his big jobs at first was to buy the property from the local people, and some people didn't want to sell. Some people just didn't like it. At that time most people had more land than they could handle. Some people did. His main thing was that he was good at dealing with people. He was a very good public relations man. He never wore a gun. He was eligible to wear a gun for the government, but the old-timers said that he never wore one. He never thought it was necessary. He believed in people. He tried to always be fair when he bought property from people.

"He was a good speaker, and he would go around and make all these speeches and try to educate the people. People had been used to burning off the forest to green it up for cattle and such. He had to get that stopped. That is why he bought the dogs. There were people during the Depression who would go and set fires in order to get a job [fighting it]. People had nothing. He bought the dogs to help catch people. And they did catch several people. When they caught the people they prosecuted [some of] the cases in Gainesville in federal court.

"They had supervisors and people who came around and helped him. People from the head offices and people from Washington came on a regular basis. They sent young people here to work with him for training. The number of people working under him depended on what the projects were. He had an assistant ranger and a clerk. Then he had these fire wardens. He had a lot to do, but he had things delegated out pretty well.

"He was the Ranger until 1952, I think. He bought a T-Model Ford and had it when they got married in 1922. That was one of the first cars in the county. He could not use it but a part of the year because the roads were not suitable. But he was a woodsman and he would come in at night and he might say, "Let's go and have a picnic." And we would load up [the Ford] and go. We'd pick up whatever Mother had ready, and we'd go eat outside somewhere."

While the responsibility for supervising a large part of the CCC program fell on the shoulders of Ranger Nick, he must have felt a great deal of satisfaction in seeing so many of the plans he had made for his Nantahala District carried out by the young men of the Civilian Conservation Corps. He wrote in the May 23, 1935, *Clayton Tribune*:

Prior to the CCC work in this county there were a great many roads that were passable only during dry weather. The least rainfall made travel over these roads impossible. With the aid of C.C. labor the Forest Service has built nearly 150 miles of good graveled roads in this county. . . .

The protection of the resources from its worst enemy, fire, is probably the most important single item in forestry practice. The value of the C.C.C.'s in respect to this phase of the work is beyond conception. Not only have the members of this organization suppressed fires thru physical effort, but they have also spread the advantages of protection all over the country.[8]

—Interviews and research by Eric Hollifield, Cristie Rickman, Shane Danaher, Mike Cook.

NOTES

1. No author, *Mountaineers and Rangers* (Washington, D.C.: U.S. Department of Agriculture, 1983), p. 5.

2. Dykeman, Wilma, and Jim Stokely, *Highland Homeland: The People of the Great Smokies* (Washington, D.C.: National Park Service, 1978), p. 128.

3. According to documents prepared by the Tallulah Ranger District of the Chattahoochee National Forest.

4. *Mountaineers and Rangers,* p. 7.

5. *Clayton Tribune,* May 16, 1935.

6. Ibid., July 31, 1930.

7. Ibid., December 28, 1933.

8. Ibid., May 23, 1935.

The CCC

THE ROAD TO RECOVERY

After carrying the November 1932 election with 472 electoral votes to Hoover's 59, President Roosevelt found himself faced with a nation lacking in spirit and money. During his first 100 days in office, Roosevelt, along with many banks, repeatedly sent requests to Congress to support proposals for alleviating the nation's suffering in the Great Depression. In 1933, realizing the seriousness of the situation, Congress got behind the President and passed the Emergency Conservation Work Act. (A succeeding act in 1937 changed the title of the original project to Civilian Conservation Corps—CCC—and the work continued.)

The CCC would provide a great many jobs for those who qualified. To qualify, applicants had to be males between the ages of eighteen and twenty-five, physically fit, unemployed, and unmarried. (In 1935, the age limits were reduced to seventeen and increased to twenty-eight.)

The enrollee would be paid thirty dollars per month, twenty-five dollars of which would be sent back to his family. If the enrollee had no family, the twenty-five dollars would be held in escrow by the Army finance officer who paid the enrollee the collected sum at the time his service ended.

Originally, the government wanted to employ 250,000 young men in the CCC, but by 1939, the enrollment had increased to

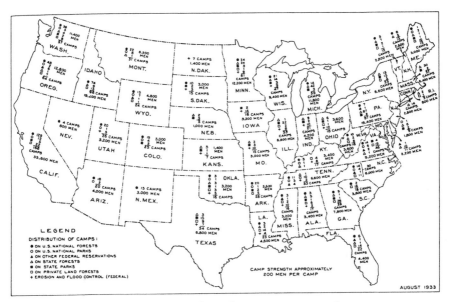

*Map showing the number of CCC camps in each state
in the United States.*

507,782. The first quota of 25,000 was called up on April 10, 1933; and the first camp—Camp Roosevelt—was occupied in the George Washington National Forest near Luray, Virginia, on April 17 of that year.

The War Department was to administer and provide for the needs of the men in this newly created army. Immediate needs included food, clothing, education, shelter, transportation, and religious services. Once underway, every state in the Union, as well as the territories of the Virgin Islands and Puerto Rico, had one or more camps. The number of camps in each state varied depending on many factors such as the number of work projects which a state had readily available and the number of enrollees from that state. Many Eastern men were sent West since there were not enough projects in the East to accommodate all of the Eastern enrollees. Nationally, 4,500 different camps operated during the life of the program, averaging 1,643 at any given time.

There were up to 300 different approved work projects that varied from state to state, but they all fell into ten general classifications, as follows: structural improvement; transportation; erosion control; flood control; forest culture; forest protection; landscape and recreation; range; wildlife; miscellaneous (emergency work, surveys, mosquito control).[1]

That the CCC had a tremendous economic and social impact, there is little doubt. The CCC had a significant social impact by taking young men off the streets to perform useful work in healthy outdoor environments that were often far from home, thereby giving them a chance to travel. Some of the men we interviewed for this section were sent as far away as Oregon, and some, like Curtis Pearson, had never been in the mountains just north of their own state before.

The CCC provided jobs, work training, and health care to about 3 million young men across the nation. The men were taught first aid, safety with tools, equipment, and machinery. Their KP chores gave them experience in good housekeeping, such as how to make a bed and clean their clothes and themselves, and they learned about a proper diet. They learned how to accept responsibility, to get along well with others, to be disciplined, to be punctual, and to take orders. They also learned how to appreciate their surroundings and take care of their natural resources.

From the educational adviser, many enrollees learned to read and write, and many learned trades such as how to use typewriters and adding machines and how to do bookkeeping. From the foremen in the field they learned a number of other occupations. Some young men, like Bill Southards, entered the corps illiterate and left with the equivalent of an eighth-grade education and a lifetime trade. In fact, according to one of our published sources:

> One of the most significant features of the CCC was its educational program. . . . Over 60% of the enrollees took part in the courses presented. In addition, several thousand attended night school in adjoining communities. At the end of the school term in June, a large number were granted eighth grade [or] high school certificates or diplomas.[2]

The tremendous scope of Roosevelt's Civilian Conservation Corps can be partly derived from overall statistics. In Georgia alone, for example, the aggregate number of men given employment was 78,630, including "72,379 junior and veteran enrollees and 6,251 non-enrolled personnel of camp officers and supervisory workers."[3]

See Table 1 for a brief summary of some major tasks accomplished at the state and national level.

TABLE 1.

	Georgia	National
Total Number Employed:	78,630°	3,190,393°
Some Major Work Accomplishments		
•Telephone lines, miles	3,638	89,900
•Check dams, erosion control⁕	425,829	6,660,000
•Erosion control, planting, seeding, sodding, acres	25,082	21,000,000⁕
•Gully-trees planted, number	1,672,905°	
•Fighting forest fires, prevention, presuppression, man-days	153,022	6,459,000
•Trees planted, reforestation, number	22,915,095	2,356,000,000

°These are aggregate numbers. Some individuals enrolled more than once, thereby increasing the total number of those employed.
⁕"Acreage covered in trees, plant disease and pest control."
°There is no separate national category for this.

Figures come from Merrill.[4]

As the nation's first such large-scale reforestation program, the work undertaken by the CCC was regarded as experimental. All their commanding officers were sure of at the outset was that after their training at Fort McPherson, the enrollees would work "under the direction of experienced forest reserve men," to cut fire lines and undertake other fire protection measures in the forest, plant trees where timber had been harvested, and build whatever roads they needed to accomplish this work.

As you read the reminiscences of those involved in the program, we think you'll agree that they did much more than that. We also think their stories will give you a better sense of the impact this national work program had on the lives of these young rural men than all the statistics of all the official publications put together.

—Tallie Cilbrith
Interviews by Jimmy Andrews, Dinah Beck, Jeff Black, Joe Blume, Tim Burgess, Kurt Cannon, Kenneth Coalley, Mandy Cox, Chris Crawford, Rita Darnell, Eric Deering, Frankie Dunlap, Frank Dyer, Rance Fleming, Danny Flory, Bartley Gragg, Kenny Hensley, James Houck, Gwen Leavens, Leslie Luke,

Tammy Maloney, Robert Mitcham, Rita Nichols, Alan Ramey, April Shirley, Scott Shope, Carlton Speed, Brant Sturgill, Jerry Taylor, Richard Trusty, Karen Varnes, Regina Watson, Curtis Weaver, Belinda Welch, Walter Welch, Leah Woods.

James Cartwright
CCC Forester

While James Cartwright spent two months supervising work in Rabun County at Georgia Camp 10, on the west side of Lake Burton, he spent most of his career as a CCC Forester in North and South Carolina and Tennessee. As the only CCC administrator we have interviewed, Mr. Cartwright's story fills in a big piece of the puzzle and sets the stage for the enrollees' stories that follow. We first met Mr. Cartwright at a CCC camp reunion in Mountain Rest, South Carolina. We found out that he had been a forester, or cultural foreman, in several CCC camps, and he had many old pictures and interesting stories that he had collected during the years he had served. He invited us to come to his house in Easley, South Carolina, to talk with him some more about the CCC days, and we accepted. He talked first about his early years. Mr. Cartwright was born in Ohio and reared from the age of five on a farm in Commodore, Pennsylvania. He was educated in a one-room schoolhouse and at a teachers' college. After teaching school for a year, he became interested in forestry and studied it for two years at Pennsylvania State Forestry School, then transferred to a new forestry school in Raleigh, North Carolina, from which he graduated in 1931.

—Scott Shope

Interview by Scott Shope, Carlton Speed, and James Houck.

It was in the spring of '33 when Roosevelt took office that all the foresters began getting telegrams offering them jobs. I had offers from several places. I had been in the Nantahala Forest—visited there while I was a student—and had fallen in love with that country, and, boy, I grabbed that one. That's how I wound up in Mountain Rest, South Carolina, and I was with the first group of men who opened that camp.

When I reported for duty, I checked in at the Forest Supervisor's office in Franklin, North Carolina. That was the office in charge of all the camps in the Nantahala

James Cartwright.

National Forest, which at that time spanned over parts of three states. I was brought to Camp 1—later named Ellison D. Smith—outside Mountain Rest, South Carolina. That was in June of 1933.

The project superintendent was an old road construction contractor whose bonding company in Asheville had gone broke in 1929. He had had a lot of money at one time, and he had worked huge crews of men with mules and slip sloops and all that; so with the road construction projects we were doing here, he was a good one to be in charge.

I wasn't working on the roads, though. In 1934, my main work was timber stand improvement in areas where the best trees had been logged out and a lot of cull trees had been left. We were girdling the big old cull trees and taking out the undesirable species so the young timber could come up through that canopy. Most of the cull trees were scarlet oak, which tended to have persistent dead limbs all the way up, and the heartwood tended to become doty [decayed and crumbling]. We had to be awfully careful in girdling one of those. We learned to chop a notch in, and if we found the heartwood was doty, somebody stayed back with that tree till the crews got way on away from it because when you cut around it, you didn't know which way it was going to fall—and it wouldn't give any warning.

From the Mountain Rest Camp in South Carolina, I next went up to Highlands, North Carolina, where they were building a new camp in Horse Cove. I was there through the winter of 1934. Then in the middle of April 1935—in fact, just a week before I was to be married and I'd already made arrangements for my wife to stay in Horse Cove with a local family—they transferred me over to Georgia Camp Number 10, a National Forest camp on the west side of Lake Burton in Rabun County near Moccasin Creek. One of the main projects there was building the Tiger Road—the one that still today circles all around the west side of Lake Burton and goes across the Lake Burton Dam and comes out in Tiger at the old Clayton to Franklin highway.

I was there just two months when the Forest Supervisor came out and had a nice talk with me and told me all the good reports he'd had on my work; and he told me that Mr. Smith, the project superintendent at Highlands, was being transferred to a camp closer to his home in Asheville, and they would like to make me acting project superintendent of the Highlands camp. At the time I had passed the junior forestry examination and I was still on my probationary appointment under Civil Service. That meant I'd have to stay at my junior forestry salary, but I would be the acting project superintendent.

Well, I was there about six months and they transferred me to Camp 12 over at Rainbow Springs, North Carolina. At that time, Rainbow Springs was quite a place. The Ritter Lumber Company had a big band mill there, and they had a big commissary and a lot of dwellings, and they had their logging railroads all around there and were still cutting out the virgin timber up in those hollows. Had a post office there, school and church, all that; and the CCC camp was over across Black Gap, just two or three miles from Rainbow Springs on Buck Creek. The enrollees there were all Negroes. It was an all-black outfit with all-white officers. I think most of those fellows had been brought in from Asheville, and being black, they had no contact with the local people whatsoever. They just didn't dare get out by themselves around there, so every week or two, they'd load up two or three trucks of them and take them into Asheville and give them a night on the town there, and then line them up about ten or eleven o'clock and bring them back to camp. So that was their recreation.

Otherwise, though, everything was just the same as it was in the white camps—same barracks, meals, clothes, jobs, and everything.

The big job there, though, was building the road from Rainbow Springs to Aquone, where there was another CCC camp. That was one of the most difficult jobs I was involved with. For one thing, that was in the *coldest* location I think I have ever been in. The cold air drained down off of Standing Indian right down the hollow, and, in fact, there was one morning when they just refused to go out on the project. The temperature was about twelve below, and there was snow all over the ground, and they just wouldn't come out to work call. When we did work, some of the area we were building on was on north exposure and those banks didn't thaw out all day long, and by jolly, we'd have to have barrels all along there with fire in them so the men could warm up occasionally. We were also suffering from a lack of heavy equipment. A whole lot of the work had to be done with a pick and shovel since we did not have equipment like jackhammers and compressors that we needed for drilling and for blasting boulders out of the road. They had to just put the charge of dynamite on top of the boulder, cap it over with mud, and set it off.

A few months before I went to that camp, they were about to blast, and everybody got back out of the area and around a turn, and this one fellow got down behind a great big boulder in the shoulder of the road. He was safe there as long as he stayed down, but he wanted to see that thing go off and he stuck his head up to watch it, and when it went off a rock just about took his head off practically. It killed him instantly. That was a rough thing to have happen. I'm glad I wasn't in charge of the proceedings there at that time.

But they finally built a pretty good road out of it.

Then in the first part of 1936, they brought me onto the Forest Supervisor's staff. I stayed in that office fifteen months or so. Of course, I was low man on the staff, and they passed everything down to me. I was the I and E man—Information and Education— making talks around at schools and organizations and setting up fair exhibits and so forth. I was also the safety officer for the forest, which kept me pretty busy.

Later, while I was still working out of the Forest Supervisor's office, I got involved in the training programs in conservation that taught the men fence construction, road construction, erosion control, quarrying, etc.

Then they shifted my duties again and put me on timber survey for a while. That lasted up until about August of 1937. That same summer, the whole CCC program was cut back drastically—almost cut in half—and we lost a number of camps, and a lot of personnel was let go or transferred out to other forests. Since I was one of the very few under Civil Service, I was taken care of, but they transferred me over to east Tennessee in a TVA unit. I spent four years there in CCC camps that were run by the Forest Service, but TVA had contracted them to accomplish certain projects they wanted done in the area. I'd go out and map eroded areas—draw in all the gullies and scalded areas and everything—and the TVA engineer would come out and decide on the work that we wanted done to control that. Then I'd take a crew out there and do it.

One of our jobs was to reforest what had been cleared farmland. Another was to tear down a number of log homes. That whole thing was rather a sad chapter in this story. In the first place, many people hadn't wanted to sell their land, but were talked into selling by just being sold a bill of goods on how isolated they would be—and cut off from everything—once the reservoir filled up. They were told they just wouldn't be able to stand living back in there. But many of them still didn't want to sell. No-o-o indeed. So, in some cases I think the land had to be condemned.

Anyway, after the people moved away, squatters kept moving into those log homes that were left behind. Back in those hard times they'd do that. TVA had had some trouble with it, so they decided they would just eliminate that. They tried to sell them first. I think they advertised them, and people that bought them could come and dismantle them and move them out. Then they saved a couple of the very finest ones—ones that had the logs hewed on all four sides and were really fitted out—and left them standing. They were still there the last time I was in there, but there were very few of those. The rest were tore down and burned to keep squatters from moving back in.

The CCC's came to an end completely in 1942. The Forest Service organization got thinned out a whole lot after Pearl Harbor. Lots of the rangers were reserve officers and so on. I was working then in a national forest in Arkansas, and I enlisted and put in two years with Uncle Sam in the Army engineers.

The CCC camps pretty much disappeared completely. Many of the buildings were portable. They were made in panels that you could just bolt together. The floor was in panels, the walls were in panels. They were built at a factory, complete with windows and doors, and when they got them to a site, they'd just bolt them together. At the end, they were unbolted and hauled away.

The CCC program, though, was one of the better things the government did. We had these boys twenty-four hours a day, and they were young, malleable material, and they were up at the age where they *could* become responsible and they had nothing to do. No jobs. Their families were on welfare. But when a boy went into CCC, his family came off of welfare. He became the breadwinner for that family. He drew a little money in the camp, but most of his money went to his folks, and so it made him think a lot more of himself. Plus he was learning skills and discipline and being well fed and well clothed, and he was in a good environment. It just straightened an awful lot of young fellows out who were headed for trouble. It sure made men out of boys. And the work they did was *so* beneficial. There is a lot of it still needs to be done, too.

Then when the war came along, these fellows were ready. There were cooks, you know, and others who had been leaders and squad leaders and used to being in charge of men and used to discipline themselves and to exerting their influence to maintain discipline. Uncle Sam built an army real fast around those fellows.

We made men out of them. We got some crabby material to make men out of, too, but most of them straightened up. Programs like this and Job Corps and CETA was costly. They're expensive. But they're very, very good. The American Forestry Association is pushing the idea again, and I'd be happy to see it happen.

Enrollment and Camps

"We had to pull off everything—our shoes, socks, everything. I mean you were just bare"—Ed Huffman

Ed Huffman.

Ed Huffman: I was born in Marion, North Carolina, on a one-horse farm. Our family was rather poor, and there was seven [of us] plus Mother and Dad, and ten acres was not much for a family that size. Times were hard, and people were out of work. They needed the work, but there was no work to be found. We did not have any food stamps, and what welfare we did have was very [little]. So when President Roosevelt came up on this idea to help the poor people, [the welfare people] called around to find out who was in need of help. They would say, "If you have a son or husband, y'all come on in here and let's talk." [So] we went in and talked, and [I went into the CCCs]. I was the only one out of my family [who went in]. My father worked in the furniture factory, and so did one of my brothers. The [brother] next to me—I am the baby—was finishing school and working whenever he could find something to do. And I was going to school, and in the summertime I did all of the plowing. I was plowing [at an age] when I had to reach up to the plow handles like this [extends his arms upward].

They got 100 of us out of McDowell County that really needed the help. They sent 20 of us out of McDowell County to Charlotte, North Carolina. They put us on a train, and then at Charlotte there was a bus waiting on us [to go to] the courthouse for our examination. We got down there that morning about ten o'clock, and we went right straight on. One of them guys was pretty talkative, and I asked him how many they had run through there that morning before we got there, and he said 1,500. There was 550 of us from different counties, and we went in about a quarter till eleven, and at twelve o'clock we were down at the place where they had reserved us a place to eat.

They examined us in the courtroom. Everything was sealed up

to that floor, and nobody was allowed up there. We had to pull off our clothes out in the hallway and roll them up. I mean we had to pull off everything—our shoes, socks, *everything*. I mean you were just bare. Then we lined up and went through [the courtroom]. Each man had his specialty. [He would examine you, and] then he passed you right on through. A paper followed you through. As you walked up, that paper slid right on up to the next man, and all he had to do was look at that one place. If you passed him, he just put a check there. You knew you passed [the whole examination] at the last man in line. I believe that only about six got rejected that day because of physical disabilities.

After that last man, they took us back into a room, and we got our clothes back on. Then they took us in another big room and called roll. Then we had to line up and walk down to the depot. They had special cars for us because there was so many men going through. They had some going north and some going south. We got on the train and went down to Cornelia, Georgia. The train stopped there, and the conductor cut our two cars loose and put us on the side. We were to wait until the next day until the [Tallulah Falls Railway train] came and brought us into Franklin.

I will never forget that night. There was just enough room to walk between the cars and the siding, and down below there was a street with houses. Well, the old sergeant was about half drunk, to start with. He was in charge of bringing us up here, and he had all the paperwork and everything. He was up there in a little cubbyhole by himself. Well, some of these boys slipped out and went downtown where they got ahold of some whiskey, and they got drunk that night. Me and another boy took the seats apart and laid them down and made us a bed. Well, we were trying to sleep when them drunks got to rocking them cars. And every time that it would rock over that way, you could see that street and them houses down there. We got out of there! Of course, we were sleeping in our clothes except for our shoes, and we got our shoes on, and we got out and set down beside the railroad in front of the depot. And them drunks in there was a-rocking that thing. [The] cars have safety chains on them, and that body comes up so far, and then that safety chain takes over. Well, that brings them wheels up, and I have seen them wheels come up that far [holds his hand about two feet off the ground]. If they would have turned them cars over, it would have went over that bank and killed Lord knows how many people down there.

Fred Kelly: I went in 1936, when I was about twenty. I went out to Clayton to an office they had in the courthouse and signed up to get in. They sent me to a camp in Morganton, North Carolina. I guess all the camps in Rabun County were full at that time, and they didn't need any men here, and those over there needed some. Now, you could ask for a transfer and, generally speaking, it would be granted so you could go back home. At one time, a group of boys from our camp there at Morganton was sent to Oregon. I tried to get them to let me go, but I'd been doing a good job with all those boys there in that educational department, and that was against me as far as getting a transfer out because they wanted to keep me there. But I'd loved to have gone to Oregon.

There were boys in our camp from something like ten different states. The government furnished everything. They furnished all of your clothes and your shoes. And you had winter clothes and summer clothes. In the wintertime, for instance, they gave you "long-handles," and before you would go out to work, they would have inspection to see that you had them on. They gave you those clothes to keep warm, and they meant for you to wear them. They had property inspections frequently to see if you had the amount of blankets you were supposed to have and the two pairs of shoes, and your socks and your underwear. You had to lay all that out on your bunk, and the commanding officer and a sergeant would come through one barrack at a time. If you didn't have something, you were charged for what

Fred Kelly.

you had lost and issued some more. There was always a scheme going on inspection days. Sometimes a man would borrow a blanket from one way down there and slip it in because he'd lost his.

Payday was once a month. Now you could borrow some money for the canteen, but you couldn't get over five dollars' worth of credit in a month there because that's all you'd have to pay back since you only got to keep five dollars of your pay.

A full camp was 200 men. Your supervision was provided by the Army for the care of the people there in camp. Matter of fact, it was just exactly like an Army camp. The clothes were Army clothes, and the rules were Army rules, and you had your Army officers there in charge of the camp. You would have a lieutenant or a colonel that would be the commanding officer of the camp, and then you'd have under him a second lieutenant, and then you had the sergeant.

There were about twelve buildings in our camp. You had the officers' quarters, and we had a doctor so we had an infirmary. Then we had the mess hall, and we had the laundry. And then we had the forestry headquarters and the toolhouse. And all the buildings in the camp that I was in were made of wood with tarpaper roofs. Practically all of the camps were built on one style. They were all just about the same size, and the buildings were portable buildings that were made and carried to the site and erected.

Each barracks would sleep fifty-two men, twenty-six cots to a side. Your cots were turned head-to-toe down each side. One's head would be out to the aisle, and the next one would be next to the wall. That was all the way down. You had an aisle down the middle, and then on the other side you had another row of bunks just the same way.

The barracks were crude and made out of rough stuff, but they were really clean. They had a stripe put down on the floor, and every bunk was sitting on that stripe so every one was in line from one end [of the barracks] to the other. The cots, when they were made up, had marks on them, and the blankets were folded a certain way so that when you stood at a distance and looked down the barracks, you would see one long straight line where each sheet was folded back six inches.

You didn't have a closet. You had a locker—it was just a wooden box—that you could keep your private belongings in. Each man

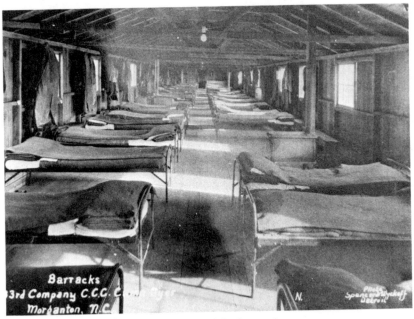

Barracks
3rd Company C.C.C. C...
Morganton, N.C.

Inside view of the barracks.

had his locker against the wall in the aisle between each bed on the right side of his bed; and you didn't have many clothes, but the clothes you had that needed to be hung up were hung over that locker when they weren't at the laundry. You had your suit of dress clothes and your work clothes and your raincoat, and they would hang up there on a rafterlike thing with the raincoat first and all the other clothes hid behind it. Then your rubber galoshes and your two pair of shoes—a work pair and a dress pair—had to be setting under the bed in a certain position.

Then you had all your other buildings. You had a common bathhouse there with eight shower heads across the end, and all that was scrubbed and kept really clean. You had your officers' quarters—it had about six rooms in it—and a lawn out front that was kept real pretty. Then you had the Army office building where your commanding officer was and your second lieutenant and your company clerk and all. The company doctor had an office in there.

You had a woodworking shop that at one time had been a barracks until they made a shop out of it; and a big recreation hall with a canteen in it where you could buy your candy and tobacco and gum and stamps and picture show tickets and stuff like that; and the education building where we taught classes, with the supply house behind it where you kept the extra blankets and shoes and shirts and underwear. Then you had the mess hall and kitchen with a separate room for the officers' mess. They didn't eat with the rest of the men. And you had your forestry building and tool house and the area where the motors supplied our direct current.

It was a pretty big operation, all in all.

Initiations

*"By the time you got through, you had
some blisters on you"—Buck Carver*

Buck Carver: They had a little bit of everything for initiations [into the CCCs]. Usually, they threw you in the lake or something similar to that. If they wouldn't have got so rough with you, they could have been a lot of good clean fun in it, but they got to getting a little bit too rough. They would run you through the belt line with fifty or a hundred fellows on each side. Some of them had two-inch leather belts, and the rest of them would pull off their canvas belts, and you'd run down that line and them striking at you. By the time you got through, you had some blisters on you. That kind of stuff was just a little bit too rough.

Finally, what stopped it was a man that's still living here in the county. He had served fifteen or eighteen months in CCs, and got an honorable discharge, and then they rehired him. And this LEM [Local Enlisted Man] man came in that year and went around with a bunch of boys getting them new guys out to initiate them, you know. He went to this old man's tent, and he told him to get out of his tent. The old man said, "I've been here before, and I've done went through all that initiation stuff before, and don't come in here." Well, this LEM thought he had him a little bit afraid of him or something, and he started laughing and raising Cain and started coming on in anyhow. That old man met him there in the door and give him a rake across his stomach with his knife, and that LEM went to the first-aid tent holding his intestines in his hands!

Well, they put the old man in jail until they seen whether this other man was going to live or not, and when they seen this boy was out of danger of dying, they discharged the old man. But a heck of a lot of us thought—and I still think—they done the old man dirty. We hated him losing his job over it. He needed it, and he was a good man anyhow. I think they ought to have let him stay right on in there and probably give him a medal, for that put a stop to the initiation business. It was high time that it was being quieted down, I can tell you that.

The Specific Jobs

"I've got up at the dead hour of midnight to crank my trunk to take a load of men to the woods to fight fire"—Robert Cannon

Minyard Conner: I was working for the Smoky Mountain Park when the CCs come in here, and they had to have a few local people to help 'em get started, you know, so they hired me [as a Local Enlisted Man, or LEM]. Most of the boys in the camp was Northern boys, and them boys didn't know what a crosscut or a ax was, lots of 'em. A foreman would have five or six or eight boys, and there wasn't nobody that knowed how to fall a tree. It looked funny to see so many men, and none of 'em knowed how to fall a tree. We built a wooden bridge—it may be up there yet—and we used a poplar tree that was three-foot through here on the top, and we used a broadax. And out of all them hundreds of men, there wasn't but one man up there that could use a broadax. He could use it, though. He could just hew that log and it was just like you'd planed it—like you'd sawed it.

But I had to teach a lot of them boys how to use an ax so we could trim out these four-foot trails you could ride a horse through for fire protection. Most all them leading ridges had trails like that on 'em. Built trails all over them mountains.

The way I trained them boys was cutting logs for firewood. I'd give 'em an ax, and I'd hit it on a rock or something and dull it. It'd be so dull you could just beat with it. He had to learn to chop with it. Then everytime I'd see where a beaver'd cut a tree down, I'd send them boys with that ax and tell 'em to chop that tree down and just gnaw it down just like that beaver. [Laughter.] We was gettin' wood for that damn barracks, and I was in charge of thirty-five of them boys, and they finally got to where they could cut wood and haul it to the camp. Then I'd begin to give 'em good sharp tools—something you could *do* something with—and I learnt them boys how to fall a tree and tell which way it'd go and all. They learnt good, too. They was several of 'em made awful good workers, just extra good workers. One boy I remember just kept a-thankin' me for what he'd learned off me about cutting them trees.

And then we had fire duty. Someone had to be on fire duty there all the time. In '35 or '36, it was a real dry season, and lightning hit a tree and went down and set that ground on fire back in those Smoky Mountains. I can show you up there now where that there big timber's standing where that fire hit. And them CC boys carried water pumps plumb up there to the head of that river and made 'em a dam and pumped that water for a mile up that mountain trying to put that fire out; but I'm telling you, it just burnt that mountain shed off just as bare as it could be. That old dead moss and stuff was under there five and six foot deep, you know, and it had dried out, and couldn't nobody stop it.

Most of those boys wound up making good workers, finally, but it took some work to get 'em that way. They was awful green. There was one old boy—I can see him to this day. They had him in old-timey Army shoes. Big old leather shoes, you know. And he'd never walked up a mountain in his life. It had always been flat where he was from, you know. And the leaves, you know how slick they can get. We was a-workin' on the sunny side of the mountain, and it was just slopin'. He went up through there, and he'd slip like this. He went, and down he'd go; and he'd get up and his feet'd slip again, and down again. But he wouldn't turn his feet sideways or anything. He'd keep trying to walk straight up the hill. He just learnt the hard way.

Another time I had a crew of them boys tryin' to dig a big septic tank about thirty-foot square. Every once in a while they'd run into a rock, and them big old stout Northern boys'd just wrestle around with it, and I'd get down in there and just lift it out, you know. Or if it was too big, I'd bust it with a sixteen-pound rock hammer. I'd show 'em where to hit it with that hammer so it would bust, but they never could catch on. They'd dig down to a big rock in that septic tank, and they'd say, "Oh, here's one Conner'll never bust!" and I'd get in there and show 'em where to hit it, and it'd bust and we'd pull it out.

Well, they got one in there one day, two big old boys, [and got up on a rock], and they just beat on that thing. They'd just beat,

beat, beat, beat. Waller that thing around and beat it some more. And every time they'd beat on that and waller it some more, they'd knock off another corner till they had that thing just as round as a ball! Finally one of them boys turned and said, "Now then," he said, "we'll have to do something. We'll have to get some kind of a lift to get that out of here with!" I went up there and turned it over and looked at it and seen the way the grain of the rock was running on it, you know, and I just picked up the hammer and hit it right—and, by George, it just fell open. He said, "I'll be damned!" [Laughing.]

And they was always quittin'. I know one boy told me he was gonna. He said, "I'm gonna let you send me in."

I said, "Why you gonna let me . . . ?"

He said, "I ain't a-gonna work. I'm gonna lay down on you. I ain't gonna work and I'm gonna let you send me in." He said, "I want to go home."

And I said, "Now, listen," I said, "I know a better way for you than that." I said, "This way you'll get a dishonorable discharge," and I said, "that'll go down again' you on your record." I said, "You just write home to your mammy or daddy one and tell 'em to write back and say they got you a job. They'll pay your way home, and you'll get a honorable discharge."

So he said, "I hadn't thought about that."

I said, "I'd hate to have to send you in. You just lay around here and do nothing, and it'd be a dishonorable discharge." I said, "I'll work it out. If you just have to go home, get your mammy or daddy one to write you a letter." Homesick. Lots of 'em was. But the ones that stuck it out made fine men.

Fred Kelly: If you worked away from the camp, what you did depended on what kind of a camp you were in. You might work stopping gullies and erosion, or setting out trees, or putting out kudzu or terracing, or stonework on the sides of roads and bridge abutments, or running phone lines to a fire tower wherever they had one. We worked on what they called fire trails, and I guess we worked out twenty or thirty miles building those fire trails through the woods. Sometimes you'd drive two hours to where you were going to work.

Those fire trails went all through the forest up there so that

Fred Kelly, Wig, and Kurt Cannon discussing the work Mr. Kelly did in the camps.

equipment and personnel could get in to a fire. Sometimes they widened old roads. Where they cut roads that were not old-timey country roads or mountain roads, they'd go out there and clear the timber off—just push it off on the sides out of the way—and the people that wanted to could get wood if they wanted, but didn't anybody get it 'cause everybody had plenty of wood back then. After the bulldozer got through, we'd gravel them. They wanted all-weather roads so they could get in there when it was wet, but that's never when you had a fire—when it's wet and muddy. [Laughter.] But anyhow, it was an all-weather road. Now they were just one-width roads, but they had a little side ditch on 'em. And you couldn't always pass when you'd meet another truck coming. You might have to wait, or the other one back up a little bit so you could get by.

Our crew was ten men and a foreman. We had our own truck, and when it was cold you had plenty of clothes to put on, and you bedded down in the back like a gang of boys to keep from freezing to death. At the job, we had a big old Caterpillar that pulled a portable rock crusher, and it would pull up about six feet at a time. The road had already been channeled by a crew ahead of us, and then another crew had to haul rock and place them along the road in the side ditch. Our boys picked them up by hand and would throw 'em up into that crusher, and it would crush them. Two boys tailed it, and they would shovel the rock and place it out on the road, and when they got that space filled in, the man that drove the tractor would pull up six more feet. He just stayed on it, and every little bit, he'd pull up.

I was a water boy. They wouldn't let me do anything—just told me to get out of the way—so I just carried water. Sometimes you were way up on the mountain, and the water was way off, and they'd send the truck to haul it. If we were in a rural area with big old apple trees, I'd go down there and get us a bag of apples. It was real interesting to me.

After that, I was working with the educational adviser instead of going out on the road all the time. My duties working with the educational adviser were to do anything that we could do to help the boys because several of 'em couldn't read and write, even.

Oakley Justice: When we first went in, they put all the new ones out cutting wood. They had us on the Forest Service land to cut wood for the kitchen, heat, and everything. This here forester, he'd come out there and watch them and pick out his crew for the Forest Service from the ones he thought would make the best. They already had a crew there, but he would pick out new ones to take on, and that's the way I got my job.

They would put the new ones on them lines for two or three weeks at a time and let them follow the old boys. I was following a crew, and we came to a big old white pine that we had to girdle, so they put me and another boy girdling that tree, and it was a big one. I started chopping my side and he started chopping on the other, and he was just hacking his side up. He was out of the city, and he didn't know how to do nothing. Actually, the bigger part of those boys came out of the city. But I girdled mine and then went around and finished his side up.

The next day, they put me to carrying the line. There would be one boy eight or ten feet from you, and you carried a line. We stayed about like that, girdling trees and cutting grapevines and trimming out over little white pines. It usually took about two to three weeks before the new ones started carrying the line, but I knowed all about it before I went in the CCs. My daddy was in the CC camps on Coleman River, and that's what he done. He told me everything that they did, so I knowed what to expect. I could have got that forester job like my father had if I had had a good enough education.

I don't remember anybody ever getting hurt on the job, but I do remember some of the boys getting drunk one time when they run across a still. We was out fighting a fire. I believe that was the fire that burnt over 800 acres, and there was men from three CC camps fighting it at the same time. Those fires would get up in the tops of the timber, you know, in them pines, and it would sound like an airplane or something. You never heard such a racket. That time we was going back into the fire to mop up, cut out the stumps and trees that was on fire. We was going up a branch to the top of the mountains when we came across a still. Some of the CC boys found them a bucket in there and they got them some of that beer that was in the barrels. They carried it to the top of the mountain and set it down while they fought the fire. It had got hot by the time they quit, and it was summertime. A bunch of them drank that beer and by the time they got to the truck, they was drunk. The officers didn't do nothing. They just let them go. We run across several stills. That little old forester would tell us to be *sure* we didn't say nary word about that when we got to camp. If we had, the moonshiners would burn them mountains out. They would set fires, you know. We seen one boy coming out of the woods from where a fire was set, and we knowed he set it. They'd just stick a match out in the leaves and let her start because they'd get mad at the CC camps or something and set her out. A lot of people in that country made liquor, and if you made them mad, they'd keep you fighting fires all the time.

Robert Cannon: I was hauling the boys in and out of the woods to where they was girdling timber. Then I went from that to a dump truck hauling gravel. While I was taking boys to the woods, after I dropped them off I stayed with the truck till they come back to it. That's all I had to do. Stay right there till they come back. I stayed there in case someone got hurt so they would know where to find me. Not many got hurt, but I've seen them boys come in there that didn't even know what a axe was. They used doublebits all the time, and the blacksmith man kept them things just like razor blades. But they didn't even know how to use a axe. Instead of using the cutting end, I've seen 'em hit flat thisaway! [Smacks hands together.] [Laughter.] And some of 'em did get cut pretty bad. When that happened, I'd bring 'em back to camp where they had a company doctor. If it was beyond him, he'd give first aid, and an ambulance took the boy out.

Then we were all on duty to fight fires. I've got up at the dead hour of midnight to crank my truck to take a load of men to the woods to fight fire with fire rakes and dig fire trails. Sometimes we could get ahead of it and set another fire to burn back to it and cut it off that way, but that was a tough job.

Clyde Harkins: I worked over here at Winfield Scott Lake, putting sand on the beaches and whatnot, and we built some barbecue pits. The second job I went on was over here on Duncan Ridge, busting rock in a rock hole. I was in that rock hole in July and August. It faces the south, and you talk about something *hot* about three o'clock in the evening! Those "sprawls"—little rocks flying where your hammer hits the big rock—they would cut the blood out of you. And some of those boys would pull their shirts off and would be speckled like you poked them with a fork.

We [busted the rock] by hand. We wore goggles—shields, you know—that covered your complete eye, sides and all. We called them safety goggles, and, boy, they were aggravating, and they were hot and heavy. You would put them around your neck and your eyes, and you would get to sweating, and your goggles would fog up your eyes [until] you could hardly see. And a few times—it was not far from this rock hole [to where I lived]—I could have went through what I call Yellowjacket Ridge and to the house. [But I couldn't go because] my pride wouldn't let me. They laughed at me when I came up to join the CCCs because I was so small and so young. I was so glad that they accepted me that I toughed it out until it was time for me to go.

We would bust the rock just big enough to pick up, and then there was dumps that we throwed them in. The dump moved and carried [the rock] to the crusher. The rocks would weigh fifteen, twenty pounds—just whatever the crusher would take. Then we had a crusher man. I fed it a little bit [and] I did not like it. You had a big crowbar, and you kept working those rocks around when they would get jammed so that they would go on down into the jaws of the crusher. It was dangerous work, and I was small, you know.

They had sixteen-pound hammers—we called them "calf-heads," big ol' rock hammers made especially for busting rock manually. My first morning on the job when the truck stopped [at the equipment shed], I noticed that everybody got off the truck and run real fast. Well, I had been working on Lake Winfield, so I just kindly drug around, and when I got down to the toolshed, they did not have any hammers left but the sixteen-pound hammers. I looked around, and the fellow there at the door, the leader, said, "Get you a hammer, son." His name was Black. Well, I drug that big old hammer up there, and, mind you, I was five feet three inches tall and weighed 109 pounds, and I was fifteen years old.

I got up there, and they put me on a rock [that] would have filled a pickup bed up good if they would have had some way to load it. He put me on that rock. I noticed that Mr. Berry Lunsford was standing a-watching, and Preacher Parson, and several of the people I knew that was raised with my dad. Well, I beat on that rock for a while, and this taught me something—I learned something from this experience. [Black] said, "Just bust that rock down to where you can handle it, where it will go in the little dump and then into the crusher." Boy, was it hot, and I frailed on that rock. The leaves were not too full at that particular time, and there was not a thing in this world between me and the sun but the sky.

Well, after while I decided to just lay the hammer down and go to loading rock. There was two dumps come all the time, and I just followed over in the gang and went to throwing rock. I thought, "I got it made," and just the hammer lay there by the big rock. I could see Black, the leader, and Berry Lunsford and different fellers talking and watching the work crew. After while, I guess thirty or forty minutes, Black came over and said, "Did you get that rock busted?"

I said, "No, sir, I just was not doing a thing with that rock. I can do better here."

"Well," he said, "I believe that you had better go back and get on that rock. I did not tell you to come over here."

That was [the first] time when I thought it would not take me long to get through Yellowjacket Gap and right out through Cooper's Creek and into the house. Then I [thought], "No, they will laugh at me when I go, so I am not going to go."

So we go over to the rock, and he looks at the rock and says, "You are doing all right there." Little ol' sprawls like the end of your thumb, I had knocked off many of them, you know, whamming that thing on that rock. Black said, "See there, you have knocked off some small pieces here."

I said, "Okay." So I got back on that rock, mad and disgusted.

We went on to noon, and of course they brought the truck out loaded with food, you know—big cans with ladles to dip out with, and we had our own mess kits. After twelve, Black came over and said, "Harkins, we are going to put you out on the road." So, I got to go out on the road, and I worked on that awhile. But finally, I made a good rock crusher.

We did a lot of good work, like roadwork and setting out trees. One of the things I enjoyed about the CCCs was building pools on the trout streams, cutting logs and placing them. And [we stocked] some of the areas that did not have the trout in them on account of falls. The CCC boys had five-gallon cans that the military uses now [with] a big lid on them and a hole. We put small trout in those cans, and we would pack them on our back over the falls. We would put them in different areas. I do some good fishing now in some areas that did not have any trout before the CCC boys carried them over and started them higher above the falls. [Back then] we carried them up on trails, not like the roads they have now.

This is something I remember as a kid, a boy about ten year old when the CCCs first started. They were building this Duncan Ridge Road from Wolfpen Gap to Mulky Creek. It goes straight across, following high ground all the way across for several miles. And you could hear that bulldozer. I could hear that thing a-running, and me and my two older brothers would go all the way across from the house, about a mile and a half or two miles to where that 'dozer was running and get back up on the mountain and watch that thing run. You talk about something interesting, that big 'dozer! It was a big "scooter." We had it at the Forest Service. It was a big gasoline bulldozer, one of the bigger ones. We would watch that 'dozer push that dirt and move those trees. I would stay there for thirty minutes or an hour and just watch that dirt move.

Ed Huffman: At Camp 9, we made fire trails on the mountains, and we worked in rock quarries. We had two big crushers and made our own gravel, and we made our own roads. If you have ever been across Wayah Bald, we built all those roads from down at the foot of the mountain all the way up to the bald. Up here at the experimental station at Otto, we built Shope Creek [road] that goes off to the right, and Bald Creek [road] that goes off to the left. We built Buck Creek road. We built it and graveled it all.

If we was not working heavy equipment, we was out cutting right-of-way. Out on the job we had this boy. I can't remember his name—all I remember was we called him "Snake Eye." They would put him up front, and if he stopped, *you* had better stop. I said, "What is going on here, Snake Eye?" and he would say, "There is a snake right up there." In front where we had not cut he would go in and beat it out. He could smell them. The foreman kept him out in front all the time.

Man, I have seen some of the biggest rattlesnakes up there, on that Bald Creek side, especially. I guess they were five or six foot long. We was up on Shope Creek side about a mile up in there from the camp grading, and I seen something coming. You could see its head up here and its body down there, and that thing was black. I hollered to one of the boys that was on the Bald Creek side and said, "What in the world is that coming there?" And he jumped behind the bulldozer and smacked him right in two. The foreman—he was a local man—said that it was a black racer. That was the first one that I had ever seen. And they will run you.

Clyde Harkins: At camp time, after we came in and eat our supper, we had an hour or two. You had an hour that you had to work around the camp, cutting wood or something like that. I never spent a week in KP. To keep from getting KP so that I could go home every weekend, I would take the job as table waiter. We would bring bread and whatnot to the table when the boys came in to eat and sat down. You just walked up and down the aisle, and when the bread plate got empty, you took it and filled it up. And after everybody ate, you cleaned up the mess hall; you cleaned the tables, wiped down, and did that, and that kept you from getting KP.

Food—The Mess Hall

*"First thing I had to do after I was inducted
at Fort McPherson in Atlanta was peel
potatoes"—Alton D. Story*

Alton D. Story: They had an Army sergeant who was our mess
sergeant. I don't know whether he had any direct orders to go by—
what we're gonna have tomorrow or whatever—but he would plan
the menu. And he instructed all the men on what to do and how
to cook. I was one of the cooks. I believe there were three cooks,
as best I can remember. And, of course, there were KPs, people
who worked in the kitchen. When I first went in the kitchen, they
put me as a KP instructor. The way that come about, one of the
fellers there that come from my home—same place that I was born
and raised—somehow he got a job in the company commander's
office. They wanted somebody who could type, and I took some
typing in high school and could do a little typing to a fashion, and
this boy came for me. And then, later on, they wanted somebody
in the kitchen. So they chose me to go in there, where I went from
KP boss to cook, and then cook to mess sergeant.

I had an experience one morning. The mess sergeant was a
good fellow. His sleeping quarters were in the very end of the
building, and he overslept one morning. I was cooking, and I had
the whole thing by myself. Don't remember what caused it, except
that he slept and I didn't want to bother him. So it came time for
breakfast, and I wasn't quite ready for that outfit. They'd come and
line up in way long lines. I didn't call them in, and they got all
excited and got mad, and they started at the door. And I told them,
"You're not coming in here yet. I'm not ready." So that made that
company commander mad, and they fired the mess sergeant. If I'd
known that was going to happen, I'd have gone out there and waked
him up. But it was too late then. That's when they moved me up
as mess sergeant.

So nearly all my work was in the kitchen. The last of my work
was as mess sergeant where I was in charge of buying the food and
all. Mr. Jim Dillard and Pete Dillard and their father [of the Dillard
House in Dillard, Georgia] used to haul produce, you know. And
they furnished food for the camps. I bought my meat up at Leon
Bleckley's market here in Clayton, and, of course, I bought stuff

from wholesalers out of town from Cornelia and other places. And then bread from the bread man. The milkman was local.

It was a balanced diet most of the time. The meals were just about like you have at school. Course you could figure on having Irish potatoes every day. First thing I had to do after I was inducted at Fort McPherson in Atlanta was peel potatoes.

They ate breakfast and supper in camp, and then they had trucks to haul dinner to the men who were out on the road. They had these big old vat things, you know—Army equipment is what it was. And we would put the food in those things and carry it out in the woods or wherever they might be. And if they didn't have their food, they'd get hungry, and they'd get sort of excited. So we had to get it there on time!

Fred Kelly: We had plenty to eat. That's for sure. We had good food and plenty of it. We had a supply truck that went into Morganton every day to pick up the mail and to pick up fresh produce at a produce market. So we had good food. In the wintertime the food was a little different. We had more dried food than we did in the summertime because there were not the fresh vegetables. They were not plentiful then like they are now. I suppose now you can get most any kind of fresh vegetables the year around in these big supermarkets. Well, it hadn't reached that stage back then. But it seemed like about once a month in the wintertime we'd have duck for the meat. We had a lot of fish and seafood. Every week, the year around, on Friday, we would have something special. It might be oysters or it might be oyster stew or fish, but once a week we would have seafood for supper.

For breakfast, we had sausage and biscuits, and it was good. Then for dinner, we still had hot chow no matter where you were. The men had mess kits they carried with them, and the chow truck came from the camp out there, and they had those insulated containers that would keep the food steaming hot; they'd come right out on the roads where the crews were working and feed 'em their dinner, and then they would go back in. While they were there, you just formed a chow line through there, and you had your mess kit, and you'd just go down through there and get some of this and some of that. Whatever you wanted.

Then you headed for camp. We had to leave the job in time to get in by about an hour before supper. Supper was six o'clock, so we had to be back in camp at five. You might travel two hours out there and two hours back, so nobody was overworked. [Laughter.] Now, when you got in from work, you had to wash your mess kit and cup and then take a bath and put on your dress clothes. You had to have your shoes shined, you had to have a necktie on, you had to have a button everywhere a button was supposed to be on your clothes, and you had inspection just before supper. We formed in Company Street, the main street right down between the barracks. It was a twenty-four or thirty-foot highway—just a long, clean place in there—and that's where you formed. You went up to the flagpole, and they lowered the flag every day, and then from there you went on to the dining hall.

And we ate well. People out in the rural areas are used to that, and they expect plenty to eat. I remember kinfolks from Atlanta used to come up here in the fall, and we'd have just all kinds of good vegetables; and, of course, we killed two hogs in the winter and cured our own meat, and had our chickens and milked cows and all that stuff. And those people from Atlanta'd just carry on: "My, how good you folks eat up here." Well, we just thought everybody ate that way. We never had been out anywhere. That's how we'd always been eating. We thought that's the way everybody was eating. But they said rich folks in Atlanta didn't eat like that. [Laughter.] I can tell you, rich folks in the city don't eat like that *now*. I've been around eatin' with some of them, and they give a little old three-cornered wedge of cracker and one of the little old fancy cups with them little teensy handles on 'em, you know, and clear soup in it. [Laughter.] You'd starve to death!

Recreation—Free Time

"It was a wonderful life. It was about the carefreest life I ever had"—Bill Southards

Fred Kelly: All the profit made in the canteen—every dime— was spent on the boys in one form or another. How that money was spent [was up] to the commanding officer. We had one there that liked to see 'em scramble for it. He'd get his, say, fifty or a hundred dollars, and get out there with a box, and get everybody out there on main street and throw it out, just to see 'em scrap for it. Everybody got to keep all he could pick up. It was all change, and he'd just get it and throw it out there, just like feedin' a gang of chickens. But now I'll tell you, I didn't get in there for any of that. Why, you'd a got killed. [Laughter.] They come in there meanin' business when they come in there pickin' up that money. I used to help the boy work in the canteen, and it did lots of business. We'd make about $800 profit a month. So when the man got him a bucket full of coins to throw out, he could throw out a good bit.

We had others who would give it out as prizes. Like when you would get ready for supper and get out here, each one in front of his barracks, for inspection, the commanding officer would go down through there and look at everybody. The neatest two people in each barracks or the ones who had the best shoe shine, say, he'd give 'em a carton of cigarettes apiece, or he might give 'em five dollars apiece. And then others would hire an orchestra to come in and give a dance in the rec hall. Or several times they'd pitch a party like a Thanksgiving party or a Valentine's party, you know.

And then, say, three times a week, you could go into town to a picture show. The picture show tickets then would cost us eighteen cents apiece. We had a form of credit in the camp there. You could buy a canteen book, which was just a credit book, and it would be broken down into nickels, dimes, quarters, and dollars. And that was just the same as money in the canteen. And you could trade him one piece of paper for another that would get you into the picture show. Or get your Sunday clothes sent into the presser in town. But nothing was real high back then. All your drinks were a nickel apiece and candy was a nickel.

If you had a good enough reason—like a death in the family or serious illness in the family—you could go home on a two- or three-day pass, and they didn't dock your pay. You still got paid.

They had lots of ways to break the routine. Over around Morganton [North Carolina] they used to do a lot of rooster fighting. We had a sergeant there in the camp that liked it mighty well, so he got some fightin' games and kept them off in the woods, off behind the mess hall over there. I used to help him exercise 'em some. We'd put boxing gloves on 'em. They'd cut those natural spurs off and put those little old boxing gloves on there for 'em to exercise. And then we'd put them back in the pen and take some more out and just give 'em a workin' out. He had about twenty-five around there.

I never did go to one of the real fights, but one time the sergeant said, "Let's buy us one of these hillbilly roosters around here and put the spurs on one of mine and see what happens." We went over there and bought us what we called a "hillbilly rooster," and the one with spurs on never did kill it. After the fight was over, we killed and skinned that hillbilly rooster. The other one had hit him lots of times, but he never had hit a vital spot.

Another time, we took two young roosters out of their pens. The neighbors lived around there close, and their chickens would run out wild like everybody's did. They weren't fenced up. And we held those fighting roosters—he held one and I held one—in our arms to be sure they saw that old mountain rooster way out down yonder in our ball field, and they got to jumping, wanting to go to him. We finally turned 'em loose—it was about, I guess, 300 feet down there—and when we got down there, that hillbilly rooster nearly had them other two killed. He'd whipped 'em both. He was a big old white chicken with good, long spurs and them good and sharp. He liked to have killed both of them. We had taken them out of a pen, and they weren't too well used to fighting, and, I guess, running down there they were about out of breath when they got there! [Laughter.]

We also had dances. We would invite girls from Morganton and go and pick 'em up at certain places—maybe at a church or some-where—or their folks'd get 'em out there. Oh, we'd have maybe a hundred girls. And then, later on, they had a girls' camp about forty or fifty miles away, and once in a while, they would come over there to visit and have a dance. Always we'd have an orchestra in there for that.

Now, on payday, they always had a lot of poker games, and they always had a lot of candles 'cause they'd play after lights out. They had to get these old candles, you know, and stick them on the back of a bunk and pull old boxes out to play on. Most of it was penny poker, with a nickel the highest thing, 'cause didn't any of 'em have any money. Lot of 'em would be playing with matches. But it was something to pass off the time.

Right in the outer edge of the camp, we also had a baseball diamond, and we had a baseball team. We would go and play other camps or other schools in the area that weren't too far away. I know one time we played the deaf and dumb students from the state school over in Morganton, and I kept score with their guy. We'd just write to one another anything we wanted to know and just got along fine.

The forestry people's main thing was horseshoe pitching. That's where I learned to pitch horseshoes. If you couldn't put on a ringer pretty often, you wouldn't get to play with them. I got real good, and after I come home, I kept it up. I could almost always be sure of getting a ringer ninety-eight times out of a hundred. I'd just pitch and pitch and pitch until I got good.

Ed Huffman: During the summer months we had to practice baseball after we got off work. The other boys were off playing checkers or poker with what little money they had. We had to try out just like if you wanted to get into professional ball. You had to go out there and prove yourself. I was catcher.

[The games were] officially organized. We were in the Fourth Corps area, working out of headquarters at Fort McPherson. We had teams from Georgia, South Carolina, North Carolina, and Tennessee. We had a scheduled season just like the major leagues. We had to put in five days a week during the week, and so the only time we got to play would be on Saturday and Sunday. Unless it was a holiday—on holidays, they would schedule make-up games or a regular game.

For a while, we had a crackerjack baseball team. We won the Fourth Corps area championship in the summer of '35. The ball team rode the stake body trucks with seats, where we had a little more room. What men got to go to the ball games [as spectators] had to ride in the dump trucks. Of course, they had covers in case it rained. We had first-class equipment just like the pro-teams.

We got our umpires out of the towns we played in. If we could not get a local umpire, we would get one from over in the next town or something. Mostly we had only two umpires. The umpire that stood behind the pitcher called the balls and strikes, and the man on base would stay out there pretty close to second base. If the base man had two or three men on base and he was having to watch second and third, the ball and strike man would call first base from behind the pitcher's mound.

Most fields had bleachers built behind home plate around to first and third base, and they would step up about thirty or forty foot high. We would have good crowds. All the camps that were pretty close by would bring their boys to pull for a team if they did not have a team. If they couldn't get a seat, they would line up behind first base all the way out toward right and left field. A lot of these places had banks that would come down pretty close to the playing field [and people] would sit all around them banks. We didn't lack for spectators, [because] the camps would advertise games. They would notify all the schools around the county, and the school kids would be there. After we got through with the ball games, they would put the ball team out there cleaning it up and smoothing it down. The fields were raked and swept.

[We played the Rabun County CCC boys.] We played ball on the old high school's ball field. We even played the high school boys down there. I played in an exhibition game over in Asheville, North Carolina. It was against the Asheville Braves, I believe. We split with them. We had some good players in the CCCs. [Hackett] Beber was the pitcher, and Shorty Coontz was the shortstop. They ain't nothing got by that boy. You had to hit it over his head. If it was between shortstop position and second base, he got it, or between that and third base.

[One time] they took us to Asheville to try out [for a professional team]. I knew I did not have any chance because there was so many catchers. But they didn't have the pitchers and the shortstops. They had called the camp commander and wanted to know if he could bring the pitcher and the shortstop over there, because there was a talent scout that wanted to talk to them. He said, "No, let's just have a game. Bring your whole team." Said, "Let him look at all of them." [The scout] looked at me. He said, "Huffman, we got too many catchers now, but I sure would like to take you." He told the camp commander and the rec director that he would get back with them on those two boys [the pitcher and the shortstop]. I left before they did, and I don't know whether they got called up or not.

I first met my wife at the ball field. We slipped and got married while I was still in the CCCs, but nobody knew it. They did send one or two home because they caught them. I got a local boy I knew [to give me his] A-Model Ford, and we left here one Saturday morning and went to Clayton, Georgia, to the clerk of court. We had three old farmers from out of the county there as witnesses. [Laughs.] I was twenty-one years old, and my wife was twenty.

Jake Waldroop: Sometimes some of the men would bring a guitar or banjo in, and they'd have music until lights out at nine o'clock.

Going to Franklin [North Carolina], was the main thing. They'd take about fifty every Friday night. The next Friday night they'd take another fifty. Swap it around that way till they all got into town. Then you'd start back up at the first bunch again and take them again.

Sometimes them fellows would get drunk, and they'd put 'em in jail, and the captain would have to go down there the next morning and get 'em out. They would get bootleg liquor just anywhere. There was one man just over the ridge from the camp that sold bootleg liquor, and they'd take their blankets over there and swap them for liquor. We got so many blankets lost the captain [got involved] and found out where they was at. He took a truck and went over there and told him all that was stolen property, and he could get him for receiving stolen property. That man knew it—he just couldn't resist, you know—and he told them to just come on in and get 'em. The captain came back with one of them big dump trucks piled with just all the blankets and stuff they could pile on it.

Now if they got drunk in camp, or if the captain had to go get 'em out of jail, they'd get extra duty. They'd make 'em clean up around camp and have some kind of pretty rough job for them to do. Sometimes they'd put 'em on for a week at a time. Every evening after they'd eat their supper, they'd just have to go out and work till about dark. And if one got too rowdy, the captain would discharge 'em—take them and get them a ticket and send them back home.

There was no women in camp. There was families that lived around there, but they didn't have nothing to do with them boys. No visitors. It wasn't too happy a place!

Bill Southards: We'd gamble and play cards. And we had a basketball team and a baseball team, and we would visit different camps and play 'em, just like the schools would. And we got government holidays off, unless there was a fire or something. It wasn't much, but we played baseball and football, and it was a wonderful life. It was about the carefreest life I ever had.

I finally got me a car, and I'd haul CC boys around, and I made pretty good after I done that. I bought me an old A-Model [Laughter.] You wasn't allowed to have a car in there, but we'd steal it off and hide it, and oh, we had a good time. And the girls went wild over CC boys! They did!

Hugh Holcomb: On weekends we could get a pass and go into town as long as we had on our khaki uniforms and ties. When I first went to Oregon, the first time we went to town, they closed the doors—the stores, the barrooms, everything. They just closed up the town. We really didn't know what was going on, and we got to inquiring around, and they said there'd been at this same camp a bunch of boys from up North. Said they'd come into town and just take over. We had a time building up a good name. They would have weekends where we could invite girlfriends out, and when they found out that we was all right, they would come out there— maybe fifteen or twenty girls on a weekend—and bring their parents. And the officers would have a meal cooked for them.

But we had a time building up our name. We had some trouble with some of our boys that we had to treat pretty rough to get 'em straightened out. If they went to town and one of 'em got drunk, why, he caught it when he came back because it was a good town, and we wanted to build up a good name because we was from the South.

Education
"I had to get somebody to sign my name. I couldn't even write a letter home"—Bill Southards

Fred Kelly: I worked with the education program part of the time I was in CCs. We had a wood shop, for example. You always have boys that like to work in a wood shop. After work they would make things like cedar chests. A lot of them made elementary things to start with, like a shoeshine box, you know. That's about what they start with in schools today—just something to get [them] using those power tools in there.

And then we had an education building on the main street of the camp where we taught reading and math in the evenings. During the day while the boys were out at work, we would get in touch with our teachers over in town and make preparations for things we were going to do on the nights that we were going to have these classes. It was adult education, but it was very elementary because you were dealing with people who didn't know, and you had to start back where you could start and then go from there. We had people in there that couldn't sign the payroll, and everybody has to sign the payroll. So first thing that we would do was teach them how to write their name, and then, from there, simple reading. Just the very simplest of things, but all with words that they were used to and should know. And numbers. Most of them would catch right on to it. They already knew the terms, you know. They just had to see what they looked like, and then they'd come right on with it.

Then on evenings when we didn't have classes, I'd be in the building anyway, and after the boys would get in from work, they'd come in there if they wanted help. I'd help them any way I could. I'd write letters for them and read their mail to them.

We had one utility man that was real smart. He was an older man, but he had never had a chance at education. He could measure a room, but he went by a different method from figures. It'd just be "this measure here so many times," and "to this notch," and so forth. I worked with that man, and we got us a ruler. And we just did very simple arithmetic: how much flooring you'd need to do a room in something, or how much sewer pipe we'd need to do a job. And I believe he was one of the happiest fellows I've ever seen. He'd say, "Now, give me another problem!" They were all easy; that's the way you teach people. Never have them feel embarrassed. They all had confidence in me because I helped them all. I never made fun of them. I always helped them like they wanted to be helped, and they all liked that.

Oh, he was so happy that he could just measure anything. And he was smart. One time the commanding officer kicked him in the seat. Now, he liked him very much—he was just going on with him, and he kicked him in the seat. And that man stuck out his hand and said, "Give me a quarter for that shoe shine!" The old commanding officer just pulled out a quarter and give it to him! [Laughter.]

Bill Southards: People back then didn't think much about education. The kids didn't think about nothing but helping Daddy on the farm. So there was over a third of 'em that couldn't even read or write their name when I went in. Well, I couldn't either. I hadn't never had a chance to go to school. You had to sign the payroll, you know, and I had to get somebody to sign my name. I couldn't even write a letter home. I had to get somebody to write me a letter home.

Well, after I got in there and seen how much of a disadvantage that was, it bothered me. It made me feel ashamed because you couldn't even write your name. You could see where you was hurting. You needed to know how to sign your name anyway!

Now, you'd meet some pepole in there that if you'd give 'em a gold mine, they wouldn't take it. They had an education program, and you could take it or leave it, but to me it meant something. I went to school three nights a week, and I could read and write when I come out. I come out of there with the equivalent of an eighth-grade education. That was really worth something. You knew you needed it, and it meant something to you.

That's where I learned to blast rocks, too, and that's all I've ever done. It meant a trade for me, and it's a trade I wouldn't never have learned if I hadn't been in there.

Punishment

"Those boys couldn't stand at attention very long. Before long, there'd be six of 'em laying on the floor that had fainted"—Fred Kelly

Fred Kelly: Some boys' job was KP-ing all the time. That was their regular job. But on weekends they got the extra help of people who had not followed their rules exactly—someone who forgot to button one shirt collar or shirt pocket when he was out in the inspection line and got to work in KP on the weekend. Or he didn't have his shoes shined. Or his bed wasn't made up exactly right. That was a form of punishment, always, as in all Army camps, I reckon; they'd get KP, or extra duty, or whatever you want to call it, for breaking the rules. And they got extra help on the weekends that way all the time.

One time, the man who was the flunky around there was unstopping a sewer line. One old boy went by and laughed at him because he was down in there. It was kind of soggy and muddy and nasty, and he was laughing at him and [the sewer man] said, "Well, you need not laugh." Said, "Tomorrow afternoon, you'll be helping me." When they went out to work the next day, [the sewer man] just took that fellow's bed and turned it back down, and that fellow got extra duty. They assigned him to that man, so that evening he was out there helping on that sewer. [Laughter.]

And there wasn't anybody there with long hair. They had a barbershop in the camp there, and you had to keep your hair cut. One time two boys went to town and had their heads shaved, and the commanding officer grounded them. They couldn't leave camp except to go work till their hair grew out, so they didn't gain anything by pulling a prank like that.

You always had boys drinking home brew, and sometimes they would have fights, same as anywhere where there are a bunch of people together for a long time. They'd get extra duty.

But, like in any camp, you also had men getting away with things and not getting caught. We had this motor that kept the lights on, and the night guard would cut the lights out at bedtime. [That was at ten-thirty.] Anybody that he saw coming in after the lights was out, he was supposed to turn them in to the lieutenant. One of the barracks had twelve steps at the back of it. He would just come in the front and go out the back and go down those high steps after lights out. They knew the pattern that he would walk every night, checking beds to see who was in bed and who wasn't, and they got tired of him telling on them. So they stretched a piece of wire about six inches above the floor, and when he went out of the barracks, he tripped and went tumbling down them steps and skinned himself up pretty good. Of course, the next morning he told the lieutenant, and the lieutenant got the sergeants, and they went down there to make the person tell about putting the wire up. He made them all stand at attention. Well, you know, those boys couldn't stand at attention very long. Before long, there'd be six of 'em laying on the floor that had fainted. You can't really stand at attention if you are not trained to it. You just can't do it. So some of those men just fainted, and the rest wouldn't talk, and they never did find out who did that!

Robert N. Mitcham: Once in a while there were fights, and they'd just put 'em in a ring and let them just fight it out till both of 'em would usually just fall out and lay there. Both of 'em got a good whippin'. [Laughing.] And they had some caught selling whiskey. They'd slip it in there in camp. And stealing. But I never was involved close enough to know too much about any of it. But I know they had trials, and about the worst sentence you could get would be a three-dollar fine. If it was bigger than that, it was a dishonorable discharge. Now they did try some of 'em and discharge 'em. I know they did. I didn't see the discharge, but you could hear everything that went on, you know.

And some of 'em "went over the hill." A lot of 'em left like that. I don't remember 'em every bringing any of 'em back.

I got in trouble one time. I had already planned a trip, and they were out there waiting for me. I went to talk to the man that made the rules. They would let you get somebody to work in your place, but you had to get permission and get it okayed. [But I couldn't get permission because] he had to go off and didn't come back, so I just hired somebody to work in my place [anyway] and took off. He gave me Christmas KP for the whole week for taking off. But I had a good foreman there, and he talked [the captain] into letting me out of it. So I got Christmas week off, and I didn't have to make my Christmas KP. I never *did* have to make it. But that was my punishment for leaving without permission. It would've been all right if I'd'a waited and got permission, but I was in too big a hurry. [Laughing.] I had to go.

Accidents and Deaths
"There was one old boy that died up there.
I never will forget that. He was just as fine
a boy as you ever seen"—Minyard Conner

Buck Carver: Our camp was the only one in Rabun County that had a doctor and an ambulance. If somebody got sick in one of the other camps, they'd bring him over and let the doctor work on him and then send him on back to camp or to the hospital at Fort McPherson.

I remember one time an old boy over there at Camp 5 on Tallulah River got rattlesnake bit. Him and two or three more boys had been out about all night. They was drinking pretty heavy, you know, and they laid down under some walnut trees before they got back to the camp, and that guy got onto a rattlesnake, and it bit him. Them other guys got him up, and the boys had already been drinking some, you know, and they got him to drink about a quart of liquor before they got him over there to that doctor. You talk about a doctor raising Cain. He cut his leg in several places, put suction faucets on it, loaded him up in an ambulance, and they took off to the hospital. Then he had the first sergeant blow that reveille whistle and lined us all up out there. It was raining that morning, and we didn't have to go out to the woods to work. He lined us up out there, by the way, and you talk about a doctor giving us a going-over about if we ever get snake-bit to be sure to keep that liquor away! Lots of people then thought liquor was a good remedy for snakebite, but that doctor sure told them different! He said be sure and never give anybody whiskey if they got snake-bit.

But that guy that got bit was crazy. While the doctor was still working on him, the doctor said, "This is going to hurt."

And that boy said, "Doc, ain't the average man got about forty-eight feet of guts?"

He said, "Yep."

That boy said, "Well, I'm a little above average. I got fifty-two feet." Said, "Just pour into it!" And he just laid there and went on with all kinds of talk like that, and that doctor cutting on him like nobody ever seen. Cut them gashes in an "X" shape about a quarter of an inch deep, right over each fang mark.

We was awful lucky there at Camp 6. As long as that camp operated, there never was nobody that got bit by one of them things, but, boy, we sure did go through some snaky country. We had canvas leggings we wore that laced up the sides to protect our legs from snakes. I told them if a snake seen them darn things, they'd run themselves to death getting away from them! Most of the men would wear them in the winter when it snowed to keep their pants dry, but they sure hated to wear them in the summer when they needed them most because they were so hot. But they tried to make us wear them anyway.

Ernest Dotson from down here at Wiley got spinal meningitis. They transferred him to Fort McPherson, but he didn't make it. He died. And they quarantined the whole camp. I don't remember how many weeks that quarantine lasted, but it was several. That was after I had done got out of the camp and got dis-charged, but I still had three brothers-in-law down there and lots of friends.

Then there was a foreman named————[name withheld] that got killed in a car wreck. That was after they abandoned Camp 1 over at Mountain Rest, South Carolina. They transferred quite a number of them boys including my brother-in-law, Buford Garner, over to Georgia F6. Buford was a Civil Service guy down there over at the rock quarry at Hale Ridge Road. He was working on some machinery up there one morning, and he couldn't get it to go to suit him, and directly he said, "I'm a s-o-b!"

A little boy from South Carolina said, "I knowed you was a s-o-b, but I don't know where you're from."

He said, "South Carolina, where the rest of the s-o-b's come from."

That little boy said [to Garner], "No, Mr. Garner, [the foreman] ain't from South Carolina." Well [the foreman] was from Georgia, and he overheard him, and my brother-in-law said he thought he was going to hit that little boy. But everybody disliked [that man], I don't even think his wife liked him. He didn't make no efforts to make anybody like him. Seemed that he tried to see how many enemies he could make. When he got killed in that wreck, I was out of the CCs, but I didn't see nobody shedding no crocodile tears. Didn't get no reports of it either.

Minyard Conner: They was one old boy that died up there. I never will forget that. He was just as fine a boy as you ever seen. It was Thanksgiving or some kind of holiday, and they had beer there. It used to be dry way back then, and beer hadn't been in long, and this boy come down there. He was just a friend to every-body, and he said he'd never had as much beer as he could drink in his life. Well, every boy, I guess, tried to give him a can or two of beer apiece, and he took their beer and drunk it just as fast as they give it to him. And he drunk enough of that, and I reckon he couldn't belch or something, and he died, by George, with the doctor right there. Musta busted something in there.

Women

"We were taught that we shouldn't be a-flirtin' with a CCC guy"—Edith Cannon

Edith Cannon: The boys that were in the CCC camps were unmarried. They wouldn't [let] any married men in the CCC camps, I don't think.

Whenever the first of the CCC boys came, we didn't have much [of a good opinion of them] because they liked to flirt with the girls. They were away from home, most of 'em, and we were taught that we shouldn't be a-flirtin' with a CCC guy. It was not proper for us to flirt with a CCC boy.

Most of 'em wasn't from here. They were from somewhere else. I dated a local boy, but my sister-in-law dated a boy from out of the county, and another one of my friends dated a boy from out of town. As far as they were concerned, they were real nice boys, but when they got out of the CCC camps, why, they went on back to their hometown. I believe one of 'em was from Lavonia [Georgia], and one of 'em was from Hartwell or somewhere like that. They didn't stick around. Up here, all the girls married boys that had been in CCCs, but after they got out.

Ruby Callenback: [I first met my husband, Ralph, when] my daddy hired him to work. We had a cane patch.

Edith Cannon, widow of the late Robert Cannon.

We were about the same age, so we just got to going together, and first thing you know we was married. I married him while he was in the CCC camp [F9 in Lakemont, Georgia].

Mildred Story: Alton was stationed here at Camp F6. His father had died the year he graduated from high school. With no prospects of going on to college [he joined the CCCs]. He came on a truck convoy from Concord, Georgia.

The first time I saw him, I was the director of the Baptist Training Union and the Clayton Baptist Church. He and several other boys came the first Sunday they were in Clayton. Now, our local boys, you can imagine how they felt about them. They would not give them the time of day, and if you looked [at the CCC boys] you were off their list from then on. Well, I figured that there must be something to this fellow, or he would not come to church the first night. So, bit by bit, we [met at] parties and things like that, and I began to go with him. After his term, he got a job with Leon Bleckley at Bleckley's Grocery Store, which was in one of the buildings where Reeves is now. He worked for him there and stayed in Clayton in the Bleckley House [a boardinghouse], which was owned by Leon's mother. So the courtship progressed until 1933. I guess [that] was when we were married.

The Final Analysis
*"I'd never have been nothing but a plowboy
if it hadn't been for CCC"—Bill Southards*

Carlton English: Roosevelt did a good job with what he had to do with. People talk about what a bad shape this country's in now. Why, we're 200 percent better off now than we've ever been. This country was then, I'd say, a poor country. The farmers weren't getting enough for what they made to pay the fertilizer bill. They just barely made a living, and some of them *didn't* make a living. You couldn't get a day's work nor a nickel anywhere. There just wasn't anything to do. The country's in so much better shape now because it's better educated. We've got educated people now that run and manage and look after and care for the country—that know how to take care of it. In those days, they didn't.

They fell behind from lack of knowing what to do ahead of time.

In those days, people didn't have money and didn't have work, and there wasn't plenty of clothing and things like there is now. Back then there weren't any shirt factories nor pants factories around here. With what clothing they gave you in the CC camp, you had more'n anyone else. And they had a good laundry and kept 'em up. So you were clothed real good, and we had plenty of bed sheets and blankets and all that; and you had good food, and a clean, decent place to stay that was run on a clean order, and you had a job with pay. That's pretty good, now.

So that scattered a lot of dollars and a lot of jobs. It gave work all over the country. With the road building and all the work they did, and the money they spent—it helped. It helped those boys get out and get started, and it made good soldiers out of a lot of them.

If they could ever crank up some idea now that could give work to the boys or men that don't have work, it would help the unemployment situation here today. You take local boys across here that're not in school and that don't have a good job—they'd be glad to get in a CC camp if they'd pay 'em like average pay is going now. And there's plenty of work here for 'em to do. There's plenty of roadwork, park work, and everything else they could be doing. It would take a load off the county and state. Where the state works up and down these roads and the county works up and down these roads, they could set up some kind of an organization like the CC boys was, and it'd be a help. I'm sure it would.

Bill Southards: We've got to have goods and bads at different times of the world, but for his time, I believe you couldn't beat Roosevelt. If I had any good word to say about any man, I'd say that he done one good deed for poor people, because he put the CCs in for the poor class of people, and it was really a good thing. It meant a dollar a day and three good meals a day and a bed to sleep in, and that's something we wasn't used to. We worked, now. We had to work hard, but the CCs meant more than being in college to me. I'd never been nowhere but on the farm, and we wasn't financially able to go off nowhere. So it really meant something to me. I'd have never been nothing but a plowboy if it hadn't been for CCC.

Robert Cannon: The only [place] in Rabun County where you can tell there was a camp is over there on Moccasin Creek. You can still see the old concrete they poured down there to set the mess hall on. There isn't nothing left of Georgia F6. They tore it down, and it's growed up in white pine trees. You wouldn't even know where the camp was at now.

NOTES

1. Merrill, Perry H., *Roosevelt's Forest Army: A History of the CCC* (Barre, Vt.: Northlight Studio Press, 1981), p. 9.
2. Ibid., p. 122.
3. Ibid., p. 19.
4. Ibid., p. 122.

The WPA

As Frank Adams Smith says in his interview, "When the Depression came, we had a terrible time. Anyone who didn't go through it can't really appreciate what the Depression meant. There was absolute hunger. I had men that came to work that were so weak from hunger that they couldn't stand up. It was awful."

Established on May 6, 1935, the Works Projects Administration was one of several work programs President Roosevelt enacted to alleviate the suffering of the Depression. FDR appointed Harry Hopkins, who had advised him to enact the program, as head. Because it was a program for economic relief, as in the CCCs, some of the money earned by WPA employees had to be sent to their families. Each employee was paid $15 to $90 per month, depending on the job he or she had. The workers also received food and housing when their jobs required it.[1]

When the WPA began, it was called the Works Progress Administration, but in 1939, it was renamed the Works Projects Administration. The name change reflected the plan of the program: to create projects that would be useful to the people and would also make good use of America's natural resources such as land and water. The vast majority of WPA workers were unskilled laborers who were frequently accused of being less productive than their privately hired counterparts. In "Personality Portraits," Granny

Frank Smith's altruism and vision helped bring Rabun County out of the Depression years.

Toothman talks about the poor reputation of WPA workers and comes up with a plausible reason for it: "[The WPA people] always got the name of being lazy, but they really weren't; they just had too many men on their projects." The fact is, however, that even if the charge was true in some cases, rather than receiving direct relief with no obligations, the workers accomplished an enormous amount of useful work. In the first two years of operation, for example, the WPA had accomplished the following projects across the nation:

School Buildings Constructed	1,634
Air Strips	105
Tennis Courts	3,000
Storage Dams	3,300
Golf Courses	103
Traveling Libraries Established	5,800
Health Clinics	1,654
New Rural Roads, Miles	36,000
School Lunches Served	128,000,000
WPA Home Nurse Visits	2,000,000

Theatrical Productions	1,500
Fish Hatcheries Constructed	134
Braille Pages Transcribed	1,100,000
Literacy Classes Conducted, Per Month	17,000[2]

WPA labor was also used by the Resettlement Administration (in reclaiming submarginal land from which farmers had been relocated), the Rural Electrification Administration (in extending power lines to farm homes not served by private utilities), and the National Youth Administration (in building shelters to house transient youth). The latter program was formed in 1935 and put under the control of WPA. It not only provided shelter for homeless youth, but it also provided job training for sixteen- to twenty-five-year-olds who had dropped out of school or graduated and could not be supported by their families.[3]

In June of 1943, at the conclusion of its eighth year, the WPA was phased out. These were some of the primary national accomplishments of those eight years:

Highway, Miles	651,087
Repaired Bridges	124,087
Public Structures Constructed	125,110
Parks Established	8,192
Air Strips	853[4]

Now that the overall national view of the WPA has been reviewed, it can be examined in terms of its effects locally. In Rabun County, Georgia, the WPA was quite productive. Through it, three school buildings were constructed in the Tiger, Dillard, and Persimmon communities. WPA crews also erected the old courthouse, the old Rabun County High School gymnasium, and the Clayton community building. Except for the old courthouse, all of these structures still stand as the most visible legacy of the WPA. But we wanted to know more: how did the program affect the lives of the people in the county who worked in it? What else did it accomplish?

In order to investigate the WPA in more detail, we had to find someone who had firsthand knowledge of it. Among other people, we found Frank Adams Smith. Not only did Mr. Smith know and have direct personal experience with the WPA, but he also knew of many other events—some of which he made happen—that oc-

These buildings were built by the WPA and are still in use in Rabun County. This is the old Rabun County High School gymnasium, which is still used as a gym by the county's recreational department.

The old Persimmon School, now the Persimmon community center.

The cannery at Dillard, Georgia, where local people still bring their summer produce to "put up."

curred during or following the Great Depression. In his interview, he unleashed a stunning wealth of information.

Mr. Smith was county ordinary and probate judge from 1937 through 1951. Before we interviewed him, we didn't know that he had helped establish Black Rock Mountain State Park, which draws many thousands of tourists each year. We didn't know that he had created a bookmobile program that still serves the people of Rabun County. He also was responsible for administering the school hot lunch program that has continued—but not without a fight—to this day. And he was active in other, non-WPA-related activities, such as setting up a maternity home for Rabun County—the first of its kind in the state.

Mr. Smith comes from a family of achievers. He is the brother of Lillian Smith, famed author of *Strange Fruit,* the novel about racism in a small Georgia town. Like Frank, Lillian was well educated. She studied briefly at Columbia University and traveled worldwide, writing *Strange Fruit* in Brazil. Altogether, she wrote five novels and a collection of short stories before her death in 1966.

Now in his nineties, Frank Smith is a healthy, mild-mannered man with an energetic attitude. Mr. Smith lives in a small home in Clayton, and still drives his car and is not dependent on anyone. At this time of his life, he is very concerned with stopping war. He constantly writes to politicians expressing his views on the need to make peace and rid the world of the bomb. He has many books on that subject, some of which he recently donated to the Rabun County Public Library—also begun by him with WPA support.

His wife, Maud Derrick Smith, has died but remains Mr. Smith's inspiration. She encouraged him throughout his years of public office. Mr. Smith has established a scholarship for Rabun County High School students in the memory of his wife. It is awarded every year to qualified college-bound students whom he interviews personally as part of the selection process.

As he helped edit some parts of his interview, Mr. Smith added interesting anecdotes that happened forty or fifty years ago, bringing to life for a high school student an era only read about in history books. The stereotype of failing memory at his age in no way applies to this high-spirited walking encyclopedia of a man.

When he was head of the Depression-era Federal Emergency Relief Administration (FERA) in Rabun County, Mr. Smith administered the local government work programs. Following the interview with him are several that look at the WPA from a different angle—that of the men and women who found in the program the dignity of employment and relief from grinding poverty and near starvation.

—Roger Groening

Frank Smith

"Would you like to know why we came to Rabun County? I was born in another century. I was born October 31, 1895, in Jasper, Florida, Hamilton County. That's in the central north section of Florida just below Valdosta, Georgia. My father had a big family of nine children, and he was in the lumber and turpentine business on quite an extended scale. He had a twenty-mile railroad to get his timber.

He had come up here in 1911 because he needed a rest and he liked it here. The county surveyor was talking to him at that time and said, "Mr. Smith, if you really want to buy some property up here, I can take you out where it's a marvelous buy and nobody in Clayton is interested because it joins colored town."

We didn't have a color problem, and Papa said, "That makes no difference to me. Let's go and see it." So he took him a mile and a half out Chechero Road and showed him a hundred and eighty acres that Papa bought at a ridiculously low price. He remembered that when he was starting out in business, my mother, who had inherited a little farm in Hamilton County, gave it to him to start his business. So he said, "Well, she ought to have something back. I'm going to put this mountain property in her name." [It was] just lucky [he did that because he lost everything he owned when he went bankrupt later].

We had come up here in 1912, '13, and '14 just for the summer months, and the first summer we built a little cabin for the family. My older brother, Joseph, and I were to help build the cottage, but Joe and I hardly knew how to even saw a piece of lumber. My father had to get some other help, but we'd tote them the lumber. We built a little cabin with a little shelter on the outside to cook, and our family had the best time we ever had when we came up here. We thought we were many miles out in the mountains, in the wilderness, cooking outside. We had a grand time, and we enjoyed it those three summers.

[My father] was overly optimistic with his business dealings, and he was overexpanded when a severe recession came along in 1913 and '14, just before World War I. At the beginning of the war years, he lost everything he had. After my father lost his property down there in Hamilton County, our family moved up here. I wasn't around then. I had gone out to be with the Mormons in Utah and

Mr. Smith stayed after school to discuss the Depression Era. He is shown here in the Foxfire classroom at Rabun County High School.

was there one year [during 1914 and 1915]. They sure made me feel like I was an intruder, too, in a way. I was a "Gentile." I didn't realize I was a Gentile before, but I was a Gentile to them. The non-Mormons had developed a church and a school. I was teaching school out there so I missed that trauma of breaking up in Florida and coming up here. It was hardest on the three youngest. My brother Wallace was the youngest child. Then there was Esther, who's still living out there on that same property on Chechero Road, and Lillian, who died in 1966. My father was in his middle fifties and broke. How in the world he even made a living, I don't know, but he got hold of a little portable sawmill and began. That was what he was used to. While in Florida, he had employed two hundred men. Up here, just two or three men and himself began a small sawmill operation.

He would accumulate some lumber and have a little cottage built. The larger place for our family had already been started so he was able to complete that building. Then they built several cottages, as they could, for summer people to come to. When he got the first cottage built, my parents rented it to people, usually our friends who knew we were up here. My father built one, two, three, four cottages that way. When they got several cottages built and occupied, they called it Laurel Falls Hotel. The name was bigger than the business to start with, because it took several cottages to make a hotel. However, we did get to where we could handle eighty or ninety people.

Later, in 1920, we decided to start a summer camp for girls, and I still don't understand how we had the nerve to do that when we had nothing to go on but a beautiful site and a number of cottages. All the cottages were finally connected with a covered walk. Then there was the beautiful little Laurel Falls. We had to build a little dam up the creek, back of the place. How in the world we did it, I don't know, but we opened with sixty-five girls [see p. 74 in the Tallulah Falls Railway section]. My father and I ran it for five years. My sister Lillian was over in China for three years, and when she came back, we turned the camp over to her. Then we moved it up to a ridge of Screamer Mountain where she ran it for about twenty-five years.

I took over the lower place where the camp had been and established a summer hotel. We called it Woodland Lodge and had cottages on both sides of the road that could each take care of eight or nine people. My wife and I ran that for about twelve years.

Back in those days, trips to Rabun County for the summer were mostly to rest and eat. Almost every hotel in the county had really good food. The visitors would ride horseback, and a lot of young people would walk up to the top of Black Rock Mountain. Some would go fishing. They didn't come to be entertained back then. They usually came from hot sections of the country just to relax and enjoy the climate and eat a lot and have a good time.

Then Georgia Power came in and began constructing a power plant at Tallulah Falls. They began the building of their dams, which brought in jobs and some money, and they finally bought about 15 percent of the county acreage. An elderly lady [Helen D. Longstreet], widow of a confederate general, put up a magnificent fight against construction of the lakes because they would destroy the beautiful waterfalls at Tallulah—but to no avail. When Georgia Power built these lakes [Rabun, Burton, Seed, Tugalo, Tallulah], the real movement of vacation homes started.

[Then came the Depression itself.] The stock market crash, of course, was in 1929. Up here we had felt some pretty bad times even before that, for several reasons. One was that we felt the effects of the boll weevil, as all of the South did. Then we felt the effects of the bankruptcy of the banking system where our bank was a member. We also felt the effects of the Florida boom bursting; we felt that very much. So we were having rough sledding for a number of years. Anyone who didn't go through that can't really appreciate what the Depression meant. There was absolute hunger. Hunger. Ordinary Will Smith (no relation) had appointed me as head of the FERA (Federal Emergency Relief Administration) in Rabun County. I had several men coming to work who were too weak to stand up unless supported by holding onto a shovel. I would send them home with a grocery order and tell them to come back when they had regained their strength.

I had known poverty in a casual way and took it for granted, you know; it's just one of those things. But when you come face to face with people starving to death, it's a different thing.

The first job I had due to the Depression was as manager of the Rabun County Employment Service. In 1933, before they even started the federal relief, the U.S. Government set up employment offices all over the United States, not to give jobs, but I think to determine the actual extent of employment. We were down on Savannah Street where we rented an office. We got a few people jobs, but not too many. The government did get a pretty good idea of total unemployment, but it also incited hope that there were jobs available for everyone. Many people were disappointed.

I remember the first day of registration it looked like the whole county was coming in. I had to do something about it. We had five or six people working—taking applications—but we still couldn't handle it. So I said, "We'll have to issue numbers, about the number we know we can take care of every day, and give tickets to all the others. There is no use in their standing all day and not even getting in." So we did that and carried on that way until all the county was registered, and it was a big registration because a large number wanted jobs. It was too bad because I knew they were going to be disappointed. We found maybe seventy-five or eighty jobs for several months.

Most of the time during the Depression, we didn't make very much money, but I did some accounting in the winter; I was also preparing myself in law studying on my own through correspondence courses on those long winter nights. I went about six months, one session, to Atlanta Law School. I passed the bar examination and I could have practiced law if I'd wanted to, but I never did. After that, I studied and became a CPA, which was harder for me than the law.

When Judge Will Smith died, his son Lamar Smith, a lawyer, filled out his term, which was just one year. He didn't run again, so that was when I ran. I was running Woodland Lodge when I ran for ordinary, and I knew I couldn't do both, so I just turned the hotel over to my younger brother to run. I began my term in 1937. The title of my job was Judge of the Court of Ordinary, and [so] for seventeen years I had the wonderful title of "Ordinary Frank Smith"! [The office of county ordinary also served as county probate judge and commissioner.] The term "ordinary" is an old Anglo-Saxon term. It was the original form of county government in Georgia. The probate judge, or county ordinary, was chief executive of the county. He ran the county and he really had to ask no one anything, except to talk it over with the grand jury. When I held the office, if any project with any expense was proposed, I discussed it with the grand jury. I wrote the checks, but the grand jury, when in session, represented the county. There was no other agency that did. I would go before them every time and discuss things. Luckily, for my sake, I had audited the books of the county for three years before I went into politics. During those three years, I became familiar with every phase of the county. I had audited every penny they'd spent, so that helped me a lot.

When I got in office I discovered a man was walking eight miles to work, working all day, and having to walk eight miles home. I just said that can't be—we can't let that happen. The county hadn't been doing anything about that. So I sent out county trucks, which we enclosed with tarpaulins for the winter, and we would haul men that were quite a long distance from the work, to the work.

For the first time, I think I began to understand poverty. [Now] that was a change in my life. I'd seen a lot of poverty, but I didn't understand it [until then].

The WPA had started in 1935. Before I came in office, some of the projects had already been established. As ordinary I had nothing to do with the WPA except the supervision of the county work. I handled that, and I nearly always had at least a hundred men working for me on the county roll. Three hundred was the highest number of workers the WPA had in Rabun County at any one time. In the end, the numbers had gotten down with the development of the Civilian Conservation Corps and everything.

Some of the ideas for the projects were federal and some local. The federal government made some sociological and economic surveys in various counties until they got an idea of what they really needed. The WPA, of course, was a federal job, and then the states had to set up [their own] organizations. The [state] organization [had] to cooperate with the federal government and [also work with] the counties.

In the early period of relief work—the early 1930s—the county didn't have machinery, so a lot of that work was pick and shovel. That was when we could only pay fifty cents a day. Later, we could pay more, and the county was in position to buy some heavy machinery.

We got some good workers out of the WPA. We built a lot of roads, but one thing that I liked was whenever we had to rebuild a bridge. If we had a bridge, it was wood, and we would do a lot of rock work with it. [Many] of those are covered up now, but a lot of men in Rabun County had a natural talent for rock work, and they did some beautiful rock work for those bridges. They took pride in that.

We also had women working. A lot of times there wasn't any man head of the family. That's why we had to have some projects for the women. One of their projects was making mattresses. Thirty or forty women from needy families made the mattresses and they were then given to those that needed them. They also made clothing, and let me tell you another thing: some of the experiences those women had helped a lot when we got a shirt factory in our county later.

There were two canneries built which furnished jobs for the canning, and that was a real help for the county. And the gymnasium down here for the high school was built. A rock school was built in Tiger, and several other schoolhouses were built.

Another project that we worked like the devil on was making outhouses for homes and schools that didn't have them. They would pay for the material if they were able, and if they couldn't then we'd make them anyway. Three of the schools didn't have any outhouses, so I immediately went to the county board. I said, "Hey, you buy the materials, and we'll fix them right quick"—and we did.

I would cooperate any way I could with the school board. The schools were county business as much as anything. If the county school board wanted a school built, and they wanted WPA labor to build it, we would work together. If there was any grading to be done, the county would do it—things like that, you know.

I've always liked books. I knew that in the county there was not a great deal of reading matter because it was such a [hard time and the people couldn't get to any books]. [They had] maybe the Bible or the Sears Roebuck catalogue [or] a bulletin that came out from the Department of Agriculture. It occurred to me [that if] we could start a library the government would help some. Up here, we didn't have much money, you know.

The Rabun County Library was set up in 1937. I have to be frank. It could not have been done except for the WPA paying the librarian to get it started. I don't know that the grand jury would have authorized me to pay the money or not. I talked over those things—all the finances—with the grand jury.

The library was started up in a little office up in the old court-house. We had a little room upstairs about four by six feet. That's all the space we had. I fixed it up with shelves and everything, and I gave them about 100 of my books. The Women's Club had had a library in Clayton a number of years before. This library had been inactive for twenty-five years, so they gave their books, and about a hundred citizens came in and contributed, making the total about 300. I never will forget the first day. We only had one visitor, but we soon outgrew that little place. Then an idea came to me [that] the large grand jury room with the space of an empty office room back of it would be big enough to move the library to so we opened it up. We made a nice room with about five windows overlooking Black Rock.

In 1939, I decided we just had to have a bookmobile. That wasn't an original idea; in fact, there are not too many original ideas. The point is when you see a good idea to accept it. Well, I read somewhere that the Tennessee Valley Authority had decided to put in a little bookmobile to carry books in the mountains of Tennessee. I said, "Well, if they can do it, by George, we can do it in Rabun," because I knew the families needed that. We began talking about it—the first in the state. But a county down in South Georgia—Thomas County where Thomasville is—heard about this little county talking about a bookmobile. They said, "Well, while they're talking about it, we'll go ahead and do it," and they did. But here's the funny thing: theirs didn't last a year, while ours is still going.

You could hardly understand how eager [people were for] the bookmobile. We had two people, a driver and a person to look after the books. They said [people] were just so eager to see that bookmobile they couldn't believe it. They were checking books out all over the county.

At that time, our circulation of library books in Rabun County was 79,000 a year, which was three times the national average. This was more than ten books for every person in the county. I was proud of the way the library developed.

We got a tremendous amount of good out of the WPA in Rabun County. There wasn't any slack work going on here, I'll tell you that. We didn't do any of what has been referred to as "leaf raking" jobs. Every job we tried to do meant something, and that was true all the way through. It was good without any question. Many of the buildings we built are still being used. The old gymnasium is still here. It still is used quite a bit. The canning plants are still here and used. We built the school at Tiger, the one at Persimmon, the school at Satolah, and the one at Bridge Creek—Lake Burton.

Another program initiated through the WPA was the hot lunch program in the public schools. Mr. Smith regards that program as one of the more important ones.

We [in the county] didn't do anything to initiate the hot lunch program. That was done in Congress. It was under the WPA and couldn't have been started any other way. Some kitchens were within the school, and some of the larger schools had separate buildings. We built some of the buildings with the help of WPA. It was a matter of cooperation. WPA and the U.S. Government, and state, and the agencies within the county all cooperated. That's why we had such a fine program, and there was no doubt that it was one of the best for a rural county in the whole country. Before that time, students and teachers brought their lunches to school or went home at lunchtime to eat. For some children, the hot lunch that was served at the school was the only well-balanced meal they ate each day. They were delighted to have a hot lunch, you know, and I don't blame them.

Melvin Taylor

Well, after Roosevelt come into office, things began to pick up. That's when come the WPA, and my dad worked for that. They normally paid sixteen cents a hour, but my dad was a stone mason, so he covered walls and stuff and got twenty cents a hour, which for the times was good. While WPA was in Rabun County here, they built the gym at the old high school, and they built that rock building in the center of Clayton, the community house, it used to be. Now they built that all in that time. They wasn't no money a'tall back before then.

During the WPA, they had a sewing room, they called it, put up by the government up there where the Mountain City Playhouse is now. And ladies, that was a job for them. Best I remember they didn't have these electric machines; they'd pedal with their feet, you know, old-timey. Well, they made pants, made shirts, and give 'em out to people that needed them in the community. That took care of the clothing. They made some good clothes. The pants were made out of blue demin, and the shirts were made out of light blue denim.

Before they come in with the WPA and all that, we never had a mattress in our lives excepting a tick full of rye straw packed in it. That's what your mattress was—pack all the rye straw in there you could get in good thick ticking where that stuff wouldn't stick you through it. When they got wore down in a while, we'd either change the straw or pack more in it, you know. It wasn't bad. Straw is not a bad thing to sleep on. It's soft. A lot of 'em we used to put hay in 'em, but most of the time they had rye straw.

Then when they put up the factory up there where all the families could go, we made our own mattresses. That's the first [cotton] mattress I ever saw. Every family could go up there and make enough mattresses for everybody to have one. They'd furnish the cotton and the ticking and everything, and some lady would show you how to do it. Boy, that was a job a-beating that stuff with a paddle, and I got the sore throat and everything from that cotton dust. I never will forget that. We made enough mattresses and fixed 'em, nice ones, to have us all a good something to sleep on.

Also, back then they wasn't no plumbing much. Your water run into the house [from a spring], or you got it out of a well. [WPA] built a lot of outdoor bathrooms and stuff. They made 'em out of concrete and everything and took it to their house and put it up. For most people out in the country, that was the best there was in that day.

The WPA worked on roads, and built roads, and built a park at the Lake Rabun beach down there, and they were real assets. They worked all the time. Mostly what they did was build roads— Warwoman through to Hale Ridge, all over Rabun County—that's what they did. Most of these roads in Rabun County was built by 'em. They had machinery, you know, good stuff to work on 'em, and that's what they did. Most anybody at that time who would work, they could find a job. Of course it's kind of like it is right now, I mean the jobs are scarce and stuff, but anybody that's really hunting a job, it may not be the best job in the world and pay the most money, but they can find one of some sort.

That whole golf course, and the swimming pool [in Clayton], that was all built then. If you ever go to that golf course, you can see where those outside bathrooms had been. There are also springs up there that's built out of rock with a spring in under it. There's a beautiful one up there at [hole number] seven. It has a big hole carved out in the rock, and that water runs out of there. Everybody stops there and gets water. Even got a water can up there. About every time I go by there, I stop and get water.

Harold Brown

I had to go to Franklin to sign up for the WPA. [The only requirements were] that you be able to work and not have any other income. I just don't know what year that was. There wasn't nothin' else to do [except the jobs around home]. We put in a pretty good bit of crops—corn, 'taters, beans. My woman had a good garden. We had our milk and butter, and most of the time a hog to kill. Nowadays we have to live out of paper pokes [sacks of groceries from the store]. I told someone the other day now it was bills and pills—that's all. [Laughter.]

The work I did was on the roads. I helped build headwalls for the culverts in those big streams across the roads, and we'd dig banks off and slope them. I worked on that Dillard-Highlands road. We remodeled and widened it, and then they paved it. Then I worked on the road that goes to Georgia up by Otto through Dillard.

Whenever I went to work up there [near Otto], I'd had rheumatism a long time and I was drawn over and my head was just about that high [three feet] off the ground. My hip was drawn out of place, too. My daddy lived over that way, and so my brothers took me to a chiropractor up there at Mud Creek. She'd get my hip back in place. Then I'd come back to my brother's over that bumpy road and it'd go out again. Finally she had to come down [to his house] and put it back in place. She taped me up and it never did come back out that I know of, but it still gives me trouble.

When I got to where I could go back to work, they gave me the nail keg to sit on [and I was a flagman]. They was that good to me and let me go back to work. [Two of the men who were over us were Mr. Burgess and Mr. Scott.] Mr. Burgess must have been from South Carolina or somewhere over that way. Mr. Scott was a local man. He lived down there on the river.

They'd transfer the boys once they got their job done. When the Dillard road was finished, they transferred me up here to the rock quarry at Highlands [but there were so many men on that job they sent me] up right this side of Highlands. They had poured a cement form for the big creek over there, where it comes onto the road, and wanted us to tear the form out, get down in that water and tear that form out of there, and I wouldn't get down in there. I knowed they couldn't make me [since I had] flagman's papers. If I'd gotten hurt, they would have gotten the bossman, wouldn't they? I wasn't signed up for that.

They had me laid off, so I went to [Franklin] to Miss Franks down there. She was in the WPA office down there, and I told her how everything was. She gave me Mr. Hanes's address at Asheville for me to write him. Whenever I heard from him, they never did bother me anymore. I went to work [on a job] up toward Buck Creek. I worked on that road, and then I worked on the Flat Mountain road from Highlands. I carried water to the boys that were working on the road there, so they wouldn't keep going up there to get 'em a drink of water. They were putting up locust posts and barbed wire along there. The boss would put me in the car [for me to get a ride]. [Laughter.] I guess I was about forty-five then. Time passes and you don't think about it. You don't keep up with time.

I just quit the WPA. I told them I was gonna go home and rest up a while, and I never did go back. That's what I told them, and I never went back. I don't know how come [the WPA] ever quit. They were good for our community.

NOTES

1. Rauch, Basil, *The History of the New Deal 1933–1938* (New York: Creative Age Press, 1944) pp. 163–65.
2. Ibid., p. 164.
3. Loucheim, Katie, *The Making of the New Deal* (Cambridge: Harvard University Press, 1983) p. 296.
4. Ibid., p. 177.

Sources

Leuchtenburg, William E. *Franklin D. Roosevelt and the New Deal.* New York: Harper and Row, 1963.

Loucheim, Katie. *The Making of the New Deal.* Cambridge: Harvard University Press, 1983.

Nash, Gerald D. *The Great Depression and WWII: Organizing America 1933–1945.* New York: St. Martin's Press, 1979.

Rauch, Basil. *The History of the New Deal 1933–1938.* New York: Creative Age Press, 1944.

PERSONALITY
PORTRAITS

STUDENT EDITOR, JENNY LINCOLN

This section showcases personal experience narratives of three of our contacts whose lives resonate with the same issues of Depression-era survival, railways, timber harvesting, and federal aid programs featured in the early sections of this book.

Ellene Gowder talks about her family background and her life as a teacher in a logging camp on Moccasin Creek during the Depression. The only professional woman in the camp, she ate in the mess hall with seventy-five men and lived in a boxcar. Teaching the children of those logging families was challenging, and Mrs. Gowder tells a story so detailed that it brings to life the camp and its characters.

Walker Word was reared in a little community called Waco, Georgia, a few miles west of Atlanta. His family owned a mercantile business where his father bought and sold cotton. When Walker was about sixteen, his family lost everything in the Depression; alone, he traveled to Atlanta to find work. A born storyteller, Walker Word vividly recounts rich tales of his life before and after the Depression.

Lyndall "Granny" Toothman is one of those personalities who, as we say, "broke the mold when she was born." Born in West Virginia, she started her adult life as a housewife; but when her coal miner husband was laid off, she began to work in a federal penitentiary where she taught weaving to World War II spies such as Axis Sally and criminals, including Machine Gun Kelly's wife, Katherine. (Granny, by the way, had learned weaving not from a female forebear but in a WPA-sponsored weaving school.) For much of the rest of her life, Granny Toothman has driven her van to crafts fairs and shows all over the country, spinning and weaving stories as well as thread. She is now in her eighties and still hard at work.

Ellene Franklin Gowder

"I was the only lady in the mess hall."

Ellene Franklin Gowder is a career teacher, now retired. She taught all her life in a number of different North Georgia towns—Clarkesville, Robertstown, Turnerville, Amos Creek, Leno, Nacoochee Valley—and at a logging camp on Moccasin Creek during the Depression. After she earned her basic certificate, she studied at Piedmont College and the University of Tennessee to get her two-year certificate and then completed her degree several years later by attending night school and summer school: "You perhaps taught school six or seven months during the year on fifty-five or sixty-five dollars a month, and you were also expected to . . . work toward your college education. It was pretty hard. [But] there are so many new things being discovered and developed. Teachers need to know these things, because how are they going to teach about them unless they know themselves?"

She believed in the importance of using community resources in the classroom, inviting local people to talk to her class and taking her students on many field trips: "I'd have them write about the trip when we came back. You would be surprised at the things first-graders write about: 'Yes, I went to Atlanta. I went to Grant's Park. I saw an elephant. I went to the airport. I went into an airplane.' They wrote short sentences, but they never will forget it."

While she was teaching at Robertstown, Ellene Franklin married George Gowder from Homer, Georgia, with whom she had two children and, eventually, grandchildren: "We could have settled anywhere, but we both liked the mountains. We decided to come here, and we built this house. We also built a little store and ran a business." Although she has retired and her husband has since died, Mrs. Gowder remains active; at the time of our interview she was planning a trip to Africa to visit missionary friends. In her travels, she says, "I've been all over Europe twice and the British Isles, and I've never found any place more beautiful than the mountains of North Georgia."

Like many of our other contacts, Ellene Gowder laments some of the changes wrought by modern life upon the social fabric: "[In general], people were more together back then. The families were more together. They were very close. What was mine was yours, and what was yours was mine. If you needed help, you'd have it; if I needed help, I'd call on you. That's the environment I grew up in. All the neighbors used to pitch in and help each other. I miss that now, because I can't get any little odd jobs done at all. We used to have men and boys in the community who would come help prune your shrubs and clean out your drains. They'd cut your wood if you needed it. People don't do useful things anymore. I'm living in a community of retired people, and of course they're not going to come here and work. And the young people in the community know so little about how to do anything. . . . I had some boys from Georgia Tech visiting today. I know how to hook up my electric wire to my charger for my garden. They're from Georgia Tech, and neither one of them can do it.

"[I think we need to] respect the past and to [use the wisdom of the past] to build the future, because the world goes on. If future generations know what we have done and accomplished, and if we have that foundation to base their lives on, it's going to help them."

The part of Ellene Franklin Gowder's career we were most interested in was her very first teaching job in a Depression-era logging camp operated by the Morse Brothers Lumber Co. on Moccasin Creek, in Rabun County. It was the same logging camp that Bennie Eller talks about in his interview on p. 178. The vividly detailed description Ellene Gowder gives of her experiences in the camp as a rookie teacher brings to life that place and time.

The moment we met Ellene Gowder, we were impressed by her courage, spirit, and determination—as real in her now as they were half a century ago when she got out on her own to teach at Camp Moccasin. We noticed how she used her hands energetically to emphasize strong points. We also noticed what an amazing memory she has. Her precise details about the different jobs at the logging camp, students she has taught, Dr. West and his percolator, and home entertainment and herbal remedies certainly show an extraordinary person who has the wisdom and practical experience of age but the spirit of youth.

—Jenny Lincoln
Interview and photographs by Jenny Lincoln, Leigh Ann Smith, Joanna Chieves, Taphie Galloway, Lori Gillespie, Annmarie Lee, Heather Scull, Jennie Shoemaker, Brooks Adams, Andy Ruth, David Volk, and Al Edwards.

I was born right where I live today [in Batesville, Georgia]. My people pioneered this area. They were here since 1818, and then they got their papers and deeds in 1823, I believe, through the land lottery. We've been here ever since. [The way the land lottery worked], the best I remember, was you had to go out and stake a territory and live on it so many years before you could apply for a deed. They would camp, cut logs, and build a log house to live in until they decided they wanted to settle permanently. It was practically free. I think some of them paid as little as twenty cents an acre for the land.

My great-grandfather, Joshua A. Sutton, was a pioneer man who did a lot for Batesville and the surrounding country. He settled on the Soquee River in Batesville district. He first built a little log cabin. When he decided he liked living there pretty well, he built that sawed plank house that's just below this house and brought his bride there. He reared a big family of children. He had slaves, too. They took his name after they were freed.

I [remember the last slave he had]. [She was] Suzie Sutton and she married [and her name became] Suzie Trammel. When she married a Bean Creek Negro, she moved to Clarkesville and lived in a little cottage behind my great uncle John Hill's house for the remainder of her life. She always lived with my people: never left them.

Joshua Sutton's house. Behind Mrs. Gowder, the horizontal mail slot cut into the front door is barely visible.

Joshua Sutton's house is going to pot now. I'd give anything if I had the money to restore it. It's the first sawed plank house in Habersham County. It was built by slaves. It also served as the first post office in the Batesville district. There's a slot in the door that people would drop their letters in. And it has the first formal garden.

He was pretty well off. He had a commissary or some kind of a trading post, where everyone in the community at that time traded with him. There were no teachers, so he hired tutors to teach his children. They were very well educated. You look at some of the letters they wrote, and the penmanship is just unsurpassed. You couldn't believe it—that a person who had never gone to school could write a letter like that: intelligent, beautifully written—just unbelievable.

My great-grandfather was very active in the land grant business. He was deacon and clerk of Providence Church. He founded the church with two or three other men. Prior to that, they'd been holding meetings in the home. They saw the need for a church, so they established one, and it was built on his property. He also gave the land for the church cemetery.

He also saw the need for a college, so they built one. It was a wooden structure, and the name was Providence College. It was an interdenominational college and was very small. There were only between 200 and 250 students there. They came here from as far away as Elberton, Young Harris, and Gainesville, Georgia. [The professors] taught Latin, Greek, calculus, and premed.

The college was very good for the time. It was particularly noted for producing good teachers, musicians, doctors, lawyers, and preachers. They went from here to all parts of the northeast Georgia area and other places, where they became very prominent citizens.

Providence College thrived from about 1848 until around 1880. The college burned three times [and it was rebuilt the first two times]. After it burned the third time, they decided to move the college to Demorest, Georgia, and call it Piedmont. [*Piedmont survives today, and it provides an affordable education for many people in the area—Ed.*]

I suspect I'm the only one living today who knows anything about [the original Providence College]. The Batesville people do not know anything about it now because that's been a long time ago. The only reason I know about it is that my family was connected with it, and it was on our property. I know where it stood, but there are no documents or anything left, as everything burned.

Anyway, my grandmother, Elizabeth Sutton, was left a widow at the age of twenty-three, with three small children. Because she was an excellent cook, whoever was in charge of Piedmont College at that time asked my grandmother if she would come down and be the dietitian and matron of the girls' dormitory.

Well, her father, Wilson Lumpkin Hill, had moved in to take care of her because it was unheard of for a young widow twenty-three years of age to live by herself and get a job. No, that couldn't be done. When he heard that they had made this offer to my grandmother [Ellene's voice deepens], he says, "No. It's just not fittin' for a young widow to go out and work." And she didn't go.

My grandmother was said to have been the most beautiful girl of her time in Batesville. She was beautiful, but she never remarried. Most women would have at that age. But she didn't.

My mother, Effie Sutton, and Aunt Cora, and Uncle George had to get their education by attending a small local school. I don't know much about that time because before Mama died, I didn't think that information was so important. You know how young people are. We're all alike. We don't think things are important until it's too late.

My father's name was Paul S. Franklin. My mother's name was Effie Mae Sutton Franklin, and she was a teacher and a very intelligent person. She knew the names of every wild plant, every tree, all the bugs and insects and birds and butterflies. She taught all of this to us. We didn't learn that in school; we learned that at home.

I never made a complete list, but I knew both the botanical names for plants and their mountain names—they're different, you know. We call flame azalea "wild honeysuckle." Wild iris is "flags." Laurel and rhododendron is "ivy." Sweet shrub is "bubby bush." And there's a wild snapdragon that is very yellow and grows in damp places. We called them "poopies." Why, I don't know. But every year, we'd go find the poopies. [Laughter.] I still know where there's a bed of wild ginseng; and I know where there's one stand of a vine that's a kind of birch that grows on the ground like trailing arbutus. You mash it, and it has the birch flavor.

I love flowers. It's one of my hobbies still, but I haven't been able to do much with it this year. There's a place I'm going to soon if it's not pouring rain. When I was young, we used to call it Fairyland. It's a mountain stream about a mile from the house, and I'll have to wear my boots and wade. On this stream there's the most beautiful wild plants in the world: grass of Parnassus, bottled ginseng, daisies of different types. It's just a wonderful experience to be able to go out onto a stream like that when you're a child and learn the things we were taught at that time.

When I was a child, part of our education was learning how to do things and make things that were needed in the home. One of the first things we learned to do was to piece quilts. Teaching children to make quilts back then taught many things. It taught color coordination. It taught children the different stitches, and it taught patience.

Quilting at that time was a necessity. Even when a girl first got married, she always had to have twelve quilts to start off with. The bride usually made some of the quilts herself, and then the community usually got together and quilted a quilt or two for the bride.

Our mothers and grandmothers gave us a needle and thread and a little thimble when we were eight or ten years of age, and we were taught how to make a running stitch, a backstitch, a lazy-daisy stitch, and many others. We were also taught to cut patterns from paper for our quilt design. They would show us how to join those different blocks together to form a square. After we had so many squares, we would set them together with stars and bars, and it became a quilt.

Some of the quilt designs we made were the nine-patch, the bear paw, the step-around-the-mountain, and the whirligig. There were any number of arrangements of stars and patterns. And of course there was also always the crazy quilt. You took the scraps as they were, and you fitted them together, usually on a piece of paper. Then after you fitted the blocks, you would trim off the excess around the paper, and you would have a quilt square.

It was during the winter months that people worked the most on piecing quilts because in the winter you could not get out of the house to do anything on the farm or the garden. Once the weather began to warm up in the spring, they would have quiltings at different homes. They'd quilt out perhaps three quilts here. Then they'd go to the next neighbor's house, and quilt out two or three there until they got all the tops that had been made during the winter quilted. People then did not piece quilts on machines, so it took quite a while to make a quilt by hand.

Another thing everybody did [when I was a child] was hunting. People at that time hunted because they needed to rid themselves of varmints. Another reason they hunted was to collect the pelts to sell to the fur companies. It helped them out a lot financially, especially when people had a large family and had to buy school-books. We had to buy all of our schoolbooks. No schoolbooks were free. But many times, the young boys of the family would catch enough possums and raccoons and other animals to buy the school-books, and their winter clothes.

Another thing about hunting was that it was a pastime. It was recreation; it was fun. A lot of times, the girls went hunting with the boys. Often they'd sit around the campfire waiting for the dogs to tree. People enjoyed getting together to hunt, especially if they had an unusually good hunting dog. [Each person] wanted his dog to be the best dog in the pack. [Someone would hear] barking sounds, and he would say, "Now, listen. Old Blue's treed a possum. I'd know Old Blue's voice anywhere."

Someone else would say, "Well, I hear Old Rags. He's picked up a trail."

[We also prepared a lot of good food back then.] Of course we had plenty of pork, and butter and eggs and chickens and things of that type. Families were poor moneywise, but they all had something to eat.

People didn't do very much canning [back then] because they didn't know how. And of course freezing was unheard of. So the early people in this community depended upon root cellars, sauerkraut, and pickled beans. They also dried a lot of beans; they called the dried beans leather breeches.

There were two main types of beans. The tender bean was a green bean that we could use for cooking fresh or making leather breeches. The tough hull bean was the bean they shelled out to make soup beans for the winter. People usually had sacks of soup beans.

[We also made pear preserves.] Usually you would peel and quarter your pears. Sometimes you would cut them up into smaller pieces. You knew exactly how much sugar to use per pound of pears. You would sprinkle the sugar over the pears, and let the pears sit overnight.

The next day, you would boil the pears in their own juice; you had to do that very, very slowly to keep your pears from sticking. Eventually, the juice would begin to thicken. If there was any juice left over, you'd let it sit until the next day, and then you'd cook it again. Usually the pears would absorb all the juice, or it would evaporate; and this would leave your pears rather tough. Your best pear preserves are slightly tough and dark.

We used lots of pottery. My people bought pottery from Meaders Pottery for as far back as I can remember. [See Foxfire 8— Ed.] Most people always bought from the Meaders, and most of them needed [all the pottery] they could get.

It was very essential back then because people used crocks so much. It was as necessary back when I was a child as Frigidaires, deep freezers, electricity, electric fans, and so forth are today. We used crocks to store our milk and butter and to make pickled beans and sauerkraut, and for preserving. We'd take a little cylinder-like cap and a piece of cloth, dip it in beeswax, and [seal it].

They stored molasses—syrup, as we call it—in pottery jugs.

They rendered out their hog fat and stored their lard in churns for the next season's use. They stored whiskey in it, too. They had a special type of jug for their whiskey. Most of them were little brown jugs.

We had a lot of fun, too. We lived on one side of the river, and the Wilbanks family lived across the river from us. Well, we had to hoe these long rows of corn, and when we'd get to the river, we'd have bathing suits, and the Wilbanks children would come from their side of the river over to our side and we would all go swimming together. Then we would put on our field clothes and go back to work. For snacks, while we were working, we would boil potatoes or eggs in an old tin can. [Later] we'd fish or go possum hunting, fox hunting, or coon hunting, and sometimes we'd run into polecats. One time when I was really small—I guess I was about four years of age—some local farmers wanted to see who had the best team of oxen, and they hitched them to some logs they had put together with hooks. The team of oxen that could move those logs so many feet always won the contest.

We had pound suppers where usually all of the younger people of the community would [get together] and bring a pound of some kind of food. Sometimes these pound suppers were held at the local school building, but more often they were held at the homes. Each person who would attend the pound supper would make a cake or a pie or a bowl of beans, more or less like a covered-dish supper now. Each person would put whatever they brought on a long table and all get together and enjoy the feast. Sometimes they had a local string band, often accompanied by an organ. Nearly every home at that time had an organ, and somebody in the family could play the organ. Whether they had ever had a music lesson or not, they could pick up those songs and play them through.

Usually the pound suppers would turn into square dances, and everybody had a good time. Today they do the Western square dancing; we did the mountain square dancing. Wherever we went, our parents went, too. The parents danced with their daughters and their friends' daughters, and everyone danced together. It wasn't a boy-girl dance; it was a family affair.

All of these entertainments we had back then were family-connected. And I think that's good. I think we've gotten away from that too much.

They didn't raise peanuts in this section, but we grew a peanut patch just to have some for home use. We parched them and ate them. It was a great treat. We also grew our own popcorn and made our own sorghum syrup. We had candy pullings after we cut the cane, carried it to the mill, and boiled it down into syrup. We would take some sorghum syrup and boil it down until it was very stiff, and then we would put a tablespoon of soda in it to kind of whiten it up a little bit. When the candied syrup would get cool enough, we would usually grease our hands so that the candy wouldn't stick. We would get a big handful of candy and start pulling it. When we first started, the candy would be dark, but the longer we pulled it, the whiter it got. Eventually, it would be very white and brittle. Then we laid it down on an enamel pan, and we could pick up one of those sticks as a whole and take a knife and hit it, and it would chip off into little pieces. It was a lot of fun for the courting couples to pull the candy together.

We also had cake walks. Mothers and young ladies of the community always made the cakes for the cake walks. If a lady made some kind of especially good caramel cake, she always baked a caramel cake. The lady who made the best coconut cake in the community usually made a coconut cake. There was a band consisting of a violin, a banjo, and a guitar or a uke, and they would play while partners would walk around and around in a circle. The circle had sections with numbers in them from one through sixty. When the music stopped, the person who was in charge of the cake walk would call a number, and if the number was thirty-five and you were standing on number thirty-five, you were lucky. You got a cake.

People used to tell stories at night. Usually they'd sit around the fireside. I remember my great-grandfather telling stories, and I also remember Nicodemus Fain. He was a widower and was lonely, so he would visit different neighbors each night and tell them ghost stories. He would make his round each week. [When he came to see us], our eyes would get as big as saucers. We would be afraid to go into another room to get a drink of water, he would tell such hair-raising ghost stories!

Well, one night after supper, he was down home telling ghost stories, and some of them were very colorful. He told one that was so big and so scary that he had my brother scared stiff. It was necessary for my brother to go get some wood for the fire from the back house, so he got up and started to the back house. [Then he ran back] pounding on the door.

"Let me in! Let me in!"

We opened the door, and he was scared to death. So we asked him what was wrong.

He said, "I saw that thing! I saw that thing out there! I saw that thing that Mr. Fain was talking about!"

My daddy says, "Well, you show me where that thing is, and we'll take care of it."

We went out and looked for the thing, and it turned out to be a large tub where my father had taken the ashes out. It had two live coals in it that looked just like two eyes.

They would also tell hunting and fishing experiences, and they always elaborated on them and told them bigger than they were!

I also remember that corn shuckings were a very important thing back then. The last one I went to was about seventy-eight years ago. There was a young lady named Lela Smith who lived just above us and who was planning to get married. That was in October, and I hadn't started school. My brother was going to school, but I wasn't, so they let me carry my lunch to school with him. That day, after school, we went out to Mrs. Smith's house where the men had been shucking corn all morning. They shucked and they shucked, and every time they'd find a red ear, the boy would get to kiss his sweetheart. Anyway, they shucked until they got pretty well into the center of the [pile] and they found a jug of whiskey. Well, that had to be passed around, and everybody had to have a drink of whiskey, before finishing up the corn shucking.

The ladies had a quilting that afternoon, where they finished up two or three quilts. That night they moved everything out of the living room and had one big square dance. And that was it. It was a small living room, but they had a dance. I wasn't even in school at that time, but I remember it. I learned things when I was young. I even remember who was there.

I finally got to go to grade school. I never went to a nine-month school in my life. Never heard of such a thing. Four- and five-month terms—that was it. And that was split. You had a summer term of six weeks, which was called "the laying by season." That is when you have finished up plowing, hoeing, fertilizing, and all you have to do is wait for the crop to grow.

Then after that six weeks' period, we were out of school for six weeks while we had to pick peas, pull fodder, strip cane, dig potatoes, dig the peanuts, and go back to the woods and round up the cattle that were out on free range. Also, the wood had to be cut for winter, and bedding had to be seen to. There was always something to do. My first year in grade school was spent doing nothing. I sat up on a high desk, and my legs and feet lacked ten or twelve inches from hitting the floor because my desk was so high. I sat between two grown students who were very protective of me. We were not supposed to eat anything except at recess or at lunch. Well, these two grown students were so protective of me that they would slip me food, and I would duck down under the desk and secretly eat apples, peaches, and corn.

The teacher would just maybe have time to give me two minutes during the day, in which I might read half a page which I had memorized and had already read many times before. Back then, we had to do a lot of memory work, especially to memorize a lot of poems. We were also taught arithmetic, English, reading, and spelling.

I remember that after they had more than sixty students in the room, they decided they needed two teachers. Of course they did not have a building for two teachers. So they got gunnysacks and made a partition. They hung it up on a rope from one side of the building to the other.

One time, one of the boys across in the "big room," where they had the upper grades, threw a huge baked sweet potato over that rope. It hit kerplunk!!! on the floor, and splattered all over everything. Well, someone over here in the "little room" just couldn't take that. It would not do to let them get by with it. So the little fellow went to the lunch pail, got two ears of corn, and tossed them back over there.

When I was ready for high school, we didn't have one around here. So I had to go away to a boarding school called Hiawassee Academy. I had to borrow $150 to go, but I went ahead; and in 1928, I finished and obtained an A-1 teacher's certificate, which at that time qualified you to teach in rural communities.

At the time that I grew up, there was nothing for a young lady to do unless it was teach. They frowned on a young lady becoming a nurse or a stenographer. Also, it was more or less something I wanted to do because my mother taught school. My aunt, my uncle, and my grandmother were also teachers. I had heard all of my people talk about what a rewarding thing it was to be a teacher.

So I was in debt. I had no earthly idea how I would pay the money back. And I didn't know where I could teach. Because the Depression hit at just about that time, there was no money. Here in the Batesville district, we all had plenty to eat, and we also had enough to wear, so we did not feel the Depression like a lot of people. Each family had a garden. Each family had hogs, cows, chickens, and a potato patch. When you have all of those, you make out very well. But there was no money. A lot of people didn't have enough money to mail a letter unless they took an egg to the store to trade it for money to buy a stamp, and, by George, they didn't know when that egg was going to be laid, either. It was that bad a lot of the time.

I applied to Habersham County and White County boards of education for a teaching position, and they said that all the teaching positions had been filled. Mrs. Greer who lived in Nacoochee Valley, had been up [at Moccasin Creek in Rabun County to a lumber camp, and] saw what a deplorable situation it was. I think she was the person who decided to do something about it. She talked to the men in the office at Helen who owned the camp about getting a teacher up there.

When Mrs. Greer heard that I wanted a position as a teacher somewhere, along about the first of August she came to my house. She said, "You have a teacher's certificate, don't you?"

I said, "Yes, I do."

She said, "We're looking for a teacher to attempt to teach school up on Moccasin Creek."

I said, "Moccasin Creek?"

She said, "Yes, it's at a logging camp."

I said, "Well, I'll think about it."

And she said, "You know, they'll pay you forty dollars a month."

I said, "I didn't know that. What would I do about room and board?"

She said, "The company would furnish that."

Well, I was desperate for a job, and I looked forward to a great adventure. Barely eighteen and just out of high school, I said, "Yes, I'll go." I had no experience as a teacher, but even a poor teacher was better than none.

It was rather amusing when I first went to the camp. I had no way of getting up there. There were not as many automobiles then as there are today, and they were not as good-looking, either! I didn't have one, because I was too young to have saved up the money to buy one.

Well, I didn't know how in the world I was going to get to camp. It was just beyond me. But I had a friend who lived about three miles down the road. I said, "Jeff, would you, by any means, have enough time to carry me back to Camp Moccasin?"

He said, "Yes, when do you want to go?"

[He had an] old '23 model, long-bedded truck. I got in that old truck, and we huffed and we puffed. The road wasn't paved, and we'd bump and we'd bounce to this side and to that side and the other.

Finally, we arrived at camp. I didn't know what to do going into a place like that. There I was, standing there with my suitcase, not knowing a soul—not one. Then their sheriff, Mr. Sullivan, came up and asked me what I wanted. He was a graduate of Piedmont College, believe it or not. He was a clubfooted man, and the nicest person you ever saw. I told him I was the teacher, and I was supposed to open up a school. He looked me up and down like, "I'll give you two weeks, and that will be the end of you." But anyway, he said, "Where are you going to live?"

I said, "I don't know! The company said they'd furnish room and board."

He said, "I know there is no place at all for you to live."

That's when the sheriff took pity on me. "Well, I'll tell you, the school is very, very important, so I'll just move out of my boxcar and move into this building over here where you'll be teaching."

Well, he moved out, and I moved in. That boxcar had one bed in it, a potbellied stove, and two straight chairs. Someone brought me a dynamite keg, and I had a thirty-five-cent mirror, and that's what I had for my dressing table. My closet was an Army blanket stretched across one corner. There were two little windows up near the top, and no curtains. No electric lights, no running water or

Ellene Gowder entertains a group of students in the Foxfire classroom.

facilities. I burned coal in the heater. At least someone would always bring coal to my door so I didn't have to go out and get the coal.

For water, I had to go about 200 or 300 yards to a spout where they piped water out from a spring. I would fill up a pitcher or bucket or whatever I had. I had a washpan and a washcloth. That's all I had, but you could be presentable. It was very crude living, but you could survive.

I think I could cope with it better at that time than you could now because I knew how. We didn't have electric lights when I grew up. That came after REA in 1934–35. Didn't know anything about central heat. We didn't have any bathroom facilities or anything like that, so I could cope with living in a boxcar. I was never in the [boxcar] much anyway, so I could cope with the bed and two straight chairs. I have always [been] more or less of an outdoor person, and if I can be outside, I'm not going to be inside.

The Morse Brothers Lumber Company gave me my meals, and I stayed in Sheriff Sullivan's boxcar, so I was out nothing for room and board. I was paid forty dollars a month by the Rabun County school system. They paid us in scrip. They'd give us a little piece of paper saying, "Please permit Ellene Franklin to draw a certain amount of money on this paper." [It was] kind of like a check. We could go to the bank and get money on it. The county board issued it, but they didn't always have the money. Sometimes there would be two or three months before they would pay us that, which made it pretty hard. But I made out fine.

The schoolroom was heated with a fireplace that burned logs, and, of course, there were no lights in it. We used oil lamps. I moved the sheriff's bed back into the corner. I would go in early in the morning to tidy the room, and [chances were] one to ten that I'd find the sheriff's pistols lying on the bed. I would pick up the pistols and hang them up because I didn't want some child to be [tempted by them]. Someone up there could do very good carpentry work, and he made me six or eight long benches where three people could sit on the same bench. I took a sheet of linoleum and painted it black with enamel paint like a chalkboard, which worked very well. You could get chalk at most any store.

I also had a word rack, which was a large manila-like chart with strips pasted across from one end to another. There was a series of them, from the bottom to the top. They were more or less like pockets. We'd pick a word, for example, "Baby Ray." Then we'd pick up a card with "Baby Ray" on it, and we'd put that in one of those pockets. You could see "Baby Ray." Then we'd pick up an-other one. Maybe it would have the word "can." We'd put that by the side of "Baby Ray." Then we'd pick up another card, "run," and put that up there. "Baby Ray can run." The children enjoyed the word rack a lot.

That's the equipment I had for teaching. There was not a book, not a library. There was nothing. So I hired someone to carry me to Hiawassee to a schoolbook depository where I bought a series of *Baby Ray* readers. I had to buy all of the books myself. Sometimes I would get paid for them, and sometimes I wouldn't, because a lot of those people had no money to buy books. But the ones who could pay me did.

The children were from many different backgrounds, financial and otherwise, but most of them had some connection with the camp. Before the camp moved in, there were some native Rabun County people living in there, and their children walked three to five miles to school. I remember there were some Rogers and some Ellers, some Thompsons, and it seems like some Powells. Their descendants still live up there. Then there were six or eight families who had children and were camp-connected and were from Helen and Robertstown and would live right in the logging camp. Some of them had never gone to school a day. I had children from fourteen, fifteen, and sixteen years of age who had never gone to school one day. They were very smart. They were culturally deprived, but they were very anxious to learn.

The first day of school, I had books and chalk and a chalkboard and everything pretty well ready. The majority of them, as I said, had never been to school, and they didn't know what school was all about. The children began drifting in one by one, and they would look around the corner, not knowing whether they were supposed to come in or not. They would come to the door and look and look and look and look. I would have to go outside and say, "Come on in. This is the school. Come on in."

When they got inside, they didn't know whether to sit down or run. There were around twenty-four of them. They were awed; stunned. They stood around with their eyes glaring and their mouths open. They waited for directions, but they were very nice in every respect. They waited for me to tell them what to do and where to sit. They were not students who were headstrong, who would go into anything without some forethought or someone telling them what to do.

Finally, we just sat there and talked awhile; talked about school, how many people were at home, if they had any pets, and all that. You have to do things like that sometimes. I gave them their books and tried to tell them what I expected out of them. Some of them could understand, some of them didn't, but the children always looked forward to their classes, and the chalk seemed to fascinate them. They didn't know whether to pick it up or what to do with it. They had to adjust to a lot of things.

We started classes at eight o'clock and stayed until three-thirty. We had three recesses: forty-five minutes of a morning, one hour at noon, and thirty-five minutes in the afternoon. During recess, we had games to play. We played tag, drop the handkerchief, antny-over, blindman's buff, and little white daisy—a singing game where you would form a circle and go around and around and sing a song.

The boys liked to play with slingshots. That wasn't a good idea, but they did, and I let them because they didn't know any better.

They were also interested in guns and fishing. The boys [also had] pole vaults. They would just cut a pole, and each person would see how far he could jump on that pole. They also had wrestling matches.

The children brought their own lunches and ate them at noon. They didn't eat at the camp mess hall where I did. They usually brought their own lunch in a tin pail or a lard bucket, or something of that nature. Some of them brought rather attractive lunches, while others had very little for lunch. They would often have a biscuit with syrup—a syrup sandwich. And sometimes they would bring baked potatoes, or a boiled egg, or maybe an ear of boiled corn. I think they got on pretty well. They ate under a tree or in the yard or on the porch or anywhere—picnic-style.

We had one room for all the grades, and I had to do the best I could with no help whatsoever. It was trial and error for me to determine what grade they were in. I would start them out with the *Baby Ray* books. If they could read that and do simple math— addition and subtraction and so forth—I gave them the Zaner method writing books, which taught a method similar to the Palmer method used today. We used cursive writing only.

I also made a card chart, and I had cards with one, two, or three words on them. I would put words up on the chart for them to recognize, while I would teach phonics at the same time. The fact that I was so inexperienced myself made it hard, but you'd be surprised at the amount of education they got.

The oldest child I had was sixteen years of age. She couldn't read or write. I had to teach her to write her name. I said, "Now, Grace, this is the way you must learn to write your name." So I would put her name on the chalkboard, then take her hand and guide it along a line and say, "Now, Grace, we make a 'G' like this and we make an 'R' like this."

She was kind of in love with the cook's helper, and she wanted to write letters to him. I finally got her to where she could write a little bit, and then she said, "Miss Ellene, I want you to teach me to back an envelope."

I didn't know what she meant by "back an envelope." I finally figured out she meant address a letter. Years later she told someone the most important thing she ever learned in her life was learning to back an envelope. She was a very nice person. Later she married, and I taught her children, her grandchildren, and her great-grandchildren.

Most of the children really learned a lot, since they had never been to school. If I assigned them anything to do, they would willingly memorize it. We had spelling bees, usually Friday afternoon. We would more or less go over everything we had had during the week. I'd say, "How many of you can spell so-and-so?" Hands would go up.

[Then I'd say,] "How much are three plus four?" It was amazing the progress they made, because they really wanted to learn, and the parents were well pleased because they had no earthly way of sending their children to any other school. One of the boys I taught went on to finish at Georgia Tech, and I was proud of him. The others mostly settled down in local areas, sent their children to school, and believed in education. They got along fine.

I tried to do a lot for those children because they seemed so deprived. You have no idea how deprived those children were. I taught [the children] how to write their names, how to count money, and practical things that they would need. I thought that that should come before anything else. I still think so.

We also had Bible reading. We had devotion every morning, and some of those children said that the only Bible verses they ever heard read were there in that one-room school building. We studied history and geography as well. We did a lot of reading, because I felt that they were so behind in it. I felt that if they could read they could eventually pick up other things as they went along.

[The women at the camp] had phonographs, and they brought a lot of records and played [them]. Most of [the records] were the religious type, but some weren't. One of the ones I remember was something about, "St. Peter done called me and I can't go, 'cause I owe my soul to the company store." I can't quote it verbatim, but I remember they had that record, and they'd play it over and over again. They also had a lot of songs like "Hand Me Down My Walking Cane" and "Will the Circle Be Unbroken." That was another one they'd play over and over.

[The women] would memorize these songs. Some of the children had beautiful voices and would sing them at school. They thought it was great entertainment to get up before the other children and sing. Well, it was, and it took a lot of nerve. They really did all right.

For other entertainment [at the school], we had school plays. We found that school plays were a form of teaching. You never know a child's potential until you try that child out for a play. Some of them were very good. All children like to be noticed, and if you put them in a play, they're going to do their very best, often beyond all expectation.

In camp we put on a lot of plays, especially around Thanksgiving, and Christmas, and at the end of school. The children looked forward to being in the plays, and the parents looked forward to seeing their children on the stage. We had many Thanksgiving programs. The children enjoyed being Pilgrims. Some of them also enjoyed being the turkeys, and some the deer, and some the Indians. A Thanksgiving program was easy to arrange because [we had a lot of enthusiasm from the community].

[I got along well at the logging camp.] Because the sheriff kept everything under control, there was very little crime. He told the people that now we had a teacher coming to live here and to teach school, that they had certainly better behave themselves. And they did. They were very respectful, kind, and understanding. They seemed to appreciate me a lot. They felt very fortunate in getting anyone to come up and teach.

[No other women] had jobs at the camp, but there were a lot of mothers up there. They didn't have much to do unless they crocheted or knitted. I don't recall a book or magazine in that camp, but they had Bibles. Every home had a Bible.

I told you that the company furnished my meals. Well, I ate in the mess hall, which was about 300 to 400 yards from my boxcar. I ate with the men, usually—seventy-five men and boys. Sometimes I would wait until after they were gone to work in the morning because they had to go so early.

I was the only lady in the mess hall. The men were all on their p's and q's to be nice to the teacher, and they were. I have never been treated nicer in all my life than I was treated there. They were very rough men, but I didn't know it. They were very, very nice to me.

There is a lot to be said about how the men lived and how they worked and how each job had its own particular crew of men. Each trade had its own particular name. The bushwhackers were the first crew out. They followed the surveyors, cut the underbrush, and blazed out the route for the railroad [that would have to be built into the area being logged].

Then they had a dynamite gang that went ahead. They called them blasters. They blasted the right-of-way through rock for the railroad so they could lay the tracks. The gandy dancers were the ones who actually laid the tracks for the railroad. Then they had the fellers: "There goes the gang of fellers up there." They were the people who cut the trees down.

Another crew would come in behind the fellers and take the limbs off the trees and cut the logs into a certain length—maybe a twelve-foot log or fourteen-foot log. Sometimes they had orders for particular lengths. The mule skinners were the ones who snaked the logs down the mountains with mules.

There was one guy there that they called a lobby hog. They'd say, "I see the old lobby hog coming." He was the man who kept the boxcars and living quarters of the men cleaned up. [He] made their beds and mopped the floors and cleaned out the buildings. [Many of the men had nicknames.] If a person operated the cranes and lifted the logs, he was also known as a crane. Some of the gandy dancers were nicknamed "Spike" for the railroad spikes. There was a Mr. Allison we called "Payday." "Payday" Allison— his real name was Clarence—got that name because he was always going to pay off his debts after payday. And Clarence Palmer was the man who bought the cross ties, so he was known as "Cross Tie" all the time.

A lot of the people were from New York. They could not understand our ways of doing things. Our language was somewhat different. We didn't speak at a fast pace like they do. We were slower of speech, and we used a lot of local words that they had no idea what we meant. And it's possible that they knew some long words that we didn't know about.

One of the things that amused me very much was when a man named Gary Payne came South to the lumber camp there. We liked to play practical jokes on him. We had a lot of rain at that time, and a lot of big mud holes. The men told this man from New York that those mud holes contained the biggest fish he could catch anywhere. So they gave him a line and a pole, and red worms for bait, and told him to sit out there by that mud hole and cast his hook out.

Well, he sat there for an hour or so, and then [decided to call it quits]. He finally realized that they were pulling his leg.

We had one man named Pearl Nelson who cooked for the Waldorf Astoria. He was head chef up there and was roughing it at the lumber camp that summer. He came down to spend his vacation with us. We really had swell food then because he was trying to show Claude Allen, our cook, how he cooked, and Mr. Allen was trying to teach him how to cook for logging people. They seemed to have a lot in common, although the cooking and the menus were worlds apart. The loggers and the people who laid the railroad tracks thought Mr. Nelson was wonderful. They respected him and tried in every way to make his vacation enjoyable.

Mr. Allen was a really good cook. We had great meals. He could make the best cakes and pies, and, of course, they served a lot of beans and peas and potatoes and things like that. They had to, because men had to have heavy food in order to work. He had one other man who helped him. They cooked for about seventy-five men and boys, and those meals were always on time. They weren't anything you would call fancy, but they were clean and good and substantial. We had the best raisin pie I had ever eaten in my life, and also apple pies, peach pies, and plenty of rice.

[The camp also had a doctor.] Dr. S. A. West, who was from Dahlonega. He was a small man and was very well educated. He was at the camp full time. If anyone got hurt out on the job, two or three miles out of camp, Dr. West had to go. He had to walk, but he had to go. The company had several camps—Camp Moccasin and Camp Plum Orchard and so forth—but he would have to go to them if anyone got hurt or sick. Sometimes a person would get hurt out in the woods, maybe sprain an ankle, or skin a shin, or something of that nature. Dr. West had very little to do, though, and if there was anything of a serious nature, he would always put the patient on the train and send him to Helen or to Gainesville, where he could get better treatment. He just sat up there and drew his paycheck.

He was kind of a little smart aleck in a way. He was a doctor, mind you, and he asked me how to spell Cicero. I said, "If you've gone all the way through medical college and haven't learned that yet, you come on and start in my first grade!" He didn't ask me any more questions after that, either.

One Monday, Dr. West brought a percolator to camp with him. He said, "Claude"—that was the cook's name—"when you make my coffee every morning, you be sure and make mine in the percolator. It'll be better than the coffee [boiled] in that old pot."

Mr. Allen said, "All right, Dr. West, you'll have your coffee perked." For the first three or four mornings, Mr. Allen religiously made coffee in the percolator for Dr. West. Dr. West would drink that coffee, put that little finger up there and sip it and say, "This is delicious. This is so much better than the coffee cooked like you usually cook it."

In the mornings, I would usually get to the [kitchen] before Dr. West did. The cook said [one morning], "Oh, Lord, I forgot to make Dr. West's coffee." He saw Dr. West coming down from his room. So he took a big old dipper and filled it up out of the boiler where the rest of the coffee was boiled and put it in the percolator. He took it back and put it on Dr. West's table. And Dr. West poured himself a cup of coffee, and he said, "Claude, this is DELICIOUS! DELICIOUS!"

He called me over to his table and said, "Miss Franklin, will you have a cup of coffee? This is *so* much better than what is brewed in the pot."

I knew what was in that percolator, and I said, "Yes, I think I shall."

Mr. Allen looked at me and winked, and I thought I would [break down laughing].

The blacks worked on the railroad most of the time. I never saw one do anything else. They did the heaviest work there was to do on that railroad. Laying the steel and putting the cross ties down was about the only work they did.

Some of them were from Toccoa, some from Cornelia, some from Helen and Bean Creek. There's one woman in Toccoa today that worked up there [at the black men's camp]. She was the wife of this big man called Barrelhouse. He was in charge of cooking. They had their own cook, their own dining hall, their own everything, just like we did [except for a teacher]. No little blacks came up to our school, either, because that wasn't done back then. Some of the white children were afraid to pass their camp when I would occasionally arrange a little outing for them. All the time I was there, I never saw a black person at the white camp.

I don't think they needed to [separate the two races, though]. I don't think they would today. [There were] never any incidents between the black and white lumber camps. You were likely to see a 200-pound Negro steeplejack driving spikes into the ties over there, and working side by side with a white man.

They were all very nice to work with. There were no problems whatsoever. If there was ever any disturbance or anything between them, I never knew it. But that was the way it was done back then. They didn't want the whites and the blacks having trouble, drinking and carousing around [at night]. And for that reason they kept a night guard on duty [every night].

Back then, they did not have tractors to log with. At that time, everything was done by mules and horses. They skidded the logs down the mountain to the railroad with mule teams and horse teams. I remember one man who was killed when they were trying to slide logs down the mountain too fast, and the logs ran against him and killed him. In fact, there was a saying in camp that it was all right for a man to die on that skid trail, but you better not kill a mule or horse because that was a terrible thing. They didn't care much about the life of a person. They had about three or four teams of mules and horses. And each man thought he had the best team and could do the most work!

They had many, many train accidents. It was a narrow-gauge railroad, and any little thing could cause the train to turn over. If the track got out of line, if they were running too fast, or if it was too heavily loaded, the train would jump the track. Occasionally, there were people killed in these accidents. I think there were two or three killed.

We had four trains, and each train had a whistle with a tone that was decidedly different from that of the other trains. You could tell from the whistle which train had wrecked. There would be so many longs and so many shorts for a wreck, and so many longs or shorts for a railroad crossing.

On weekends, the camp was dead from Friday night until Monday morning. They looked forward to Friday night and Saturday, so they could go into Helen. At that time, Helen was the head-quarters for the logging business that carried all the logs there by train to be sawed into planks and other building materials. I have seen fifteen acres of sawn plank timber there.

In Helen they had lots of dances, where the men used to get drunk. [There were] two big hotels in Helen. One of them was a famous summer resort, and the other more or less catered to the lumbering crowd. A lot of them could [also] go into Gainesville for shopping or see a show.

My home was eight or ten miles as the crow flies from Camp Moccasin, so when I wanted to go home on weekends, I would walk about three quarters of a mile to where the track was at, and then flag down one of the little lumber trains that would pass. I could hear the trains coming, and I would get ready and be there at the crossing in time. They would always stop and pick me up, and I would ride in a boxcar down from Moccasin Creek [to the main road]. Then I would stay the weekend at home. When I would get ready to go back, Sunday afternoon at about four o'clock, I knew that the train would be going into camp. I would walk up to the railroad tracks and stand over a track. The train would stop and pick me up.

After Morse Brothers Lumber Company cut all the timber out of the area on Moccasin Creek, they moved further up the rail line to Plum Orchard. They could pick up these boxcar-type houses, put them on flats, and carry them right into the next camp and set them up. The women didn't go, because it was a very wild country out through there. The men didn't stay there too long either—only until all the timber was cut out of that area. Then the company bought a tract of timber in El Paso, Texas. They ripped up all the steel and sent all of the trains and steel to Texas.

The year they moved to El Paso was 1931, I guess. Some of the logging families stayed, and some of them went on to El Paso. We called the ones who had come from other states the drifters. Some of the people who had roots in and around Helen and Robertstown moved back home.

I was going to go with them to El Paso. I wanted to go, but Mama said, "No, you're not going." At that time she thought I was just a little too young to go that far away from home with that kind of people. But "that kind of people" had treated me well, with the greatest respect. There was nothing amiss whatsoever as far as honor is concerned. Those people treated me like a queen.

The next job I got was at Turnerville, Georgia, where I taught for three years. I was paid fifty-five dollars a month and had to pay room and board out of that.

Then I taught over in Robertstown. This was during the time when President Roosevelt had decided something needed to be done so people would have a better way of making a living. So they started a program called the Works Progress Administration. It hired men to build roads and power lines, clean cemeteries, and do a lot of things that would never have been done otherwise. Some of them did carpentry work. One of the school buildings at Clarkesville was built by WPA labor.

I remember one project where they had to go through the forests and eradicate all of the cedar trees because they thought that the cedar trees had a disease that caused apples, peaches, and things of that type to rot. They also had a group of WPA people searching for Indian relics. The people who worked with the WPA had to put in so many hours a day, and it was sad that a lot of the projects they worked on were not worthwhile. A lot of the people who worked on the WPA did exactly what they were supposed to do, but they were accused of just leaning on their shovels a lot of the time instead of working.

There was a truck that passed through our community each day to pick up the WPA people; at night it carried them home. One morning, it must have been zero weather—and that was before small girls were permitted to wear slacks or jeans to school. I had a little first-grader whose parents started her to school that morning, and the little thing froze down on the side of the road and couldn't go any further. She had on a little dress that went halfway between her hip and knee, and little anklets. And she was more or less anemic anyway. Her sisters and the Tipton children who walked with them to school decided she was faking, so they went off and left that child frozen down. She could not go any further. Along came the WPA men who picked her up, but the child had no identification, so they didn't know what to do. They brought her up to the school building.

I had to send down to my boardinghouse to get a blanket to

wrap her in. The lady fixed warm milk and heating pads made of warm bricks wrapped in old quilts to put around the child to warm her up. It took me about half a day to get her straightened out. Well, I decided something needed to be done.

"Well," I said, "I'll tell you something, little girls. It's just too cold for you little girls to walk two miles and a half to school with your legs bare that way. You have little brothers, and most of you have little overalls and things you wear at home, don't you?"

They were embarrassed to think about wearing pants to school. I said, "I'll tell you what. In the morning, I'm going to wear my slacks to school, and I want you to wear your slacks to school, or long stockings or something so your little legs won't get so cold." Well, they didn't believe that I would do this. Right across from my boardinghouse was the post office, and that was the gathering place for the "Cracker Barrel" gang. As I walked up the street with my slacks on, the deacon of the church called through the door to the postmaster and the postmaster called to the policemen. And I walked to school with my slacks on. I had my skirt on under them.

When I got to school, I kept my slacks on until all the children got there that morning. I said, "Now, I told you I was going to wear my slacks today, and I don't see a one of you with your slacks on. Now, I'm going to wear mine in the morning again, and I want to see all you little girls wear your slacks to school." I said, "If you don't want to wear them all day, then that's all right. We'll just slip them down and have our little dresses on." So the next morning, four or five children wore their slacks to school, and the next morning a few more, till eventually they all got to wear slacks.

I was afraid I would [get into trouble for that, but] I thought the children's health was more important, and it was. I suspect I was the first teacher in the state of Georgia who ever wore slacks to school. I don't know, but I suspect it.

I went back to Camp Moccasin a few years ago, and most of the trail has grown up—pine trees and shrubbery and so forth. I did find a piece of an old water pipe where we got our water from after we [piped] it from the side of the mountain, but everything else is gone.

Walker Word

"I just believe that my horse will outrun that train."

Walker Word is age eighty-one. In one of our lengthy discussions about his childhood, I made the mistake of stating that he was eighty-one years old. Promptly correcting me, he said, "I have eighty-one years of age. I am not eighty-one years old."

Unlike many men his age, Walker does not consider himself old. However, he has told me that he has known men just thirty and forty years old who were, nevertheless, old men. As you might infer, Walker believes that age is only a frame of mind. I think so, too.

Walker has told me this: "At eighty-one, you can relax. Nobody expects much of you. If you forget your name or someone else's name, or forget to fill an appointment [it's not a problem]. When you reach a corner and hesitate, you may change directions. Don't fight it; just go down that street. No telling what you will find. At eighty-one, people will forgive you of anything. If you ask me, life begins at eighty-one."

To prepare this interview with Walker, I have listened to his stories on tape many times. I have enjoyed them more and more each time I hear them, and each time I have gotten a clearer sense of what his life was really like. Although his childhood sounds like something out of Fred Chappell's I Am One of You Forever or Olive Ann Burns's Cold Sassy Tree, Walker Word has been through many hardships, especially as a teenager having to support his *family through the Depression. I often wonder if I could have done any of the things he did.*

I feel very fortunate to know Walker Word. Although he is eighty-one and I am seventeen, I consider him to be one of my best friends. He has positively influenced my life in many ways. As you will find, his stories of dedication and hard work are truly inspirational.

—Interview, photographs, and introduction by Chris Nix

When I was young, I lived in Waco, Georgia, which was near the Alabama line, in Haralson County. My father was very affluent. He was president of a bank. My uncle Grady Word ran the Waco Mercantile Company. He and his brothers had a cotton gin and a sawmill. My father was chairman of the Board of Deacons for years and years. He was chairman of the school board. His name was on a plaque as one of the builders of the high school. We had everything that anybody could want. I remember when we had the only car in town. I remember when we got the first radio in Waco.

Waco was a trading area for just about the whole county. Farmers were supplied with anything from a horseshoe nail to a casket. Groceries, dry goods, eyeglasses, you name it, just everything. Everything was on credit, and in the fall, my father would grade and buy their cotton. This would go on their accounts at the store and the bank.

We went broke when I was about fourteen years old. The boll weevil ate us up. We were gone with the boll weevil. Waco was cotton country. Cotton was king. My father thought that cotton would go to sixty cents a pound. Then one day he got up, and cotton was worth about six cents a pound.

Uncle William Heaton was a brother to my grandmother Word. Uncle William started our mercantile business in Waco. After a few years, he brought my father from Texas. I believe that was in 1908. My uncle Grady came from Texas in 1910. There was also another uncle in this business on my mother's side—he was Uncle Tupper Rowland. Uncle Tupper was the bookkeeper. His wife, Aunt Naomi, was my mother's half-sister. Another one of my uncles that ran this business was my uncle Arthur Walker. They called me Little Walker, and they called him Big Walker. It was my father and so

Walker Word.

many of my uncles in Waco that involved me in many things during my childhood there.

We had behind the mercantile store a horse stable. We had stalls and barns, hay and corn. A man named John looked after the horses. One day I was with John, watching him look after the horses. I said, "John, my daddy likes nice horses, doesn't he?"

He said, "Let me tell you somethin' about your daddy and his horses. A long time before your daddy married your mother, he and I went on Sunday to Salem campground. I handled his horses. We went to a preaching service, ate a meal, and was sitting down on a bench by a spring. [All of a sudden] your daddy-to-be jumped up and said, 'There goes my wife.' [There were two ladies that we had never seen before riding in a buggy.] I asked him which one was his wife, and he said, 'The one under the umbrella.' "

Well, Daddy didn't meet her that day, but he sure found out who she was. She lived in Bowdon, Georgia. The next day, he told John to hitch up his horses and ride down to Bowdon and tell his wife-to-be that he was busy buying cotton, and that after cotton season was over, he'd like to come courting.

I think it took my daddy three years to convince my mother to marry him. I think she was also going to college at that time. They finally married.

[My earliest "courting" memory involves a runaway horse.] One Sunday afternoon, my mother, father, my little sister Margaret, and I were on our front porch. Down the street, on the sidewalk in front of our house, came my father's pretty secretary and a young man who was a new teacher in Waco. I said, "Where're they going?"

Mother said, "I think they are having a date."

I said, "What's a date?"

She said, "That's when two people that are interested in each other go someplace together. That's what you call having a date."

I thought that was a pretty good deal. My aunt Naomi had a daughter, who was my cousin Mabel. She was a sweet, pretty girl who was ten years older than me. She was sixteen and I was six. I saw her, and said, "Mabel, I want to date. Will you date with me?"

She said, "Well, sure, Walker. When do you want to date?"

I said, "If they will hitch a horse up for me on Sunday afternoon, let's go for a buggy ride."

She agreed to that. We got into the buggy, and she said, "Where are we going?"

I said, "Let's go to Bush's Mill." It was two or three miles away. It was a beautiful place. Mabel and I had got almost there at Bush's Mill, and came to a railroad track. We crossed that track. Right after that, a train came along. The train blew its whistle. Our horse, Bob, was frisky. That whistle scared him half to death. He took off running. Mabel got hold of the reins, because I was too little. My feet wouldn't even touch the floorboard. I held on for dear life. Bob ran down a gully, up a bank, and across a big cotton patch. After a bit, he stopped. That ended our date. We went home as soon as we could. After that, I thought having a date could be a very dangerous thing. Later on, I found out that the statement I just made can be true throughout life! The older you get, the more dangerous having a date becomes.

I had very happy times in Waco. There was a swimming hole [at Price's Creek] half a mile from my house. Before breakfast, I would ride my horse, Maude, down to the creek to let her get a good cool drink of water. I think she looked forward to it.

There was one Indian that lived in Waco. His name was John Plummer. Mr. Plummer's wife was not Indian. I had my first gun given to me when I was twelve. I wanted to hunt, but my father wasn't a hunter. So, I went to see Mr. Plummer one day and he said, "Come here, I want to show you something."

He had a little baby girl in there. I said, "If she were a little boy, she could hunt with you."

And he said, "Yeah. She could. But she can't, because she is a

Walker Word developed a great admiration for the American Indian as a result of his relationship with Mr. Plummer. Over the years, he has found many arrowheads and other Indian artifacts. He made this eagle from arrowheads in 1960.

girl." As I was leaving, he said, "Walker, what did you come to see me about?"

I said, "Mr. Plummer, I want to hunt with you."

Now this was the Depression. Ammunition was scarce. He said, "You know, we can't waste ammunition."

I said, "My father has a store, and he said if we keep him in quail, he'll furnish our ammunition." I hunted very much with Mr. Plummer. This man meant a lot to me. He showed me a lot about shooting.

Mr. Plummer told me this. He said, "When we hunt turkeys, don't shoot the first one. Just be quiet. When they all get close, don't shoot the one closest to you. Shoot the farthest one away that you can hit. It doesn't disturb them as bad."

One thing that I learned from Mr. Plummer was not to panic. During life, anything can happen. One day, I was hunting arrowheads down on Clark Hill Reservoir. I came up on a pretty creek. I thought, "Well, I'll walk up on this creek." I heard a little old dog barking. It sounded like he was hurt. So, I went to see about him, and there he was tied to this tree. About that time, I got a big whiff of moonshine. There was the biggest still I ever saw in my life. I could just feel eyes looking at me. I don't know how many guns were pointed at me. I thought, "Well, I'll walk backward and sing." I can't sing at all, so I whistled. I whistled, "Nearer My God to Thee," and got out of there. I got away with it, but it was a very close call.

Mr. Plummer taught me how to fight. I've never lost a fight, and I've never been as strong as the people I've fought, either. Mr. Plummer said, "Now a lot a' them boys are stronger'n you are, but you've got the longest arms of any of 'em. If you can, grab 'em at their shirt collar and push that way and pull him back and forth while you hit him. Before he hits you, the fight's over." And that's certainly true.

There was always a bully in school. We didn't have water works when I was a kid in school. Before recess, the teacher would send a few boys out to draw water. I was selected one day to do just that. I had just had me a drink, and up walked this pretty little girl named Dixie Holloway. I got about half a dipperful of water and handed it to Dixie. She was drinking that water and up came the school bully and jerked that dipper out and broke one of her front teeth. Well, I knocked the hell out of him. Blood flew everywhere. I looked up, and here was the school principal. He was a nice fellow. His name was Preacher Cook. He took us back to his office and made us bend over his desk. He really gave us a whipping. Well, I didn't think I needed a whipping. Anyway, that afternoon, after leaving school, I saw the preacher. I picked up a rock and threw it at him. I knew that if I'd hit him solid it would have killed him. It just grazed his ear. I shouldn't have done it. He went and had a little talk with my dad. He said to Dad, "Mr. Word, Walker threw a rock at me today."

Preacher Cook wanted me to make a public apology the next Monday morning at the assembly. Well, it came Monday and the auditorium was filled because everyone wanted to hear me apologize. When the time came, I got up and said, "I threw a rock at Preacher Cook, I missed him, and I'm sorry." So I never did really apologize to him because I said that I was sorry that I missed him.

I never did think about the fact that my family had more things than most of the other people in our community. It didn't make a difference to me if anybody had anything or not. You know, it's not

*For this photo, Mr. Word switched clothes with a fellow student
so the student could have better clothes for class pictures.*

what a person has that makes them special, it's their actions. That's what counts. [I have this school picture.] The boy in the front row is dressed up. The reason he's dressed up is that morning he came to school and told the teacher, "I'm not going to have my picture made. My overalls are all worn out." In school, our teachers said to wear nice clothes the next day if you were going to have a group picture made. My mother dressed me to perfection. I said to him, "Bill, at recess, let's go down to the creek and I'll swap clothes with you." In the picture, he is the boy in the front row with the biggest smile. I'm toward the back with his worn-out overalls on. It didn't bother me, for I knew all I had to do was to stop after school at the clothes department and tell one of my uncles that I needed a new outfit. Several times I traded my clothes for the worst ones in school. I've spent my life giving. It seems the more I've given, the more it's come back to me. I know I've been blessed.

[When I was young, I liked to "help out" when I could. Sometimes I made a little money at it, and sometimes I didn't.] My uncle William traded for a mule one day in Waco. He had a business in Tallapoosa, which was nine miles from Waco. Uncle William said, "Walker, I've got this mule. I want you to do me a favor. I'll pay you well if you'll take this mule to Tallapoosa for me."

I agreed to do it. We had a platform at our mercantile business that was used for loading and unloading cotton. Well, I got up on the platform and hopped down onto this mule. I thought I'd ride him without a saddle. I was wrong. I couldn't ride him at all—he threw me off. I thought I'd walk down the road a little while with him and try to get back on him later. I came to a gully after two or three miles, and I got him down in that gully. I got on the bank and stepped down onto him. He threw me off again. I finally reached my destination, on foot, in Tallapoosa. During the course of the trip, the mule threw me three times in all, total. When I got to Tallapoosa, I was all beat up and bruised. I was too tired to walk back to Waco. I walked up to the train depot. Mr. Newman was the depot agent at Waco a few years back, and was at the time the depot agent in Tallapoosa. I knew him when he was at Waco. I walked up to Mr. Newman, and said, "Is the train going to be on time?"

He said, "Walker, you look like you've been in a fight. What happened?"

I said, "Mr. Newman, I brought a mule over here for my uncle. That mule threw me three times. That's why I look the way I do."

He said, "Yeah. The train is going to be on time, as far as I know. Do you want to buy a ticket?"

I said, "Yes, sir. I only have a quarter that my uncle gave me for bringing the mule over here. Would you take my quarter and give me a ticket, and let me pay you the rest the next time I see you?"

He agreed to that. I had to use the payment for bringing the mule to Tallapoosa from Waco to buy a ticket back home. I didn't think using the payment I got for bringing the mule over there was really fair, but at the time, my main concern was getting back home.

Daddy sent me one time to deliver a bull. We got about halfway, and I guess that bull got tired. He laid down right in the middle of the road, and absolutely would not move. So I went out in the woods, looking for a stick to hit him with, to try to make it move. I saw this rich pine stump. I kicked it out and took a piece of that rich pine and stuck it under that bull's rump. I struck a match to it, and in a minute that bull took off. I chased him as long as I could hold out. I never knew what happened to that bull. To this very day I have yet to see him! I hope he found a good home.

As a youngster, I would ride in a buggy with our Dr. Robinson to make calls. People would send for him from all directions. He would get so worn out sometimes that he would ask me to drive him in the buggy and let him rest. He was overworked, and would ask me to go with him at night. I would drive the horse and let him rest. Sometimes it might be midnight and miles away when we would head home. We would wrap ourselves in a blanket and both go to sleep. The horse would take us home. Dr. Robinson was a wonderful man and did great things with what he had to work with.

Most people did not have any money. They would give him a ham or a pig, or most anything. We had a cage built on the rear of the buggy to handle such things. One time a man gave us two goats. Dr. Robinson said, "Walker, you take the goats." I turned them in our large pasture, and soon I had thirty-seven goats.

One of these was a huge billy goat with tremendous horns. He was a real pet. One Christmas Santa brought me a nice wagon which could seat two. One of our businesses was a leather factory. I went to see the foreman and asked if he thought they could make a collar and harness for my goat. He said, "I don't see why not." They did, and that goat seemed to take pride in pulling me anywhere I wanted to go.

During our childhood at Waco, my cousin Reese and I would often get in Price's Creek to fish and swim. It was rather wide, but shallow in most places. Sometimes we would take our shotguns down the creek and kill the big moccasin snakes we'd see. We'd have contests to see who could kill the most snakes. One day, we were standing rather close together, about two feet apart. We shot our guns, and about that time, a shot was fired toward us. A bullet hit directly between us in the water. It scared us so bad that we immediately took off running. Really, I think our reaction to being shot at was quite normal. Anyway, later on down the creek, we stopped and got our breath. Reese said, "You know, Walker, we both have guns. I don't know who shot at us. I don't think we should have ran . . ." I said, "Reese, I was thinking the same thing!"

We went back to where we were shot at. Together, we devised a plan. Reese stood on my right and I was on the left. We decided to begin shooting up in the woods. We'd start in the middle, Reese would shoot from the middle to the right, and I would shoot from the middle to the left. We did that, and before long, we saw this man running up the hill, holding his rear end. The next day, I got a message from Dr. Robinson. He came to get me so we could make some house calls. He said, "A man got shot yesterday in the rear end with some buckshot. I want you to help me get the buckshot out of him."

So he put this man to sleep. He had twelve to fourteen pellets in him. We must have hit him with just one charge of shot, because a double-barrel buckshot 12-gauge ordinarily has about twelve bullets. They were not very deep, but I'm sure they were very painful.

I picked those things out of him. As we were getting ready to go, I started laughing about it. The man was still asleep, of course. Dr. Robinson said, "What's so funny, Walker?"

I said, "I don't know if it was me or my cousin that shot him, but we are both responsible for him being here." I told Dr. Robinson about the whole ordeal. I found out later that the man had a liquor still up there. He was trying to scare us away from it. I still don't think he had the right to shoot at us, though.

I remember one time my mother was about to get after me about something. Her beautiful brown eyes were flashing, and I said, "Mother, before you say anything, I just want you to know that I have the prettiest mother in Waco." From then on, I don't remember my mother ever getting after me about anything. She sometimes would say, "Walker, I don't think you should do that."

My family would go ride every Sunday afternoon. Of course, my daddy would drive. Anyway, I remember one time when he had just bought himself a new car. My father always bought Buick automobiles. He thought they were the number-one car. We drove up toward Bremen and Buchanan. I thought that I could drive it myself. I knew everything except how he put it in reverse. Anyway, this Sunday afternoon, for some reason, he turned the car around and backed it under the shed. That gave me an idea. I asked Daddy, "I want to drive this car."

He said, "Son, you're too little to drive this car. Wait until you get a little bit bigger. Then I'll let you drive it."

The next day, I said to my mother, "I know I shouldn't do it, but I've got to drive that car. Daddy won't let me. I know I'll get a whipping, but I've got to drive that car."

She said, "I don't think you should." But I cranked that car up.

Daddy was out buying cotton at the store. He heard me coming. Daddy recognized the sound of his car. He came out and tried to wave me down. I just waved back at him and started toward Tallapoosa. The thought occurred to me about the fact that I didn't understand how to turn the car around in reverse. I thought I would just go on to Tallapoosa and go around the courthouse square. I did that. After I came back home, Mother said, "Walker, your father said to come to the store and see him."

I said to my mother, "Don't worry about me. I know he should whip me. I knew what I was getting into. He never has whipped me before, but after what I've done, I believe he will now. I think I'll put on an extra pair of pants just in case he does." I did that. So I went up there and to my surprise, he didn't whip me.

He said, "Son, I see you can drive an automobile. You see that truck out there? You're going to drive that truck from Waco to Tallapoosa and bring fertilizer back here to Waco every day this summer. We're not going to pay you anything in the world for your time. Do you understand?" I promptly agreed.

For the business, Daddy had bought a Model-T Ford truck. I remember the price was $636. They were having a big sale at the mercantile store, and Daddy wanted circulars to be distributed. He had me get up a big bunch of boys to help me do that. Daddy let me take the truck because it would go places where a car would not. We left, and came up on the railroad track. We had to cross it. I had the idea about easing one wheel over at a time. I got the left front wheel over and then the left rear wheel. About that time, I heard the train blowing for the crossing. I told the boys to run down the bank and get out of the way. I killed the engine trying to back the truck back down. I jumped out to crank that thing. It would not crank. I stayed with it until that train was almost on me. I jumped off down the bank. I was terrified. I sat there on a rock and shook until somebody came after me. I was that scared. The train stopped, but it took them a mile or so. They scattered that Ford. The next day, Daddy didn't get after me because he knew I didn't mean to do it. For reasons obvious, I now try to stay away from the front of a Model-T! You know, those things will kick the fool out of you when you try to crank them. I think I've broken my arm twice while cranking Model-Ts.

[I had some other adventures because of the store. One] story is so vivid in my mind. I was age twelve when it happened, and I can remember it like it was yesterday. Anyway, people kept breaking into the stores in those days. At Waco, we had no law enforcement. These thieves in particular had robbed my family's mercantile business before. My father was determined to put a stop to the robbery that was going on at our business.

My mother, father, and uncles talked it over one day, and realized they couldn't hold out to stand watch every night. Somebody thought to let Little Walker stay up and be the lookout. It didn't bother me beause I wanted to do it anyway.

We had a system set up. One of my uncles was at the front of the store, one was in the clothing department, and my father was in the livery stable. I was to let them all sleep where they were. And in the event of a break-in, I was to wake my father up. Then, my father was to shoot a gun up into the air. That would wake them up, and also sent a signal to my uncle in the front to throw a master switch that would flood the store with light.

I stayed up there for several nights. One night, here they came. I counted them as they got out of their Model-T and walked up the steps. I saw seven. I ran and got my father up. I said, "Daddy, they're here."

He said, "Now you stay right here."

Of course, I didn't. I followed him to the store. He fired a shot into the air. My uncle up front turned the lights on. That sent them running back to the way they came in. They didn't make it. They started shooting, and my father and uncles started shooting. There was a lot of shots fired. Only one man was killed. He was one of the thieves. After that, they gave up.

Those boys that robbed us had an uncle that was a lawyer. They decided to try to figure a way out of their mess. So they picked one of my uncles and made a case for murder against him.

This came to a court case. It was apparent that the attorney for the thieves had told them what to say on the witness stand. They all said the same thing. Now I was called into a room to speak to my uncle's lawyer. He said, "Walker, we did not want to call on you, but now it looks like I'm going to have to. Will you testify on your uncle's behalf?"

I agreed to do just that. We got into court. Judge Edwards was presiding. I was called to the stand. The judge said, "Walker, because of your age, I'm not going to swear you in. Now, I know you'll not tell a lie, so I'm just going to trust you will tell the truth about what you saw that night."

I began to tell what I saw. I said, "I think . . ."

The other lawyer jumped up and said, "This court does not want to know what this boy thinks; they want to know what he knows."

That got my goat. I said to the judge, "You know, I've got some people in my family that are lawyers, and I heard one of them say to the other one that some lawyers talk without thinking. I don't want to do that. If you don't mind, I'd like to think before I talk!"

Everyone kind of laughed at that. Soon after, I continued my story. I said, "Judge, I think this uncle in question is the poorest shot I know. One time he bought a new Winchester rifle. We were going to try it out down at his house. I set up a can for him to shoot at. Well, he took five shots and missed all five times. Now, I don't know who killed that man. But there is one thing I do know. I was right beside him when that man was shot. I saw that man fall to the floor. My uncle had a double-barrel 12-gauge shotgun. I used that gun often to hunt with. It had two hammers; one side had bird shot and the other had buckshot. Now, my uncle aimed his gun at this man. Just as he fired, one of those thieves hit him in the elbow with an ax. This caused his gun to jerk upward. Because of that, he shot into the ceiling instead of the man who was killed. The store had plastered walls and plastered ceilings. My cousin, Mabel Rowland, has a camera. She took a picture of the hole in the ceiling. So, I have proof that my story is true. Judge, that's all I have to say. I know my uncle didn't do it."

The other lawyer didn't have any questions for me. The jury was out a short time, and they came back in and announced that my uncle was not guilty. I remember that whole ordeal word for word. I'll never forget it.

My mother had about nine or ten brothers and sisters. They were all great people. I could stay a week at anybody's house, but I couldn't stay an hour at Aunt Naomi's. She was so neat about everything. She had waxed floors and old scattered rugs. My feet would often slip out from under me. I'd end up knocking a lamp off, or something else disastrous. Well, Aunt Naomi enjoyed ninety

years of poor health. I don't know how many times they called me
to tell me that she was dying. By the time I got over to her house,
they would have her sitting up. They'd be waiting on her hand and
foot. Finally, my sister Mary called me and said, "Walker, Aunt
Naomi is dead."

I said, "Mary, are you sure?"

I was a pallbearer along with my brother Burrell. We were on
our way from the hearse to the grave, and there was the biggest
storm I had ever seen. Burrell was on one side of Aunt Naomi and
I was on the other. About that time, lightning hit a tree right close
by. It made the biggest racket you ever heard. I said, "Burrell, Aunt
Naomi has reached the promised land!" He got tickled, and I did,
too!

I wanted to be around my family as much as possible. Every
one was so different from each other, but they were all rich with
knowledge. Now, some of them I could talk to easier than others.
I guess I was around my uncle Grady the most.

Whenever I needed money, I went to my uncle Grady. He
would take the money out of the cash register in the store and
charge it to my daddy as apples. It was funny how we began to do
that. One day, I told our help, John, to hitch the horse and buggy
up in front of the store. I asked Uncle Grady to get me sixty cents
out of the register. I told him to charge it to my daddy. He said,
"Where are you going?"

I said, "I'm going to Chatauqua. Write down on a piece of paper
sixty cents, and out by it, put Chatauqua."

Uncle Grady said, "How do you spell it?"

I said, "I'm not sure. I think it's got a k and a q in it."

He said, "I'll just put it down as apples."

I remember one time when we were having a revival at our
church in Waco. Dr. Parrish was the preacher. He was a fine
evangelistic preacher. The week he was there, he lived in our home.
Preachers that came in like that always stayed at our home. It was
usually my daddy who brought them in. Anyway, that preacher was
preaching about this train that was going down this hill so fast with
brakes that wouldn't hold. The train wrecked. He said some of the
people on the train were saved, and some of the people were not.
Those that were saved didn't have anything to worry about. How-

ever, those that were not saved were going to the devil. I thought to myself, "If anything was to happen to me, I'd like to be saved. I believe tomorrow I'll join the church."

The next day, he preached about how it was easier for a camel to go through an eye of a needle than it was for a rich man to enter into the kingdom of heaven. That worried me. Of course, I was young then. I didn't understand the true message the preacher was talking about. Anyway, I consulted my uncle Grady on the matter. I didn't ask my daddy because he would only tell me to take the Bible and study it. I said, "Uncle Grady, I was going to join the church today, but the preacher talked about how it was easier for a camel to pass through the eye of a needle than it was for a rich man to enter into the kingdom of heaven."

Uncle Grady, being the great trader he was, said, "Walker, wait until tomorrow. Maybe he'll make you a better proposition. . . ."

Uncle Grady traded for a Stutz Bearcat automobile. It was a sharp car in those days. It had two extra wheels. It was the sportiest looking thing. My daddy had to be at the bank at Atlanta one morning. Daddy had a Buick, a good automobile, but it wasn't very fast. He asked my uncle Grady, "I'd like to borrow your car and drive it to Atlanta."

Uncle Grady said, "If little Walker would drive you, I'll lend you my car." So we were going to Atlanta, and we hit a straight stretch. I said, "Daddy, this is a running automobile. We're making thirty-five miles per hour." [About that time, our rear wheel came off and passed us, rolling down the road.]

One time my uncle Grady traded for a beautiful old racehorse. Somebody said to him, "Is that a fast horse, Mr. Word?"

Uncle Grady said, "That horse will outrun any horse in the county."

Somebody bet that the racehorse couldn't outrun the Number 40 passenger train that went from Birmingham to Atlanta, and to Waco from Bremen. Bremen was two and a half miles away from Waco. Now, the train would stop at Waco to get coal, and at Bremen to get water.

Uncle Grady said, "I just believe that my horse will outrun that train. And I'd just bet you that if little Walker would ride him, he'd sure do it."

Everybody lined up between Waco and Bremen. The train

stopped at Waco, and that was where we started. The road wasn't paved. It went right alongside the tracks all the way to Bremen.

Well, we got a pretty good start with the train taking off. The train passed us, and slowed down to stop at Bremen. We beat that train by about two horse lengths.

It was a hot day in August. The horse was covered in perspiration. I was, too. Nearby was a watering trough. Before I realized it, this horse walked over there and began to drink that water. About that time, he dropped over dead. I never should have let him drink that water.

When I was young, I liked to do anything I could to earn a quarter or a dollar. A time or two at Christmas, my grandparents would give me ten dollars. In about seven years, I saved up a hundred dollars. By then, I was age fourteen. I said, "Daddy, I've got a hundred dollars. What should I invest it in?"

He said, "Why don't you invest in the Citizens Bank?"

I thought that sounded like a good idea. I went to Mr. Stamps, the cashier, and said, "I want to buy a share of stock. I understand it's a hundred dollars for a share."

He pulled me out a pretty yellow certificate and I gave him my hundred dollars. I thought that it would really be worth something. It wasn't long after that when the Depression hit, and the bank went broke. I lost the first hundred dollars I ever earned and saved. I learned a hard lesson about life that day.

[One day] after the closing of our business, my mother said, "Son, would you believe we are out of coffee? What can I tell your daddy?"

I said, "Mother, hold off a bit and I will see what I can do." I grabbed a big fat Dominecker hen from the yard and walked to Mr. Logan's store and asked how much he would pay for this nice fat hen. He said he thought a dollar would be about right. I asked the price of coffee. He said thirty-five cents a pound, and I said, "I'll give you this nice fat hen for three pounds of coffee and a large stick of that peppermint candy." He did and I felt mighty good giving the coffee and candy to my dear mother. Mr. Logan said that I drove a hard bargain.

The Depression was quite a unique period in my life. I believe my experience there molded me into the type of person I am today. The Depression was odd. It was like waking up one day and having everything gone. You were in the same house, but you didn't have access to anything. The groceries were getting scarce. You didn't have access to the bank anymore. I saw my parents go through the hardship. It was absolutely horrible. I suppose there was nothing Dad could have done. It was the boll weevil that hit and ate up the cotton. And with our cotton crop gone in Waco, there was nothing for us to do. There was no income throughout the community. People could not pay off their debts.

My father went to work in the insurance business in La Grange, Georgia, after all the other businesses went broke. Times were very hard. I said to my mother and daddy, "I'm going to Atlanta and get me a job." By then, I was fifteen years of age. Well, they reluctantly approved, and my daddy said that he'd give me some money. I said, "No, sir. I know where a man is building a house, and he said if I help take shingles up on his house for two days, he'd give me five dollars." I bought a bus ticket to Atlanta from La Grange for three dollars. By the time I got to Atlanta, I had twelve cents in my pocket. I walked down the street and saw this policeman. I walked up to the curb and he said, "Somethin' I can do for ya?"

I said, "Yes, sir. I'm lookin' for a job."

He said, "Better go on home. Ain't no jobs. It's Depression."

I said, "Well, what's the best part of town?"

He said, "I like West End Atlanta."

I said, "Well, how do you get there?"

He said, "You can catch a streetcar right here."

I got on that streetcar, and I don't know why, but I got off at Langhorn. I walked down that street, and I saw a neat little white house with a white sign that said: ROOM AND BOARD—$5 A WEEK. I walked up, and this little gray-haired lady met me at the door. I introduced myself. I said, "I've come to Atlanta to get me a job."

She agreed to let me come and stay for two or three days. I put my violin, which was in a suitcase that I carried all the way to Atlanta, under my bed. I walked down the street about three or four blocks in the afternoon, and I came to a little grocery store. I looked in there and saw this big fat man who weighed about 300 pounds. I walked in, and he said, "What for ya?"

I said, "It looks like you need a man to help you."

He looked around, and said, "Where is the man?"

I said, "I'm the man! Tomorrow's Saturday. Let me come help you tomorrow, and if I do you any good, you pay me. If I don't do you some good, you don't owe me a dime."

So he agreed to that. We worked about fourteen hours that Saturday, and he paid me five dollars, which was a lot of money back then. Well, that was my first week's board money. I made that the first day. He said, "Now, don't you come back no more, because I can't afford to pay ya."

Well, Monday morning I was right back down there. The grocery store was surrounded by a picket fence. He said, "Boy, did you spend the night by that fence?"

I said, "No, sir. I got me a boardinghouse. I haven't missed a meal. I've been doing all right."

He said, "Well, you mighta' been doin' all right, but you haven't got a job!" [I talked with him for a while, and] he said, "Come on. Let's go to produce row." I worked for that man for ten years. He raised me. I was making forty-five dollars a week. Back in those days, that was a lot of money.

After I got to Atlanta [and worked there for a while] my shoe soles were getting mighty thin. I had six dollars in savings. [One time] I got on a streetcar to go home after the grocery store had closed at night. The stores back then would stay open until midnight, or perhaps even later. It was Depression, and they wanted to get the last dollar they could. I got to Mitchell Street. I saw a shoe store that had big red letters on the front that said SALE NOW ON. I got off, and went into the store. The little fellow running the store said, "What for you?"

I said, "I need a pair of shoes."

He said, "How much money do you have to spend for a pair of shoes?"

I said, "I've got six dollars."

He said, "Oh, I've got a fine pair of shoes here for five dollars and ninety-eight cents."

Well, I bought that pair of shoes. I was five or six miles from where my boardinghouse was. I finally realized I had spent my last dime on shoes. That night, I learned one of the greatest lessons I have ever learned throughout my life. It held good, and still does.

That lesson is to always plan ahead. Don't jump into anything you're not prepared for.

Anyway, I had two cents in my pocket. Now, a streetcar ticket in those days was seven cents. I didn't have the money, so I had to walk home. I walked down from Mitchell Street to Spring Street. There at Spring Street was the old railroad terminal. Now, going home, I took a shortcut through an area that was real tough. It wasn't safe for anybody, especially at that time at night. Anyway, as I was walking through this area, three young fellows a few years older than I blocked my way on the sidewalk. One of them said, "Man, what are you doing down here of a night, walking barefoot?"

I said, "Well, I bought me a pair of shoes. Those shoes got stiff as I was walking home. I decided to take them off."

He said, "I don't believe you've got any business being in this place."

I said, "I am in this place, and you're in my way."

I guess saying that kind of took them by surprise. They realized I was tired and didn't have any time to fool around. They moved out of my way.

In the grocery store business in Atlanta, one of my jobs was to answer the telephone. People would call in and place orders for their groceries. One day, I answered the phone, and I was told that my father was dead.

By that time, it was two years after I left Waco, and Daddy had moved to Roanoke, Alabama. Well, I didn't have a car. The only way I knew to get to Roanoke was to ride a bus from Atlanta to LaGrange, and then find some way to get from there to Roanoke. I got into LaGrange about midnight. The bus terminal there was empty. It was raining out there that night. I looked out the window, and I saw a man in a Model-T asleep. He was a taxi driver. I woke him up, and got a ride to Roanoke.

When I walked into the house, I saw a door open down at the end of the hall with the lights on. By then, it was two o'clock. I heard them talking. I remember hearing one of them say, "I don't know what they're going to do."

I saw another door open with a dim light passing through. I went in there. There was my father in a casket. I moved closer to him. I saw a note that was for me. It said, "Tell Walker to sell everything, and move the family to Atlanta."

I started to pray. I prayed, "Lord, it looks rough. Everything looks black. I don't know if I can do it or not. But I will work. Please see that I don't make too many mistakes. Don't let anybody get in my way. I will do my best to look after my mother, brothers, and sisters."

I looked at my father. I said, "Daddy, I promise you I will certainly do my best to look after our family."

I was seventeen years of age when I moved my mother, brothers, and sisters to Atlanta after my father's death. I bought this house on South Gordon Street. I remember one time when we had a little problem. Now, the thought of owing taxes did not occur to me. One night I got home and my mother said, "Walker, we have a bill today for forty-two dollars for taxes. I just don't see how we are going to pay it. We've got a month before it's due."

I said, "I'll see what I can do."

The next few days I was at work like usual. One of my job requirements then was to get up early and go to produce row around five o'clock in the morning. I'd buy the store's produce there and have it back in the store by seven to open. It was a fast operation. I'd always look all the produce row over and see what I could see. One day I noticed there was only one cabbage truck at all of produce row. There was a lot of people lined up buying cabbage. They were ripping this man off. They had bags that would stretch. They were bushel bags, but you could fit more than a bushel in them. This man that owned the truck was selling the people that cabbage by the bushel. Those stretch bags sold for only a bushel, instead of what they actually were, a bushel and a half. The owner didn't realize that fact. I walked up in front of the truck to the man and said, "I see you have a lot of business."

He said, "Yeah. I do."

I said, "Do you realize that these people here are ripping you off? They are using stretch bags and getting a bushel and a half, instead of a bushel."

He said, "You don't mean it!"

I said, "I do mean it. I'd like to buy all your cabbage at a fair price, and pay you an extra ten dollars if you stay here and help me." He agreed to that, and sold me all his cabbage at three cents a pound.

I stood up on that truck so everyone could see me. I shouted,

"Now I know what y'all have been doing. Put all the cabbage back on the truck. Forget using those stretch bags. He was selling you this cabbage by the bushel. I'm going to sell it to you by the pound, for twice the price it's actually worth. It's all the cabbage in Atlanta, you can buy it or not."

Well, I sold all the cabbage. I had for my part, fifty-five dollars, and I gave him back ten. So that morning, I had enough money to pay our taxes. I got home and gave my mother the money. She said, "Walker, where did you get all that money?"

I said, "Cabbage."

I think age is a frame of mind. When I was young growing up in Atlanta, I had to think and act a much older age. How else was I supposed to survive the Depression? It was a hard time for me, like it was hard for most of the other people in America. Boys had to become men. My thoughts now are not that way. Like I said, I am age eighty-one. I'm retired and free of worry. Now, I think like a much younger age than what I am.

Lyndall "Granny" Toothman

"If you can spin a few yarns
while you're spinning yarn,
then you're really spinning yarn."

On July 9, 1991, I did one of the best interviews I'd ever done
in my life. When you consider that in the three school years and
three summers of work I've been with Foxfire I've done around
sixty or seventy interviews, saying this means a great deal!

At the beginning of the summer of 1991, Wig suggested several
people for me to interview for the Personality Portraits section of
the Foxfire 10 book, and the very first person he mentioned was
Lyndall "Granny" Toothman. She had first been interviewed several
years ago, and an interview with her about Christmas dinners was
published in A Foxfire Christmas.

Wig told me she was coming down to visit in early July, so I
wrote her, and we later set up the interview for eight in the morning
at the guest house on the Foxfire property in Mountain City, where
she'd be staying on July 9. Celena Rogers and I arrived there that
morning in an excited mood. We asked her one question, and she
gave us a whole tape of material in response to it! We went on to
ask another question and another question, and we just kept putting
tapes in. By two o'clock in the afternoon, when we'd gotten through,
we had a total of five and a half hours of tape.

She showed us lots of pictures of her family and friends and of
various events in her life, and she showed us various things she'd
made, including a pocketbook woven out of ten different kinds of

animal hair. She demonstrated spinning on the flax spinning wheel, which she does with dog's, cat's, and rabbit's hair as well as sheep's wool. (She can even spin a person's hair!) She let us touch the soft, silky dog's hair that she spun with.

Granny Toothman turned out to be the most fascinating person I have ever known in my life. She was born in the mountains of West Virginia. She was a loner and a tomboy as a child, and she didn't like school very well.

Granny Toothman was married three times and had one daughter, Jean. She says one of the few things she would change about her life is her marriages, which didn't work out because "They always want to change me, and then when they start to change me, I get unhappy."

When she became older, she lived and cooked in a small van, and she taught weaving and spinning at craft festivals that took her all around the country. She often stayed at various camps, and one time she stayed at a nearly deserted camp for about six months, living "off the earth." She even stayed in hippie communes. At one point, she was required to go to a weaving school in order to continue to teach. It turned out that she knew more than the teacher! At that time, she said, she had probably woven more than anyone else in the country.

Granny first came to Kentucky's Morehead College, where she now works as weaver in residence between road trips, through a federal nonprofit organization assistance program called "The Green Thumb." The program paid her salary at Morehead, and the college provided her with an apartment. When her term under the program expired, the college took her on their payroll and continued to provide her living quarters: "[I plan to stay here as long as I can.] I told them, as long as I can get one foot in front of the other, I would like to stay, so they keep renewing my contract every year. I just renewed my contract to the next first of July."

Granny Toothman is really an adventurer, and she has gone to many places alone where most of us would be afraid to go. She says that God has always protected her and that He warns her if there is any danger. She is a deeply religious person. Although she is officially a Methodist, her religion is a personal one, and includes many different and interesting beliefs. It shines through her whole life and through the advice she gives: "Have faith and have goals."

*She radiates a wonderful energy and spirit, and she puts every-
one around her in a good mood. (The day I interviewed her, I was
the happiest I'd been in several months.) Now in her eighties, she
is still working and still driving. She has the heart and energy of a
teenager, and she is as bright, vibrant, and alert as any twenty-
year-old.*

*This interview had a weird, destined quality to it, and I know
it will make a difference in my life. I have finally found someone
who is a true hero and who has lived the kind of life I would like
to live someday.*

*—Jenny Lincoln
Interview, article, and photographs
by Jenny Lincoln, Celena Rogers, and Eric Hollifield.*

I was born on May 1, 1910, early on a Sunday morning in a log
cabin back in the hills of West Virginia, right in the heart of the
Appalachian Mountains, in Greenbrier County. It's one of the prettiest counties of West Virginia. It's more farming than it is coal
mining. My grandmother died the day before I was born. I was a
breech birth, and I was stillborn, so they had to put me in hot and
cold water and work with me for a long time before I ever breathed.

We lived very primitive; in fact, the first log cabin I lived in
had only three rooms. The cabin was a story and a half. It was
about eighteen by twenty, and it didn't have a porch on it. However,
we still got plenty of good air because we had a front door and a
back door just straight across. In the summertime, when we'd get
hot, we opened both doors.

I was a very imaginative child. I played by myself, and I had to
find ways to amuse myself, because my sister was six years older
than I was, and I was twelve years old before my brother was ever
born. My sister and I had nothing in common; she worked in the
house, and I worked outdoors. I was through grade school when
my brother was born, and I graduated from high school the year
that he first went to school. So I grew up almost as an only child.

My daddy was a lumber grader and a stone mason. He built
lime kilns. I would go with him and stay all day and help him. Then
I would go out in the woods when he calculated timber. He'd have
big calipers, and they could measure the width of a log and estimate

Eric Hollifield interviews Granny Toothman as she talks and spins at the same time. So accustomed to doing both, she prefers to have the spinning wheel close at hand so she can get some work done— even during an interview.

the height of it and tell how many board feet were in a tree. We would ride our horse back out in the woods and stay all day, and take our dinner out in the woods. He also farmed a bit. We had what we called a one-horse farm. We had about fifty acres. We would put out about two or three acres of corn, and we'd have an acre or two of grass to cut down for winter feed. We usually kept two cows so we could have milk. We bred them so they would calve at different times, so that we'd have fresh milk and butter year round. I went out and helped Dad with the hay, and we got our hay put up each year before our neighbors, who had two boys that were older than I was. Those boys taught me to shoot a rifle. We'd fish and hunt, and we'd do things that boys liked.

Another neighbor had a boy who was two years younger than I was, and we played together from the time we were babies. We'd slept together in the crib when we were kids, and we just grew up together. We would get together on Sundays and play ball. At that time, we had a Western pony, and I would ride that pony over to his house.

We were playing ball one day, and I had my pony tied up to the fence. There was [another] boy there. He wasn't a mean boy, but he was very spoiled, and he was just about my size—maybe a little bit younger. He scared my pony and made it break loose.

I never said a word. I went up and got that pony and tied him back up to the fence, and I took my fist and just beat that boy! He had his eye blacked and his nose bloody. He went home a-bawling and a-crying, and of course his mother got mad at my mother because I'd beaten him up.

Mother was very good with her hands. She would take bulrushes, plait them and sew them together, and make us pretty hats. [She taught me how to do it, too], and I can still do that plaiting. She also made paper flowers, and if people were going to a wedding or something, they'd come to her and get her to make paper flowers for decorations She made them out of tissue paper instead of crepe paper. She'd take screen wire and take the wires out of it, and use it for stems. Her specialty was roses, and she would make roses that you could hardly tell from a real rose.

[Of course, I also went to school.] I wasn't exactly an ordinary, run-of-the-mill kid. I had one teacher that I went to three or four years, and she said that she had a bad bunch, she had a good bunch, and then she had me. I never done anything that the bad bunch done, and I never done anything the good bunch done. I was in a category all by myself, and I kind of went through school that way. I was a loner, and I still am. I don't remember that I've ever been lonesome.

I first went to school when I was five, and I had a bad experience. The teacher scolded us, and so I went home that evening and put my dinner bucket and my books down, and I said, "I'm through school."

I never went back until I was eight, and I had to walk a mile and a half through the mud, rain, snow, ice, sleet, and everything else. I'd have to wade in mud up to my knees, and ice would freeze on my hair. I had seven gates to open, because there were different farms. [My parents and I lived on the] last farm against the mountain, the last farm on the dirt road, [so I had longer to walk than anyone].

I didn't enjoy school too much, but I liked to read, and I read, I reckon, more than any other person. To give book reports, the teacher generally assigned you one a month. I read far more than she assigned. Sometimes I would read five or six, maybe ten in a month. I read every book we had, sometimes, two or three times. Then we got a library at the school, and I was permitted to bring books home. My biggest pleasure was reading. But I never could spell; I still can't spell today. They gave us a spelling class when I was in high school. I could give the definition of each word, but I couldn't spell it.

I went two years to high school [to the tenth grade]. Then they were wanting nurses, so when I was just sixteen years old, I went to the hospital and went in nurse's training. When I'd been there a year, they made a ruling that you couldn't take [the state board nursing exam] unless you were a high school graduate. So I quit the nurse's training and went back and took the other two years of high school. My class graduated in 1930—it's been sixty-one years since I graduated from high school. In my class when we graduated, there was fifteen of us.

After I graduated from high school, I got married. My husband worked in the mines. Then the Depression struck. The mines were shut down. We were living in a little shack on my dad's farm. I was nineteen years old when the banks shut their doors. At that time, we had a bank in our little town, and if the cashier hadn't panicked when all the banks around were closing, our bank would have been all right. He panicked and killed himself, and then they shut the bank door. I had nineteen dollars in it when it shut. I got about fifteen dollars out, though [so I only lost four dollars]. They wouldn't have lost anything if they hadn't had the appraisers and everything to pay to settle it up. That bank never did open its door again.

In the town below ours, the cashier also killed himself. He just walked out of the bank, and he got his car and ran it over the bridge down to the waters. They hunted and hunted for that cashier's body, and they couldn't find it. Then they found his body shot behind his barn. [They found out that] when he wasn't able to kill himself going over the bridge, he got out and walked home about a mile and got his gun. His wife was asleep, and he went in and got his gun and went behind the barn and shot himself. It was about twenty-four hours before they ever found him.

During the Depression, we lived on a little farm, and of course we'd been poor all our lives [and so] we lived just about the same. I couldn't see a bit of difference. If you had anything, you could always trade it to someone else who had something you wanted, so you didn't need much money. We grew most of our vegetables, and I remember we had an enormous garden in the thirties. The miners would come in that were out of work and starving, and we would give them bushels and bushels of stuff that we didn't use that we grew in the garden. We had our own meat. We had our own chickens. We'd can chickens and have them all winter, and then we'd kill hogs, and we'd can some of the meat and then salt the rest down for salt pork. We hardly ever had a beef to kill, but the neighbors would kill beef, and maybe we would trade a ham for a piece of beef. Things like that. I'd take vegetables to the grocery store and trade them for flour and coffee and stuff like that.

I never was a good salesman, but I'm a good barterer. I remember I'd get half a cent a pound for cabbage. A hundred pounds of cabbage would be worth fifty cents, and thirty-five cents would buy a twenty-five pound bag of white flour. A dozen eggs was worth fifteen cents, and fifteen cents would get you a yard, sometimes two yards, of nice cloth.

I would make my daughter, Jean, little woven skirts and blouses and things like that. She wouldn't tell me for a long time, but she hated those things. She wouldn't wear them if she could get out of it. Then after she was grown and married, just a few years ago, one of her girlfriends said to me, "Do you know what I remember about Jean the most?"

I said, "No, I wouldn't know."

She said, "Them pretty little skirts and blouses and things that you made her. I'd have given my right arm for one of those." But there she was a-hating them, because they were different [from what the other kids wore].

[During that time, the WPA was started.] Instead of handing out money to the people that needed food and clothing for their children, the WPA paid their people to work, and they had many, many, many more men than they had work for. If you had a little work project you needed a man or two to do, you could call them up.

They didn't do it for people who were able-bodied, but if you were a widow woman who didn't have any help, you could call them up and tell them you had a project to do, and if you were able to pay for it, you didn't pay the men; you paid the headquarters for this project work. If you were on assistance, they didn't charge you, but people who could paid the project so they'd have a little more money in the fund to get the people to work.

Not many people wanted to pay them, though, because [the WPA people] always got the name of being lazy, but they really weren't; they just had too many men on their projects. [Some of them] just got in that habit of sitting around while others worked.

There's this joke they was always telling about the WPA. A man called up [the WPA office] and said he wanted his lawn mowed. [He asked if they] would send a WPA man down to mow his lawn. When they came, there were eight men, and on the back of their truck they had a two-holer toilet.

Well, the man looked out, and he saw the crowd out there. He said, "What's this?"

They said, "This is the men the WPA project sent to mow your lawn."

[This man] called headquarters and said, "Oh, I didn't want anything like this. One man or two at the most is all I can use."

[At the office, they replied], "Oh, that's all right. They work in shifts." They had their two-holer toilet, and they'd set it down on the bank. They said, "We work in shifts. Two a-coming and two a-going. Two in the toilet and two a-mowing."

[During that time, they also started] these special WPA classes to teach people to do things for a little money. They got a weaving school in the small village of Williamsburg, West Virginia, in an abandoned two-room schoolhouse. I went to one of the WPA classes in weaving, and then afterward I taught at a state school in weaving. I reckon that changed my life; it was a turning point. It was when I was in my twenties, in 1934.

We had an old teacher who had taught in the high school but had retired from there. She had learned as a child to spin and weave, so the state hired her for our teacher. She taught knitting [as well], but weaving was her big thing.

Now, I was at loose ends, and I had nothing much to do, so I thought, "Well, I'll go down and learn to knit." She was excited about my coming, and she said to me, "I know you're going to make a good weaver. We'll learn you to knit on the side, but I want you to start with the loom."

We didn't have an awful lot of equipment, but she had an old warp that had been handspun years before. I will never forget the first thing that we did. We threaded the loom, and it took us about four weeks. Now I can thread the same loom in four hours. I think we put in about six hundred and fifty thread-ins in that loom. It was a four-harness loom, and we threaded it in a little block pattern. I was the first one who got to weave on it because I had done a big part of getting the warp in the loom.

I knew a little bit about weaving [already when I took that class because] we had had a little rug loom in our home. However, I didn't know anything about a four-harness loom weaving that made patterns. On the four-harness looms, the old people used to make coverlets and dresser scarfs and other fine weaving. The two-harness looms they generally just used for rugs and rough cloth if they used them for cloth at all. So the WPA school was where I learned pattern weaving.

[Now let me give you some general background on these weaving schools.] They didn't generally hire women to help in the WPA in the country, but of course they had to hire teachers for all the schools they had, and these teachers were usually women.

They would teach us many different crafts at these schools, mostly as a vocation that we could go out and use for the rest of our lives. They also taught the women nursing. [They couldn't teach them to be registered] nurses or anything like that, but they taught them to be [what today would be considered] nurses' aides. They taught them bedside nursing.

[But weaving] was the big thing in this project. For several years, there hadn't been any weaving in the country at all. After they got automation in the weaving, there just wasn't any home weaving. In our community, I just knew of one woman who kept her old loom. You brought your rags in, and she would weave carpet and rugs from them for so much a yard. [Otherwise], people took their old looms down and put them in their barn lofts. The old looms were big six-by-eight beams with big heavy rollers, and they were clumsy and there wasn't much room for them in the homes.

So the WPA brought hand weaving back into existence again. [This revival] lasted for about four years, and people learned to weave. Then people [put their looms away again]. They usually put them in the barn loft and stacked the hay over the top of them.

Now when you find one of these old looms, they call it a barn loom because it may have laid in the barn maybe fifty years.

I know one family who had a beautiful cherry loom. I had made all kind of plans for getting that loom, but then when I went to get it, they'd cut it up for kindling, and it was gone. [It makes me so mad.] That was beautiful lumber, and even if they didn't want it as a loom, they could have done a lot of other things with it instead of making it into kindling. There were hundreds of these old looms cut up for kindling because they just looked like a pile of wood. The old people would be very angry about it, but the younger folks didn't even know what the looms were for because they'd never seen any weaving done.

[So the craft of weaving had] just about died out, and then the WPA revived it. Then even the wealthy people began to enjoy it. It began to be used as occupational therapy at hospitals. I don't know a veterans' hospital anywhere that doesn't have a weaving department because it's a gentle exercise with your hands and feet and back. I'm eighty-one years old, and there have been very few times when I've ever had any trouble with backache.

Looking back, it's interesting to see how much being at that WPA craft school influenced my life. After I left I said, "Never again. I'll not weave, I'll not spin."

But it followed me wherever I went. I've picked fruit, and I even picked cotton one winter. Yet every time I settled down, spinning and weaving was what people wanted—that was it. I guess my experience at that WPA school turned my life around more than any other one thing.

[Toward the end of the Depression,] I said, "I'm going out and get a job."

At that time, in 1939, Alderson Reformatory had been there about five years. Alderson was a railroad town right on the Greenbrier River [in West Virginia]. They had 500-acre farms there, that was bought to build this big reformatory—the first one that was ever built for women alone.

I went to the federal reformatory office in West Virginia and just walked in and asked for a job. And I got it, though afterward I had to take a Civil Service examination. My daughter was six years old when I went there.

I went as a correctional officer. [Some of the first prisoners I knew were] Machine Gun Kelly's wife and mother-in-law, Ora Shannon and Katherine Kelly. Ora Shannon was Katherine Kelly's mother.

Now, Ora had this little farm in Texas and a house way back off from anything. [Machine Gun Kelly and Katherine] kidnapped a Chicago banker and put him in this house that Ora owned. That's about all Ora had to do with it. [She owned the house, but it was the other two who were responsible for the kidnapping.]

In 1939 [when I first started working at the reformatory], I was one of the youngest officers. The old officers didn't take to us very well when we first came. The first day, they showed me the grounds. The next day, they put me in a prisoners' cottage next to the greenhouse. Katherine and Ora ran the greenhouse.

I went to the cottage, and the officer threw me this handful of keys and said, "Here it is. They put you here; you can have it." She gave me the keys in the hall, and then she just walked out the door and left me with those thirty prisoners.

I was twenty-nine years old then, and it was my first job. I had never even seen a prison or a prisoner before. Ora saw how pitiful I looked. She came up to me, and she said, "Honey, I've been here a long time, and I know this cottage even better than that officer does. You can trust me, and I hope you will, for your sake. If you'll trust me, I'll get you through this mess."

Ora told me [all kinds of useful things]. She told me who to lock in and who had the run of the cottage. She told me what to do in the kitchen. She said, "Now, this kitchen crew knows what they're doing. They've been here a good while, and you can trust them. The only thing you have to do in the kitchen is to take the keys and get the supplies that they need. If they tell you they want sugar, you go get 'em sugar. Whatever they tell you they want, go get it." When the evening came, she told me what doors to lock and what doors to leave unlocked.

Katherine was real nice to me. I never worked with anybody, even out on civilian jobs, that treated me nicer or more respectfully. [But I liked Ora the best.] I always had a soft spot in my heart for that woman. A long time after I left the prison, they finally let her out.

Now the warden was very much of a go-getter. I'd only been there a very short time when she came along with a tablecloth and a few handmade things that they had woven in a man's prison in Oklahoma.

She said, "Look what they're doing in Oklahoma."

I said, "Oh, I can do that."

She said, "What?"

I said, "Yeah, I can do that."

She said, "Well, have you got something I can see?"

I had a shopping bag, some table runners, some placemats, and a dresser scarf made out of linen. She looked at that, and she said, "I'll have a weaving room fixed in the morning for you."

The next day, she had two girls and two harness rug looms. [A little later, a prison in Oklahoma] sent us six or seven old handmade looms. They were just like the old barn looms that you see around, built on the same heavy beams and everything.

[Then she got even more looms from the WPA.] You see, in 1939, the industry was just beginning to come in, and a bunch of WPA schools had been shut down. This prison warden found an advertisement for these looms in Detroit, Michigan, from a WPA school that had shut down. They had twenty-one beautiful looms, four-harness and everything, ranging in size from eighteen inches wide to sixty inches wide.

The prison warden got all these looms and set them up, and I started the weaving department in that prison; I began doing a lot of weaving. That was only about six months after I came as a correctional officer.

The warden put about twenty girls [in my group], though sometimes I'd have as many as thirty. I always got the girls that was recovering from drug addictions. Sixty percent of the girls in there were drug addicts, and they were all there on federal charges. Then we had the bank robbers and the kidnappers and the prostitutes. Anyway, they gave me the misfits because weaving is classed as occupational.

I first put them back in the corner making rags for rugs and unwinding sweaters. We had a lot of wool sweaters that the girls used that had worn out. We made enough bedspreads and drapes for all of the officers' rooms, and all of them were navy blue and wine colored. The wine wasn't so bad, but that navy blue looked nearly like you were in a morgue. I never will forget all that navy blue and wine.

Anyway, I put these girls back there unraveling those sweaters and cutting carpet rags and doing other things like that. I never bothered them much until they would begin asking questions. Then, if I felt like they were ready, I asked them if they wanted to work on a loom. I got some awful good weavers out of those girls.

During World War II [a lot of the spies got sent to Alderson]. They were all very intelligent. [Among others], I worked with Axis Sally. Axis Sally was a mean ol' biddy who had gone from the United States over to Germany's side and helped them all during the war. She was born and reared up around Columbus, Ohio, and she had been in Germany about twenty years before World War II took place. She was very much a Hitler follower, but she never had become a German citizen. When World War II began, she broadcasted against the Americans, trying to make our boys homesick and unhappy. After the war was over, she was sent back to the U.S.A. to stand trial. She had a thirty-year sentence, but she only done ten years of it. I had her directly under me for seven years.

She had hot flashes, and lots of times she would put up the window when she had them, not regarding anybody in the room. People would freeze to death. She would get awfully mad if you even mentioned that she shouldn't put the window up that way. She would just do so many annoying little things.

I think that she was the cause of me leaving the reformatory after twelve years of work. She was a most obnoxious person, and she felt like she was so much better and smarter than any of us. [She thought that] nothing in the United States was good. She had done so many annoying things that I wanted to take her by her feet and dump her out the third-story window.

So after twelve years, I went in one day and said, "I quit."

The warden said, "You can't quit a job like this. You've just got seven more years before retirement age, and you haven't got any other [job opportunities] in sight."

I said, "Before I came here I ate, and I'll eat after I leave."

Then she began quizzing me, and I said, "Well, one of the reasons why I want to leave is Axis Sally."

She said, "If that's all, I'll move her."

I said, "No. I got to the point where working here is getting on my nerves. I said when I came here that when it began to get to me, I was going to leave. It's getting to me now, and I'm leaving."

I quit. I traded my furniture for a little house trailer [and I started out to see and do some of the things I had always dreamed about]. I made a trip to the West Coast, and I stayed ten months on the road.

I said, "I'll never pull a house trailer again."

Just shortly after that, they began to get the cab-over trucks. Right away, I got a cab-over camper truck, and I went back to California and stayed fifteen years. I made thirteen trips from California to West Virginia in that pickup truck. That was twenty-six times across the United States! I kept that pickup truck fifteen years, and I had 155,000 miles on it when I traded it off.

I done my first demonstrating at Knotts Berry Farm in California. I demonstrated weaving, and that was a really fun job.

On the trip through the country after Knotts Berry Farm, I went to the Retarded Children's Foundation at San Pedro, California, and worked there a long time teaching weaving. I was quite successful in teaching them. I started out with one little loom, and before I left there, we had made things and then sold them, and bought eleven new looms.

It takes them a good while to catch onto something, but when they've got it, they've got it. It's theirs. They just love weaving. [Once they got started weaving], they didn't want to go play. They didn't even want to go eat. We had to just force them off their looms. They were just so anxious to get there in the mornings.

The children who went to our school were supposed to be the unteachables. Most of them were Down's syndrome or brain-damaged. I had this nice-looking fifteen-year-old boy. This boy did such nice weaving, and so I tried to teach him pattern weaving on a one, two, three, four design. I'd say one and two on the pedals, and then three and four. But he could never go above two. He just couldn't handle figures. But he knew his colors red, blue, yellow, and green. So I put red, yellow, blue, and green on his treadles, and I taight him by color code to do four-harness weaving. He done beautiful weaving.

I remember one time I told him, "I have to go to the doctor today."

He looked at me, and he said, "Will you get a shot in your butt?"

I said, "I wouldn't be surprised, Lloyd, maybe I will." And he never said any more. Then I was getting my sweater ready to go, and he said, "I'll go with you and take that shot for you if you want. I don't mind it too bad."

[He didn't realize] that if I got a shot it was for me. It wouldn't help me for him to get it. But he thought that if the shot had to be done, he'd rather take it than have me suffer for it.

They had a national seminar for the teachers of the retarded children, so they sent me up to the seminar with some placemats and purses and rugs the children had made. Really, after they got the process straight, they done better work than an ordinary person because they were so careful. Their edges looked just exactly like they were factory done. They wouldn't have a thread out of place. Everybody was wanting to buy them. Nobody else had anything that could compare in quality. In about a month I got a plaque for outstanding work with retarded children.

I went on to Silver Dollar City, Missouri, to work. It was in 1960, just when they were first opening. I went there for a festival. Then, in three or four years, I went back and was hired full-time there. At Silver Dollar City they paid well. That's when I decided to go into adult vocational education.

I taught adult vocational education in West Virginia for about four years. It was in a one-room schoolhouse they'd abandoned. They had looms, and they set me up there. I taught the farm women to weave, and then they made things and sold them to get added income to keep their kids in school and clothed and so on.

That was when I learned to spin, while teaching vocational education. We did a lot of weaving, and the folks kind of got bored with so much of it. One of them said, "Can't we do something different?"

So I asked them how many had spinning wheels. I didn't know how to spin, but I knew a mountain woman that did do spinning. So I went to her, and she taught me, and then I taught them.

But you don't really *teach* anyone to spin. They've got to learn by trial and error. You've got to get it in your hands until your fingers do it without your thinking. You kind of get in a rhythm. You'll think you're spinning a long time before you're spinning, because you'll be making pretty good thread. But until you get to the point where you can think about something else and spin, you're not really spinning. If you can spin a few yarns while you're spinning yarn, then you're really spinning yarn. You've got to get it in your fingers instead of in your head.

[It's like that with] any kind of craft work. If you don't get in a rhythm, you're not really doing it right.

One place where I was demonstrating, I had a big crowd around me. Now, I hadn't done dog hair or anything but sheep's wool until that time. A woman came up and said she'd been saving some of her dog's hair, and would I spin it for her.

I told her I'd never spun dog hair, but I'd try it, and that I would spin it for half the yarn if I could do it. So she brought these big twenty-pound lard cans—two or three of them. When I got through with the yarn, we had thirteen pounds of yarn, and it only takes a pound and a half to make a sweater. So I had six and a half pounds, and she had six and a half.

I made a coat and a sweater and little caps and things out of mine; she made a coat. [I'm glad I got started doing that], because dog hair is much easier spun and much softer than sheep's wool. I do a lot of dog hair spinning now. Of course I do wool, camel, llama, and all the traditional spinning yarns [but I like spinning dog hair the best].

Sheep wool has to be washed and picked and carded before it is ready to spin. Dog hair is easier because you just pick it up from the combings and run it through the wheel. You don't have to do all this carding. You just wash your dog and comb him when he's shedding.

Cat hair doesn't spin as well as dog hair does. They only have one coat of hair, and you have to be very gentle with cat hair. You can't handle it or anything, or it will wad. Cat and rabbit hair both wad, but rabbit hair is not so bad. Angora is made out of rabbit. Mohair is made from goat, and the llama, musk ox, and camel are all ordinary animals for spinning.

I even spun some penguin fur one time. You know how baby chicks have the fur on them, and in just a week or so that's gone? Well, the baby penguins keep their fur about a year. They're brown. They look almost just like brown bears. When they begin to get their feathers, they shed all of their brown fuzz off. I got a nice big bag of this brown fuzz, and it spun beautifully. I can't spin the adult penguin feathers, however, because they are so stiff. Now, I can spin duck down if I just get the down [and not the feathers].

The only dog hair I can't spin is the Mexican Hairless, and I'm working on that. I can even spin little Chihuahua hair that's not more than half an inch long; if someone can comb one with enough shedding, I can spin it.

[I can even spin a person's hair.] I done a show in Kalamazoo, Michigan, at the Western State University. They had me up there doing a demonstration. I had a big crowd of college kids around me. There was this boy who walked up and down who had a beard clear down to his chest. I'd worked at Silver Dollar City where I'd spun lots of beards, and I said, "Oh, yeah, I can spin beards, too."

He never said a word. He just turned around and walked away. I said, "These boys are a little touchy about their beards sometimes. I believe that I've offended that boy."

About half an hour later, here he came with a paper bag. He'd shaved his beard and brought it back to spin. It spun real well. I sat there and spun it right before him, and made a little skein that was pretty long.

He was so proud of that. I wouldn't have been able to recognize him if he hadn't brought his beard to me because he was clean-shaven. He said that he had been getting ready to cut it off anyway. It had been bothering him, you know.

Every kind of hair has to be handled just a little bit differently. If a person is first learning on sheep wool, they can't go from sheep wool to dog hair. They have to learn all over again to get the touch. It's the touch—I don't know how to spin, my fingers know. I let them do my thinking for me.

Spinning and weaving and all of those trades are coming back a lot. I don't know whether there's a purpose for it or not. Of course, someday we might have to use them again. Somebody was recently saying something on the news about World War II, and I said, "Well, maybe we'll come back to all this. If they put out a few atomic bombs, like the Bible says, a few will live, and they'll have to start all over again. We've got a good start right here."

After Granny Toothman taught adult vocational education for a while, she "retired" from full-time work, while continuing to travel and demonstrate her crafts. For about ten years, she demonstrated in a reconstructed "frontier village" in Cedar Point amusement park on Lake Erie. She "retired" from Cedar Point in 1982.

Then I was seventy-two. I went to one of the senior citizen retirement apartment houses. It had beautiful apartments and everything, and it was just as nice as could be. Now you didn't have any responsibility there. If your light bulb went out [hired people] would come and put a light bulb in. If your windows needed washing, they came in and washed your windows. It was a beautiful place. Some of them there were younger than I was, but everyone was complaining. I stayed a year and a half, and then I couldn't take it any longer.

Granny went back out on the road.

[I've lived in a van and worked at craft festivals for many years now.] I've made lots of friends in camps. I go in the camps, and I meet them and talk to them, and then we'll probably eat together and exchange foods and all of that. I've done a lot of outdoor cooking. I'll take a stick and cook my meat on it. I know about all kinds of wild greens and things. I go out and pick berries, and I get apples off the tree. One of the things that I make when I camp is apple dumplings or berry dumplings.

Today I don't know anybody else who still makes it, but I still make a corn pone every once in a while. You make a corn pone like you do salt rising bread. [You start out with] three cups of cornmeal and a cup of all-purpose flour, a tablespoon of sugar, and a teaspoon of salt. You boil four cups of water and pour that water over the mixture and stir. Get it all nice and even; get all the lumps out.

Now, you set it somewhere [overnight] in a warm place. Of course, when I was young we always had the fireplace going, so we would set it close to the fireplace where it would keep good and warm. Don't put a lid on it; put a cloth or something on it so that it will gather yeast out of the air and make it better. Since I've got a gas stove, I always set it over the pilot light and leave it sitting for at least twelve hours.

The next morning [it will stink]. The more it stinks and the more it has soured, the better corn pone it's going to be. In fact, sometimes you think it's going to be something rotten. By morning, it will also have a different texture. It will be more watery.

When you get ready to put it in the oven, you put two table-

"Corn pone doesn't taste like corn bread. It doesn't taste like spoon bread. It doesn't taste like hoecake. It doesn't taste like any other bread you've ever eaten. It's a moist thing, and kind of solid, like fried mush."

spoons full of sorghum syrup—that's the best sweetener to use, though you can use any molasses. [Also, you should add] two tablespoons of grease of some kind. I like meat fryings. Just take your bacon and fry it out and put two good spoons full of that bacon grease in it. If it seems like it is too thin, put a little bit of raw cornmeal in it; if it seems like it's a little too thick, add a little bit of buttermilk.

We baked in a Dutch oven with a lid that looked like it was upside down. You could put the coals on top if it and the coals underneath it, and every time we went to stir the fire up, we would look about the corn pone and put new coals on it. It wasn't any trouble at all, but it took a long time to bake—about five hours.

We always wanted the corn pone to stick to the pan so we could get a piece of it hot. If it stuck to the pan and Mother would get a chunk out, then she would let us get some butter and eat that. She would rather it come out whole and cool it. Then we either steamed it later or fried it like mush. [The way I prefer it is] to take some butter and put it in the skillet and slice it and fry it like mush.

Corn pone doesn't taste like corn bread. It doesn't taste like spoon bread. It doesn't taste like hoecake. It doesn't taste like any other bread you've ever eaten. It's a moist thing, and kind of solid, like fried mush. I don't believe I've ever found anybody that doesn't like it. Even if they've never heard of corn pone before, they still like that corn pone taste. [If you cook it in butter], you can have a whole meal of it. You can [also] eat it cold. My brother just loves it cold with butter.

I hardly ever go to doctors. I am supposed to get a checkup every year. Last year I entered for my checkup, and they said, "Your cholesterol is way high, and you're going to have to do something about it."

I said, "Well, I feel good. What will happen?"

[The doctor] said, "Well, you'll have a heart attack."

I said, "Well, what a beautiful way to go."

He said, "Well, if that's the way you feel about it, just go on."

I'm getting some cataracts on my eyes. Things are kind of scummy, especially on bright days like this, and I had a checkup here not very long ago. I said, "Well, if I get to where I can't read and I can't drive, I don't want to live any longer."

I do whatever makes me feel good. If I stay in my apartment two or three days, the first thing you know, I'm sick [so I have a new van I can camp in, and I keep going to craft fairs].

Last year in Florida early one morning, I was driving along a big double highway. There was not a soul on the road that early on Sunday morning. A police car popped over the hill. I looked down and saw that I was doing seventy-five in a fifty-five-mile zone, and so I slowed down real quick!

But the police had already clocked me by radar, and he came up to me. He said, "Where are you going so fast?"

I said, "Just like the old horse. I'm headed for the barn. I'm going home."

He said, "Well, you're going too fast."

I said, "I didn't realize it. I was thinking about something else, and I wasn't watching the speedometer, and I just didn't realize it."

He said, "Give me your driver's license."

My age was on it, and he said, "Eighty years old?"

I said, "Yeah."

He said, "Well, I don't believe I've ever fined an eighty-year-old for driving fast."

"Well," I said, "don't break a record."

He said, "No, I'm going to have to fine you."

So he went in and wrote me the ticket, and told me I could go home and send him back a certified check or money order. I took the ticket. It was for $135, and I said, "It's not too bad." After you get to be eighty-one, you don't ever know what's going to happen. But I pray night and day that when I go, I just go.

There's just a few times in my life that I've ever been afraid. My dad taught me [not to be afraid]. Now, he was quite religious. He grew up in the Methodist church, and he was superintendent of the Sunday school for years, and he had this incredible faith.

He always told me that there's nothing in one place that's not going to be in another. He told me not to be afraid at night [out at a camp] because I would not be in any more danger there than I'd be sitting on my porch at home. He built up this immunity to fear in me at an early age, when I was four or five years old. Then we lived about a fourth of a mile from the main store. All the men went there at night and gathered at the store. He'd let me go with him down there, and then when I got tired he let me walk home by myself. He always told me just go on, that nothing was going to bother me, and nothing ever has.

Have faith in the universal life that you are connected to. Some people think of God as a man sitting up on a high throne with a long beard and white hair, but God is everywhere. It doesn't make any difference what you call Him. You can call Him Universal Mind, Allah, Jehovah, or anything you want to call Him, but He is still everywhere. I always think of it as electricity. You can't see it, but you know it's there, and you can always plug into this Universal Mind and have faith, and that will take care of you. It's just like electricity. You can take an iron, and you can't heat it unless you plug it in. You've got to be in connection, and if you're in connection, there's nothing in the world that you can't do that your mind can conceive and dream.

I think that's what's made me do the many things I've done in my life. I didn't play so much like other kids did. I lived in an imaginary world. I know some kids hated to go to bed. [But I was different.] I'd be real anxious to get into bed at night, and it made me mad if I went to sleep too soon, because [before I slept] I so enjoyed imagining all the things I would do. I'd see pictures or read a story about being out West and I imagined being out there and doing [the things that I read about], and then I tried to make them come true.

They say that young people dream and old people have visions, so I don't guess I'm old yet because I still have dreams—not night dreams, but day dreams. I still dream about places that I want to go and things I want to do. I want to live and enjoy life. When I can't, I pray that God will let me fade away into the night to another life with more dreams and another big adventure.

CRAFTS

STUDENT EDITORS, CHRIS NIX
AND ROBBIE BAILEY

Just as the world has changed, our crafts contacts have also evolved over the years. Foxfire students Chris Nix and Robbie Bailey edited this chapter and have been closely associated with a number of crafts people. Chris observed, "In the past, our contacts would use their skills and incorporate it into their lifestyle out of necessity. Foxfire students would interview people who turned pottery, made chairs, or planted by the signs. The contacts would use what they made because it was a necessity. Today, society no longer has a need for [utilitarian] potters or chair makers. Factories can now manufacture all the things we need. One of the main attributes of our present-day contacts is that they do what they do because they want to."

In this section are artists like Max Woody and his son Myron, whose family has practiced the chair makers' craft for seven generations, and who wax elegantly philosophical about their age-old practice. Jimmy White is a young man who turns wood on an old device: a homemade foot-powered lathe. Chair maker Clyde Runion is an old friend of ours who also talks about his Depression experiences in an earlier chapter. Jerry King is a shy and gentle man who loves the creatures whose likenesses he carves on his snake canes. Introduced to us by venerable Foxfire contacts, Jerry practices crafts influenced by the *Foxfire* series but infused with his own aesthetic. (Perhaps it is inevitable that Foxfire itself would have some effect on the very same artists we interview; after all, the first *Foxfire* book has been in print for twenty years.) Michael Crocker and his brother Melvin are young men who grew up in a whole neighborhood of folk potters and learned to make pottery under the watchful eyes of taciturn, experienced older jug throwers.

Then there is R. A. Miller, who has a yard full of wind toys, and who makes wonderful paintings of dinosaurs, devils, angels, seven-headed dragons, and all sorts of things (many of which he encounters on television nature programs). The folk art dealers pick clean his supply of work on a weekly basis. Even though he is nearly blind, Mr. Miller always has dozens of pieces to take their place by the next week. Like Mr. Miller, Minnie Black began her career as a gourd artist late in life, and operates purely out of a self-generated sense of aesthetics. Minnie, at nearly ninety years of age, took her gourd art to both "The Tonight Show" and "Late Night with David Letterman."

These artists and crafts people obviously run the gamut from the traditional to the original—even the idiosyncratic. But they do have several qualities in common: an integrity of vision and purpose, a willingness to share what they know and do, and a real kindliness of spirit toward the young people who came to learn about their work.

Max and Myron Woody

"Being happy in what you do is worth more than
making a lot of money."

There are several families in North Carolina named Woody who
make chairs. Max Woody is one of the best. The chair for which
he is best known is a black walnut or cherrywood rocker with a
fifty-two-inch-high back and six horizontal slats. Max works with
his customers, easily accommodating special requests like extra-tall
or extra-wide backs, and once we saw the craftsmanship of several
of his chairs, we knew we wanted to visit him.

Upstairs at his shop in Marion, North Carolina, beautiful chairs
sit in rows against the walls, greeting the customers who walk along
admiring all that they see. This is actually just a showplace for the
beautiful works Max Woody creates in the cluttered, machinery-
filled downstairs level of his shop.

Descending the narrow wooden staircase, we notice the large
bench at which Max works among the woodworking tools and machinery. Max Woody has been in the chair making business since
1950, and it is easy to see why his customers leave his shop with
a smile and, most likely, a new set of chairs. Max's good-natured
personality, talent, and skill make him a terrific person to talk with,
and he accommodates any guests with handmade chairs, should
they want to sit and visit. Although Max's son, Myron, worked at
his father's shop while he was growing up, after he graduated from
college, he worked in other furniture industries. Four months before

this interview, Myron had returned to work in his family business,
thus becoming the seventh generation of chair makers in his family.

—Heather Scull
Interview and photographs by Heather Scull,
Robbie Bailey, and Chris Nix.

Max Woody: On my mother's side [of the family] there were
three Arringtons who made chairs, and on the Woody side there
were three who made chairs for other people. [So] I learned, really,
from both of my grandfathers. My granddad Arrington was a gentle-
man, and he was a good one, known throughout the community as
a peacemaker on Painter [Panther] Creek in Haywood County. He
was a farmer, cabinetmaker, and chair maker by necessity because
he had to make chairs for his family. In that day and time, they
made what they had to have for their mountain homes and farms.
They made wagons and sleds and anything they needed. They made
watermills, grist mills. If you didn't make it or grow it, you didn't
have it. When crops were "laid by" in July, Granddad Arrington
always had a barn or house to build for someone. This brought in
cash to buy shoes for his wife, himself, and thirteen children. Other
clothes were "homespun."

The chair makers on the Woody side made chairs as their profession. We can trace seven generations of chair makers on that side.
We start with Henry Woody, who was the father of Wyatt Woody,
who was the father of Arthur Woody, who was the father of Martin
Woody, who was the father of Claude Woody, who was my father,
and, then, Myron, being my son, makes seven generations. It's
rumored that, when my grandfather and great-grandfather came to
this country, their name was Anderson, and because of their profession, their name was changed to Woody. Some of them settled in
Tennessee, and some of them in the Waynesville, North Carolina,
area, but most of them were living in other parts of the country.

My grandfather and his father worked in a shop for a period of
time together when my father was a little boy, and he remembered
working with them. Great-grandfather's name was Arthur A.
Woody, but everybody called him Uncle Art. At that particular
time, as well as chairs and the furniture and their family needs,
they also made some wagons.

Grandfather helped his father and grandfather when they

Chair maker Max Woody.

worked on wagons. He told me that his job was to gather up enough coal and coke to heat the wagon tires. They learned that a saucer-shaped or dish-shaped wheel was stronger, and with a shorter axle you could put a wider wagon box in it. They did some pretty good arithmetic to put those spokes in and to put the felloes together. Then they'd take a [tool called a] traveler and roll it around the wheel [to measure it], and then they'd roll that out on a [steel] wagon tire. They bought the steel in giant rolls, just like a giant clock spring, and they would [cut the steel for the tires long] enough to lap over, and they would heat those ends. On the forge they heated and hammered [the steel] and hammered the weld. Then they had adjustments on these rollers, and they'd put it in there and roll it, and it would round that wheel.

Then they would lay the [wooden] wagon wheel down on the ground. They'd lay the [steel] tire down on some rocks and then build a circular fire under it. While it was heating, they would carry about three buckets of water [with] gourd dippers, and set [the buckets down in] three positions around [the tire]. When that [steel tire] was red hot, they'd take the tire off and set it on the [wooden] wheel, and it would burn its way down on the wheel. When it was down just where they wanted it, the three of them would start taking dippers of water and pouring it around that, and he said you could see that wheel contracting and those joints coming together and hear it start popping and cracking, and you could see the outsides moving up, in addition. [*See* Foxfire 9 *for a detailed description of wagon making—Ed.*]

[So] they made wagons, and my great-great-grandfather was said to have patented the brakes for a wagon. He was a small man who lived to be almost ninety-seven years old. He made chairs on a water mill lathe, and he even made a few after he was past ninety years old.

He logged his wood in with big red oxen. They split out their wood [because] they didn't have the kinds of saws they have now. They split out [the parts] and made 'em into chairs. They didn't need anything from the hardware [store], and they didn't do much sanding. They didn't have any sandpaper. They did some scraping [instead]. They dried their rungs, but the posts were green in the upright chairs. They would cut the timber one day and make it into chairs the next, and if they warped one up [it didn't make that much difference]. They were just ole rough mountain chairs. During the Depression, chairs used to sell for fifty cents apiece, and finally when times got better, they got a dollar apiece for 'em, and they'd sell you a set of six for five dollars.

My dad made chairs when he was a young man, and then for a number of years he worked on the railroad. It was while my father was working on the railroad that he met my mother, who worked in the cotton mill in Marion, North Carolina. They married and moved to Rutherfordton. [Dad worked on a crew that] built bridges. They were the bridge crew, and they built the coal tipples and water tanks. They took wood and made water tanks—and they had to make pretty good geometry. Now, my granddad and my dad both could frame a house and order their building material [so accurately that] it was verified that you could haul the [leftover] scraps away from the house in a wheelbarrow. My dad was working on the railroad there until he was injured in an accident. Imagine this: they had a new home, a new automobile, money in the bank, and in six months' time that was all gone. There was no compensation or insurance in those days, and the hospital and doctor bills added up. Finally, they left there and came to McDowell County and moved into an old farmhouse. They scrounged enough money to buy a mule and started farming and were doing pretty well until the Depression hit.

My dad made chairs by hand, of which I have one upstairs. He didn't have any machines at all—just a hammer, and a saw, and a square, and a chisel, and a block plane. He didn't have sandpaper; he used broken glass to scrape the wood smooth. He didn't have any movement in his shoulder. He only had movement in his elbows and his wrists. He was stooped to where he could just take half a step, but he forged, and he made a garden tool in about 1940 that I still have today—a little garden hoe made out of a Model-T Ford spring. I still have most of his hand tools in the old toolbox. When I was about three or four years old, I guess, I would get into his toolbox. If I'd catch him a little ways away from home, I'd get in and get his hammer and saw. And I used the toolbox for a work-bench, and I would drive nails and them going into the toolbox. When he caught me at it, he put a lock on the box. I found out then that I could go to the back of the shop and knock the pins out of the hinges and lift it up that way. He caught me doing that, and he run a long rod through the box and stapled it down in the corners, and he stopped me awhile, I guess. I just wasn't happy unless I had something I could make out of wood. I was fifteen when my dad died.

Now my great-grandfather never made any refined furniture, but Granddad made a more refined chair. Although he didn't do any finishing, he sanded. My granddaddy worked with the water wheel up until the time that he went to work with the railroad company. Grandad worked for the railroad for twenty years until he got laid off from his job and moved in with Mom and Dad. It was then that Granddad started his chair business, and that's how I got to know him better. He made chairs from about 1930 till about 1963. [Later on] when I was working with my granddad, we'd quit about once a hour, and I smoked a pipe then, and he'd roll him a Prince Albert cigarette, and we would sit and smoke and talk for maybe ten minutes. I gleaned all the knowledge that I could from him. There's a lot of things I would love to be able to ask him now. One thing I tell many young people is to be attentive to their elders and ask all the questions that they can ask. If you're thinking of something, if you don't think you will remember it, write it down because one of these days there won't be anyone to ask. There's a lot that I write down that I will never use, but I did retain a lot that I had learned from my granddad.

Granddad was struggling to make a living in the chair business after the Depression hit. A lady stopped in his shop one day and bought some unfinished cherry ladderback chairs; Granddad never finished any. She took those chairs to Birmingham and aged them and finished them, and she put an article in the women's section of *Progressive Farmer* on how to finish a cherry ladderback chair. It was Miss Sally Hill, editor of the women's section of *Progressive Farmer*. She couldn't advertise for him, but in the article she wrote that if anybody wanted the address, they could send her a stamped envelope, and she'd send it to them. Granddad told me many a time how much that meant to him. He sold a lot of chairs from that.

I had worked in the furniture factory and saved some money and got my tools and machines before I went to work for my granddad. I told him that I wanted to make chairs, and finally I went to live with him. After breakfast one Monday morning, Grandpa Woody slid back from the table and made a speech to me. He told me that he felt obligated to help me with all that he could on the machines. He had a lot of work to do, and he knew it was going to take up a lot of his time, but we went on down to the shop after a while, and he showed me how to cut up the rungs, and I cut them up. Then he showed me how to mark out the backs, and I marked out the backs. Someone called him out of the shop, and while he was gone, I belted up the old bandsaw and cut the backs out. He came back in, and he almost got angry when he found out I had sawed them; he was afraid I'd ruin them if I did. But we went on and assembled six chair frames that day, and that was more than he had ever done. In his eyes I was still a child, really, but then he realized that I was a grown man, and he realized how badly I wanted to do this, so he hired me, and we were in business together. I did a better job of sawing than he did, actually, because he was old and was blind in one eye, but he never admitted that I was better than him at sawing.

Back in school I was [considered] the least likely to do anything worth while, according to some teachers. The teachers didn't give us backwoods kids the attention that a lot of the other students got, because our standard of living wasn't conducive to studying, and I didn't try hard. Every once in a while, I'd get a teacher that would take interest in all of us. I loved to read, and that helped me, but it seemed like everything was against me. I'd never done anything worthwhile. But [I found out that] chair making is something I can do.

So we started working together in 1950. I hadn't been with Granddad six months when Korea come along, and I was drafted. I could have stayed out on account of my mother being alone, since my father had died, but I didn't. I did well in the service. I got along with my officers. I worked hard. I drew a good pay, and I probably would have stayed in if I hadn't got my machinery and wanted to go into chair making. When I got back, we kept working together until 1955, and in my spare time I built my own shop and went to work in it and was on my own by 1955. My granddad died in 1964. I still use some of his machinery in my shop today.

The slats and posts of this mule-ear chair were bent by boiling them. They then were placed in frames to dry.

[Some of the chairs we make in our shop are our original design, and some go back a long way.] Back during the Depression, the old [mule-ear-style chair] was a standard. They were a dollar apiece, or six for five dollars. I think the mule-ear chair was designed in this country. It was made for comfort. They boiled and bent these posts, and [my great-grandfather] and Granddad built them during and after the Depression. That chair that has been our bread and butter for years is an Early American ladderback reproduction.

I remember one time a friend from Charlotte was getting married, and he wanted one of my forty-eight-inch-tall ladderback rocking chairs for his apartment after he got back from the wedding trip. Well, I went back to the shop, and I didn't have any forty-eight-inch posts. All I had were some fifty-two-inch posts, and they were so nice I didn't cut them. So I made some chairs with six slats in the back of them, and when those chairs were completed, I got more comments on them than any chair I've ever made. I just call my fifty-two-inch ladderback rocking chairs the Woody Rocker. It's my own specialty.

Max Woody is famous for his rockers. Here he goes through some of the steps in their assembly.

LEFT: *Max uses glue when attaching the arms to his chairs.*

BELOW: *With the arms held by clamps, Max then drills a hole through into the chair's front posts.*

Max drills holes into the rockers for the two posts. A block on his drill press keeps him from drilling through the rockers.

Having glued the post, he drives the rockers on with a mallet.

If someone requests an old [shorter] ladderback style, we duplicate them from a picture. Granddad and I designed and built a deacon's bench that was popular for many years. This bench was copied by a company that turned out a cheap imitation. We just

Finished rocking chair.

quit making them. Over the years, I've made chairs for governors and senators. I suppose I take more pride in getting to make one for Billy Graham.

I've had a couple of boys who wanted to come work as an apprentice and learn chair making. I'm willing to do it, but I don't encourage them to; if I were to have a disaster of some kind and my things were destroyed, I couldn't go back to chair making. Some of these machines couldn't be bought. They're ancient. It would cost so much money to set back up again.

Don't get me wrong. I've not made the most money. Some of my classmates have made a lot more money, but I'll bet none of them have had as much pure enjoyment as I have. We work about twelve hours a day, and we get people from all over the world to come in. If people have questions, you know, I'll answer them. I like to find out where people are from. Last October, I went to the Folk Art Center in Asheville for a weekend [craft show], and the weather was so nice I stayed for eight days! I had people from all over the world to come visit my display there. I learned lots of things from them, too.

[At those shows, sometimes], I'll get a chisel and sit with a piece of wood and fiddle around with it, and people will stand around and watch me, you know. You can make it look a lot more difficult than it actually is! People will crowd around and watch me. I enjoy it.

If I was going to [build chairs] without electricity, I'd want a water wheel and have a lathe powered by water. I've always wanted one. There's just something about a water wheel turning, you know? The place we bought had a creek, and I tried to figure out how I could get a flow of water from that and have a water wheel, but I couldn't.

I will spend five dollars' worth of time hunting for a two-dollar piece of lumber that I know I have somewhere around, and I've got a good reason. I grew up in hard times, and things were hard to come by. I don't like to waste anything. My great-granddad told me about a man that got all the good out of his chewing tobacco. He chewed his tobacco. Then he would lug the chews up and let them dry out. He crumbled them up and smoked them. Then he used the ashes for snuff and blew his nose and shined his shoes with it. Loyal Jones of Berea College used that one in his book titled *Curing a Cross-eyed Mule*.

The one thing I'd want to change, if I could, would be to work because I wanted to, not because I had to make a living. I'd love making things and just giving them to people. If I could throw a switch and make everybody happy, I'd do it.

Myron Woody: People always come up to me and say, "You mean, you do this? You're awful young."

I say, "I am nearly twenty-nine years old"—but that is still young compared to the older generations. There's not many young people carrying on any kind of traditional craft work. When you are someone who does what I do, you sometimes think long and hard about what it actually *is* that you do.

I guess I am about the same way my father is. Since I can remember, I have worked here at the shop, whether it was setting chairs outside or sweeping up sawdust. I grew up learning how to [make chairs]. A lot of it was learning, more or less, by watching. You stand and watch how it is done, and listen. I guess the first machine that I can remember operating was probably a turning lathe, and I remember standing up on a five-gallon bucket to reach it. I can remember Pop putting weights on the old mortise machine so that I could get it down. I couldn't have been too old then, I would say eight or nine.

Through high school, I worked here in the afternoons and all summers. I guess I did this every year all the way up until I was a senior. Chair making was what brought the family close together. Late nights. Staying and finishing together. You worked together doing the same thing. After high school, I went off to college to Appalachian [State University], and figured on [learning about the] business end of chair making. I received a double major in marketing and management.

After college, I spent some time with other furniture industries. I always stayed in the type of thing I wanted to do. I was with the Lane Corporation. Then I came back here, and we built chairs for about a year, and then I went to work for General Marble Corporation out of Asheville. We did oak and birch bathroom cabinets.

I left there four months ago as an assistant plant manager. I knew [when I was away that], sooner or later, I would come back to making chairs. But first you have things to prove to yourself— and you have things to prove to your father. The whole time [I'd been away], though, I'd never really changed. It's sort of like riding a bicycle. It is just automatic. The first day after I came back [to work with him], it was not like learning how to do anything over. The skill or the trade is in the blood.

My pop has been a pretty good teacher. Without him, I wouldn't have learned the trade. He's always telling me that I'm a lot farther along now than he was when he was growing up. So somewhere down the line, either I had to have been listening, or he had to have been doing a good job showing me what was going on.

Pop and I are occasionally going to have differences of opinion. Both Pop and I are hardheaded or stubborn. Years ago, when I started here working at the shop full time, my father and I had a collision. He wanted to make a *living,* and I wanted to make a *killing.* You know, he always would say, "One of these days, we're going to get back to doing this. . . ." I explained to him that it is good and healthy to have [differences]. If he doesn't like my opinion, he doesn't have to listen to it. I told him that I would respect that, and that he should also respect it if I didn't like his opinion. There's an old saying: "There's your way; there's my way; then there's the right way."

But we both say something like, "Let's do it this way," or "Let's try it like this." [And if one of us says], "I don't like it this way; I want to do it that way," I guess two times out of three, we will do it that way. If he and I aren't getting along, we're not happy. So

Myron Woody, Max's son, explains why he became interested in chair making.

I've come a long way, and he's come a long way so that both of us can see each other's sides now.

In chair making, there is a lot to learn. I think we have both got a lot to learn from each other. You don't want to let that pass. It is sort of like the song, "The Cat's in the Cradle." Over the years Pop was busy making chairs when I was growing up. We had no time to do anything else. Then when I left, it was sort of like I never saw him. There was probably a full year that we never saw each other much. The older you get, you begin to realize that something is getting ready to pass you by if you don't grab hold of it.

My values have changed since college. I don't value the dollar as much as I did. Of course, everybody needs money to live. But I guess I value the time with my pop a lot more now than the money I make. My mom passed away two years ago. There's a lot of things that everybody said: "I wish I had said more. I wish I had done more. I wish I had been around more." Well, that is all true, but sometimes you can do something about it. Most people don't have what I have—being able to come back and do what I'm doing. Most people are out there and have to continue doing that [same] job over and over and over again. [That's all right] if they enjoy doing it, but if not, they need to get out of it. There's always options.

You don't ever *have* to do anything—[it's just that] your standard of living may have to change some to do something else.

Somebody asked one time, "Do you make as much money as you used to?"

And I said, "Oh no. Not really." But there are always the other things that go along with it. There's that extra twenty years I'm gonna live by not having the stress. This job can be stressful when somebody wants their chairs real soon, but I just sic Pop on 'em. You know, he will fix them real good! We don't take orders; we take requests!

We try to get out six frames a day. That is a lot for what we do. Pop thinks that there is no problem turning out six frames. I think that four is good. That emphasizes how much I have changed as far as the "making a living/making a killing" thing. We want to satisfy our customers and get their furniture out as quickly as possible, but [the important thing] is still the art of doing it. We could change a lot of things. The machinery you see around our shop is old. A lot of these machines are what Pop started with. We could buy an updated mortise machine for one thing. That would make our operations a lot faster. We could buy lathes that would go through the whole process a lot faster. Somebody said, "You could use this and do this, and you could do that much faster." Well, that is true, but I don't think that you would get the same piece of furniture that you normally would get.

Sooner or later that mortise machine is probably going to lay down on us, and then we will have to change that. But the tools that have been around for a long time will continue to be around for a long time, because we want them to be. We bought some machinery that is going to always be kept the same way.

As times change, people change, too, to a certain extent. You change from generation to generation. You get it from overalls to blue jeans. It would be nice if it was back in the barter time when you traded a chair for some shoes. But it is no longer that way. But there are a lot of things that you don't have to change to keep the craft or the art alive. If you come up in it [grow up practicing that craft], there is a lot of things that don't change—your mind, your heart, and whatever you've gone through. To keep it alive, you don't want to be doing it for the money. I'm not in this business with Pop for the money. If I was, there would be a lot of things different.

People come down here and "ooo" and "aaah" over the artwork. To me, creating it is easy. [There is a lot more to the business than just building furniture. Actually, doing it is only 25 percent of the business.] There is the public relations aspect of the business. We don't discount to anyone. If they are willing to listen to us a little, we will explain why a chair is a certain price. Give them an incentive to buy that chair. It is made for them.

Maybe young people are getting smarter. They can see the value in buying a good piece of furniture. Whether *we* make it or not doesn't matter. Good furniture is an investment instead of an expense. You can buy it, and it will last three or four generations. If you buy furniture at discount houses, why, in ten years or less you will be buying another set.

Pop and I both have pretty outgoing personalities. We both like to talk. I talk to people just as much as Pop, only a little differently. Pop has always had the appearance of a craftsman. I would like to think that he has got a little more on me in that respect! I learn a lot from what he says.

I can remember Pop talking to some potential customers one night. They talked for a while. I finally had to leave. I went out with some friends, and I left him sitting there with them. The next morning was Saturday. I came in about eight o'clock, and when I walked in the door, they were each one sitting in the same chair that they had been sitting in when I left. I looked around and said, "Boy, Pop is really wanting an order real bad!" It was funny. They had stayed the night! He had talked to them and taken them out to supper, and they'd spent the night at our house. They ordered chairs from us. I guess that is my favorite story as far as what a public relations man we really have here. Ingenuity. Pop will always come up with something!

I always believed that no matter what you do, you need to enjoy it and love it to do it well. I really enjoy [making chairs]—to get out of a tie and back into jeans. I think I do this better than anything. I tell everybody that Pop has been "retired" for years and years now, because my idea of being retired is to stop doing what you have to do and start doing what you want to do. You know, that probably almost puts me on "semiretirement," but the government doesn't look at it that way!

Max Woody: Being happy in what you do is worth more than

making a lot of money. It truly is. About a year ago, a young couple visited here at our shop one evening. I took about twenty to twenty-five minutes and talked to them. I took a while to tell them about how worthwhile it is to sacrifice to do the thing you want, and how important it was to be happy. I said, "If you go through life and your life is drudgery, if you go through life not happy and satisfied with what you're doing, it doesn't matter how much money you have made, you're not a total success." This young lady looked at her husband, and he at her, and they said, "Mr. Woody, it appears that God has sent us to you. We are on a trip to find ourselves." Her husband was almost through medical school. She was about halfway through medical school. They decided that they were not sure whether to pursue a career in medicine. I told them that I could not see anything that would bring more satisfaction to me than being able to treat sick people. So they left happy. We're not put here just for ourselves. I think that we are all put on this earth to be a help and encouragement to others. I have had a lot of people to help and encourage me.

I have another son who is older than Myron. He is in the furniture industry. Someday we are going to have him back here with us. He has got good benefits in the job he is in. We couldn't afford to drag him away right now. He worked with us the same as Myron has, and I hope that someday we will have him back. I take great pride in having both of them.

Some of the most proud moments I have had in my life were when Myron was a little boy. I remember one time when this elderly lady came in the shop. She had an alcohol problem. She accused me of lying to her. Myron was about six years old at that time. He bellowed up to her, "Don't you accuse my daddy of being a liar!" That backed her up.

Actually, Myron is not working *for* me now. We are partners. I think it is better than when he was working for me. Anytime that you feel like you have done a day's work, it is better when you are working for yourself than doing a day's work for someone else.

Forty-plus years I have been building chairs. This machinery I use is kind of an extension of me. Some of my friends [who have had] woodworking shops have died, and their widows have disposed of their tools. Most of the time those shops were a part of the person that they belonged to. At times when I felt like my sons were going to work at something else, I thought that someday somebody would have to sell *me* out.

But I always hoped that my sons would come back and do this, because I wanted them to have the pleasure of the fellowship they would have and the association they would gain with other people. I think Myron knew right well that it was a lot of pleasure. But he is going to find out more and more. There is a lot more to it than it seems.

The chairs we make are also an extension of me and Myron. Most, if not all, of the people that buy our chairs feel like there is a personal touch to them. You don't go to Kmart or the local furniture market and buy anything like it. It doesn't have any kind of guarantee with it like ours does. If they want us to personalize 'em we'll build the chair to suit their heights or their size. We engrave the chairs as to who they are for. If we give them to someone as a gift—birthday or anniversary—we sign our names and date the piece. There's a lot more than just actually building furniture. You gain the respect of people by being a crafts person.

We never have advertised for our business. If you make people happy with what you sell them, they are going to tell others. If you make them unhappy, they are going to tell others. Sometimes going the extra mile does not cost—it pays. It really gets to some of the people who come in the shop wanting us to advertise in their paper or magazine. We say, "Look here. We have not been caught up [on our orders] in nearly forty-two years!" Making chairs is something that we don't need to do. The chair that we make is something that we *want* to do.

Jimmy White

"The old-timers call it simply a 'pole lay' "

On a sunny fall Friday, Robert Murray, Stephanie Kennett, and I (Shane Danaher) went to Maynardville, Tennessee, to interview Mr. Jimmy White. Arrangements had been made to stay with Bill and Billie Henry in Oak Ridge, Tennessee, the folks who had introduced us to Jimmy. When we arrived, we were greeted with a delicious meal, and had some great conversations.

The next morning we met Jimmy and his daughter, Angie, at the Museum of Appalachia in Norris, Tennessee. The museum, located eighteen miles above Knoxville, is owned by John Rice Irwin and houses a large collection of Appalachian artifacts. After a tour of the museum by Jimmy and Angie, we went to Jimmy's house and conducted the interview.

Jimmy was born September 1, 1945. He has brown hair and a brown mustache that shows a slight tint of gray. He has a wife named Pauline and two children, Angie and Anthony.

Jimmy's workshop is to the right side of his house. When we walked into the workshop, the first thing we saw straight ahead was the lathe. On the left side was the shaving horse and his workbench. On the right, a small flight of steps led to a storage area where he keeps the different types of wood he works with. Jimmy shows many of the crafts he makes at festivals and in craft shows. As he says in his interview, after he entered his first show, "I realized

394

Jimmy White.

*that some people enjoyed some of my work." We certainly did—
both his work and the interest he has in original methods of production. As we found out in our interview with Jimmy White, it is
not just the older generations trying to keep traditions alive.*

*—Introduction, interview and photographs
by Shane Danaher and Teddy Watts.*

Woodworking is a longtime tradition in the White family. I have
uncles that were blacksmiths, and my grandfather was a chair maker
[and farmer]. My dad was a woodworker, carpenter, and I used to
play around in the shop. He used to make coffins for people back
in his younger days. I think you inherit certain traits [the same] as
you inherit your looks. I made a rolling pin out of red cedar at a
very young age. I still have it. My wife gets after me every once in
a while with it! My first turning, I was probably about eight or nine
years old. However, it was an electric-type lathe. It was a home-
built one at that, and my dad built it.

Many of my toys I made while I was growing up. We were poor,
but we always knew someone that had less than we did. In the

wintertime we always liked to get out and ride sleds. Normally an old car hood is what we would ride.

I shared a pair of snow skis I made once when I was ten years old. I just took the notion to make them one day. I had the white oak lumber shaped like snow skis, except I didn't know how to turn them up on the ends. My dad told me how to do that. [You] just boil the wood. I boiled it about four hours. I found two trees out back and bent it [between them] to shape the form of the skis. All of us kids enjoyed those.

I am kind of like the country boy that goes to the city and sees all those nice items, but doesn't have the money to buy them. So I came home and made them myself. The fly swat [in my shop] was just a picture in a book. With my knowledge of basket making, I just adapted my skills to build the fly swat. If you have a real deep interest in this, by looking, and with a little practice, then a person can do it. Classes are good, too, but I am self-taught.

I have never been to a woodworking class, or a basket making class in my life. However, just because I have never been to a class doesn't mean I don't read. I do a lot of reading. Basically, woodworking came easily to me. There are a lot of pieces I have made that I am not proud of, but if I want to reproduce a piece, I keep practicing until I get it right.

The principle behind the lathe I made dates back to 500 B.C., and probably it was brought into the Appalachians by the English settlers. However, it was used in all different countries, and there are different variations. This is the simplest lathe known, and it predates all the other lathes. It's probably the first woodworking machine that was devised by man. The pole lay was a very important machine for the craftsmen who made chairs, bedposts, table legs, etc., and was considered high-tech in some of the remote areas, until recent years when electricity was brought into the Appalachian area.

Sometimes I will call it "lay" and then "lathe." The old-timers call it simply a "pole lay." That's what my dad called it. Where the tool gets its name is the pole, which plays an important part—it does half of the work. You always keep the tension on it. [The lathe] uses a leather strap. Most did, I think. The piece of leather hooks to the pole and wraps around the piece you're turning, which goes

Jimmy White with his pole lathe. The lathe is sixty inches long, and thirty-two inches high from floor to bedstock.

to the foot treadle. I have also found that you can use rope or cotton instead of a leather strap. I think the leather lasts longer, though.

This [pole] is aromatic Tennessee red cedar. [When] I found it, it was approximately one and a half inches in diameter. The total length of the pole is ninety-nine inches. I took the bark off while the tree was still green. I wrapped [the tree] around a fifty-five-gallon drum, tied it off with a rope, and let it sit in the sun for a month. [That's how it got] its basic shape. Cedar is one of the few woods that has a memory to spring back, even though it's dry. When I store this turning lay, I always keep a little pressure on the pole to keep the bend. Of course, it's shrunk some [but] that really hasn't bothered it. Since I've had this pole lathe, I haven't had to replace the pole. The pole is in the same condition it was when I first made the lathe. [There is one other pole lathe I've heard of] in Hancock County. The pole is at least eighty years old.

The simplicity of the machine is what catches most people's attention when they see this lathe. There's lots of crafts people who would like to turn wood, but they don't have the $2,000 to spend for a lay. This lay is so simple it can be made out of scrap material. With a little human power and a few chisels, you can go to work. I can stand here for hours at a time and turn.

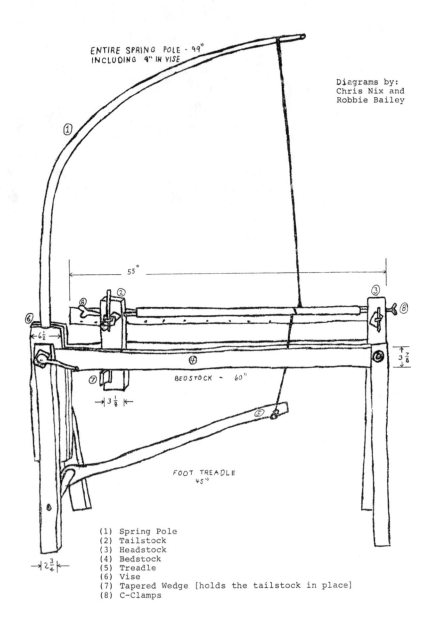

ENTIRE SPRING POLE - 99"
INCLUDING 9" IN VISE

Diagrams by:
Chris Nix and
Robbie Bailey

55"

BEDSTOCK ~ 60"

FOOT TREADLE
45"

(1) Spring Pole
(2) Tailstock
(3) Headstock
(4) Bedstock
(5) Treadle
(6) Vise
(7) Tapered Wedge [holds the tailstock in place]
(8) C-Clamps

Jimmy displays the pole from his lathe.

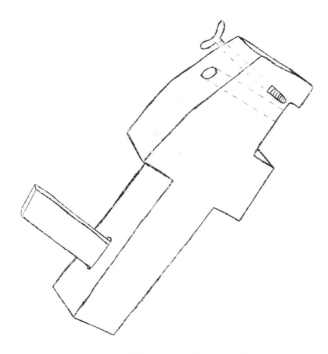

Diagram of headstock.

Holes in the tool rest allow for adjustment.

Pins and spacers in place.

Jimmy uses a drawknife to shave the wood down to the desired size. He then drills a small hole in the center of each end to accommodate the pointed screw on the head and tailstock of the lathe.

Jimmy fastens the wood to the lathe. The holes in each end of the wood have been lubricated with beeswax.

Jimmy makes his turning.

Most normally, the pole lay was a stationary machine with the pole attached to a beam of the shop or shed [but I wanted mine to be portable]. This presented a problem for me when I built my lathe, to make it portable with the pole attached to the lathe, without getting in the way of working. The plans show the clamping device I came up with, which works very well. This idea came to me one night when I was about to go to sleep. [When I take it down] it looks like a pile of wood. I think it has been down twenty or thirty times. With a little help, I can put it back together in five minutes. Other than the way in which the pole is attached to the machine, it is basically like the ones used hundreds of years ago.

At one time in my life, I would not have taken my homemade things out because I didn't think that people would appreciate them. Mr. John Rice Irwin several years ago gave me the chance to be in his annual craft show at the Museum of Appalachia. It was then that I realized that some people enjoyed some of my work, and then Mr. Bill Henry told me about some of the craft organizations, namely the Southern Highland Handicraft Guild. They have and maintain high standards of workmanship and design. I am a member of the Southern Highland Guild both in woodworking and fiber basket making.

Turning wood the old-fashioned way is slow, but I enjoy demonstrating the machine at the various craft/folklife events I attend, and usually I have some of my handcrafted baskets and bentwood Shaker-style boxes for sale. Sometimes we have to look at how things were once done to appreciate where we're going.

Foxfire student Robbie Bailey watches intently as Jimmy demonstrates how to use the turning lathe.

Here Robbie tries the lathe for himself.

Clyde Runion

"I don't try to make two that match."

Clyde Runion is an average man with special talents. We had never met him before but were interested in how he went about making the furniture of rhododendron and laurel which he has sold to people who live in our area and to those who travel through and have known about his skills throughout the years.

Clyde and his wife, Ethel, live in a small house on several acres of land in Mountain City. A porch surrounds two sides of the house, and Clyde does much of his work in the summertime right there on the side porch. The porch is cluttered with tools and pieces of furniture in the process of being finished. He has stacked up pieces of ivy on the porch there to keep them dry until he uses them to build a chair or swing or table.

In his yard are samples of other types of furniture he makes besides the chairs. There are small tables and rocking chairs in different sizes, from standard to miniature. Hanging from the eaves of the porch are several wooden spiral windmills. There is a gazebo that Clyde built about twenty-five feet from the porch. It contains a grill where he occasionally barbecues a ham or a goat for a large cookout. He does have a shop in his backyard, but he says it's easier and more convenient to do much of his woodwork right on the porch.

Clyde also makes wooden toys and windmills, for which he was

Clyde Runion.

featured in Foxfire 6. *He had an exhibit of his chairs, tables, wind-mills, and other wood items at Foxfire's 20th Anniversary picnic in May 1986. Clyde is very dedicated to his talent. He works long, hard hours getting his furniture just the way he likes it. He prepares each piece of wood with care, and he picks just the right ones for the type of furniture he is making. He doesn't use a standard pattern, so that every chair is special and each one comes out differently.*

Clyde's uncle, Kenny Runion, was a furniture maker, wood-carver, and longtime friend. Over the years, he provided us with hours and hours of stories about mountain life, many of which have appeared in other volumes in this series.

—Cathy Wallace and Dewey Smith
Interview and photographs by OhSoon Shropshire, Dewey Smith, and Cathy Wallace. Diagrams by OhSoon Shropshire.

I've lived in Rabun County all my life, all but two years that I spent in the Army. I was born about half a mile right over there [in Mountain City]. The old house where I was raised was torn down. I bought this house here in 1961 or '62. Moved down here and got married.

I've made these chairs off and on ever since about 1946, I guess. Wasn't much else to do, so I'd make them, and I'd also cut pulpwood. I'd do a little bit of everything. [The first thing I ever made was a chair.] I don't still have it. I made me several big chairs special to keep for myself, but somebody bought 'em. Good stuff. They went in a hurry.

In '75 and '76, I done regular everyday. That was just my everyday job. I was about twenty-five when I took up furniture making full-time. Me and Kenny [Runion] made 'em together for years. He was my uncle, and I just learned how to make 'em from him. Now Kenny, he was the furniture maker. That furniture making came in from Grandma's side. Her daddy was a furniture maker, and old man Doc Dover and my grandma was first cousins. A lot of people now have got furniture that Doc Dover's daddy made.

Kenny died about four years ago. As far as I know, I'm the only one now who makes this type of chair. I never have [shown] anybody else how to make 'em. There's a man across the road here who's got one that's been made thirty years [ago] and I helped Kenny make it. It's as good today as it was when we made it.

Some call ivy "rhododendron" and some call it "mountain ivy." And then there's laurel. There's a difference. They grow together in the woods. They're probably the same family of timber. The laurel's got a little-bitty leaf, and the ivy's got a long leaf. I've used laurel, too, to make these chairs. It don't look the same [as ivy]. You can't peel it like you do ivy. You can't take the top bark off of it at all, and it ain't as crooked as ivy.

I get out [in the woods] and get ivy about every week or two. I don't like to keep too much cut ahead 'cause if it gets wet [before it's varnished], the wood will turn black. I let it season out there [in the yard] about a week and then I bring it in here on the porch where it doesn't get wet. If it's green, you can't do much with it. I have to wait till the ivy dries to [chip sections of the bark off]. If you don't, [the bark] will all come off together [and you won't be

Clyde's uncle, Kenny Runion.

able to get a dark brown and white pattern]. Ivy won't shrink, though. It dries out and stays the same.

If I ain't got nothing else to do, I peel wood. Then when I start making a chair, I've already got the wood ready. Then it only takes about two hours to make a chair. It takes a half a day or more to make one chair when you start from the beginning and peel your ivy and all.

I make different-size chairs. I can make little chairs and use this little stuff [that's not long enough for the regular chairs]. That way, I don't have no waste. They use these little chairs for those Cabbage Patch dolls. Sometimes I get a long post, and sometimes I get a short post. What I do is I make a high-backed chair if I get a long post. I hardly ever measure the posts. I just find two to match.

Kenny's love seat.

I don't try to make two [chairs] that match 'cause it would be hard to ever make another chair with a piece like that to match it. I just make 'em however they turn out. Usually every one comes out good, but there's a lot of work to it. I may make 'em about a month or two and then quit and do something else. Right now, if I was able to work [regularly] though, I'd sell all I could make. I still make 'em, oh, one or two days a week.

I've got [furniture I've made] scattered from here to California and New York, and as far down as Florida. I guess I've sold more [to people] in Florida than anywhere. Putting [furniture made of ivy] outside in the rain will rot it. Just keep it on the porch like this and it'll last. I know it'll last fifty years 'cause I've got one here that's that old. Kenny made that chair in 1935.

Jerry King

"The scraps from my banjo-building make the kindling for my fires, and that way it all blends together."

Foxfire *came to know Jerry King at our annual Mother's Day picnic, to which Appalachian crafts people, most of whom we have featured in* Foxfire, *come to demonstrate their skills and show their work. Most of the crafts people we interview have learned their skills by practicing them as a way of life. Generally, the skill is passed down from generation to generation.*

When we first met Jerry King, we thought of him as a normal contact. Jerry is, foremost, a woodworker. He carves walking canes, builds fretless banjos, and makes chairs. Jerry is also an accomplished painter. He uses the same techniques and had the same skills as many of the Appalachian old-timers. But we discovered that Jerry didn't develop his skills in the same fashion as the ordinary contact; after growing up and working in the Atlanta area, he deliberately set out to learn them on his own. And one of the resources he used was Foxfire—The Foxfire Book *and* Foxfire 3.

In the tradition of Appalachian individualism and self-reliance, Jerry King wants to be in control of his own life. He used to live in the busy modern world like most of us, but he got tired of it and decided to do something about it. As Jerry says in his interview, when he was a child, "I was kind of on the tail end of a different way of life." After he was grown and had raised a family, he decided to simplify his life and recapture or learn for himself the ways of earlier times. Nowadays, he grows his own food and cooks it on a wood stove. He builds many of the things he needs: chairs, jigs for his drill press, and even a sawmill.

In his house there is evidence of his self-sufficient way of life everywhere: he has two wood stoves, one to cook on and one for heat; tools hang neatly on the walls, most of them very well used but kept in top shape. There is no refrigerator in the kitchen because he keeps his food cool in a root cellar outdoors. Walking sticks he has carved are stacked in corners of the main room. His paintings of American Indians hang on the wall; a few are propped in corners.

Jerry practices several crafts; the ones he focuses on here are his banjos and his carved snake cane. Jerry learned how a banjo was constructed from Foxfire 3. From there on, he added his own touches, and now his banjos have traveled around the world. The figures on the walking canes Jerry carves include people, animals, and other designs. We were amazed when we saw his remarkable collection of canes, which are prized by collectors.

To fully document the process Jerry uses to make his snake cane, it took us two interview sessions and a number of other trips. Jerry went through the entire procedure step by step and made sure we understood what he was talking about. He wanted us to feel as though we were doing the cane, instead of him. We found that not only does it take many hours to carve a snake cane, but it also requires a lot of energy, motivation, and determination.

We have never met a man more knowledgeable about wood-carving. Jerry is also the friendliest person you will ever meet. For example, he let total strangers like us come to his house and document for hours the way he does his work. He made us feel welcome, and he even made knives for us as keepsakes. He always had a smile on his face while we were there, and as we left, he reminded us to come back and see him again. As we said earlier, we have never met a man like Jerry. Like the work he produces, Jerry King is one of a kind.

—Chris Nix
Interview and photographs by Chris Nix, Robbie Bailey,
Cris Bessette, Scott Crane, and Bruce Beck.

I was born outside Atlanta in 1935. It was real different times then because my momma and daddy cooked on a wood stove, and we had an outside toilet. Some time since, I remember, my father built an inside toilet, so that era was just changing. I was kind of on the tail end of a different way of life. And now for nine years, or longer than that, I've just simplified my life [again]. After my children were grown, why, I pretty much did what I wanted to, and so I went back to living a real simple lifestyle. I went back to cooking on wood about ten or eleven years ago. I had real fond memories of that when I was a child.

The sparkle in his eyes and the flash in his smile reveal Jerry King's good humor and easy manner.

My daddy was a jack-of-all-trades, master of none. [Laughs.] I guess I kinda took after him. He was an electrician, and before that, he ran a store. We were all raised in the store. All us children, three girls and two boys, and Momma and Daddy lived upstairs, and the store was downstairs. The old building is no longer standing—it's all gone.

We rented the store, and our house, too, from a woman named Ms. Tindall. I called her Aunt Pete. She had run the store at one time, and then my daddy took it over. Aunt Pete had a great big old house that had all kinds of antiques and stuff she brought from out West and other places. She lived in a little-bitty house down below [the big house]. She was a real unusual person. She did a real unusual thing for a woman to do in that day and time: she took a horse and buggy and a couple of dogs and went from Atlanta to New Mexico and Arizona and back, all by herself. She had a lot of photographs of that trip. She stayed with the Navajos and the Apaches and a lot of those Indians out there. She was a real influence in my life, and I guess maybe that's why I've been interested in

American Indians, too. She also got me interested in art when I was real young. She told me something that has always been an influence—she told me to learn everything I could, didn't matter what it was, just learn anything. She said, "Someday you'll use it," so I kind of use that philosophy.

My daddy and sisters ran the store, raised some hogs and chickens, and sold dressed chickens. The store was in one room, and there was a barbershop on one side of the store where Daddy cut people's hair, and there was a back room that was a back porch that had been enclosed. That's where Momma had the stove, and Daddy used to get back there and just make the biggest mess you ever saw cooking fried pies. A fried pie is just a round piece of dough, and you put cooked peaches or apples on it, and then you fold that over like a half moon; then you fry that in deep grease. He'd cook those fried pies up back there and serve them out to the store, sell them.

They also sold whiskey and fireworks and had pinball machines in there. It was a pretty rough place—lots of drunks. I remember one time, it was a Saturday night, and everything had closed down. My folks wanted everybody to leave, and there was one man who wouldn't leave. He just wouldn't leave. He was just raising Cain, and my daddy said, "Well, you're gonna have to leave because we're going to bed." He wouldn't do it, so my daddy forcibly put him out the door. As he was going out the door, he grabbed these Roman candles. He went out into the road and started those Roman candles. Daddy sold kerosene on the front porch, and this man was shooting those Roman candles up at the kerosene can. I was standing in the window looking out, and I got scared that he was going to burn the house down. So my daddy went on out and took the Roman candles away from him and made him go on. I guess it was kind of an exciting childhood. [Laughs.]

People would come to the store and hang out. Right between the barbershop and the store part there was a window and there was a radio sitting there, one of those old kind of radios with a little-bitty dial on it. They'd all pack in there listening to the Joe Louis fights and the World Series ball games. I liked to listen to the "Grand Ole Opry" as a child. My family always listened to it, and I listened to it and still do.

*Jerry's work overflows his workshop: canes line the outside walls,
worktables dot the yard.*

An impressive array of walking sticks hangs on his workshop wall.

And then we had the pinball machines. I don't know when pinball was invented, but there was always somebody there shooting pinball or playing checkers. I was a little-bitty boy then. These guys would play pinball and run up all these games and couldn't play them all, so they'd give me the games to play. One time I was dragging a stool over there to play the games and fell backward and that stool hit me right on the finger and flattened it out. They never took me to the doctor, so I've had to live with that all my life. It looks a little weird. Actually, I hardly notice it and I'd forgotten about it until just now.

We had a big old potbellied stove. That was my job—to keep that stove going and make sure it had coal. I'd go under the house and bust up big old lumps of coal and bring them back in and keep that stove going. After I got in school, I ended up with the same job. My older sister ran the counter and sold stuff in the store. She had a rough time of it. I remember one time she broke a bottle over this guy's head that was trying to get fresh with her.

My brother kind of took after my daddy—he drank a little and smoked cigarettes. But none of my sisters would. All my sisters, they never smoked or drank or anything, and I never did either. I never did care for it, so I never did do it. I don't know how we came out of that store and ended up not drinking or smoking or anything.

I must have been five or six the first day Momma took me to go to school. She was talking to the teacher, and I got real shy and didn't want to be in there, so I ran outside—and the only place I could find to hide was in the outhouse. I got up in the attic of that outhouse, and they had to come and get me. The teacher decided, well, I wasn't ready for school yet, so they put me off for another year, and I started school the following year.

That [first] school ended real quick. I think I went there two years. By the time the second year was over, they were building a new school, and you couldn't go barefooted to the new school like you could in the old one. You had to wear shoes. There were about twenty or thirty people in the old school. The new one was a lot bigger. I went there till the seventh grade, but I got real far behind. I didn't really learn anything much. I missed the fourth grade twice, and they don't let you miss the fourth grade three times. They just put you on up.

I learned to read and write, and then I began to study what I wanted. I was beginning to study American Indians and race cars. I loved old race cars. I started designing them and drawing stuff like that in school. There was kind of a little group of us, and I guess our interest wasn't in school. One guy was a real good musician. He could play just anything.

My seventh-grade teacher was a pretty good teacher, and she encouraged me in art and stuff. She encouraged me to start high school although I was so far behind. I started high school, but I was completely lost there so I went just a few months and quit. I never went back. But by then I was old enough to quit.

Aunt Pete died one week, and my father turned around and died the next week, so it was one right after the other. I was about fifteen then. I got married at nineteen. My wife and I moved into an old basement, and then later on moved out to Smyrna and then out to Douglasville [Georgia]. I guess I was married for about nine or ten years, and part of it was good, and part of it was bad. I have never been married again. I just stayed single from then on. I had three daughters and one son. My son died at the age of three days, and I lost a daughter at the age of four years. I raised my other two daughters as a single parent.

I worked in the printing trade some; then I got into my own business later on and found a lot more freedom in working for myself. I ran a little sign shop out of my house in Douglasville and made a living painting signs for about ten or fifteen years. I wish I could have done it a lot earlier. It would have been a lot easier raising children.

I guess I was born to have a love for the mountains, but it took me a lot longer than I thought to get here. Raising children and having a secure feeling of having a job [is what kept me from coming sooner]. It's hard to make a living here.

I started making banjos about fifteen years ago. I got interested when I heard a fretless banjo being played, and I started playing about the same time I started making banjos. [My instruments] aren't very widely known, but they've gone a long ways. One guy from Europe bought one at the Hiawassee fair. One time this guy bought one and took it to Russia as a gift. I've got one in California, and a woman bought one who lived in Texas. People that are traveling, and musicians that have heard that I build banjos, seek

Three of Jerry's star design banjos.

me out now. I guess buying a banjo is a one-time deal, except for one guy who has bought two of my banjos, and now I'm building a neck for him to build him a little fretless banjo.

Most of the banjos I make are fretless. I've built maybe four fretted banjos. I don't even have a fretted banjo here, believe it or not. I traded it to a woman who really knows how to play the banjo well. I make one, and somebody wants it, and I let it go, and so I'm down to what I got here. Fretted banjos are a lot harder to build than the fretless ones because you have to put those frets in there, and that's hard. It's not actually doing the work; it's just getting the spacing. They have to be dead on it. If you are off just a hair, it makes a difference [in the pitch]. You've got to be right dead on it.

People gave me some of the tools I have, and that kind of got

Fretless banjo.

me started. Some of them were from people who owed me money, so they gave me tools instead. I build the old-time way with strictly old-time tools, and then I build using modern tools. I don't like power tools, though—they're dangerous! I don't feel that the old-time tools, the handsaws and hewing hatchets and so forth [are as dangerous]. I've never had an accident with one of those, and I've come close to having an accident with a table saw. I really prefer to use the old hand tools. There's something really enjoyable about that that you don't find in the power tools.

Foxfire was kind of responsible for [my getting started]. I needed to see a picture of a banjo taken apart to learn how to do it, to get the basics. A friend of mine gave me *Foxfire 3,* and so I built my first banjo by the instructions in the book. That banjo is hanging in the back room. It doesn't have strings on it anymore, but it could

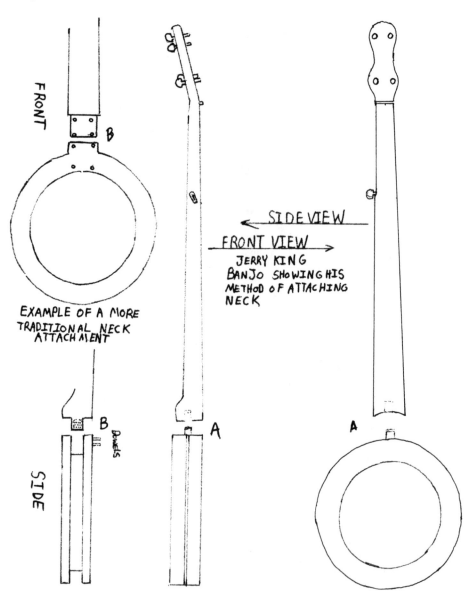

FRONT

EXAMPLE OF A MORE
TRADITIONAL NECK
ATTACHMENT

SIDE

SIDE VIEW

FRONT VIEW

JERRY KING
BANJO SHOWING HIS
METHOD OF ATTACHING
NECK

still be playable. The next banjo I built, I began using my own construction methods. I varied off of several different banjo makers' designs. The banjo that influenced me the most was one of Dave Sturgill's. I just really liked the looks of the star in the back, so I used the star design, although not exactly the same way, on a lot of my banjos.

I came up with a way of attaching the neck to the body which is easier for me (A) and just as strong as the way they are usually attached (B). It's as good a joint as the one in *Foxfire 3*. It's not any better, but it is simpler and easier to do. It depends on the tools; if you've got a drill press, it's easier. If you don't have a drill press, then you're kinda out of luck. I wouldn't attempt to do this without a drill press, but drill presses are pretty available. I think most home shops now have one.

Over a period of time I learned to get my cuts more precise, and now they don't have gaps [between the neck and the body] like the first one did. I designed several jigs especially to do the cuts. Turning the drill press table up and down each time you want to make a cut takes a lot of time, so if you are doing two or three cuts, using a jig makes it a lot quicker. That's the idea of the jig, but if you're just wanting to build one banjo, then you wouldn't need the jig. What the jig does is put the hole [on the neck where the body attaches] at a three-degree angle. It slants the neck back three degrees, which is real necessary to have a good playing banjo. If you just built a banjo and you didn't slant the neck back, then your bridge would be real close to the head and the strings would

This is the jig Jerry designed for drilling the hole on the neck at a precise three-degree angle.

be way out high off the neck and wouldn't note properly. If you slant it back, then you can have a higher bridge and your strings will be closer to your fretboard so you get good notation. Without that, you don't really have a good playable banjo.

[I set my shop up so] I could make three or four banjos at a time and really save some time, but I've never done that yet. Hopefully, some day, when I get some other projects out of the way, I'll be able to devote more time to it and maybe build two or three [at a time]. The thing about it is, there just hasn't been a market for them. If I were selling five or six banjos a year or something, then I could, but I get orders for only a few at a time.

I cut some of my own wood and split it and dry it in my attic. Sometimes I buy wood if somebody has some good wood in their attic, and, on occasion, people will even give me the wood. They might also trade wood for building, so I do trading, too. I've only stained one banjo, and after I stained it, I really regretted it. It's like cheating. I'll never stain another banjo. I would just like for it to be whatever it is. I use a real variety of woods—native woods from around here: poplar, maple, walnut, dogwood, persimmon. A friend wanted me to build him a banjo from hickory. I wouldn't use hickory again though; it's too brittle for building banjos. I'm going to start using persimmon all the time for making the pegs. I found out recently that it's kin to ebony—that's why it's so hard. It's real hard, dense wood. Real heavy.

I use a hide head on the traditional banjos and a plastic head on the more modern ones. On a rainy day, with a hide head, you don't have near the tone that you do with a plastic head. That's why a lot of people like plastic heads. My neighbors around here give me hides—either deer- or calfskins. I prefer calfskin over any other skin—it makes a better head. It seems to be smoother and you can really stretch it on tight. One day someone gave me a groundhog, and I put it on a banjo. Groundhog is a little thicker, so it has a little different tone. Different skins do affect the tone some, but if they're stretched on tight, they basically sound about the same.

I also used cat hide. The most sought-after hide by the old pioneer banjo builders was the tomcat hide, and it was still used by some up until fairly recent times. You know, all us old-time banjo builders have a bad reputation when it comes to house cats.

Jerry King talking with Foxfire student Cris Bessette.

And I guess it has even spread around to most cats, for you don't see many hanging around fretless banjo builders, especially those that use hide heads. Well, there was a large, wild, yellow tomcat hung around here for some time, catching many a mouse in my garden. He never would come close to my house. Lots of times, I would go out and sit on a bench and play banjo, and that old cat would just waller and twist and turn on its back in the warm sand and just act like it was enjoying my banjo music. And I kinda liked that old cat hanging around. One time I made the mistake of going outside to work on a fretless banjo I was building, and that old cat looked up and saw that banjo without a head on it, and [took off]. Now I wouldn't kill anyone's cat. But I guess it didn't know that. And I don't guess it was about to take that kind of chance. Now I believe them cats are smarter than we give them credit for.

It wandered back in that spring, and I was real glad to see it back. One chilly fall day I was sitting in my workshop next to my wood-fired stove carving on a walking stick when I heard a ruckus up on the hill. Here they come, two big dogs chasing after that old cat. They passed right under my window just a-flying. I jumped up and ran out the door and grabbed me a stick and took right after them. I could hear the ruckus. I could tell they had caught him up against my chicken pen. I've never heard such screaming! That big

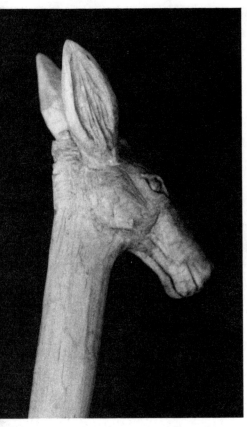

Jerry carves a wide variety of walking sticks.

old tomcat was fighting for its life, and it sure put up one heck of a fight! One dog would run in, get its fill, and come out a yelping, stay out a second and right back in. Fur was just a flying from both cat and dogs alike. I never saw that cat touch ground once. He was either on top of a dog's head or up that wire fence. On my way I picked up a few rocks and was throwing them as hard as I could. I hit one dog, but it didn't even faze him; he was into the kill. They begin to pay me some attention as I started to beat them with a good hefty stick. When I finally got them beat off and gone, I wanted to help that cat, but it wouldn't let me get close to it. So I just left it alone. I guess I should have put it out of its misery. I just thought after it had fought so hard, it might have some fight left. I found it dead the next morning. I guess it was just too injured to survive. I was very saddened to have lost my cat friend, although this was as close, physically, as I had ever been to it.

It was a large cat indeed. Now I was faced with a decision. Here I was with a perfect opportunity for a real tomcat hide for one of my fretless banjos. Or would I just bury him intact and forget about it? You probably can guess my decision. I now have an authentic fretless banjo with a real tomcat hide head. I think, after all, my friend did have an inclination of his destiny.

[For me, going back to the old-time ways has] been a gradual process over about thirty years. Having a strong interest in American Indians and their lifestyle might have had something to do with that. I lived in the woods for a while and built a teepee one time, just to do it. We put it up on some land back up on a little hill up in the woods. [My daughters and I] camped in it. We didn't live in it full time, not like a lot of people. But teepees are not meant for this country. They're Plains dwellings. They're not meant to be woodlands dwellings. The mildew [causes the canvas to] rot out real quick, so it's not a good dwelling for this area.

[I'd thought] many times [about buying a place where I could live off the land and even generate my own electricity], and I searched for the piece of land that would do that, but I never could [find it]. At one time, a couple of other people and I were interested in buying land together, and we looked for a long time, but it just didn't happen. So I just got tired and said, "Well, I'm going to have to do it pretty soon." And this is the best I could find. Some friends of mine told me about this place, and I came up and actually lived here about a year or maybe two years before I thought about buying it. I just cared for the place. It's a nice piece of land, but it doesn't have what I was really looking for. I

The handle of this cane displays a Native American theme.

wanted a good high spring and good stream where I could generate some electricity, but you can't always find what you're looking for. You just have to settle for something else.

I'm not where I want to be yet. I'd like to know what it would be like just to live way back in somewhere—just camping, using just old tools, no electricity, no power tools. Really simplify my life. I don't know if I'm ready for that or not. I guess I'll still keep going in that direction, and I might end up moving away from here [eventually]. There is a place up in the higher mountains that I'd like to move to and just build a real simple cabin without any electricity. I could have gravity-flowed water to my house so I wouldn't have to have any electricity.

Right now, my main reason for having electricity is for running my tools and to pump my water to the house. I could do without electricity for light. [I'd probably use] beeswax candles for that. I would just go to bed when it got dark and get up when it got light, which is a good way to live. I think that the land has a lot to do with how easily you can become self-sufficient. I mean, you can become self-sufficient [by bringing] your water from a spring in a bucket, which I did for about a year. There are rewards to that, too, but I prefer not to have to do that; I'd rather have my water gravity-flow into a sink. But I'm content to not have my toilet in the house. I just have an outhouse. There's no plumbing in here except for a sink. I did have a solar bathhouse for a while and plan on using it again in the future. The disadvantage of it is that [you can only take a bath at certain times], but that can be corrected too, you know. You've just got to find a way to insulate your water and keep it warm till nighttime, which wouldn't be real hard to do.

I think one reason I [wanted to become self-sufficient] is I really wanted to get into growing my own food. There's something real satisfying about growing my own food—something real satisfying about growing a plant, putting a seed in the ground and watching it come up. Growing something. I would like to be where I don't even have to go to a store at all. It's just so much better right out of the garden. You just take something from the ground right to your body. The less time away from the source, the more nutritious it is, I guess.

Growing my own food this past season really hurt [though]. With the drought and all, it was really bad. I had a real hard time getting a garden together this year. My tiller tore up at the end of last year, so I worked my garden by hand, and I really got behind. I had a lot of other projects going, so I don't have a root cellar full of food this year like I have had in the past. I guess I'll have to make a little more money this year. I bought me a tractor, an old model Ford tractor, and I've been working on it and got it running

Jerry prefers old tools. These are some of his favorites.

real good, so I think next year I'll be able to raise a lot more food easier, hopefully.

I raise chickens for the eggs, and I just like to watch them hatch out and have little biddies each year. The hawks and the foxes take their toll during the winter, and summer, too, as far as that goes. I don't really mind that too bad. I mean, they might need the help. But I do shoot them off. I don't kill them or anything, but I discourage them. They don't get the chickens easy; they have to work for it. There's something about predators—when I'm away, they know it. So every time I go away for a long festival, a three- or four-day festival, I'll come back, and most of the time I'll have chickens missing. I don't mind losing a few to the hawks and foxes, but I don't like losing them to domesticated dogs and cats. One time, I think, a dog got in here and got about three or four. Just killed them and left them strung out. Didn't eat them. Most of the time, if it's a wild animal, it doesn't take more than it needs, but if it's a domesticated animal, it'll kill just for the pleasure. Makes me mad. If I could have caught that dog, I'd have put his hide on a banjo right quick.

I don't like to kill the chickens for myself. It's hard for me to kill a chicken that I've raised. If somebody's here that requires a chicken more than I do, then I might kill one. But just for me, I don't feel like I need it. If I got hungry enough, then I'd go kill a chicken, but I'm just satisfied with the eggs.

I eat mostly a vegetarian diet. I don't eat any red meat. There's a little pond over here where I go and catch some fish on a rare occasion, so I can't say that I'm a strict vegetarian, but I'm real conscious of what I eat. Some time back a friend of mine said to me, "Hey, you ought to change your diet. You're eating too much sugar." He showed me the book *Back to Eden.* I began to analyze that and think about it and got to studying it more and more. The more I studied it, why, the more it made a lot of common sense to me. Then I got more into health, knowing the way my father and all lived and how young they died. My family has a bad record— the men in my family die real young, in their fifties. I didn't want to die that young, and I think that most of their problems came about because they were eating a lot of bad food. Of course I may die tomorrow, and I wouldn't be any older than they were, but at least I'm changing, doing something different than they did. I've been a vegetarian for about fifteen years, and I'm pretty healthy. People tell you that you can't be healthy and be a vegetarian, but you can. In fact, I think that they're saying on some of those public announcements on the radio not to eat so much red meat, to back off it. Maybe they're coming around a little bit.

It's a lot easier [to be self-sufficient], I think, if you're vegetarian. I've raised animals. I've had goats and chickens and a horse, at one time. They're a burden to you, really. Especially doing what I'm doing [selling my banjos at fairs] where I need to go away for a week at a time sometimes. My chickens, I can just leave them. They can fend for themselves, especially since I have a self-feeder for them.

It takes a lot longer to cook a meal [on a wood stove] but, you know, you allow yourself that time, and you go out and cut your wood and keep it dry. It is a real enjoyable way of life. I wouldn't have it any other way. It all fits together, working with wood and the things that I'm doing now. I'll always have scraps, for example, so the scraps make my kindling for starting my fires, and [that way] it all kind of blends together.

It's not really a hard life for me. I enjoy it. Of course, I'm not having to live the way a lot of people here have had to in the past.

I can turn around and go to a supermarket, if I don't grow this or that, whereas they couldn't do that. If they didn't raise it themselves, they really had a hard time. So it is not as hard on me, living this way, as it has been for a lot of people that considered themselves homesteaders. I consider myself a modern-day homesteader.

[There are a lot of reasons for becoming self-sufficient] and I use all of them: [because it saves money, because I like to take care of myself and not have to depend on other people, and because] I don't like to damage the earth any more than it already has been. I don't want to contribute to it. I kind of even feel guilty about driving an automotive vehicle. Sometimes I wish it had never been invented. Of course then y'all wouldn't be here, and it'd be a different world. I guess it would be made up of a lot of little self-sufficient communities if there were no airplanes, or trains, or automobiles. Of course, that's not where we're at. We're just in the middle of what's here. You can either go with it and be a part of it, or I guess you can do what me and a lot of other folks have done and get out of it. Do something on your own that makes some more sense to you than being in there and making a lot of money or *trying* to make a lot of money. I don't like where the modern world has gotten us. I don't like nuclear anything. I would like to see more passive solar and development of things that don't pollute the earth.

I'm happier with this than anything else I've ever done—I'll say that. I'm less lonely here. I used to live in a place that was really growing and had a lot of people around, but people don't necessarily make you less lonely. I'm less lonely here than being around more people. Just being close to the land, growing my own food, I really just get a different sense of contentment or value or something, I don't know. It feels like I'm in control of my own life.

My carving really goes a long ways back. My daddy used to make these whistles. Have you ever seen a poplar whistle? In the early spring, you take a poplar sapling and cut it. You trim it down and make a little whistle out of it. The back end of the whistle will slide up and down to give you a variation of tone. I'd carve those whistles and like the feel of the knife cutting the ridge around.

I could see snakes in the canes I was cutting before I actually ever carved one. It interested me, and from there I started. Snakes are pretty gentle creatures. Black snakes and garter snakes are very gentle, and they are useful. People shouldn't kill them. They are a help in your garden. If you have a garden, you need those snakes. They keep your mice problem down. Snakes help keep other varmints away, too. They keep the rabbit population in check. Snakes keep everything in balance. I don't kill any kind of snake.

Most snake carvers put fangs on them. It kind of makes them look fierce. But if you notice, my snakes don't look fierce. They look pretty gentle. They're not fierce creatures. I don't know of any other creature that you can go out in nature and pick up and not have them bite you. Of course, you have to pick them up the right way, not to scare it. But I don't really choose to pick up snakes. I let them go about their way.

[Occasionally I do pick them up, though.] I was up on this mountain one time, and it was a cold fall day. I seen something black up in a fork of a limb. I got a better look, and I discovered it was a black snake. It was so cold it couldn't get down. This early spring, I found a black snake over here on the road. It was too cold, also. It had started to go across the road, and it was having a hard time getting out of the road. I went and picked it up and got it out of the road and got it over in the leaves. I didn't want it to get run over. I kind of like snakes. I used to want to catch them, but then I really don't want to scare them. I like them to hang around here and eat rats. I build habitats for them and other animals, too.

One day, I was going to my mailbox. This was a good while back. I saw a black snake coming up to cross the road. That was before they put gravel on the road or anything. I was back here all by myself then. They really didn't keep the road up. It was pretty rough and muddy. Anyway, I was walking to my mailbox, and I saw him coming up to cross the road. I thought to myself, "I'm just going to wait this guy out!" I wasn't in no big hurry, so I sat down. You know, a snake will freeze when you see it. Well, this one saw me and it froze. I sat down and decided to wait it out and see what it does. I watched it, and it watched me. It never did move for a while. Directly, it just got tired of me and started to crawl away. It got halfway across the road, and that snake turned around and looked at me and hissed real loud. I guess he was thinking, "What are you doing?" I guess that snake thought I was really doing something wrong! It just went on up into the pasture, and I went

Jerry begins to explain to us how to carve the snake cane.

on to the mailbox. I guess that snake didn't much like me winning. I think he sort of cussed me out in his own language.

Snake canes are my favorite, but snakes are the hardest to carve. It takes me many, many times longer to carve a snake cane than it does any other cane. Some of the eagle canes I do take a little time, but nothing like a snake cane. It just takes hours and hours to end up with a finished snake. I don't think making a cane is a tiring job, though; I could go all day making canes. Of course, I wouldn't do that, but I could. I had seen other canes that different people

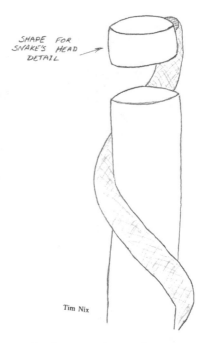

SHAPE FOR
SNAKE'S HEAD
DETAIL

Tim Nix

The saw is used to prepare the snake's head.

The diagram shows where Jerry cuts away a section of the cane so that the snake's head rises above it.

had carved, but none of them really looked like a snake to me. I wanted to carve a realistic-looking snake. This first snake I carved was a rattlesnake climbing up a stick. However, you really wouldn't see a rattlesnake climbing a stick, but you would see a black snake. So I said to myself, "From now on, I'm going to carve black snakes." That way, it would be realistic. I like following nature. I like to do things that are realistic.

I use a hewing hatchet to hew down [the small trees I make my canes from]. It's sharp on just one side. I have a round gouge, and that's what I usually start out with. I've got just a regular fat chisel that comes in handy. I use a little homemade knife for getting real close into tight places that you can't get in with a pocket knife. Then I use a smaller round gouge for fine finishing. I use a maul

Jerry outlines the body by using a gouge.

to work with my chisels and gouges. It's important to have your tools extremely sharp. You can't do anything with a dull tool. There really is an art to sharpening tools. I don't think that I've mastered that art yet. I just do the best I can when I go to sharpening them. I also use this band saw. I really don't even have to use the band saw, but since it's here, I'll use it.

I use a bench to carve canes on. It's called a shaving horse. I use it to brace my wood. It clamps my wood in so I can work with it. I made this bench. I am not really sure how many years ago. It is made the old-timey way, but it's a little different. I've seen a couple like it before, but I didn't like what I had seen, so I kind of modified it to where it was the way I wanted it. It's made to fit me. It's a split log, and it was made with all hand tools. I have a piece of leather on it to keep the horse from scarring my wood. It's an old-fashioned clamp, and it works so good that I haven't tried to find anything that works any better.

Now I don't know about other people who carve canes and do carvings. I don't know if they use old-timey tools or not, but I do. I really like using the shaving horse and the drawknife. They really work for me. Most of the tools I use are really old. I think your better tools are your older tools. They are all considered antiques now, and you have to compete with antique dealers to buy them. I don't really look for tools anymore, though. I've got all that I need. My favorite tools to use are my hewing hatchet and my drawknife. I don't really know why I like them the best. It's just something about them.

I like to work with sourwood. It is a good hard, dense wood. It carves pretty good. I'd rather carve into a hard wood than a soft wood because I can control the wood better. Green wood carves easier. The bark comes off a lot easier. I would say that you have to be less careful with green wood than you do with seasoned wood. It's easier to carve the chips off. Your knife works better. When the wood is drier, your knife works a little slower. It's basically the same. One is just a little faster process.

It's hard to find a piece of wood that is twisted just right to make a good snake, or what I call a good snake. Most of the time, when you find one, though, you'll find two, or maybe even three. The grain and the way the vine wraps around the wood is very important in your selection. I look for a cane with an even twist. I've got to look at that piece of wood and figure out just what I'm going to do with it.

I could start out with a [straight] round piece of wood, lay out the snake with a pencil, and carve it right there. But if the cane dropped on the floor or something, the head would break right off, because it would be running right opposite with the grain. [Instead, I find a stick or small tree trunk that a growing vine has naturally twisted, and I carve along that.] That way, the grain runs along the body of the snake, and I get a strong snake that won't break easy. The snake head that sticks up above the top of the cane is real delicate, but I've never had them break with me. Nature gives me something to work with.

The most important and the most tricky part is carving the head of the snake. Getting the head to look right involves some delicate work. As I carve on it, I kind of let the wood dictate what I do. I have an idea in my head, but what's in my head doesn't necessarily [agree] with the wood all the time. Sometimes I've got a knot that's working against me. If the knot doesn't go the way I want it, I may not be able to do the head of the snake just the way I want it.

I've made some canes with the snake head on the side of the wood. On other canes, I make the snake head come up off the wood and let it stand off [as the head] of the stick. That's what I'm making here. I think they are more impressive. I think I discovered it by accident. I was sawing a knot out and trying to get rid of it. I decided to try this, and it worked. A lot of times you create stuff from mistakes. If you make a mistake and try to hide it or work around it, you develop something else.

If you're going to let the snake head come off the top like it's above the cane, take the saw and saw down into the wood [until you cut the inside core of the cane away from the twisted snake's head]. You have to be really careful about sawing down because you don't want to saw down too far. I get so far [with the saw], and then I start carving using a pocketknife.

I use a little punch to make the eyes. I just push the punch in with my hand near the front of the head [where I want the eyes to be]. Most people would think the eyes would be far back on the

Here he uses the spoke shave.

head. They're not. The eyes are up toward the front of their face. After I do the eyes, I shape the head up a little bit.

From there on out, I just continue to carve down to get rid of the [surface] wood around the vine in order to give it that snake effect. I use the gouge to cut out around the vine. I go down one side [of the stick], to establish the body with score marks, and then I go back on the other side, taking some of the higher wood out. That is what I call roughing out. I use the chisel to rough it out with. I do this to give me the indication of where the snake is actually going to be. It is my starting tool, more or less. Once I've got the body outlined, I'll know where I want to go to. The head is smaller than the body. The body gets fatter. Then after you establish the central portion of the body, you have to begin to taper it down for the tail. Usually, the way the vine is, it will automatically begin to taper itself.

I use the drawknife to take out what is between the score marks. Then it starts to shape up more like a snake. Part of the time, I pull the drawknife toward me, as it's supposed to be pulled. But I also turn the knife around and use it backward. A lot of people say that I'm not supposed to use a drawknife in that fashion, but I disagree with them. Actually, it's probably the proper way. I con-

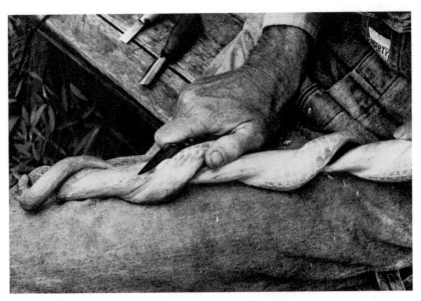

Jerry uses a pocketknife to remove a knot.

sider both ways to be right. What works for me might not necessarily work for someone else. You have to develop your own working style.

I use a spoke shave to smooth rough places. Every time I go around a knot, it wants to end up rough. If I hit a knot with the shave, I'll leave it and come back later and smooth it out with a real sharp pocketknife.

If you have a cane that's not just right, you can carve away more wood. I might slightly slip sometimes and cut an area that I didn't plan on cutting. [But it's] not anything that I can't repair. When the end of the stick is crooked, I fix it so the cane will come straight down, instead of curving.

I could leave the bark on as the snake's skin. But to make realistic-looking snakes, I take all the bark off. When I work on canes that are real seasoned out, it's hard to take the bark off. With a green cane, it's easy to take that bark off, but it's still pretty delicate work. We're talking a good many hours.

The hardest part [of the whole process] is scribing the scales. To do that, I use an extremely sharp chisel. I use a little flat chisel, because I can't work them with my flat-bladed knife. I use a criss-cross method to carve the scales. It's like making an "X," in other

Jerry burns the snake cane to give it a dark polished look.

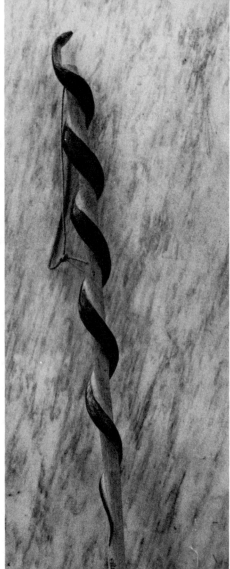

Detail of finished snake cane.   *Full-length view of snake cane.*

words. The first mark I make is an "X" in the middle of the cane. What I do is go in one direction and scribe lines across, and stop and go back and carve the other way. I put a good bit of pressure on the knife to cut into the wood, and I just go as deep as I can with one cut. This is where you really put a lot of time into making the cane, because it takes a long time to score it. As I get closer to the tail, I start getting closer between the scales. I don't draw on it [with a pencil] or anything like that. I just start closing it up as the body starts getting littler. I judge it by eye. Then, after I score the scales, I go back and notch it. I notch it by the score marks.

To give the snake its black color, I burn it with a blowtorch and then buff it down to make it shine. I don't buff it by hand. I use a machine.

I don't consider what I do as a job. I'm just doing something I like to do. I got tired of having to get out and make money—it's stressful work. I make money [carving canes and making other things], but I don't regard it as a job. A job is where you go and sign in and quit at a certain time. I don't do that. I'm surely not punching a clock! When I get tired, I stop and don't do it anymore.

Michael and Melvin Crocker

"I want to keep the tradition alive."

When times change, much is lost, as well as gained. Some people accept that loss as unavoidable. And some people don't. Two men, Michael and Melvin Crocker, refuse to let an Appalachian tradition die.

Foxfire first got to know Michael Crocker in the early eighties, when we interviewed him and other Southern folk potters for Foxfire 8. Back then, Michael had just left Wilson Pottery in Lula, Georgia, a family-owned production pottery where he had worked since eighth grade, to turn pots for Craven Pottery in Hall County. Michael has since opened his own business, in which he began by making flower pots but eventually moved successfully into folk pottery.

Michael and his brother, Melvin Crocker, produce every piece, using the same methods and designs as those of 100 years ago, when functional wares were essential for everyday living, for preparing, preserving, storing, and transporting food and drink. By doing so, they open a window into the past, preserving a traditional craft that could otherwise perish. Because there are many modern storage containers to replace the older pottery jars, the pieces that Michael and Melvin turn are sought for collecting and decorating purposes. Here Michael and Melvin talk generally about the place of their business within the folk pottery tradition and, specifically, about *the production of one of their most popular pieces, a snake jug, which requires seventy-seven days from start to finish.*

Michael obviously regards pottery as more than a job; he is passionate about the origins, traditions, and survival of the craft: "What I'd like to do is have a collection with representative pieces from the old potters that used to make pottery in the northeast Georgia area. I want to compile this information into book form. I would like to give people photographs which include all the different styles from all the different potters. Right now, I probably have around 500 pieces or more. I have pieces that date back as far as the 1830s."

—*Chris Nix*
Interview and photographs by Beth Davis,
Robbie Bailey, and Chris Nix.

Michael Crocker: I think, by definition, folk pottery would reflect what used to be made in times when people had to use pottery like syrup jugs, and butter churns, and even moonshine jugs. In my opinion, folk pottery would have to be the shapes, styles, and designs that used to be made and used by the folks that grew up in that time period.

There are a few folk potters left in the country that are representing eras and families that have been pottery dynasties for decades [but, generally, it is a dying art]. I don't think a person has to have ancestral [potter] relatives in order to be a folk potter, or even a folk artist, for that matter. These older folk potters had parents that were not potters—Cheever Meaders, for instance. [His father, John Milton Meaders, built a pottery operation around 1892, but he had to hire other local potters to turn the ware.]

So what we are doing today is actively practicing, as a way of life, a folk art tradition. Without someone continuing the tradition, it would probably perish. I'm thirty-four years old, and I want to keep the tradition alive, because I have immense respect for old-time potters. It's a part of our heritage, and it's important for us to remember it. We make utilitarian jars as well as the decorated pieces. That means that they can be used for purposes around the home. We do the decorated pieces because we have to make a living at what we do, while at the same time continuing the tradition.

Michael Crocker, potter.

We use the same tools, concepts, methods, and designs that have always been used. We try not to do anything in a modern way.

There are a few popular names that people know who were very significant potters in times past. However, in actuality, there were more than 100 northeast Georgia potteries and hundreds of potters. A lot of them would travel—some would go and work around Atlanta making distillery jugs for moonshine. They would also travel around North Carolina and throughout Georgia. They would work a few years here and a few years there. A lot of those potters were important links in continuing this pottery tradition.

My family grew up right behind a pottery. It was Wilson Pottery. At that time, Javan Brown, Mark Hewell, Caleb Hewell, and Wayne and Jimmy Wilson [all worked there]. Ricky Wilson is the youngest

Renowned for a century of pottery production, the Meaders family was featured, along with a number of other Southern folk potters, in FOXFIRE 8. Lanier Meaders's face jugs gained such notoriety that they sold faster than he could make them. Here, Lanier displays his last two face jugs. On the reverse side of one he wrote: "This is the last face jug made by Lanier Meaders 7/12/91." On the other: "Next to the last face jug made by Lanier Meaders 7/12/91."

son of Hallie Wilson. We are about the same age. Anyway, I used to go and see him. I was around eight years old, and we would always walk past that pottery shop. I could hear them slapping that clay, working it up. I would peek in the windows, but the windows in that place would be literally packed with clay because the clay would splatter everywhere. I wanted to go in there badly. It excited me a great deal. I knew they were making pottery, but I had never seen it before up close. Later on, when I was ten years old, I would still walk by that pottery. The doors on that place were always jammed shut. I don't know why they were so hard to open. Besides that, Ricky had told me that kids were not allowed in there because they might get hurt. One day, I talked Ricky into going in the pottery shop. That is about all it took for me. It was sort of dark and [had] low ceilings and I saw all those racks full of freshly turned wet clay jars, and they were just making hundreds of them. It fascinated me so much I could not stand it. I had to experience it. I had to get into it. That made an impression in my mind, and I realized I wanted to be a potter.

After going through, watching and playing, turning on the wheel, you know, making a mess, they asked me to help them work. I was about twelve years old. Primarily, my job was to unload trucks. I was real excited about that because I knew if I got connections with the pottery, I could eventually work my way into the handmade side of the business. Getting my hands in that clay was the most fascinating thing in my life. I had a desire to do it. I used to see Wayne turn these big five-gallon pieces. I thought to myself that I would never in my life be able to do something like that. That would be something unbelievable. I thought you had to have a special gift to do something like that. Of course, now I can make five-gallon jugs all day long. I have made six- and eight-gallon pieces to sell.

I worked at that pottery for several years. I was working in the handmade shop nearly all the time. I would get up before school and work clay balls up. That was for Jimmy and Wayne, primarily. I think I would get five cents a gallon to make the balls. I would do the same thing in the evenings. All this time, I would make myself a few balls of clay, and I would go up to a wheel that wasn't in use, and I would try to turn. Eventually I started getting some of the technique down. Then occasionally when one of the Wilson brothers or some of the old well-known potters like Caleb and Mark Hewell would walk through, they gave me a pointer, and I would just love it. I could not wait until they came over and critiqued me because that was very important to me for them to say, "Don't do it that way; get ahold of it like this." I learned, and it wasn't real easy. It stayed with me, though, and it was involuntary to a large extent.

After I began to turn and make pieces that I could set off the wheel, then the other potters would come and give me advice. I began to make around twenty-five strawberry jars a day. The Wilsons would give me so much apiece for making them. I remember getting better at it. They would start telling me to set the piece off the wheel before I messed it up. A lot of times when you get a piece of clay and start playing with it, it will tear down with you. A few things like that have really stuck with me. I remember one simple statement from those old potters that has helped me more than anything else: You can't rush clay. That's from the turning of it, the drying, the firing, and all the stages of operation. You are liable to have a problem with clay if you rush it. Most all potteries have a problem with cracking, but my brother and I hardly ever have a problem with cracking.

I joined the Army in 1974 and spent three years in there. Then, when I came out of the Army, I went right back to work in pottery. I spent five years dealing with sales, primarily, although I did make hundreds and hundreds of cactus pots for different nursery growers. I would make different pieces on the wheel frequently while I was in sales. That was when *Foxfire 8* was written. I was interviewed on the business aspect of Wilson Pottery.

Around the time *Foxfire 8* came out, things were not working out just right for me at Wilson Pottery. So, I decided that my destiny in life was making pottery, some way, somehow. I went to see Joe Craven on a Friday in the wintertime. I asked him about a job turning pottery eight hours a day, five days a week. He hired me on that day to come into work on the following Monday. I worked for two years there at Craven Pottery, turning mass production clay strawberry jars. When I started working there, I had never previously turned anything bigger than a one-gallon piece. The third week I was there, I was put off making one-gallon strawberry jars to making two gallons. After that, I began to turn three-gallon jars with ease. I didn't get to do that all too much because the older potters that worked there had priority on the bigger pieces. Things didn't continue to work out for me at Craven's, either. In 1984, I left Craven's Pottery.

Then, as I was thinking of my next move, I came upon a decision. I decided to start my own business continuing to make my own pottery. I had never thought of it before. When I started this business about six years ago, I had never in my life, until then, imagined doing it. It just happened, and it wasn't anything I was looking ahead to do.

I set out to find an abandoned chicken house. They make the best pottery shops. They've got windows going down both sides so the pottery can air out. It's a comfortable environment with plenty of space to work in. There seems to be no other type of building that can be built [that's better] for the purpose of turning pottery.

There is a big difference [between] a folk pottery shop and a modern-day pottery shop. Folk pottery shops that make utilitarian pottery that is either decorated or undecorated, using methods and tools that are of old-timey concept, are very, very rare. To my estimation, there are probably no more than fifteen full-time, actively practicing folk potters in the country. There are thousands of studio potters and college [potters]. It's contemporary, and there's some good-looking studio pottery out there. I respect other potters who do different things with pottery. I appreciate anybody who has an artistic ability. I think they should express it to the fullest of their ability. And, you know, I'm not throwing off on [their] pottery. With all due respect, they do good work. A lot of those studio potters could come in here and run circles around me with the technical information on the clay. They could go all the way into ceramic engineering. However, their work and folk pottery is significantly different.

Nothing is commercially manufactured when dealing with folk pottery. What a person has to do and has always done is to build their equipment to satisfy their needs. What I initially wanted to do was go into producing decorated clay flowerpots, pitchers and bowls, birdhouses, and things like that. The first thing I did was build my kiln. It is ten feet long, ten feet wide, and seven feet deep in the middle. I had never seen one like it in my life. I have never seen one similar to it since I built it. I designed and completed it in six months. The reasons I designed and made it myself were because most of the old potters built their own equipment, and all of the kilns I've ever seen before that had another design had cold spots and hot spots, so I just thought I could do as good as anybody else. I did it practically by myself. There was limited help with things that I just could not do on my own. My kiln now is just as efficient and effective as any commercial kiln with a similar capacity.

I also had to build a [clay] mixer and pug mill. I built my last clay mixer out of stainless steel, so it should last a long time to come. And I built my wheel. There's no company in America that I know of that makes potter's wheels, for folk pottery. To make the bulk, and to use a lot of clay, and to make the old shapes and styles of jars and big stuff, you just have to build the equipment yourself.

*One of Michael and Melvin's designs, uniquely theirs,
but in the tradition of face jugs.*

That's the way everybody's always done in all the old potteries all
up through the years. It is like my kiln, because the wheel is of my
own design. I made it to suit my needs. I had to build the lifters
to lift the pottery off the wheel, too.

When I first started I was producing mostly flowerpots. We
would ship truckloads of earthenware pottery out to fourteen different states. The biggest boost in business was when we finally
began making folk pottery. I have always had a respect for the
utilitarian folk pottery. I had seen it declining and disappearing
from existence. I thought it would be really important for someone
to continue it—someone who had been around pottery all their
life. So, I began to make stoneware pottery. Although I didn't [use
the traditional] ash glaze at first, I would clear glaze it over cobalt
paintings, which Melvin would come in at night and make.

Then, of course, we started making face jugs. The Indian jug
became real popular. Northeast Georgia has got a cultural heritage
dealing with Indians, and we thought the Indian face jug would be

*Michael and Melvin make their own glaze. Here, Melvin stirs
the glaze to prepare it for the jug.*

a good piece to make without infringing on anyone else's design
and keeping with the tradition. We numbered a lot of those jugs.
We made quite a few Indian chiefs and some princesses. Later, as
time went on, we had more and more interest in continuing the
traditional way of making pottery in northeast Georgia.

A few years ago, I set out to start into ash glaze pottery on
regular native red clay in this area. We changed our styles a little
bit from what we were previously doing to the more authentic,
traditional styles of the area. We use the old original ash-glazed
formula: ashes, clay, and glass. People really respect that. They like
to use and buy it. Before long, I thought it would be necessary for
us to make a more significant piece of pottery than the Indian face
jug, so we decided to first make a snake jug for ourselves. We did
that after work as an experiment to blow off a little steam. It is

common at the end of the day for a potter to make an odd piece for themselves or for someone who requested an unusual style. We had a reputation for making real detailed sculpture pieces in our work, so with that knowledge, we came upon a decision to make a real detailed snake jug. It took a long time. As we measured around the jug, we realized that it would take about a six-foot-long piece of clay [weighing] around ten pounds to wrap around the jug for the snake.

I had always been told never to make a piece of pottery and set it off the wheel with the thought of never having to make many more like it. When I worked for Wilson's and Craven, the owner used to come up to me and say, "Hide that piece. A customer will come in and want a hundred of them." And if that happened, we would have to start making them because it is hard to say no to customers.

Immediately, we began to take orders for the snake jugs. Naturally, we had them underpriced. As orders built up, we fine-tuned the style. The first seven pieces we made, we used the lighter burning clay, and we painted the colors on the pieces. We glazed those with our older, clearer glaze. With number eight, we started doing them out of the red clay. That is the way we have been doing them to this day. Now we make a coiled snake with its mouth open. We inlay white clay in the mouth. It takes longer to do the mouth on a coiled snake than to make [the rest of the] whole snake jug. We make an Indian face jug with a snake on it, also. Not many customers know about that piece. It is a piece we wanted to make ourselves to see how it did. People would come by and see us working on one. Now we have seven made, and already at this time [we have] twenty orders for them. The snake jug has been very popular, along with the Indian jug. The country scenes have also been a success.

It is hard to price folk pottery. We could make simple face jugs and snake jugs ten times quicker than the ones we make [now, but] customers seem to want what we do. They don't seem to mind our price when they consider the time and effort we put into the jugs.

Melvin Crocker: I haven't been in the pottery business as long as Michael. I worked at Wilson's for ten years, mostly loading and unloading trucks, but I always wanted to see what I could make out of clay. I would put some faces on jugs [but] I wasn't too serious

The latest line of Crocker pottery: the Indian snake jug.

about it. It was mainly just for fun. When I was in high school, I used my skill with clay to help me pass courses. You could either have a big written speech or do a project. Well, I went down to Wilson's and got me a bag of clay. I would make a bust of a president or something like that. When I started coming down here to help Michael, it seemed like the more we did, the more we had to do. Like he said, we made a snake jug, and somebody saw it. I didn't think it would go like it has. To tell you the truth, it was so hard to make and took so long, in the back of my mind I was hoping it wouldn't sell, but with the process we go through now, everything falls in place. The finished product makes it worth the whole thing.

I etch country scenes [onto some of the jars]. I use a little screwdriver. We don't want to get into anything modern. For that reason we use all the old tools. I started out with an ink pen cap, [which] was the first tool I used. When I made those busts of

Country scene jug.

presidents, I used ink pen lids to put the lines on the faces. It worked fine then, so I'm still using it. You can get into tight spots [with it]. For the scales [on the snakes], I use a coffee straw for the head and a series of larger straws for the body.

Michael Crocker: Melvin and I do individual things [but] all in all, we both make the pottery together. Melvin is very important in the process we use when we make the snake jug. He is so gifted when it comes to creating designs with extreme detail. Melvin makes things look real to life. He's valuable. We both sign every piece. On the country scenes I sign the pottery, and Melvin signs the scene. I think that is appropriate. On the snake jugs we both sign the bottom and date it. Some pieces we number [also]. We have numbered some snake jugs.

[So] we sit here in this hole-in-the-wall and make pottery. We have never, ever advertised or called on companies for business.

That makes it interesting. Of course, around Christmastime, we have sent around cards with a picture on them with our names on it, but there has been no major advertisement. We have a piece of our work in the Smithsonian. It is a snake jug. They want us to do another piece for them. Things like that, and Foxfire doing an article on us, and having some business from outside the country as well as all over this country is a real motivator. When I have a piece of pottery for sale, I want it to satisfy the retail customer. If I called on the phone right now to companies and said, "Hey, I've got a bunch of giant pots here. They're great, and we're closing them out at two dollars apiece. How about a thousand of them?" I could probably talk them into it, but if [the pots] have all got little chips and cracks, they're never going to buy any more. I would really rather make gravel out of damaged pieces of pottery than to sell it to a customer or collector. We will never have a piece of pottery to go out of here with a crack in it. We want the pieces we sell to be 100 percent museum-quality. A lot of art institutions all across the country want a piece of our pottery to represent folk pottery in their museum. You know, we don't go after that business or those institutions. They come after us. We keep that in mind and as a goal to make good stuff. It will return in compensation in the future. People never have a complaint with our work. If they do, we don't hear of it.

A snake jug takes about eight and three quarters of a pound of clay. If we were going to start to make snake jugs for next week, I would work about three or four at a time. Then comes the process where you have to beat the air out of it and wedge it. That is what intrigued me so much when I was a child. I would hear those potters beating the air out of the clay. Boy, they would have a rhythm going. The clay has to be slammed together many times and then cut. When you cut it, you have to look on the smooth surface to get out any of the pebbles and other stuff. After you knock all the air out, you roll the ball. This is important. You have to pack it real tight so when you turn the clay, you won't have any air pockets to seal up and fix.

The next step is turning the piece, making the jug. It doesn't take a whole lot of time to make the jug, but it does take a long time to do everything else. All the snake jugs are not identical. They are all handmade, one at a time. You can't have anything

Michael turns the piece, pulling it up.

exactly alike when it is handmade. The turning comes out of years and years of practice and "want to." It looks easy in a way, but it takes a lot of practice. It is according to your ability and desire to want to do it. You learn by trial and error. I try to learn from older known potters who have already experienced problems, to save me some trouble.

From there, I put a big old box lined with wax to cover the jug, to keep the air out of it. The reason I do that is, if I leave it out today, the air would dry the top out like crazy, and the bottom would still be wet. I cover the jug so it will dry out evenly.

[After the body of the jug has dried for several hours, it's time to attach the handle to the jug.] Handling [putting the handle on] a piece of folk pottery is a significant process. For handling, the piece of clay [for the handle] has to be real sticky. We used to put salt in the clay years ago, because salt is an electrolyte, and it would cause the clay to get real soft, real quick. Now what I do is mix in a little slip off of my wheel. That is real soft, watery clay that has already been prepared [by the throwing process]. Then I just take a piece of clay and roll it. Then I cut the clay about the size I want it and go to the jug. Putting the handle on the jug is not really all that [hard to do]. What I do is wet my hands real good and wet the clay good. I have got to make a handle with my hands. That is all I have to work with. I put the slip on my hands so I won't pull the clay too much. You want it to slide. A lot of the beginner potters make a round handle. I don't do that. I make a flat handle [because] it stands a lot less chance of cracking. [After the handle is on, I again cover the jug and let it dry slowly.]

On the eighth day [after starting the process], Melvin will roll the snake out and fix it on the jug. As he rolls it out, it is five and a half feet long. As we put it on the jug, it will stretch. We etch a little line on the jug to act as a guide to show us where to go. Now, if we put the snake on the [dry] jug, by tomorrow, the snake would come right off. So what we do is put slip on the jug. This slip is a little bit thicker than the slip I used for the handle. This stuff is sort of like glue. When we rub it into the jug, it will cause the jug to be real sticky, so the snake will stick on there.

We pack the top of the jug with a plastic trash bag to increase the inside air pressure slightly so the snake will not put any unnecessary dents or curvatures in the jug. When we have just got the snake wrapped around the jug, we will position the snake in the most naturally aligned position and then proceed to tap it on. We tap it with our fingers to make it adhere to the jug, and that also takes care of air pockets, too. We then smooth the edge of the snake onto the jug. [After this step, we then cover it up again to dry evenly.]

Approximately three days after the snake is fixed to the jug, we reduce the stress on the snake to prevent cracking. If we had such cracking, I'd pull my hair out! We put slip on it all the way down. Then we will come back and put one direction of pressure on the clay. We'll work that clay. If you look under a microscope, it looks like a lot of plates. They are called platelets, and they fit together. When clay is disturbed, those platelets get twisted up. They can get air between them. If they are not lined up, the clay is apt to

*Michael reduces the stress on the jug by applying even pressure
in one direction on the newly attached snake.*

have stress problems, which is why we reduce the stress. The clay
is made up of positive and negative ions. These ions have a negative
pole and a positive pole. Without reducing the stress, those positives
and negatives are pushing and pulling and everything else. Reducing
the stress aligns all the positives and negatives together, so they
will attract one another and fit together perfectly. The polarity is
aligned, and that causes it to dry evenly. It relaxes the clay. [Again,
as after each of these steps, we cover it up to dry.]

On the fourteenth day, Melvin forms and models the snake
features on the back and face. We can still move the clay just a
little bit, but it is a lot firmer now. Sometimes we will take a knife
and trim a little bit. I want to get the form just right because when
we put it up this time, it will be for quite a while. It will dry real
even.

The next step is on the twenty-eighth day. We put the scales
on the head of the snake. The reason for that is those parts of the
snake are exposed more [so] they stick out [and dry faster]. If we
don't go ahead and do that now, it will be too firm to do it later.
To make the scales [on the snakes], we use a coffee straw for the
head.

The next step will be on the thirty-fifth day. The reason we have
that seven-day wait is that in seven days the snake will temper out

Melvin scores the scales on the head of the snake by pushing into the clay with a coffee straw.

and dry out. In this step we complete the scales and rub the bottom of the jug. [To make scales on] the body, we use a larger straw and then another larger straw [and then, as the body tapers down] we use the middle-sized straw and then at the tail the coffee straw again. There are a lot of little things that you have to do which people don't realize have to be done. I rub the bottom of the jug so it will set down even. I give it a real smooth bottom.

This is where we sign and date the piece. This is the last check to see if there are any cracks in it. We put the snake jug upside down on a piece of styrofoam or something soft. We use a nail to sign our names. That completes the step on the forty-ninth day.

On the sixty-third day, we uncover the jug completely. You can tell that some jugs have a darker look in some places. If we were to fire one that has that, I guarantee it would explode. On this stage we uncover the piece completely and let it sit in the shop here and air dry. Sometimes we put fans on them.

On the seventieth day, after it has been sitting out about a week, it is almost completely dry. Then we set it out in the sun. That sun will really draw out what moisture there is in it.

Most all the folk pottery that has ever been made was not prefired. It was all raw glaze. We raw glaze practically everything we turn, but we don't do that with the snake jugs now. If we were

On day seventy-three, Michael paints the coloring on the jug.

to do that, the glaze is liable to penetrate the connection between the snake and the jug and leave a crack.

We go ahead and prefire the snake jug on day seventy-one and seventy-two. To prefire the jug, I have to set it in the kiln in the morning and let it fire all day at a real low temperature and make sure all the moisture is gone. Then, I fire it all night on a little bit higher temperature. Then the next day, I take it up in faster stages, increasing the temperature a lot higher. By the end of the day it will be completely fired. When I get through firing it, [it] becomes one piece. It totally bonds.

We take the piece out of the kiln and let it cool off. On day seventy-three, we paint the coloring on the snake jug. We use natural-occurring minerals. The black is a titanium dioxide, and the yellow is an iron oxide. [Even though] the painting under that ash glaze on the snake alone is not all that noticeable on the finished product, it takes a significant amount of time to do that.

On day seventy-four, we dip the jug in the glaze. I'll stick it

Finished snake jug.

down into the glaze and spin it three or four times. I make sure the jug gets coated real nice and even. We will usually glaze more than one piece at a time.

On day seventy-five and seventy-six, I go through a two-day firing. I could fire it quicker, but I like to start a kiln late in the evening and build it up in the morning. That way I could finish it up in the early evening. It is more convenient that way.

On day seventy-seven, we take the jug out of the kiln and call the customer that is next on the list to get the piece.

[To produce one snake jug requires a lot of steps and time, but] it is just like any occupation. If you really like what you do, it is not going to be a big chore to go out and do your job. It seems to me like it is a calling for Melvin and me to do folk pottery. I look forward to coming to work every day. I have got a two-and-a-half-year-old boy. I would be tickled to death if he would take up pottery in the traditional way. Someday, I hope that someone could catch on, and we would train them as an apprentice to continue the tradition. I would rather it be a family member. Whether they would choose to do that or not will be entirely their decision—it will have to be something that they choose to do. But I definitely would like to see that.

Reuben A. Miller

The Wizard of Windmills

As you are traveling on Old Cornelia Highway toward Gaines-ville, Georgia, in the distance on a green, grassy hill you see a barrage of whirligigs and windmills. No, whirligigs isn't a word for an extraterrestrial object. They're a type of windmill that folk artist R. A. Miller makes. He explained to us that there are two kinds of windmills at his house: the whirligigs and regular windmills. The whirligigs are windmills that have two propellers. But what makes his creations different from those of others is that he puts painted animals on them.

Mr. Miller's shop beside his small brown house was a maze of paint buckets and tin animals everywhere I looked. The smell of paint and the sounds of a brush against tin, going swish, swish, swish, filled the air. His shop was a primitive assembly line. Blank, white, rectangular pieces of tin lay to his right. Behind him were the finished products: sharks, chickens, and anteaters that had once been pieces of a tin roof or a gutter, now re-created as works of art. In the midst of it all, Mr. Miller was painting the final touches on a blue dinosaur.

Mr. Miller is seventy-seven years old. His gray hair was partially hidden by a black hat that had "The James Gang" embroidered in turquoise on it. He wore a turquoise shirt and blue work pants. The brightly colored rainbow of paint that splotched his clothes, shoes, and hands revealed that he gets into his work. His thick glasses couldn't hide the youthful spark in his eyes. Mr. Miller's smile radiates warmth and a cheerfulness that reminded me of a kid who had just gotten cotton candy at the fair. If enthusiasm reflected age, I would have thought him a lot younger than he really is. He told us that his eyes were bad and that he couldn't see well. He said, "Have you ever looked through a glass of water? That's what I see." His determination to keep on painting despite his worsening glaucoma is amazing.

He showed us some of the remarkable animals he made: camels, alligators, and dinosaurs cut out of tin. While a number of his pieces are decorated with domestic and farm animals, many of the creatures he makes he has never seen firsthand. He told us he watched National Geographic television programs all the time to get ideas for new animals to create. We left his shop so he could show us some of his real animals. He paused and removed a handkerchief from his back pocket and wiped the sweat that had formed on his brow. He then led us to his pen of chickens.

Mr. Miller used to own other animals as well—cats, dogs, goats, pigeons, hogs, and peafowls. He used to milk goats. As he said, "That goat's milk [is] good. If you got an ulcerated stomach, it'll heal it right up when nothing else will."

We then ventured into his side yard for the final showcase—a hillside forest of whirligigs and windmills turning in the breeze. As I looked around I saw some great and creative work. For example, one windmill was made out of a refrigerator fan, and one had a Georgia flag painted on it. Others had bicycle wheels, dinosaurs, cats, and chickens flying proudly.

He also showed us an interesting character called the Blow Oscar. This unusual tin figure turns out to be Mr. Miller's cousin Oscar. He explained that Oscar and he pulled jokes on each other all the time. He started calling it a Blow Oscar because every time Oscar drove by his house, he'd blow his horn at him and yell as loud as he could, and both would laugh at each other.

—Robbie Bailey
Interview and photographs by Robbie Bailey, Scott Cannon, Sharon Williams, and Leigh Ann Smith.

R. A. Miller, windmill maker.

I was born and raised here all my life. I used to go to school here. The members of my family are Pearl, Burt, Will, Jake, Allan, Morgan, and me. There were eight of us, but one died when she was little. I'm the youngest in the family. My oldest brother was eighty-five years old when he died. He got run over in Rabbit Town. He was old and crossing the road. A boy was comin' down the road, going pretty fast, and he got too close to the edge of the road. He hit him and knocked him over in the ditch and he died. My other brother was old when he died. He died up here. One of my brothers had hardening of the arteries. He died when he was seventy-five. My oldest sister died in the hospital. She had cancer or something. Me and my two sisters, we're the only three that's livin' now.

I sign my name R.A., but my name is Reuben. That was my daddy's name. I never met my daddy. He got shot six months before I was born. This is what my mother told me. He was coming out yonder at the Eastview Church. There was an old dirt road that came up through there, and my daddy used it because he had bottoms down in yonder. We owned all that land back in yonder. There was a man that had a little tract of land up there, and he

wanted to stop that road. They went to court, and they gave Daddy
the right to travel that road. My daddy was coming out there with
two mules and a wagon with a load of wood, and this man jumped
off his wagon and hid behind a rock. My daddy came up alone with
the wood, and he shot him. He shot him on Christmas Eve, and
he died on Christmas Day. They gave that man life in the
penitentiary.

I farmed before I went to work in the cotton mill. When I was
twelve years old, I walked back and forth to work. You had to walk;
there wasn't no other way to go. I worked in that mill twenty years.
One morning me and my wife were there at Mother's old house,
and thunder rolled, and my mother said, "Son, go up on the hill.
Look toward Gainesville and see. That's a bad storm." I went up
there on the hill, and I looked at Gainesville, and up in the air it
looked like houses and everything else going around and around.
It looked like it was coming this way, and by the time I left the
hill and got back to the house here, I didn't have time to shut the
door. It had done hit this house, and all these houses out here.
There were a bunch of chicken houses out that other road, and it
just swept 'em off. My brother's house on this other road on the
hill, it just swept it off. My mother went to praying, "Dear God,
don't let it blow the top off a'here where it would rain on me." The
whole side blew off, then, and another room on the back got blown
away. That was a terrible time. This old house was just trembling.
I never saw it hail so much in my life. This whole side of my house
blew off. It had those old-timey shingles, and it blew 'em all off.
It blew that room away. Lord have mercy, Gainesville was torn to
pieces, and it killed a bunch of people. You could hear the am-
bulances running. It was a terrible time. I hope I will never be in
another one. That was in 1936, and I had to tear that big house
down. I got my brothers, and we built this house back. I was working
in the cotton mill then.

I used to cut and haul wood. I bought me an old 1925 Chevrolet
car. I cut it down and made me a truck out of it. I hauled wood
and sold it for fifty cents a load. I would haul from here to Gainesville
and up to [a community where] there's just old houses made out
of burnt wood. Boy, I could sell the wood, though. Then I'd get a
twenty-five-pound sack of flour for sixty-five cents. I used to buy
'baccer and snuff in a big old plug for fifteen cents. A tin box of

snuff now costs you a dollar, and you used to get it for a dime. You could buy a pair of overalls for seventy-five or eighty-five cents up there at Jake's. I am used to a good, gracious life. I could take five cents and buy anything I wanted. Now, it takes twenty-five and fifty dollars to get what I want.

I got right with the Lord one night when I went to a meeting at the little Methodist church down there. There was a little preacher running a revival. Me and my old lady went there. One night that little preacher came to me while I was sitting on a bench in the church. He got on his knees, and I never heard a man pray a prayer like that one in my life. If you've ever been saved you know how it is. I was hard-hearted before I got saved at a revival.

Later at home, me and my wife went to bed. Just me and her lived in the house, and something spoke to me. I got to shaking, and the Lord spoke to me, "I tell you, you better get right, son." I stood there on the floor, and I believe I shook the bed where she was laying. "Lord, if you'll let me live till I get back here to Mother's house, I'll make it right." But I put it off, so one night I came in there and God said, "You better get right." I came in the house, and my mother was sitting in an old chair. I'll never forget. She said, "Get down, son. Let's go to praying." She was a good woman. We got down there and I prayed, I don't know how long, but there was a special time I can't tell you about. When I got up, I don't know what happened, but I know that somethin' came outta me. I jumped up off the floor and shouted all over her house.

[Then I decided to try to preach in church.] One night I said, "Lord, I can't do it." I had an ashamed face, but I went up there, and I never preached so in my life. From then on, I never was ashamed and could face the whole world. God took the ashamedness away from me when I went to preachin'. I preached for about seven years. I got goin' to meetings and helped 'em sing.

I got right with the Lord and bought a set of loudspeakers. I preached all over this part of the country. I bought me a tent and set up a group of loudspeakers up here and yonder and all around the tent. I went down to Spring Road off of Brown's Ridge Road, and I put up a tent down there. We had the awfulest revivals. I baptized forty people at one time down there. Some of the people said, "Well, we're gonna build a church."

I said, "Well, I'll help you all I can."

They said, "Well, we want you to help us."

I said, "All right, I'll do all I can."

I opened that church, and it's still down there. They got 'em another good little pastor.

[When I was preaching] the power of the Lord would fall, and people would shout and get right with God. Young people would get right, too. I'd baptize people, and they'd join the church. I used to run revivals up there in Dahlonega, Lula, Banks County, Jackson County, and Cleveland. I run them just everywhere. We used to have revivals, but there ain't none now like they used to be, not like I was raised up to. I used to go to old Springway Church when I was a little boy. I was big enough to know what it was. You'd go in there and that old preacher would get up there, and the power of the Lord would get on him. He'd go to walking the floors, and the old women would go to shouting. You hardly ever hear of that now. I don't know whether you're a Baptist or a Methodist, but you don't hear much of that in the Baptist churches now. If you go to a Holiness church, you'll still hear it, and if you go to the Freewill Baptist you'll hear it, too.

Then, you used to hear prayin' at all times of the night. We went down to Springway one night to a revival. A bunch of us gathered and we were preachin' together. A woman told us, "You know, [one time] I stood there in the door and a ball of fire fell over there. I promised it was goin' to burn 'em up. I never heard such noise in my life. They were hollerin', screamin', shoutin', and prayin'." She said a light came down. If she was living, she'd tell you. There were six or seven wanting to be saved. She said when that light came down, she never heard such shoutin' and prayin' in her life. We used to have good revivals. You don't hear of any revivals now that are like we used to have.

I'd get out and build a brush arbor. Making a brush arbor is according to how big you want to build it. Cut you a pole with forks on it. Dig a hole here, one here, over yonder, and one around. [Stand one pole up in each corner, and] lay some poles across them and you throw brush over the top of it to keep the dew from coming in. Build your pulpit where you preach it, and put your seats in there. That's a brush arbor. That's the first meetings I used to go to until I bought me a tent. We used to have some awful meetings up there. I liked to go to brush arbors.

The first brush arbor I ever built didn't have any electricity. They used to sell beer in old, brown bottles, and I'd fill 'em full with kerosene, twist a piece of cloth, and run it down in there. It would burn like a lamp. I'd set them up around and have the meeting.

Most of these churches you go to, you feel bound. Have you ever been that way? You walk in church and you feel bound. You feel like something's got you and holding you down. You can't loosen yourself. Now, when I run a revival, I tell everybody to loosen yourself. If you feel like prayin', you pray. If you feel like shoutin', you shout. If you feel like preachin', it won't bother me. Just go ahead and obey the Lord. We're here to serve the Lord. I'll obey the Lord. Don't worry about me, you satisfy yourself. I preached till my eyes didn't work good, and I couldn't see.

When I was a little boy, I used to make flutter mills. There's a big creek down there, and I used to take cornstalks and two-forked sticks. I'd be barefooted, and I'd get out there in the creek. Then I'd stick the forked sticks in the creek and take the cornstalks and put one across like that. Then I'd get another little stick and run it through the cornstalk—bore you a little hole through the corn-

As one tops the hill, the silhouettes of the windmills are created by the evening sun.

Mr. Miller shows us one of his windmills.

stalk and run it through, forks to hit where that water is, and it'll just fly away. You can make 'em big or put two or three [stick blades] if you want to, and the water turns it like an old corn wheel.

Later I started making windmills. I've been making windmills about ten years. I first started making windmills out of wood. I got one out there on that flagpole. They'll fly, and they'll run as good that way as tin will. You slope [the blades] off. That's the way I used to make 'em. Then I had a bunch of tin, and I started puttin' tin on it. I started making 'em that way. I just took a notion to do that. I got my tin from boys putting in gutters. They would have short pieces and they would bring 'em and give 'em to me. I let 'em dump the tin in the gutter right yonder on the side of the road. Then I went to cutting it out. They run faster with tin than with wood.

The iron pipes that I put the windmills on come from those kids' swings. A water pipe or any kind of pipe can be used to do that. I'd drive a stob up and nail 'em to that. Some of 'em have pine poles on 'em and you just nail it to that stob. There ain't no trouble to do this.

My great-grandma was an Indian, and that's how I got the idea to paint an Indian on the windmill. I make cats on some of 'em. I did have one that had a cat running a mouse on it. I have one that has a boy with a hoe in his hand hitting a snake. Before my eyes got bad, I could make one with an old woman turning a washing machine. It would move when the windmill turned. I'd take doll hair and put on the head and make it have long hair.

Then I got to watching television on Channel Eight. I got to watching National Geographic and seeing animals. I started drawing some of them on tin, and then I went to cutting them out. Bought a pair of snips and I got started on that. People got to liking it. It's been about a year since I started cutting them out.

I don't know if my artwork is influenced by the Lord, but God blesses me by it. On my paintings I put down, "Lord Love All" or "God Love You" or something like that on it. I get to studying how the devil got to the world. Nobody can surprise the devil. He's our

One of Mr. Miller's animals. Many of his ideas come from National Geographic television programs.

archangel. The devil's beautiful. They think of him as a boogerish-looking thing, but you wouldn't follow a devil if he had horns and everything else on. The devil makes you feel good. I've studied about making a painting with a devil and a pitchfork and a lake of fire on it. I would write up there, "This is what the devil causes you to do." I've had that on my mind about showing people falling off in that lake of fire. The Bible says they'll be a rolling, screaming, gnashing of teeth together, and praying for help. Nobody can get to 'em, and neither can they get to you.

When I see anything, I try to draw it like it is. I study a whole lot about how the devil got to the world. I listen to a lot of preachers, and a lot of prophesizing comes on the television every night. Preachers are prophesizing about the time, and that it can't be much longer till the earth will end. This was the last generation.

Now, I can't see too much to paint. My eyes have just got weaker and weaker. I have glaucoma. I first had cataracts. The doctor took 'em out, and then glaucoma got in 'em. My eyes have another set

The smell of paint and the sounds of a brush against tin filled the air.

of lenses on the inside of 'em, sewed in there, and they won't come out. They did that to cure the glaucoma.

That's the reason I don't paint 'em too good, but I do a lot of painting, though. I can do four or five in a night. It's according to how long I sit up to paint. I couldn't do it with a paintbrush. That's the reason I don't use a paintbrush, I use markers. Now paint won't come off. You mark on it and it won't wash off. Markers aren't like paint.

I'll show you what I draw. I see 'em on the television. I color them any color I take a notion to. I mostly use blue, black, and red. That's about the only kind of these markers you can get. Now I can get some others, but it won't stay on there. Man, it'll make you sick. It's got ether or something in it, but these ain't. You don't smell nothin' in these.

Some dinosaurs I'll paint red, green, and some blue. Some dinosaurs I make like this, spotted. I make all kinds. I don't know why I paint so many dinosaurs; I just like to make dinosaurs. I just like to draw 'em. Sometimes I make spots on snakes. A rattlesnake is supposed to be spotted. I didn't think there were any two-headed snakes, but there are. There's [such a thing as] a horned snake, too.

I draw elephants, and I also draw monkeys. I like a lot of animals, and sometimes I put crosses, the Statue of Liberty, devils, and Indians on them. I also draw Blow Oscar. Anybody can draw that. Yeah, I like to do that. The first one I ever made was a great big one. I drawed a devil Blow Oscar, and I drew snakes and dinosaurs. I had all kinds of animals on it, and they liked it. Then I believe the first one I ever made, I tried to draw this house on a windmill people wanted. They told me to draw some more. They are from Atlanta, Athens, North Carolina, Tennessee, California, Michigan, New York, Mexico, Germany, and England. They just come from everywhere. There were some people that came and said they saw me on television.

I do these Blow Oscars to get my cousin Oscar tickled at blowing at me. His grandma and my mother were sisters, so that makes us cousins. He used to be a preacher himself, and me and him ran revivals together. We're all the time goin' on to one another and pulling jokes on one another. [When he was driving by] he'd blow at me. He would say, "Toot, toot, toot, toot, toot." If he saw me

Mr. Miller's unique creation, the Blow Oscar.

he'd holler loud as he could. I'd laugh at him, and he'd laugh at me. [Well] I was sitting out there [one day] and I said, "I'll fix you, old boy." [And so I made the Blow Oscar.] We all the time were just going on to one another. I see him every once in a while; me and him used to have a lot of fun together.

Minnie Black

"I can recognize my work anywhere."

As soon as we walked in the small house in East Bernstadt, Kentucky, I knew I was in for a treat: gourd art from wall to wall. Minnie Black's living room displayed most of her favorite creations including "Mr. Rawhide and Bloody Bones," and her disconcertingly lifelike self-portrait.

Minnie never slowed down. We had only been in the house a few minutes when she took out some of her original gourd instruments and began to play them. She sang and played, and told stories about each instrument as she brought it out. She went back and forth from different parts of her house, unearthing more uses for gourds than I ever would have thought possible.

With all the gourd instruments Minnie had made, and all the friends that she had down at the senior citizens' center, she started her own band called Minnie's Gourd Band. From place to place, they played and sang everywhere, from community centers to senior citizens' centers. They played all over eastern Kentucky and in some of the surrounding states.

Minnie is a professional gourd artist and an honored member of the National Association of Gourd Artists. In fact, she is one of its best-known members. Minnie goes to their annual meeting in Ohio, where hundreds of artists show off their own personal styles of gourd artistry. She makes anything and everything with gourds:

masks, puppets, bizarre creatures, likenesses of people (including Elvis, Johnny Carson, and herself), insects, pincushions, and, of course, instruments. She's such a famous gourd artist that she and her creations have traveled all over the country, from Burbank, California, where she appeared on the "Tonight Show," to New York City, where she displayed her gourd art on the David Letterman show (on her eighty-ninth birthday).

Minnie gave Johnny Carson a one-of-a-kind Johnny Carson gourd doll. Not to be conspicuous, Minnie carried her gourd art to the Carson show in her giant gourd luggage, which measures about six feet around.

From that point on, the gourd business boomed. Minnie started getting letters from all over the country asking for her "special" gourd seeds. People thought that Minnie's seeds actually grew gourds in the shape of the dragons and chickens and dinosaurs that they had seen on TV. Minnie is a miraculous gourd artist, but she isn't a miracle gourd grower. Minnie gathered as many seeds as she could muster and sent them (free of charge) all over the United States, explaining to the recipients that, while these were indeed her gourd seeds, they didn't automatically grow into dinosaur shapes. She couldn't afford to send as many seeds as people were asking her to send. Finally, she decided that the only way she could send people her seeds was if they were to send her a self-addressed, stamped envelope. Minnie grows all her seeds in the garden in her backyard. She's very proud of her garden and works in it as much as she possibly can.

In her side yard, right next to the gourd garden, is Minnie's gourd museum, which she started long before she became famous. She has many of her creations there, from the newest to the oldest. To her, some of her creations are priceless. She wouldn't sell, no matter what you gave her. (Wig tried.) The gourds in the museum range from a chicken gourd, which you can fit in the palm of your hand, to a giant Statue of Liberty. You have to look up in order to see the top of that one. The museum is more like an attic of weird, wonderful, and sometimes funny gourd art scattered in a million different places. There are gourds hanging from strings connected to the ceiling, and gourd creatures cluttering the tables that fill the room. You would have to visit the museum two or three times just to try to take everything in, and then you would still be at a loss for words.

Every gourd there is unique. Minnie knows the exact location of every gourd in the museum, and she has a story for each one. If you have time, she won't hesitate to tell you. So, if you ever drive through a little town called East Bernstadt, in the coal fields of eastern Kentucky, stop by and see Minnie Black's Gourd Museum. You'll be amazed at what you see.

—Scott Crane
Interview and photographs by Scott Crane,
Bruce Beck, and Anna Lee.

I can recognize my work anywhere. People have learned to recognize it at the Gourd Show; they can tell my work anywhere they see it. Everybody has a different way of doing things. Even if you're doing the same thing with the same tools, it's going to be a little different because we are all different, you see.

I started raising gourds back in the fifties, and I raised them a good while. I could see things in the gourds, and I just loved them. I don't know why. There's something strange and different about

Minnie Black, gourd artist from East Bernstadt, Kentucky.

Minnie's gourd Statue of Liberty.

a gourd, and not only to me. I have had other people who do artwork with gourds tell me that it is the same way with them. The more you work with gourds, the more you love them. They just fascinate you, and you enjoy it so much.

Now the way that I got started with gourds, I didn't know what a gourd vine was when we moved here in 1947. Out there at the end of the driveway, there was a little cow shed, and right beside that cow shed there came up a strange-looking vine, just a bushlike plant. Then it began to vine. Well, I didn't know what it was, but there was an old lady here one evening, and I asked her, "What is that plant coming up here by the shed?"

And she said, "Well, that's a gourd vine."

Well, I let it grow to see, you know, because I never had seen gourds grow. I'd seen gourds, but I didn't know where they came from. So I let the vine grow. It had forty-two of these long-handled

She has many different varieties of gourd art.

gourds. They were all the way from twenty-four to thirty-six inches long, and they had grown on the ground, some of them. Their necks had crooked around, and they reminded me of a slug or something. I gave the gourds to different neighbors and friends. That's how I got started with the gourds. Well, the Lord gave me that vine because I didn't know about it, and I really learned to like them gourds. See, in the book of Jonah, the Lord called a gourd vine to come up over Jonah to shield him from his grief. He was worrying that the Lord chose him to go and tell the people of Ninevah that if they didn't repent of their sins, He was going to destroy the city within forty days and nights. He was a-worryin' about that, and he was showing the Lord that he didn't want to do what He had asked him to do, and yet he was afraid not to, so he went down in a ship and hid. There was a storm that came upon the ocean, and the people who were on the ship got scared, so they went down in the bottom of the ship and found Jonah asleep. He was hiding, and they woke him up and asked him his name. He told them, and they told him that there was a storm up on the ocean, and there was something causing it. He said, "It's because of me. Just throw me overboard." So they threw him overboard, and this whale swallowed him up. Then I guess that must have got him to serving the Lord, don't you know, because the whale spewed him out onto the sand,

A dragon gourd guards Minnie's museum.

and then he went walking away. He was sitting there a-worryin'
about it, and the Lord caused a gourd vine to come up over him
and shield him from his grief. The Lord caused that gourd vine to
come up overnight.

My friends knew that I liked gourds, and they gave me seeds
of different types. Then I got to searching the seed catalogues for
different types, and I'd get different kinds. When you plant them,
they say you ought to cover the seed with as much dirt as the seed
is long, and it's good to put them down endways so they don't rot.
It is better to have about two plants to a hill, not over three, anyway.
If you plant two or three or four different kinds of gourds in the
same patch or garden, the bees mix the pollen. Next year, when
you plant the gourds, the bees will have mixed the pollen from
different gourds, and you don't know what kind of gourds you'll
get.

You have to experiment with gourds because some people start
making gourds when they're in the green state, and that is the
wrong time. You're not supposed to work on gourds until you let
them dry out. Then you can clean the gourd, scrape the outside
skin off, and then they're ready to [work with].

You know, I sometimes get ideas in the night when I'm asleep.
I got an idea one night: I thought about a little mule, and I thought,

A freak of nature: a mule with two heads and six legs.

"Well, I'll try to make me one." So here he is, and branching out about the middle of his back there are the two little heads. The first [country] fair I ever went to, when I was a kid, the first thing that I noticed when I got there was a sideshow. A man was standing out in the front, and he said, "See the freak-of-nature mule—two heads and six legs." They say he lived twenty-six years.

A lady from Berea [Kentucky] said she wanted a chicken because she had seen the film about me that Appalshop [Film Workshop] made. When I make a chicken out of a gourd, I use real chicken feet. A lot of people frown when you tell them that because they think that the feet carry diseases. I don't raise chickens anymore, but my sister-in-law does, and she saves the feet for me. Once she gives me the feet, I take them and scald them clean. Then I put the feet in little plastic bags and place them in the deep freeze and keep them there until I get ready to use them. When I am ready to use them, I take them out and soak them in Lysol disinfectant overnight to kill all the germs, and then I take the feet, dry them off, and tack them on a board so they won't curl up. After the feet remain straight, I allow the air to hit them so they can dry out.

This interesting bird has now become a famous politician: Dan Quayle.

Now the feet are ready to be peeled and varnished, and they will stay right on like that.

I made a gourd doll of Elvis and gave it to a man in Georgia. He's got it in his office down in Atlanta. That was the first one. I made two others [of Elvis] that I dressed up just like he was on the stage. I let a dentist in Illinois have one and a museum man in Dillard, Georgia, has the other one. That man who had the museum in Dillard sold the Elvis gourd. He had Elvis's first old car, too.

[On the self-portrait doll I used] a short-necked gourd. I molded the face and hands with sculpture clay. The body is a gourd, and the legs are, too. It took me, off and on, about two or three weeks to make. [I made a gourd doll of Johnny Carson, and working on my self-portrait doll was just like working on his. With Johnny's] I'd look at him, and I'd see a mistake, and then I'd remold him a little. I can still see where I could fix him up a little. After everybody gets older, they change their looks a bit. I'm just glad it ain't no worse.

Somebody called me from Colorado and wanted an instrument, a whale harp [a whale made out of a gourd with a harmonica fitted

Minnie's gourd version of herself.

into the middle of the whale.] Her husband was really carried away with that, and she wanted to get it for him for Christmas. I told her I was sorry, but I didn't make them. I didn't want to. Just too much. I didn't go for it.

I had been making instruments [out of gourds]. I got so many, I thought, "Well, what am I making so many for?" And the idea came to me to organize a gourd band. At that time I was visiting a senior citizens' center occasionally, and I asked the recreation director, "How about organizing a gourd band? I've got a lot of instruments. Would you mind if I bring them up here, and we start us a gourd band?"

*Minnie scurried around, unearthing examples of more uses
of gourds than we ever thought possible. Here she strums
a song on her gourd instrument.*

She said, "Great idea." So I did. I took the instruments up.
Everybody just joined in and had the best time. Those old people,
it just seemed to lift their spirits; they really enjoyed it.

We started the band about five or six years ago, between '80
and '82. The director was a man that could play any kind of instrument and was a real good singer. He had a real good voice for
singing, and he played the electric guitar. He would lead us off on
the different songs, and we would follow. We would go to entertain
at these places. There were about eighteen or twenty in the band,
and there wasn't hardly a stage big enough to accommodate that
many, so I had to go and eliminate people, and that caused hard

feelings. It about killed me to have to do that. There were some that really couldn't keep time, but I let 'em because they enjoyed it so much, and I hated to turn them off. There were some that never got to go anywhere till we got that band up and went to so many nice places. People were so nice to us. We'd go to some of the family reunions and summer churches. We went to the Kentucky Center for the Arts in Louisville, and we went to Tombstone Junction and all different places. When I was up at North Tennessee last fall for that big folk festival, I came off the stage, and there was a lady outside wanting to schedule the band at Dollywood in Pigeon Forge. They were going to have a big fall festival that next weekend, and she invited me to bring the gourd band up there. [But] we've quit now. We just had to stop, and I just hate it so bad. I've got more invitations to entertain at different places, but there's a stopping place for everything.

Now I wasn't a musician. I'd just picked up mine when I was growing up. I was born in Law County at the head of Rockcastle River, where the Buffalo Branch runs into the river. My parents were Fred Links, Sr., and Rebecca Young Links. My mother had seventeen children, and I was the eighth one. Six boys and six girls lived to be grown. The boys, after they got grown, played stringed instruments like the guitar, and the fiddle, and banjo. My oldest sister took music, and she played the piano. We had a big baby grand piano, and she'd play, and the rest of us sang. The girls sang, the boys played, and the young people would gather. We didn't have any recreation—no cars, no shows, and things to go to like they do now. The young people would just gather up, you know, where there were several in a family. That way there was always a bunch of outsiders there. We always had a good time together. Well, after the girls got grown, we began to slip around and get some square dances scheduled just before Christmas. Everyone loved that.

I was married to William B. Black in 1919. We had four children—three boys and a girl. We had a filling station and a grocery store. I tried to help out in the store, but I didn't like that gas-filling. He'd put me out there sometimes. I didn't like that. I didn't like to smell the gas in the first place, and I just didn't think that was a woman's job anyway.

I didn't start making my bigger gourds until my husband retired from the store. I tried to carry on the business awhile by myself. It was just too much for me, and it was hard to find good help, so I had to quit. After I got retired from our business, I got to working with the gourds. After I had too many gourds to keep in the house, I started to use a separate building located next to my house. I soon named this building Minnie Black's Gourd Museum. The more I made them, the more I loved it, and finally my museum was full and running over.

In the summertime, I get a lot of visitors to the museum. But it's getting hard for me, I'll tell you, because [I have] nobody to help, and I need help. In the winter a few come, not too many. And I'm glad, too. I don't want to go down there in the bad weather.

[After I started my museum] in the latter part of the sixties, the Gourd Society got ahold of me someway. I don't know how they found out about me, but they sent some delegates down here to see me. The fall of '72 was my first visit to the gourd show, and I have been going every year since, except one. We swap gourd art with each other at our Gourd Society. At the twenty-fifth anniversary in 1987, everyone was supposed to bring something with a little silver on it. I was grand marshal in the parade [that year].

People that wanted to get ahold of me wouldn't know how, so I had to advertise that I was a member of the Gourd Society so that they'd write up there and get my address. Sometimes the secretary of the Gourd Show, he'd answer the requests for me, and I appreciate that so much. They are so good to me up there, just like they are at Appalshop in Whitesburg [Kentucky] and everywhere else.

I took some little miniature gourds with me to the Carson show so they could see the different types of gourds. When I got to the last of the gourds, I handed them to Johnny. He looked at them and said, "Are those gourds?"

I said, "Yeah, these are miniature gourds made to look like an Arizona coral snake." The snake gourds get bigger than this, but I made them out of the small size.

"Well," he said, "they look like dead snakes to me."

Many people have asked me for seed from that little gourd. They saw that gourd on the show, but there aren't hardly any seeds in that little old runt gourd.

I had a real time getting my things on the plane on my way to the Johnny Carson show. The box of gourds wouldn't fit in the baggage rack above my seat; they had to take it up to the cockpit. But on the way back they happened to have three seats in the back of the plane, and they belted the box on one of the seats. They were so nice to us. They aren't allowed to do that, but they made arrangements.

When I went to the David Letterman show, people told me he was a smart aleck, and I determined he wasn't getting nothing off me. There are some little boys that live in Bloomington, Indiana, and they said they had known him all their lives. They said, "He will probably try to get something off of you."

I got on the show, and he began to ask me questions, and I said, "Now look here, son. You can ask me all the questions you want to, but if I don't want to answer the questions, I just won't." He and other people treated me real nice. I wanted to see him before I got on stage, and I had already seen all the members, the producers, and the coordinators. "Now I have met all the staff— where is David? Where can I meet him?"

They said, "You're not supposed to meet him before you get on stage." Then I wanted to talk with him after the show was over and tell him how disappointed I was that he did not let me have any more time than he did.

I tell you what, Johnny Carson is altogether a different man from David Letterman. Johnny can make fun out of anything you talk about. I enjoyed it, and I think that everybody else enjoyed it because they replayed [my segment] on his twentieth-anniversary show.

People are so nice to me. After you get old, you appreciate all the help you can get. I've been lucky to hold up and be able to be active and take care of myself—up and at 'em. Boy, however long it is, I do hope I'll be able to do that to the end.

Editorial Contributors

Contacts

Ellen Alley
Donald Anderson
Ernest Anderson
Dorothy Beck
Roy Beshears
Jim Bingham
Minnie Black
Lester Blair
Dr. John C. Blalock
Clarence Bramblett
Josephine Brewer
Florence Brooks
Lawton Brooks
Harold Brown
Harry Brown
Marinda Brown
Ulyss Brown
Roosevelt Burrell
Knox Bynum
Mary Cabe
Ruby Callenback
Edith Cannon
Robert Cannon
Arie Carpenter
James Cartwright
Buck Carver

Leona Carver
Ed Collins
Minyard Conner
Ethel Corn
Virgil Craig
Dan Crane, Sr.
Melvin Crocker
Michael Crocker
J. D. Crowe
Ross Davis
Homer Deal
Arizona Dickerson
R. M. Dickerson
Terry Dickerson
Barnard Dillard
Bertha Dockins
Ollie Dyer
Thomas R. Ebright
Harriet Echols
Bob Edwards
Bennie Eller
Mrs. Willie Elliott
Carlton English
Mary Franklin
Pete Franklin
Lelia Gibson
Virgil Giles

Oma Gipson
Ellene Franklin Gowder
Ernest Gragg
Fred Grist
A. J. Gudger
Clyde Harkins
Lon Harkins
Howard Herd
Hugh Holcomb
Claude Hollifield
Coyle Hollifield
Mary Ann Hollifield
Joe Hopper
Raleigh Hopper
Ed Huffman
Tom Hunnicutt
Oakley Justice
Claude Kelly
Fred Kelly
Goldman Kimbrell
Jerry King
John Kollock
Cora Ledbetter
Margaret Marchman
Numerous Marcus
Joe McGahee
Reuben A. Miller

Robert N. Mitcham

Mrs. Con Mitchell

Roy Mize

Tom Moss

Dess Oliver

Jess Page

Don Patterson

John Lee Patterson

Curtis Pearson

Esco Pitts

Mary Pitts

Jack Prince, Sr.

Leo Ramey

Dan Ranger

Lewis Reeves

Woodrow Reeves

Jess Rickman

Carl Rogers

Clyde Runion

Kenny Runion

Will Seagle

Roy Shope

Genelia Singleton

Frank A. Smith

Joe Snyder

Bill Southards

Alton D. Story

Mildred Story

J. C. Stubblefield

Cleo Taylor

Janie P. Taylor

Jim Taylor

Melvin Taylor

Hoyt Tench

Lyndall "Granny" Toothman

Reverend James E. Turpen, Sr.

Bob Vickers

Jake Waldroop

J. B. Waldrop

George Welch

Jimmy White

Lex Wilburn

Fred Williams

Lee Williams

Walter Williams

Max Woody

Myron Woody

Walker Word

Jack Wynn

Students

Allison Adams

Brooks Adams

Matt Alexander

Jimmy Andrews

Robbie Bailey

Bruce Beck

Dinah Beck

Chad Bedingfield

Chris Bessette

Jeff Black

Joe Blume

Tim Burgess

Tony Burt

Kurt Cannon

Scott Cannon

Lee Carpenter

Bit Carver

Kaye Carver

Stephanie Cash

Leisha Chastain

Rosanne Chastain

Joanna Chieves

Tallie Cilbrith

Kenneth Coalley

Karen Cox

Mandy Cox

John Crane

Scott Crane

Chris Crawford

Shane Danaher

Rita Darnell

Beth Davis

Tim DeBord

Eric Deering

Scott Dick

Julie Dickens

Roy Dickerson

Dennis Dodgins

Frankie Dunlap

Frank Dyer

Al Edwards

Monica English

Holly Fisher

Rance Fleming

Danny Flory

Kim Foster

Kevin Fountain

Michelle Franks

Taphie Galloway	Leslie Luke	Leigh Ann Smith
Lori Gillespie	Tammy Maloney	Tonya Smith
Rance Gillespie	Kelli Marcus	Carlton Speed
Bartley Gragg	Tim Martin	Randy Starnes
Keri Gragg	Franz Menge	Allyn Stockton
Roger Groening	Robert Mitcham	Al Story
Kim Hamilton	Rita Nichols	Brant Sturgill
Julie Hayman	Chris Nix	Jerry Taylor
Tammy Henderson	Suzanne Nixon	Richard Trusty
Shelly Henricks	Stanley Prince	Donna Turpin
Kenny Hensley	Bo Queen	Karen Varnes
Tammy Hicks Whitmire	Myra Queen	Darren Volk
Dana Holcomb	Mary Sue Raaf	David Volk
Eric Hollifield	Alan Ramey	Cathy Wallace
James Houck	Tombo Ramey	Gary Warfield
Shannon Jackson	Annette Reems	Regina Watson
Laurie Keener	Cristie Rickman	Teddy Watts
Stephanie Kennett	Celena Rogers	Von Watts
Jason Kilby	Andy Ruth	Curtis Weaver
Suzanne Krieger	Becky Sagner	Mickey Weiler
Georgeann Lanich	Heather Scull	Belinda Welch
Gwen Leavens	April Shirley	Walter Welch
Anna Lee	Jennie Shoemaker	Dana Williams
Annmarie Lee	Scott Shope	Randall Williams
Lori Lee	Stephanie Short	Sharon Williams
Jenny Lincoln	OhSoon Shropshire	Leah Woods
Hope Loudermilk	Dewey Smith	Terry York

FOXFIRE 10 student editors: Chris Nix, Jenny Lincoln, Celena Rogers, Tim Martin, April Shirley, and Julie Dickens.

NOT PICTURED: Robbie Bailey.

About the Editors

GEORGE P. REYNOLDS teaches music and folklore at the Rabun County, Georgia, High School.
SUSAN WALKER is a *Foxfire* staff editor. Current and former students involved in Rabun County High School's Foxfire program conducted the interviews that comprise this book.

Foxfire Books Available from Anchor Books/Doubleday

THE FOXFIRE BOOK   hog dressing, log cabin building, mountain crafts and foods, planting by the signs, snake lore, hunting tales, faith healing, and moonshining
0-385-07353-4   U.S. $14.00/Canada $17.50

FOXFIRE 2   ghost stories, spring wild plant foods, spinning and weaving, midwifing, burial customs, corn shuckin's, and wagon making
0-385-02267-0   U.S. $14.00/Canada $17.50

FOXFIRE 3   animal care, banjos and dulcimers, hide tanning, summer and fall wild plant foods, butter churns, and ginseng
0-385-02272-7   U.S. $14.00/Canada $17.50

FOXFIRE 4   fiddle making, springhouses, horse trading, sassafras tea, berry buckets, and gardening
0-385-12087-7   U.S. $14.00/Canada $17.50

FOXFIRE 5   ironmaking, blacksmithing, flintlock rifles, and bear hunting
0-385-14308-7   U.S. $14.00/Canada $17.50

FOXFIRE 6   shoemaking, 100 toys and games, gourd banjos and song bows, wooden locks, and a water-powered sawmill
0-385-15272-8   U.S. $14.00/Canada $17.50

FOXFIRE 7   ministers, church members, revivals, baptisms, shaped-note and gospel singing, faith healing, camp meetings, foot washing, snake handling, and other traditions of mountain religious heritage
0-385-15244-2   U.S. $14.00/Canada $17.50

FOXFIRE 8   Southern folk pottery from pug mills, ash glazes, and groundhog kilns to face jugs, churns, and roosters; mule swapping and chicken fighting
0-385-17741-0   U.S. $14.00/Canada $17.50

FOXFIRE 9   general stores, the Jud Nelson wagon, a praying rock, a Catawban Indian potter—and haint tales, quilting, home cures, and the log cabin revisited
0-385-17744-5   U.S. $14.00/Canada $17.50

FOXFIRE 10   railroad lore, boarding houses, Depression-era Appalachia, chairmaking, whirligigs, snake canes, and gourd art
0-385-42276-8   U.S. $14.00/Canada $17.50

FOXFIRE: 25 YEARS   A Celebration of Our First Quarter Century
0-385-41346-7   U.S. $14.95/Canada $18.95

A FOXFIRE CHRISTMAS   Appalachian Memories and Traditions
0-385-41347-5   U.S. $15.00/Canada $20.00

SOMETIMES A SHINING MOMENT   The Foxfire Experience by Eliot Wigginton
Twenty Years Teaching in a High School Classroom
0-385-13359-6   U.S. $14.00/Canada $17.50

Available at Bookstores Nationwide